China in Africa

China in Africa

Between Imperialism and Partnership in Humanitarian Development

Edited by
Sabella O. Abidde and Tokunbo A. Ayoola

LEXINGTON BOOKS
Lanham • Boulder • New York • London

Published by Lexington Books
An imprint of The Rowman & Littlefield Publishing Group, Inc.
4501 Forbes Boulevard, Suite 200, Lanham, Maryland 20706
www.rowman.com

6 Tinworth Street, London SE11 5AL, United Kingdom

British Library Cataloguing in Publication Information Available

Library of Congress Cataloging-in-Publication Data

Names: Abidde, Sabella Ogbobode, 1962- editor. | Ayoola, Tokunbo A., 1957- editor.
Title: China in Africa : between imperialism and partnership in humanitarian development / Edited by Sabella Abidde and Tokunbo A. Ayoola.
Description: Lanham : Lexington Books, [2020] | Includes bibliographical references and index.
Identifiers: LCCN 2020039205 (print) | LCCN 2020039206 (ebook) | ISBN 9781793612328 (cloth) | ISBN 9781793612342 (paperback) | ISBN 9781793612335 (epub)
Subjects: LCSH: China--Foreign economic relations—Africa. | Africa—Foreign economic relations--China. | Infrastructure (Economics)—Africa.
Classification: LCC HF1604.Z4 A35124 2020 (print) | LCC HF1604.Z4 (ebook) | DDC 338.91/5106—dc23
LC record available at https://lccn.loc.gov/2020039205
LC ebook record available at https://lccn.loc.gov/2020039206

The debate between genuine Sino-optimists and Sino-pessimists has just begun. We only hope that the debate does not linger on for too long, or meander into nothingness before we realize that China's activities on the African continent are good or bad for the future of Africans. And so, we dedicate this volume to all those who are involved in the ongoing debates and conversations. Asante sana!

❖

And to my friend and mentor of fifteen autumns, Professor Olayiwola Abegunrin, who passed on Tuesday April 14, 2020, after many months of poor health. He was a friend and teacher to many. A Pan-Africanist . . . May he rest in peace.

Contents

Abbreviations

ADB	Africa Development Bank
ADF	Africa Development Fund
ADS	Approved Destination Status
AFCTA	African Continental Free Trade Area
AFECC	Anhui Foreign Economic Construction Corporation
AU	African Union
BGRIMM	Beijing General Research Institute of Mining and Metallurgy
BRI	Belt and Road Initiative
CADF	China-Africa Development Fund
CCTV	China Central Television
CDB	China Development Bank
CI	Confucius Institutes
CIA	Central Intelligence Agency
CPC	Communist Party of China
CPPCC	Chinese People's Political Consultative Conference
CSPC	Comprehensive Strategic Partnership of Cooperation
DRC	Democratic Republic Congo
EC	European Commission
EIB	European Investment Bank
EPZ	Economic Processing Zones
ESAP	Economic Structural Adjustment Program
EU	European Union
EXIMBANK	Export-Import Bank
FDI	Foreign Direct Investment
FOCAC	Forum on China Africa Cooperation

FRELIMO	Mozambique Liberation Front (Portuguese:Frente de Libertação de Moçambique)
FTLRP	Fast Track Land Reform Program
FTLRP	Fast Track Land Reform Program
G77	Group of 77
G8	Group of eight
GDP	Gross Domestic Product
GNP	Gross National Product
GOZ	Government of Zimbabwe
ICC	International Criminal Court
IFC	International Finance Corporation
IMF	International Monetary Fund
IMF	Monetary Fund
KMT	Kuomintang (KMT) regime
KSC	Kilombero Sugar Company
LDC	Least Developed Nations
LEP	Look East Policy
MBDC	Media-Based Data Collection
MINURSO	United Nations Mission for The Referendum in Western Sahara
MINUSMA	UN Multidimensional Integrated Stabilization Mission in Mali
MINUSMA	United Nation's Multidimensional Integrated Stabilization Mission in Mali
MMD	Movement for Multiparty Democracy
MONUSCO	The United Nations Organization Stabilization Mission in the Democratic Republic of the Congo
NAM	Non-aligned Movement
NCP	National Congress Party
NEPAD	New Partnership for Africa's Development
NHRAP	China's National Human Rights Action Plan
OAU	Organization of African Unity
ODA	Official Development Assistance
OECD	Organization for Economic Co-operation and Development
PF	Patriotic Front
PRC	People's Republic of China (Beijing, China)
ROC	Republic of China (Taipei, Taiwan)
SAIS-CARI	China Africa Research Initiative at the Johns Hopkins University School of Advanced International Studies
SAP	Structural Adjustment Programs
SEATO	Southeast Asian Treaty Organization

SGR	Kenya's Standard Gauge Railway
SWAPO	South West African People's Organization's
TAZARA	Tanzania Zambia Railway Authority
TCFL	Teaching Chinese as a Foreign Language
TTCI	Travel and Tourism Competitiveness Index
TTCI	Travel and Tourism Competitiveness Index
UAR	United Arab Republic
UCLA	University of California Los Angeles
UN	United Nations
UNAMID	United Nations–African Union Mission in Darfur
UNCTAD	UN Conference on Trade and Development
UNESCO	United Nations Educational, Scientific and Cultural Organization
UNIP	United National Independence Party
UNMISS	United Nations Mission in South Sudan
UNSC	United Nations Security Council
USAID	United States Agency for International Development
USSR	Union of Soviet Socialist Republics
WB	World Bank
WEF	World Economic Forum
WTO	World Trade Organization
ZANU	Zimbabwe African National Union
ZANU-PF	Zimbabwe African National Union Patriotic Front
ZCTU	Zambia Congress of Trade Unions
ZESA	Zimbabwe Electricity Supply Authority
ZIDERA	Zimbabwe Democracy and Economic Recovery Act

Foreword

What to do or think about Beijing's activities and growing influence in Africa, and whether such activities would advance humanitarian growth and development, is at the heart of this book.

China's incursion and unequal engagement with states and societies in Africa have impacted the continent in ways many scholars and decision-makers in and outside of Africa had not envisaged. The effects have been profound—with far-reaching consequences on the social, economic, and political development of the continent. And while some have assessed it and see it as good and beneficial; others evaluated it and pronounced it bad and injurious. But what does history show?

The last major incursion and unequal engagement were in the period immediately following the Berlin Conference (November 15, 1884, to February 26, 1885), when fourteen colonial powers seized the continent. More than five decades after decolonization, the residual effects colonialism is still visible, and partially accounts for why much of the continent is still in a daze. While the Europeans are still there in the form of neocolonialism, China has become the major player in Africa's economic and political landscape. But why?

Why is China in Africa? What are their motives and motivations? What does China want? Within and outside of the academy, many seem to have forgotten that long before the Chinese became ubiquitous on the African continent, the Indians and the Lebanese were better known. For instance, many African countries—including Sierra Leone, Ghana, Nigeria, Liberia, South Africa, Senegal, and Côte d'Ivoire, are home to an untold number of Lebanese citizens. The Indians also have a huge presence with the vast majority living in South Africa, Tanzania, Mozambique, Mauritius, Uganda, Madagascar, Zambia, Réunion, and Kenya. The Indians and the Lebanese, in modern times at least, does not arouse the same suspicion and hostility as the Chinese.

And unlike the Chinese who are considered *new arrivals* on the continent, the Indians and Lebanese have had thriving communities, and many of these communities can be traced to, at least, the precolonial era.

Furthermore, unlike the Chinese, there was no official government policy by Beirut or New Delhi that encouraged migration, trade, and investment, or official policies intended to further their government's intentions and aspirations. Members of the Indian and Lebanese communities, for the most part, simply left the shore of their respective countries in search of *greener pastures*. And while there are recorded history of commerce, connections, and curiosity in earlier times, Beijing's approached Africa formally. They wanted trade and investment links and desired to establish diplomatic relations. Furthermore, they wanted supporting partners and allies in readiness for *The Age of China* they knew would come. And it came at the height of the Cold War when they exercised great power and influence at the United Nations and its six principal organs and a multiplicity of specialized agencies.

Essentially, therefore, the Chinese were methodical in their approach to Africa and many parts of the world. And so, it was that when the modern Sino-African relations publicly began in the late 1950s, they knew not to squander it. Several decades later, not many could have imagined that such a relationship would expand to the point where the United States and former colonial would be threatened by China's ubiquitous presence, power, and influence. But here we are! During the Cold War, the international system was dominated by the United States and the Soviet Union. It was, broadly speaking, a bipolar world. Since the downfall of the Soviet Union in December 1991, the world, again, broadly speaking, is considered by many scholars to be unipolar (dominated primarily by the United States).

In the second decade of the twenty-first century, China has the largest population, commands the second-largest economy, and the third-largest military in the world. It is a country that has and continues to invest several billion in Science, Technology, Engineering, and Mathematics (STEM) and intelligence activities. And at the same time, attracting students to study in China. And with tentacles that reach every corner of the world, China is likely to overtake Russia in many areas that matter in the twenty-five to thirty-five years and be at par or close to parity with the United States in forty to sixty years. And unless there are implosions caused by endogenous and or exogenous factors, China is likely to overtake the United States in seventy to eighty years beginning in 2020. Many factors will contribute to the stagnation or decline of the United States. But until such a time, a multipolar world will be possible in another fifty or so years. That is China for you.

That is China for you—the same China that states and societies in Africa are wining and dining without being smart and alert and proactive. The history of Africa from the fourteenth century to the present has mostly and notably been a history of subjugation and exploitation of its peoples and natural resources by outside forces—done mostly with domestic collaborators. Philanthropy does not factor into National Interest (except when used as a tool). China's national interest—raison d'État or "reason of State")—as is the interest of every national state, is survival, prosperity, the well-being of its citizens, and self-perpetuation. China, in furtherance of its national interest, therefore, will have no compunction in draining all that is drainable, excavate all that is excavatable, and cart all moveable and immovable parts of and from Africa.

In assembling this volume, we have faced many vexing and irritating challenges. The first unnecessary delay we encountered was by an acquisition editor in the UK who, after five months, decided she did not want to go ahead with publication. This was followed by contributors outside of the United States who, after extensions were granted, decided they would not be able to meet their commitment. To put it in perspective, we went from fifteen chapters to ten before scrambling to invite other scholars. And of course, there was the months-long delay caused by a debilitating health crisis. Finally, and fortunately, we have made it.

Despite the challenges, we are happy with this volume. Still, we hope that another book—either an edited volume, single, or coauthored—will singularly and critically examine China's incursion and activities on the continent. But more than that: how are states and societies handling this unequal relationship and are African leaders, elites, and the masses up to the challenge China poses? Are the governing institutions strong and dynamic enough to checkmate machinations by China and other forces? And while we have not ascribed injurious motives to China's presence and activities on the continent, we do not know what China's endgames on the continent are. We can only be optimistic; nonetheless—save for Cuba—no other external force has ever engaged African on an equal footing or treated Africa with respect, dignity, and honesty.

Sabella Ogbobode Abidde, PhD
Dept. of History/Political Science
Alabama State University
Montgomery, Alabama

Tokunbo Aderemi Ayoola, PhD
Dept. of History/Diplomatic Studies
Anchor University
Lagos, Nigeria

Acknowledgments

Edited volumes have their peculiar problems and challenges. This was no different. But finally, we are here, we made it! We owe many debts in the form of gratitude. Therefore, we would like to thank the following friends and colleagues for their assistance and wise counsel: Professors Olayiwola Abegunrin (Howard University/the University of Maryland) who died on April 14, 2020, and Alem Hailu (Howard University).

We would also like to thank Chief Adekanmi Ademiluyi who made it possible for us to contact/invite Simbo Olorunfemi to submit a chapter. Additionally, we would like to thank all the contributors for their brilliant chapters. We apologize for being late in submitting the final manuscript. In addition to the anonymous reviewers of our proposal and manuscript, we owe our acquisition editor, Dr. Trevor F. Crowell, a world of gratitude. Despite our many delays and missed deadlines, he was very patient and professional. And to Shelby Russell (who took over from Trevor), thank you! Every acquisition editor we have had at Lexington Books has been great!

We also appreciate the assistance rendered by Ms. Felicia Kemp, the administrative secretary in the Department of History and Political Science at Alabama State University. And to the scholars who provided the blurbs, we say Thank you . . . We Appreciate it!

Introduction

The ongoing relationship between China and Africa is a complicated one—complicated by history, geopolitics, globalization, Cold War, and post–Cold War politics, and by Western interests and influence on the continent. China is not the first or the only country that has had a complex relationship with Africa. Hosted by Otto Van Bismarck, the first chancellor of Germany, fourteen European countries gathered in Berlin, in 1884–1885, to set the stage for the ensuing conquest and plunder of the continent. Several decades earlier, the Trans-Atlantic Slave Trade, which lasted from the fifteenth to the nineteenth century, had laid waste the continent's human and natural resources and had in the process debased and dehumanized a considerable portion of humanity.

The Trans-Atlantic Slave Trade formally ended in the nineteenth century and was immediately followed by almost a century of colonial exploitation and control. Many countries on the continent gained independence in the 1960s through the 1980s, but the residual effects of these acts of cruelty and perversions continue to impact Africa in ways that are yet to be fully understood. Several decades after independence, neocolonialism is at play with much of the continent being controlled by Western Europe and the United States (a noncolonial power in Africa). The People's Republic of China formally entered the continent in the1950s and thereafter began to show interest and, eventually, began to exercise control even if incrementally. In the second decade of the twenty-first century, it will appear that all pretenses, gentility, and diplomatic niceties are gone: China is today the dominant foreign power on the continent.

Whether real or imagined, China appears to be at the center of the new new colonialism, the new *Scramble for Africa*, even though China and some scholars do not consider China's omnipresence as the beginning of or the continuation of imperialism. The initial contact between China and Africa dates to several centuries. However, the current Sino-Africa relations began in the late 1950s under the leadership of Mao Zedong, when Zhou Enlai, the first premier of the People's Republic of China, visited Africa and signed bilateral agreements with several African states. Today, China has bilateral and multilateral agreements with nearly all African countries. Her accomplishments and level of influence in so short a time has become a source of concern not just for the Europeans but also for the United States and Africans. China's power and influence, according to many scholars, have been built by knowing how to play *better politics* and by seemingly having a better understanding of the psyche of African leaders and elites.

Indeed, there are African leaders, and a growing list of diplomats, observers, and scholars who firmly believe in the long-term commitment and righteousness of the Chinese government and firms. These are the Sino-optimists (who see the Chinese engagement as a real partnership, opportunity for growth, and the beginning of a new approach to development). But Chinese, other scholars have argued, have not come to Africa with bags full of free goodies and free of conditionalities and preferences. What we have now, according to these scholars, is a relationship that is profoundly unequal and troubling—with China gaining the most from barter-transactions which involve natural resources in exchange for low-interest loans and the provision of infrastructures. These are the Sino-pessimists. Of course, there is the third wing—the Sino-pragmatists—scholars and commentators and observers who caution patience and demand more data-driven evidence before concluding whether or not China's involvement in Africa is: Imperialistic or humanitarian, that is whether they are humanitarians wholly concerned with and interested in the growth and development of states and societies on the continent.

While there is a growing list of literature on Sino-Africa relations, the primary aim of this book is to (1) report on what is currently going on in Africa's political, economic, cultural, and social space vis-à-vis the Chinese; and (2) investigate the immediate and long-term implications of the said relation. The central questions to be answered are these: Is this a mutually beneficial relationship or is China the new imperialist? And how do we know whether the former or the latter is the correct perspective? But of course, we may never know the definite answer in this or the next couple of decades because, in the first instance—while we know what Beijing's publicly stated motives and motivations are for its expansion into Third World politics and economic space—we do not know what its unstated and secondary reasons are.

Second, almost sixty years after many African countries gained independence, the old economic, social, and political structures—left behind by European colonialists—remain firmly in place. And now there is China! The European society is alleged to be open and free and to some extent, its foreign and economic policy toward Africa would appear to be understood in both colonial and postcolonial contexts (capitalist exploitation and control). But what understanding and insight do African leaders and elites have of China's politics, motives, and psyche, especially in a situation where she still insists, she is operating a communist system? The coming decades and centuries, may, therefore, turn out to be that of control, domination, and plunder by China.

Third, African leaders—from the 1960s to the present—have not fared well when dealing with issues relating to growth and development. Furthermore, many of these leaders have been wanting in terms of leadership skills and cleverness. Do they have *cajones,* the heart, the guile, and the intellect to stand up to Beijing? The evidence, from the independence years until the twenty-first century, tells us that standing up to the Chinese or any other power for that matter would or might be a losing cause. Some of these leaders and elites are corrupt, self-serving, lazy, and appear traumatized by their contradictions and alienation from the people they are supposed to be leading.

One may want to believe that the future will be different. And that the next generation of African leaders and elites will be smarter and wiser than their predecessors who have, for the most part, failed in terms of their vision and values, ethics, and leadership ability. But really, this may be wishful thinking. If the last sixty years have been woeful, where is the evidence to suggest that the next sixty or 120 years will not be worse? Some have asked the question: How could a continent that was unable to fend off the Europeans expected to survive the *Chinese onslaught?* To this, others have stated that times are changing!

There are several books published in the United States and elsewhere dealing with the changing nature of Sino-Africa relations. And the list keeps growing. Here we have assembled a group of scholars to examine the involvement of China in Africa from different perspectives. In chapter 1—"Zhou Enlai's Excursions to Africa"—Alecia Hoffman explores the purpose and implications of Zhou Enlai's visit to Egypt, Algeria, Morocco, Tunisia, Ghana, Mali, Guinea, Sudan, Ethiopia, and Somalia between 1963 and 1964. Utilizing a micro–macro linkage approach as the guiding theoretical paradigm, she can show that forging partnerships with "periphery nations" in Africa was a part of the People's Republic of China's development goals before the opening and normalization processes which began during the latter years of Zhou Enlai's leadership in the Communist Party of China (CPC).

In chapter 2—"The Policy Framework of Sino-African Relations from the Chinese Perspective"—Wei Ye asserts that the current Sino-African relations have experienced three distinct periods which have featured different patterns and priorities initiated by China. As a result, the writer reviewed selected policy papers, bilateral and multilateral agreements between China and

African countries in each period to explore the changing policy framework from the Chinese perspective and illustrated how the domestic development in China has shaped China's changing perceptions of itself and its relations with Africa. Wei YE also argued that the changing economy of China drives Sino-African relations into a more economic-oriented direction which inspires spillover of cooperation in other fields. "Jamie Monson and the Historiography of China-Africa Relations," chapter 3, is by Tokunbo Ayoola wherein he maintains that from the 1950s and 1960s and up until the start of the new millennium, the cordial relationship between China and Africa progressed exponentially and through many critical stages.

During the Cold War era, for instance, China represented itself to Africa as a genuine partner in economic development—in contrast to the West and the Soviet Union. China's engagement with Africa, Ayoola posits, has been the subject of many scholarly research and writings. With this in mind, he critically examined the work of one of the prominent scholars of China–Africa relations, Jamie Monson who had written widely—particularly on the Tanzania-Zambia Railway project, which is "emblematic of China's enhanced engagement with Africa." And in chapter 4, "Alliance Systems Redefined," Lawrence Mhandara posits that most analyses of China's renewed and growing relations with Africa treat China as an emergent imperialist or as a benevolent global partner seeking to ameliorate Africa's plight, that is, China is in Africa for purely humanitarian objectives. Consequently, he proposed a nuanced understanding of China's hands-off attitude toward African politics that is motivated by strategic analysis. Mhandara argued that China's hands-off approach is tied to the changing approach to the whole notion of alliance-building among sovereigns, from hard to soft approaches.

Mhandara also argues that China's engagement with Africa is primarily motivated not by imperialistic or humanitarian objectives but also a not so obvious strategic calculus, one that seeks to counterbalance other global powers, not just the United States, from "taking over Africa," thereby checking their global influence. With the use of a structuralist political economy theoretical framework, Kudakwashe Chirambwi in chapter 5—"The Belt and Road Initiative in Africa"—investigates the kind of developmental power China has and its successes in its attempt to build a community of shared future. Chirambwi framed his argument around three concepts of power which he posits China employs: The first is visible power which involves China making decisions on issues over which there is an observable conflict in African states. The second, invisible power, involves ways in which China influences decisions to block other communities from the belt and road initiative. The third is a hidden power. Through the belt and road initiative, and building a community of shared values, China manipulates other countries to make them believe that common development through trade and infrastructure networks is in their interests when it is not. All combined, this produces a Foucauldian notion of governmentality characterized by domination and control.

And in chapter 6—"China in Africa: The Fifth Wave of Conquest and Plunder?"—Sabella Abidde asserts that in its ancient and enduring history, the African continent has undergone four waves of plunder and subjugation. The fifth, he argues, is the current Sino-Africa relations, which began in the 1950s and which gathered steam at the tailend of the twentieth century. According to Abidde, the ongoing Sino-African relations may not augur well for states and societies on the continent that are looking to Beijing for economic growth and development. It is a relationship, he further argues, that may lead to the eventual conquest of and the plunder of the continent's resources. Abidde's argument is anchored on three premises: The motives and motivations of the Chinese; the weak and fragmenting nature of states and societies on the continent that makes exploitation and subjugation possible; and the weak, corrupt, and self-serving leadership that has come to characterize the continent. According to Simbo Olorunfemi in chapter 7—"Changing Africa-China Relations: Colonialism or Partnership?"—the relationship between Africa and China is strengthening by the day and is one that has generated significant interest in different parts of the world—especially in Western capitals.

Olorunfemi states that the unease on the part of the West on the growing Sino-Africa relationship is particularly striking, and wonders why the Africa–China relationship is of so much interest and concern to the West that it would be issuing, in a manner of speaking, a *fatwa* against its consummation and continuation. This and other questions are at the center of his submission. In chapter 8, "China and Africa: The Beginning of a New World Order or A New Form of Colonialism," Priye S. Torulagha explored the increasing economic and political relationship between China and African countries and asserts that China's international economic strategy is designed to affect a paradigm shift to establish a new world order. Or perhaps, China and Africa's attempt to create a new world order is based on reciprocity and reject a more Machiavellian power politics model typical of Western economic relationships.

According to Alecia Hoffman and Regina Moorer in chapter 9, "China's Cultural Rapprochement: The Uses of Soft Power as a Form of Building Alliances in Africa," argue that within the context of the international system, the level of power that a state can wield varies. This power can be measured by a variety of variables such as military might, gross domestic product (GDP), purchasing power parity (PPP), and so forth. The power approaches utilized by states in the international system toward each other can be characterized as either hard power or soft power. For China, the deployment of soft power has been the sine qua nonapproach in all things about Africa and is the cornerstone of the country's foreign policy toward Africa. Hoffman and Moorer went on to examine China's utilization of soft power as a means of deploying its foreign policy objectives.

In chapter 10, "Politics and Governance: China's hands-off approach to African politics," Charles Mutasa stated that the Chinese emphasis and commitment to the principle of noninterference in the internal affairs of other countries as a key tenet of its foreign policy call for more rigorous academic scrutiny than any other developmental phenomenon in the twenty-first century. The authenticity of the claim and the evidence on the ground needs to be critically examined. Mutata proceeded to discuss the basis, key drivers, rationale, and application of China's hands-off approach to African politics. This is done with the aid of country case studies across the continent. Furthermore, the question of whether this Sino-Africa relations is a new form of imperialism or it gives Africa a unique opportunity to own its development process is interrogated.

China's presence in Africa is no longer news, but what remains newsworthy are the complexities and sometimes contradictory manifestations of Asia's largest and world's second-largest economy, in Africa. These manifestations—which broadly fall under optimism, pessimism, and/or caution—shape the responses of states and nonstate actors to Africa–China encounters. Bearing in mind the multiple arenas of contestations on the "true" role(s) of China in Africa, Surajudeen Mudasiru, and Abdul-Gafar Tobi Oshodi, in chapter 11—"Reporting the Dragon: A Thematic Study of Anti-Chinese Sentiments in 'China in Africa' News Coverage"—focused on the "news theater" with specific attention on anti-Chinese sentiments in the news coverage. Furthermore, they highlighted the anti-Chinese themes in the coverage of Africa–China encounters.

Since the year 2000, Zimbabwe has experienced an economic decline because of sanctions imposed on her by the West and other factors such as unprecedented levels of corruption. The Chinese have proved to be a significant economic development partner, notably in the last two decades. Chinese have invested in different sectors such as agriculture, energy, manufacturing, mining, tourism, and transport, during this period. It is for this reason that Charity Manyeruke, in chapter 12, "Chinese Economic Development Projects in Zimbabwe," discussed the economic projects with a view of assessing the impact on the domestic situation and Sino-Zimbabwe relations. And finally, the rapid population growth of Africa in the face of dwindling economic misfortunes means that African countries are in search of foreign investments. In its quest to bolster economic development and create jobs for an increasingly jobless and restless youth population, most African countries have opened their economies to the outside world. In the last few decades, Chinese presence in Africa has grown exponentially.

Elisha Dung and Augustine Avwunudiogba, in chapter 13, "The Match of the Red Dragon: The Geographic Footprints of Chinese Presence in Africa" examined the spatial pattern and trends of Chinese presence in Africa from a variety of perspectives, including economic, demographic, social, cultural, political, military, trade, telecommunication, and diplomatic ramifications. Drawing theoretical inspiration from colonial/neocolonial theory and the core-periphery model, the two scholars addressed these questions with special emphasis on the implications for the survival and economic development of African countries. Using Zambia–China relations as a case study, Emmanuel Matambo, in chapter 14, "Africa's new Wise Men from the East? An analysis of Africa's non-state and state actors' perceptions of China and the Chinese," compares the sentiments expressed at the level of state-to-state interaction between China and its African partners and the perceptions of ordinary African citizens who interact with Chinese citizens who do not come to Africa at the behest of their government. According to Matambo, at the state level, China and Africa present their relations as mutually beneficial between equal partners. However, the sentiments of ordinary Africans toward Chinese citizens have not been equally optimistic.

In chapter 15, "Chinese Investments in Africa: 'Chopsticks Mercantilism,'" George Ayittey tells us that after decades of poor governance, abject neglect, and destruction from senseless civil wars, Africa needed substantial investment needed to rebuild build and rebuild infrastructure. Africa, however, did not have the funds but had natural resources, which China needed to feed its economic machine. So, China went looking for resources in Africa. Unfortunately, Chinese investments in Africa did not produce the glorious "win-win" results most analysts had expected. In many countries, the "infrastructure-for-resources" deals were dubious. What many recipient African countries got in return, Ayittey argues, was infrastructure at a grossly inflated cost that might or might not be delivered and some political PR mileage.

This volume did not cover many of the topics many readers and scholars may have wanted, that is, the impact of Chinese language schools and Confucius centers in some African countries. And, is China making demands that are likely to erode state authority and sovereignty? We concede that more scholarly works need to be done on China's engagement with Africa. It is in so doing that many of the fears associated with the Sino-African relations can be allayed. Or, it could lead to the next generation of African leaders modifying the terms of the relationship. China needs Africa, and Africa also needs China; however, it must be a partnership of equals.

Part I

EARLY CONTACTS
AND CONNECTIONS

Chapter 1

Zhou Enlai's Excursions to Africa

A Case Study of Egypt

Alecia D. Hoffman

INTRODUCTION

In 1963, Zhou Enlai, the Premier of the People's Republic of China (PRC), embarked upon a decision that would have lasting implications on Sino-African relations. This decision, to expand the PRC's influence in Africa, started with goodwill tours to ten African nations. Jules Archer surmised that during the winter of 1963, the decision was made to tour the ten chosen African states to determine how to put the Chinese on par with the United States and the Soviets and also circumvent any further U.S.–Soviet involvement in Africa.[1] Prior to Zhou's arrival in Africa, several countries had already received Chinese delegations in the so-called "goodwill tours." These preliminary tours centered on "trade-union affairs, education, art, and theater," and as Archer states, these missions provided great success for the Chinese and the African nations to the consternation of the Soviets and the American officials.[2] The rationale behind the angst expressed by the Soviets to the Chinese incursions in Africa before Zhou Enlai's arrival can be surmised by examining the international environs; specifically, the agreements made between the two world superpowers and the effects of balancing and bandwagoning to maintain the existing power structure of the international arena.

Zhou Enlai served as the Premier of the PRC from 1949 until he died in 1976. He is undoubtedly one of the most important figures in shaping the PRC's foreign policy. Although Deng Xiaoping is historically noted as the PRC's pragmatic leader, it is also necessary to observe Zhou Enlai's pragmatism. His negotiation skills with foreign leaders and his ability to act in a conciliatory manner with the leader of the PRC were of utmost importance.

Hence, the reason why Zhou Enlai has been studied as one of the most notable figures of China's political history.

Background and Purpose of the Study

In August 1963, the United States, Soviet Union, and Great Britain signed the limited nuclear test ban treaty, which specifically led the United States and Soviets into a period of rapprochement. After the United States, Soviets, and Great Britain signed the treaty, 100+ additional nations were signatories to this document. The PRC, on the other hand, was not one of those nations that agreed to the particulars of this international agreement and instead called for a world disarmament conference and tried to convince other nations not to sign the US-Soviet-UK backed treaty.[3] To further highlight the PRCs disregard for the test ban treaty, the country was in the process of developing their nuclear bomb and believed that the treaty was an attempt to further isolate the PRC, label the country as a rogue state, and only allow nuclear materials to be concentrated in the hands of the major super powers.

Balancing and bandwagoning was another useful tool employed by the two major power brokers. As previously stated, the limited nuclear test ban treaty was one of the reasons for China's need to increase its influence in Africa. Additionally, the role of the United States and Soviet Union in the affairs of other "Third-world" nations presented itself as a concern for the PRC. In the 1960s alone, the PRC was involved in border disputes with India and an increasing partnership with Pakistan, nominal assistance to Latin America— particularly Cuba (at least by way of rhetoric), assistance to North Vietnam in the second Indochina War, and involvement in Palestine, just to name a few. Each of these interactions in the affairs of other nations along with the development of organizations such as the Afro-Asian People's Organization; namely the push to hold a second Afro-Asian Conference, akin to the first held in Bandung Indonesia in 1955, was a part of the PRCs foreign policy strategy and the goal of fomenting a path that differed from the capitalist/ democratic ideals of the West and the communist ideology of the Soviets.

The question as to how this feat would be accomplished centered on the nonaligned movement and the need to hold a second Afro-Asian conference following the initial conference held in 1955 Bandung, Indonesia. Although the tours commenced in 1963, the meetings between Zhou Enlai and the African leaders of the ten nations continued well after the initial tour. Furthermore, Sino-African relations did not commence in 1963. The relations between the two regions date back centuries; however, this renewed interest in fomenting relations with African countries became a central part of China's foreign policy objectives. The Sino-Soviet split of the late 1950s ushered in an interesting tripartite world structure, with the United States,

Soviet Union, and the PRC all vying for dominance in the international system. For African nations, some that had already received independence by this date and for others that were on the path to soon receive autonomous self-governance, this new international structure offered several different trajectories for alignment.

This semitripartite structure that emerged in the international system after the Sino-Soviet split catalyzes an examination of Premier Zhou Enlai's excursions to ten African nations. Commencing in 1963, Zhou Enlai embarked upon trips to Egypt, Algeria, Morocco, Tunisia, Ghana, Mali, Guinea, Sudan, Ethiopia, and Somalia. This chapter will examine the visit to Egypt and the implications for the main superpowers in the international systems—United States and Soviet Union, and the consequences for China and Africa. Through the utilization of two theoretical paradigms, triangulation and balancing, and bandwagoning, this chapter will be exploratory and it will examine Premier Zhou Enlai's tours in Africa with a specific focus on the Arab Republic of Egypt, formerly known as the United Arab Republic (UAR).

THEORETICAL PARADIGM(S)

The neorealist paradigm was introduced by Kenneth Waltz in 1979 through his manuscript *Theory of International Politics*.[4] This idea of structural realism(a synonym of neorealism) is a paradigm in which balancing and bandwagoning are aptly located. On the other hand, the theory of triangulation or triangular diplomacy became a watchword in American foreign policy circles and was utilized by Henry Kissinger, who has been labeled as a practitioner of *realpolitik*, to describe the US-Soviet-China rivalry. However, one can attest that the use of triangulation, at least from the perspective of analyzing the African states, was employed when Zhou Enlai began his excursions to Africa. The commencement of these new diplomatic ties between the identified African countries to which the Chinese Premier Zhou Enlai visited gave African countries the option of either the United States, Soviet Union, and China; at times, African nations would employ the tactic of free-riding and utilize the support that could be garnered from all three.

Although the PRC was not recognized as a major power threat at this time in history, the recent Sino-Soviet split gave way to the PRCs rise as a new state—although classified as a weak state—to which African nations could turn and thereby bandwagon under the guise of shared colonial history, counterbalancing imperialism, and the need to strengthen the Afro-Asian alliance. Therefore, the use of balancing, bandwagoning, and triangulation worked in concomitant nuanced ways with varying degrees at different times throughout Cold War history.

Balancing and Bandwagoning

To commence, the utilization of balancing and bandwagoning by the PRC with the hopes of gaining African allies was to serve a purpose that would be realized eight years after the historic tours of Zhou Enlai; gaining a seat on the UN Security Council and supplanting the Republic of Taiwan as the official China in the international community. The PRC, operating as a revisionist state, sought to disrupt the balance of power in the international arena by gaining allies on the African continent. As stated by Stephen M. Walt, "states form alliances to prevent stronger powers from dominating them lies at the heart of the traditional balance-of-power theory. According to this view, states join alliances to protect themselves from states or coalitions whose superior resources could pose a threat."[5] Furthermore, Walt surmises that with balancing, policies that promote benevolence and restraint tend to be the best types of policies.[6] This is what the PRC employed before Zhou Enlai's excursions and continued with African states thereafter.

From the perspective of bandwagoning, states align with the stronger side over that of the weaker. In an examination of the Cold War and the PRCs place within this context, the Soviet Union and the United States were undoubtedly the stronger points in this dynamic and a number of African states, or feuding factions within the states, aligned with either the West or the East during the years of the Cold War. Much of this is evidenced through the supplement of military supplies to fight proxy wars in Africa during the Cold War years, that is, Congo and Angola.

The practice of free-riding by African states was a bit more nuanced during the Cold War. With the end of World War II (WWII), several African nations were on the precipice of independence, and commencing in the 1950s many countries in sub-Saharan Africa began to receive independence from the colonial powers. Independence led to the fomenting of new relationships and the commencement of strategy in establishing partners that would be evidenced throughout the Cold War. As previously stated, Africa was the location of several hot and cold proxy wars throughout the U.S.-Soviet dispute, and with many of the African nations recently receiving independence from the European powers of years past, finding a position within the international theater was of vital importance. Many of these newly independent states were characterized as "weak states" and the differentiated aspects of colonialism is one of the culprits.[7] How African states operated as freeriders is considered nuanced, due to the aforesaid reason. As part of this analysis pertaining to free riding, most in international relations present this behavior as a problem; however, in the case of newly independent African nations, the incentive for these states to contribute to the collective public good for either the West or the East seems a bit implausible. Therefore, enjoying the benefits of protection in the anarchic international system by bandwagoning with either the East or the West without having to incur many costs can be considered rational behavior.[8]

Triangular Diplomacy

The concept of triangular diplomacy is most often associated with the Nixon administration and the foreign policy posturing of Henry Kissinger. It is known that Kissinger's visit to the PRC in 1971 was the precursor to Nixon visiting the country the following year. Furthermore, taking advantage of the China-Soviet rift would bode well for the United States' own foreign policy objectives and further containment of the Soviet spread of communism. According to the U.S. State Department, triangular diplomacy is "using relations with one country as leverage to extract concessions from another."[9] When utilizing this definition with the PRC, the applicability is just as appropriate.

The utilization of triangular diplomacy was employed by the PRC before the Kissinger and Nixon visit to China. As the rift between the Soviets and the PRC became more pronounced, China began to implement its brand of socialism with Chinese characteristics and newly independent nations of Africa were the beneficiaries of such cordialities. Furthermore, the PRC had commenced its excursions into Africa sending personnel and experts before the Zhou Enlai tour in 1963.

With the PRC entering the arena as a third possibility with which African states could forge alliances, the basic two-state analysis and possible iterations of what the Soviets or the United States would do in the bipolar international theater became a bit more complex. From a game-theoretic perspective, this new order of triangulation presented itself as an n-person game in the international arena ending the first round with some semblance of cooperation between at least two of the three players, the United States and the PRC. This can be seen with the normalization efforts that began in 1971 and when the PRC gained a seat on the UN Security Council. This, however, was not the end of the Soviet Union, as the Cold War raged on for approximately another twenty years, and the iterations changed, and the n-person games continued.

When the PRC introduced itself as a third viable option for African nations, the country proposed the non-aligned movement, indicating that it is neither the West nor the East, but one that would operate by the "Principles of Peaceful Coexistence" as first espoused at the Bandung Conference in 1955. The major caveats to this philosophy were the win-win cooperative partnerships between African nations and the PRC, mutual respect, and non-interference in domestic affairs; all of which were welcoming and assuaging to all parties, including the PRC, which all share the common history of colonialism and imperialism. The use of triangulation by the PRC fits well within the parameters of the definition provided by the U.S. Department of State. As stated previously, the main goal of using triangulation from a theoretical standpoint is to extract concessions from the other party. The PRC utilized this approach to play off the two world superpowers, foment its place in the international arena, and offer African countries a viable alternative by espousing the narrative of a shared history of struggle against imperialism, and now, the Soviet's brand of communism.

In conclusion, the theories of balancing, bandwagoning, and triangulation were all employed in some fashion by either the PRC, the United States, or the Soviet Union. Furthermore, African countries utilized these approaches as well to position themselves in the new international order that arose after WWII and upon each country's independence. Each of these approaches can also be examined from a game-theoretic perspective within the neorealist paradigm of international relations to understand the varied actions and iterations of states and actors in a system that is considered anarchic. Even though international organizations exist, the rules are not necessarily binding.

METHODOLOGY

The research for this chapter is one of a case study approach that is unobtrusive. An examination of Zhou Enlai's visit to Africa, with a case study approach of his with then-Egyptian President Abdel Gamal Nasser will be carried out by way of examination of research articles, books, and archival documents that are publicly accessible.

Premier Enlai commenced his travels to Africa in 1963 during the first wave of independence struggles on the continent. Although Egypt received independence from Great Britain in 1922, there was still a great deal of British influence in the region. Likewise, the struggle between the Soviets and the United States for dominance in those countries that were deemed "developing" was gaining steam. Coupled with Soviet-U.S.-British competition, Egypt was recuperating from the Suez Canal Crisis of 1956, and the UAR was able to show its might against Western domination and influence in the region. The significance of highlighting the colonial connection of these states is due to the period that Premier Enlai visited.

Premier Enlai's visit during this time is significant for two reasons: First, as previously stated, Robert I. Rotberg's analysis of weak states is applicable as it pertains to the time that the Chinese premier decided to take his travels. Many of the states being newly autonomous nations were indeed functioning, but to surmise that every state was functioning to maximum capability free from any colonial control would be misguided. It is a fact that even though independence occurred, the laws and institutions that existed during the colonial period were not completely dismantled. Furthermore, most economic assistance was obtained from Western institutions. As characterized by weak states, fundamental economic institutions and true political dynamism were not yet stable at the time of Zhou Enlai's tour. As Robert I. Rotberg notes:

> Nation-states exist to provide a decentralized method of delivering political (public) goods to persons living within designated parameters (borders). Having replaced the monarchs of old, modern states focus and answer the concerns and demands of citizenries. They organize and channel the interest of their people, often but not exclusively in furtherance of national goals and values. They buffer or manipulate external forces and influences, champion the local or concerns of adherents, and mediate between the constraints and challenges of the international arena and the dynamism of their own internal economic, political, and social realities.[10]

The second point pertains to the entirety of the African continent at the time of Zhou Enlai's travels. From a continental perspective, some of the important institutions that currently operate on the African continent were not yet established. For example, the African Development Bank did not become operational until 1964 and the Organization of African Unity (OAU-AU) held its signatory meeting in 1963, the same year that Enlai embarked upon his tour. Provided in figure 1.1 is an illustration of the ten African states to which Zhou Enlai traveled, between December 1963 and the spring 1964.

Utilizing archival material from the Wilson Center, this chapter will examine in detail the conversations held between the Chinese premier and the Egyptian president. The discussions will be examined in a chronological format analyzing the documents and data in order of the year that the visit occurred. In addition to the particulars of the visit to the guest country in Africa and the discussions held between Premier Enlai and the African heads of state or their designees, and analysis will also be given to communications exchanged between the PRC and the varied departments and Chinese embassies which assisted in facilitating the visits to the African countries.

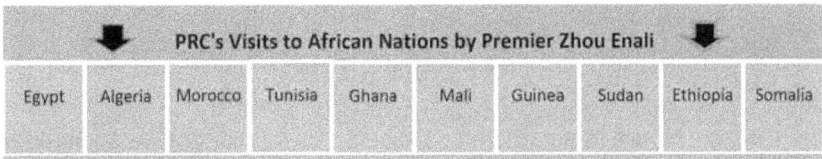

PRC's Visits to African Nations by Premier Zhou Enali									
Egypt	Algeria	Morocco	Tunisia	Ghana	Mali	Guinea	Sudan	Ethiopia	Somalia

Figure 1.1   PRC's Visits to African Nations by Premier Zhou Enlai.

The implications of the premier's visit pertain to China/Africa relations, U.S./Africa relations, Soviet/Africa relations, and U.S./China relations. It is important to examine the implications of the visits, for the exchanges made between the PRC and the African states present important repercussions for the international community. These consequences are presented objectively, although, for some of the actors, the significance of the visits causes an eventual shift in behavior that eventually leads to systemic change in the international system.

LIMITATIONS

The visits made by the Premier of China to Africa between 1963 and 1964 consisted of visits to ten African states. Due to the amount of information that is available about each of the states, a case study approach of just one state—Egypt—has been chosen for this chapter. The need to complete a comprehensive study of all ten states is still needed, as the existing literature does not provide this type of systematic analysis. Furthermore, although raw data is readily available pertaining to the visits to the varied nations, the ability to find the concrete historical sources of the exact dates of every one of Zhou Enlai's visits to the ten countries in Africa presented a challenge for this research. Although the Wilson Center Archives has recently made available significant amounts of materials that detail the communications of the Premier of the PRC, not all communications are yet provided. As with conducting a great deal of research on the PRC, the ability to obtain exact data may prove difficult, for this information is not always made available.

In addition to the lack of all communications of every African country visited, the files provided by the Wilson Archives presents dates that may not be the exact date as to when the conversations took place. This too posed a challenge in the research. There is the likelihood that the day the communications were recorded in the respective ministry offices, such as the foreign ministry, are the dates that are provided by the Wilson Center in their Archives. Further analysis will have to be conducted in future research to determine the exact dates of the meetings and conversations held between the premier and the foreign heads of state of the African countries visited.

LITERATURE REVIEW

The study of Sino-African relations has received a great deal of attention in recent decades. However, much of the literature centers on the PRC's role in Africa after the Tiananmen Square incident of 1989. Following the protests of 1989, the PRC took a brief hiatus and retreated inward to handle its domestic matters. Conversely, with the birth of the Forum on China Africa Cooperation (FOCAC), and the shifting direction of China's foreign policy goals, a renewed interest in Africa took place, and now the PRC has diplomatic ties with every country on the continent except for Eswatini, which still recognizes Taiwan as the sole China. Even though there is a great deal of scholarship being produced on China's current position on the African continent, there is a need to examine some of the early excursions to Africa, before the 1979 opening process of the PRC initiated by Deng Xiaoping.

Several manuscripts are circulating that discuss Zhou Enlai's trip to Africa in 1963–1964. George Segal, Robert Scalapino, Donovan Chau, Gregg A. Brazinsky, David H. Shinn, Joshua Eiseman, Christopher J. Lee, Ian Taylor, Deborah Brautigam, and Bruce D. Larkin are just a few of the scholars that have researched Chinas' role in Africa during this period of 1963–1964. Other scholars such as George W. Shepard, Young Chan Kim, Chris Alden, Jules Archer, and a host of others have written books and journal articles regarding the changing dynamics of Sino-African relations.

To commence, an examination of George Segal's work suggests that the reasons for China's interest in Africa during this period were due to the PRC breaking with the Soviet's perceptions and practices of communism and also the increase of independence struggles that were beginning to take place on the African continent. According to Segal, this was of importance because the PRC had already undergone this stage of revolution and African countries could benefit from China's blueprint for revolution. "Africa was seen as a testing ground for Chinese principles that were disputed by the Soviet Union."[11] In tandem with the belief that Africa could be used as a testing ground, the visits of Zhou Enlai to several African nations shored up the PRCs' early influence in Africa, as the premier's visit was the first high-level delegation to Africa.[12] To augment the work of Segal, the Rand Corporation in conjunction with Robert Scalapino published a brief memorandum which highlighted some of the important aspects of the premier's visit to the African countries, giving firsthand accounts of what some of the salient features were on the ground when Zhou Enlai took his tour of Africa.

Donovan Chau provides an interesting account of China's incursions into Africa. Unlike many contemporary scholars that examine China's role in Africa today, Chau takes a historic look at China's early "incursions" into Africa and specifically examines the period of 1955–1976, which was aptly known as the Mao era. According to Chau, those who study China's role in Africa from just a contemporary lens miss the historical significance of the PRC's early influence on the continent. It is necessary to examine the relationships forged in the past to have a clear picture of contemporary events and even future ones. Overall, Chau surmises that the role of the PRC in Africa is one that pertains to its own political, economic, and strategic objectives in the international arena.[13]

Gregg A. Brazinsky's work examines the U.S.-China competition during the Cold War and particularly addresses how this rivalry had implications for many developing parts of the world, specifically Africa. This rivalry cemented the global agendas of the two competing regions, the United States and China. Just as Chau and others argue that status was the main impetus for competition, Brazinsky's assessment takes the same line of thought.[14]

David H. Shinn and Joshua Eiseman provide a thorough analysis of Sino-African relations. Shinn and Eiseman provide a continentwide approach in the study of Sino-African relations with a particular focus on the post-1949 period of China. The book is careful not to generalize about the continent of Africa because each of the fifty-four countries that comprise the continent has its own unique set of characteristics and it is, therefore, necessary to examine the respective countries and the continent from a historical perspective. Shinn and Eiseman traversed the continent and visited nine countries, visited China several times, and conducted interviews with diverse populations which ranged from blue-collar workers to Chinese diplomats that were stationed in African countries and African ambassadors to China. The book focuses on several different themes which include, the initiation of Sino-African relations, which date back to the Ming Dynasty; the package strategy, which highlights China's modest foreign aid program with African countries, state visits, cultural exchange, and student programs during the early years of the PRC; the no China development model. From this standpoint, China recognized and still recognizes that there are differences between itself and African nations, therefore the export of a particular development model is not necessarily promoted to Africa by China; the Taiwan issue; closer political relations; moving from revolutionary support to pragmatic support of Africa; establishment of relationships with successor governments. In this aspect, Shinn and Eiseman point out that the PRC has always worked with any government that is in control in an African nation; the PRCs military presence; and lastly, the growth of Chinese expatriate communities in Africa. To conclude the study, Shinn and Eiseman examine some of the future trends as it pertains to Sino-African relations and what this portends for the future.[15]

Christopher J. Lee's edited work is comprised of many interesting chapters that discuss the importance of the Bandung Conference of 1955 and the implications of this meeting on Asian countries and those in Africa. The edited work covers several fields yet creates an interconnectedness between them. Cold War History, postcolonial studies, global history and area studies, diplomatic history, and sociocultural history are all addressed in this work to provide the reader with some semblance of understanding how important the Bandung Conference was for the developing world. It is also during this conference that Zhou Enlai delivered the "Principles of Peaceful Coexistence" message which would become the watchword of China's foreign policy and interaction with other countries.[16]

Ian Taylor's work commences with a historical overview of Sino-African relations and concludes with prognostications of the Sino-African relationship. Taylor delves into the significance of the Bandung Conference and the "Principles of Peaceful Coexistence" and their applicability to Africa. Taylor notes that during the post-Bandung era, which commenced around 1959, the PRC began to make more direct overtures to the African continent, most notably North African countries. Furthermore, ahead of Zhou Enlai's visit to the continent, several Chinese delegations trekked various countries on the continent.[17]

Deborah Brautigam provides some analysis of Zhou Enlai's connections to Africa. In chapter one of her book, she discussed the role of the Cold War and how this long-standing international event directed China's foreign policy initiatives. Just as previous scholars have discussed the importance of the Bandung Conference, Brautigam also expresses the role of Zhou Enlai at this event and the significance of the "Principles of Peaceful Coexistence." She continues with some analysis of the countries that began to receive aid from the PRC during the independence movements, Zhou Enlai's tours, and his position on PRC assistance to African countries.[18]

Bruce D. Larkin discussed China's aid to nationalist movements and the country's short-term goals and how these goals will and can sustain its commitments long term to social revolutions. The text also assesses China's revolutionary model and how this could have been employed in other states. The concluding remarks of Larkin are that "African governments that chose to create relations with China may generate useful opportunities for themselves, and lessen, rather than enhance, the likelihood they will be disrupted by China's pursuit of world revolution."[19]

To conclude, the literature reviewed in this section is by no means exhaustive. The field of Sino-African relations continues to grow creating less of a dearth in the scholarship that exists. As more students, policy-makers, practitioners, and researchers delve into the continuously burgeoning field of international relations and country studies, the growth of literature in this area will continue with more nuanced examinations of China's role in Africa as China continues to carve its place in the international arena.

PREMIER ENLAI'S VISITS TO AFRICAN NATIONS: AN EXAMINATION OF THE UNITED ARAB REPUBLIC (EGYPT)

Background

According to Jules Archer, prior to 1963, the PRC had developed relationships with only a few African states, most notably Algeria, Ghana, Mali, and Somalia.[20] However, to circumvent the Soviets' influence in Africa, the Premier of the People's Republic of China—Zhou Enlai—decided in the winter 1963 to embark upon a ten-nation tour across Africa. This tour was not the origins of Sino-African relations or exchanges, but rather these exchanges date back at least a century. Before the premier's commencement of his excursion, several Chinese delegations were sent ahead of him, and Guinea, one of the countries visited, already had Chinese experts on the ground assisting with an agricultural project.[21]

Prior to embarking upon his tour, the United States, the United Kingdom, and the Soviets signed a Nuclear Test Ban Treaty during the summer of 1963. This particular action was viewed by China as further attempts by the Western and Eastern Blocs to dampen any prospects that the Chinese or other developing nations might have on harnessing their nuclear capabilities and development. As a result, this event is one of the contributing factors for the PRC to begin shoring up its relations with other least developed nations around the globe. Records note at least two exchanges made between Premier Zhou Enlai and the leaders of other nations that comprise those countries designated as the developing part of the world. In a conversation held with Vice Premier Chin Yi and Raza, the Ambassador of Pakistan. Exchange of communications centered around the PRC's disapproval of the Test Ban Treaty signed by the major powers with the hopes of getting Pakistan to join with the PRC in disapproving of the agreement and at least conditionally signing the Test Ban Treaty.[22] In addition to this conversation, Premier Zhou Enlai also held talks with a Kenyan African National Federation Delegation on September 5, 1963. In this particular discussion, the actions of the United States, the United Kingdom, and Soviets were criticized once again. The premier noted, those allied with the United States have access to data and nuclear weapons and can conduct testing while those developing countries now have their hands tied. This was essentially called "nuclear blackmail" and "one-sided."[23]

The disapproval of Premier Zhou of the West and the East in consolidating control in the international arena, particularly as it pertained to nuclear capabilities served as an impetus to reach out to the newly independent states in Africa and to further assist any independence struggles on the continent. It is in the 1960s that the world began to see the third side of the triangle that was beginning to emerge in the bipolar structure. This was further evidenced through Mao Zedong's "Two Intermediate Zones" speech delivered in September of 1963. His address highlighted areas that were not happy with the United States. He surmised that the two intermediate zones consisted of Asia, Africa, and Latin America and the second, Europe, Japan, and Canada. Both camps were not happy with the United States or the Soviet Union.[24]

The Premier's Travels to Egypt in December 1963

The relationship between Zhou Enlai and Gammal Abdel Nasser was established at the Bandung Conference in 1955. It was at this time that the Chinese premier espoused on the "Principles of Peaceful Coexistence" and also invited the heads of state to visit the PRC. Prior to visiting Egypt (then the UAR) the PRC and Egypt had entered into several agreements and relations were established between the two countries in May 1956, a year after the Bandung Conference. Shinn and Eiseman note that during the same year, relations were established between the two countries, "China initiated a modest economic assistance program."[25] China also provided support to Egypt during the Suez Canal Crisis in 1956, at least morally.

There are at least three instances where the premier met with Gammal Abdel Nasser of Egypt during his travels to Africa. According to the Wilson Center Archives, the first meeting between the two men consisted of talks pertaining to the "domestic conditions inside Egypt, the Sino-Indian border war, and the possibilities for a nuclear-weapons-free zone in Africa and the Middle East."[26] This meeting between the two men took place at approximately 10:30 a.m. within the Cairo Presidential Palace. The discussions about the domestic conditions in Egypt largely centered on economics, employment issues, unions, trading matters, Judaism in the UAR, and land reform. Within the larger Middle Eastern region, the Premier and President Nasser discussed the nuclear situation of Israel and establishing a nuclear-free weapons zone in Africa, however, the Israel question caused some consternation for Nasser, particularly if Israel possessed nuclear weapons. As it pertains to the PRC's international affairs, the India discussion was broached, and Premier Zhou Enlai made quite certain that the PRC was willing to "establish peaceful and friendly relations with India and Pakistan." The premier highlighted further that doing otherwise would be incompatible with the Chinese system and policy.[27] On the question of India-Pakistan-China relations, Nasser assured the premier that Egypt would attempt to promote negotiations since it was a friend to both sides.[28] In the very last portion of the meeting, Zhou Enlai informed Nasser of his visits to the other respective African nations on his tour and asked Nasser if there were any particular things he should pay attention to? Nasser obliged him and provided particular details about the countries of Morocco, Algeria, Ghana, Mali, Guinea, and Sudan. There was no discussion of Somalia, Ethiopia, or Tunisia recorded from the first meeting between the Premier and President Nasser.[29]

During the second meeting between the two leaders, Zhou and President Nasser held discussions about the countries of Tunisia, Morocco, Libya, and Mauritania in Africa; and Israel, Palestine, and Yemen in the broader Middle East region. The men also discussed the significance of the non-aligned

movement and the possibility of a second African-Asian conference, akin
to the Bandung Conference in 1955. The meeting was held in Cairo at the
Qubba Palace. Of interest to this meeting were those in attendance, starkly
different from the first meeting held between the two leaders. At the second meeting, accompanying the premier was the vice premier, Chen Yi;
Deputy Director, Kong Yuan; Vice Minister Huang Zhen; Ambassador
Chen Jiakang; and Department Director Wang Yutian. The Egyptian delegation consisted of President Nasser; Vice premier, Amer; Executive Council
President Sabri; Presidential Council Member Rifaat; Foreign Minister
Fawzi; Deputy Foreign Minister Zulfikar Sabri; Ambassador to China, Imam;
and Presidency Secretary General Farid.[30]

In this particular meeting, the discussion of the Middle East continued
at length with President Nasser providing some history to the premier. The
initial focus centered on the Israeli-Palestinian situation and shifted to the
countries located in the North African region that are too considered part
of the Middle East (MENA). President Nasser provided the premier with
details on Libya's economic condition after independence and the role of
the major Western powers in the occupation of Libya after independence.
Background information was also provided on Tunisia and the independence struggle that occurred against France, Egyptian assistance toward this
struggle, and Tunisia's non-aligned stance. The countries of Algeria and
Morocco were also given a brief overview by the President of Egypt. As
it pertains to the former, the policies instituted by President Ben Bella to
thwart the French and fuel the Algerian Revolution were discussed. For the
latter, the anti-socialist policies of the country and the growing rift between
Morocco and Algeria along with Egypt's place within the feud were covered
in detail.[31]

Further discussions and briefings were held where the two leaders deliber-
ated the possibility of the PRC establishing diplomatic relations with Tunisia,
the Non-Aligned Conference, and the Second Asian-African Conference.
According to the transcripts provided by the Wilson Center, Nasser thought
of the Non-Aligned Conference as a way to attract those countries that were
still under colonial domination.[32] According to Nasser:

> I stepped forward to propose the Second Non-Aligned Conference. The main
> purpose is to encourage and attract emerging countries and those still under the
> influence of foreign countries to adopt an independent policy, to enable Non-
> Aligned Countries leaders to discuss not only their own national issues but also
> important international issues, and to emphasize that war and peace not only
> involve the great powers but influence us as well.[33]

What Nasser envisioned were nations that represented each region of the
globe. This included six countries from Latin America, specific Asian and

African countries, and three European countries. As Nasser discussed his plans with the delegation in attendance, he highlighted the difficulties of bringing this event to fruition, as there were several countries in Africa and outside of Africa that rejected the idea and refused to participate in a conference of this type and the fact that this conference did not yet have the strength that the Asian-African Conference exhibited. As it pertained to holding a second Asian-African Conference, it was believed that this would be difficult due to the diversity of views among the members who participated in the first Asian-African Conference in Bandung. Nasser quipped about how difficult it was to reach an agreement and achieve something at the first Bandung Conference of Asian-African nations.[34] The culminating points of this second meeting between the two leaders centered on Mauritania and devising a time for the third meeting.

The third and final meeting is recorded as being held at the same location as the second meeting with the same members in attendance. The context of this conversation centered on Sino-American relations, Sino-Indian relations, and Sino–Egyptian relations.[35] Unlike the previous two conversations held by the leaders, this conversation featured a great deal of discussion and explanations by Premier Zhou Enlai. To commence the discussion, the premier discussed the history of the Sino-U.S. relations indicating from the onset of the conversation that the relations between the two countries are not good and that it was no fault of the PRC.[36] A historical analysis was then delivered to President Nasser highlighting the significance of the Cairo Conference, the Cairo Declaration, and the proper place of Taiwan (ROC). The premier provided further detail of United States involvement in Asia, particularly the Korean War and the U.S. occupation of Taiwan during this event; the 1954 Geneva Conference; the situation with Cambodia; and Taiwan's recognition by the Western bloc as an independent political unit. Zhou Enlai discussed the PRC's displeasure with the decisions made by the United States on the Taiwan issue, thereby creating "two Chinas." The actions taken by the United States and the rest of the international community to create organization such as Southeast Asian Treaty Organization (SEATO) and the United States going against its word of Taiwan being a part of mainland China was considered an act of imperialism. According to Premier Zhou Enlai via the transcripts of the Wilson Center:

> With the liberation of the Chinese mainland, after Chiang Kai-shek went to Taiwan, in the latter half of 1949 US President Truman declared that Taiwan was a part of China, that the fight between Chiang Kai-shek and the Chinese mainland was a civil war, and that the United States would not interfere. In 1950 the United States published a white paper and continued with this position. Taiwan's jurisdiction and status were not at issue, but, because of the Korean War, became an issue.[37]

The idea that two Chinas were created by the United States, and the idea that the United States was not advancing the discussion of resolving this issue with the premier international organization the United Nations (UN), was highly detestable to the PRC. At this time, the PRC was not a member of the UN and was not amenable to the actions taken by the United States on the Taiwan issue.

After discussions were held about Sino–US relations, the conversation took a turn and resumed the discussion on Sino-Indian relations. Premier Enlai expressed to the delegation in attendance that India did not wish to negotiate at that time about the McMahon Line. However, a cease-fire agreement was settled upon, and negotiations were settled upon to stop the skirmish at the border in 1962.

After concluding remarks about India, the premier revisited the possibility of holding a second Non-aligned Conference and Asian-African Conference. It was at this juncture that the premier discussed the positives that emanated from the Bandung Conference, such as the "Principles of Peaceful Coexistence." It was further suggested that advanced preparatory work be conducted to ensure that a meaningful second conference is held. To ensure that the second conference is a success the premier suggested that certain issues such as technical, economic, cultural, and scientific be resolved based on the Ten Principles adopted at the first conference.[38] On the issue of Egyptian-Sino relations and adhering to the Ten Principles, particularly the issues of economic and technical assistance among the members who are to attend the second Afro-Asian conference, the premier suggested that there should be economic assistance given if one can offer that assistance to another country. In this same vein, he recognized the industrial and technological advancements made in the UAR and pledged support based on the reciprocal advancement of trade capacities between the two countries. For the economic side, the premier contributed fifty million dollars.[39]

Just as the PRC has made significant strides in promoting its culture in Africa in the twenty-first century, the country extended the same gesture during Zhou Enlai's visit to Africa in 1963–1964. The premier expressed his desire to send Chinese students to Africa to study Arabic, science, and technology. In exchange, Egypt was extended the opportunity to send the UAR's song and dance troupe to visit China.

The culmination of this third meeting between Zhou Enlai and President Nasser consisted of Nasser supporting the PRC on the Taiwan issue, offering support and reassurance on the Sino-Indian situation, and the guarantee that the next non-aligned movement will address the issue of imperialism. This is of importance due to the varying opinions and positions of the number of states that participated in the first Asian-African Conference and non-aligned movement, where some countries accepted economic and militaristic support from the United States, most notably India. With this, President Nasser reassured China that the country would not be condemned at the next conference over the India issue.

CONCLUSION

The significance of the six-day visit to Egypt is of importance because the transcripts reflect the detailed dialogue between the two nations and the process that the PRC undertook to foment its position as a viable option for African states in the international arena. This first high-level visit between both countries provides some of the groundwork for the commencement of the triangulation strategy discussed in the methodological section. That the relationship between Nasser and Zhou Enlai had some depth of substance and evidence that both men felt comfortable enough to discuss the complex international arena and where they felt each of their countries were situated within the dynamic. This exchange between the PRC and Egypt also set the stage for Zhou Enlai, as he received firsthand information about the political and economic dynamics of the other countries that were in line for his subsequent visits during his tour.

The relationship between Premier Zhou Enlai and President Nasser was not of new origin, the two men had met previously at the first Afro-Asian conference in Bandung, Indonesia. Furthermore, President Nasser was the only head of state from Africa to attend the conference. Although the countries of Ghana, Sudan, Libya, Liberia, and Ethiopia had ministerial staff represented at the conference, this one detail of a sitting head of state from Africa being present is of importance. Nasser is known as one of the first African leaders to make significant modernization reforms on the continent, and this is something for which he has been remembered. Premier Zhou, although working under Mao Tse Tung, was a pragmatic reformer himself. He too sought to make the PRC a nation that could best be emulated by other emerging dependent nations. Although Egypt had its own goals toward development, it did seek assistance from the PRC, and the PRC looked to Egypt for expertise in science and technology, something that the premier was quite impressed with.

Another important facet of the relationship and visits between the Premier and President Nasser was the unadulterated discussions about international affairs. After reviewing the Wilson Center transcripts, it appeared quite evident that both men were able to honestly discuss matters openly and sincerely. Whether it was Nasser providing advice about other African nations before the premier's visits; Premier Zhou Enlai discussing the Sino-Indian skirmish; the need for a second Asian–Afro Conference and both men expressing their concerns over whether solidarity would occur among all nations invited; the place of Israel in world affairs; and last but certainly not least, the role of the US-Soviet dilemma, which seemed to undergird every aforementioned point, were of great importance for both men. The visit to Egypt by Premier Zhou Enlai set the stage for more talks and further South-South cooperation in Africa. Because of these visits, new trading partners were developed, new allies created, and lastly, the development of the relationships as a result of Zhou's visits to ten African nations later set the stage for the PRC's place as a leader in the international community.

NOTES

1. Jules Archer, *Chou En-Lai* (New York: Hawthorn Books, Inc., 1973), 121; Lillian Craig Harris, *The Washington Papers/112: China's Foreign Policy Toward the Third World* (New York, NY: Praeger Publishers, 1985), 32.

2. Ibid., 121.

3. "Nuclear Test Ban Treaty," John F. Kennedy Presidential Library and Museum, accessed March 23, 2019, available from: https://www.jfklibrary.org/learn /about-jfk/jfk-in-history/nuclear-test-ban-treaty; Also see Jules Archer, *Chou En-Lai* (New York: Hawthorn Books, Inc., 1973), 120; For more information regarding the background of the Test Ban Treaty of 1963 see "Treaty Banning Nuclear Weapons Test in the Atmosphere, in Outer Space, and Under Water," U.S. Department of State—Bureau of Arms Control, Verification, and Compliance, accessed March 23, 2019, Available from: https://www.state.gov/t/isn/4797.htm.

4. Kenneth Waltz, *Theory of International Politics* (Reading, MA: Waveland Press, 2010).

5. Stephen M. Walt, "Alliances: Balancing and Bandwagoning" in *International Politics: Enduring Concepts and Contemporary Issues 13th Edition*, ed. Robert J. Art and Robert Jervis (Boston: Pearson Publishers, 2017), 153.

6. Ibid.

7. For further clarification on weak states and failed states, see Robert I. Rotberg, "Failed States, Collapsed States, Weak States: Causes and Indicators" in *State Failure and State Weakness in a Time of Terror*, ed. Robert I. Rotberg (World Peace Foundation: Brookings Institution Press, 2003), 1–26.

8. For further reading on free riders, collective action, and public goods, see Mancur Olson, *The Logic of Collective Action: Public Goods and the Theory of Groups* (Cambridge: Harvard University Press, 2012).

9. "Foreign Relations, 1969-1976, Volume I, Foundations of Foreign Policy, 1969-1972" US Department of State—Office of the Historian, accessed 29 April 2019. Available from: https://2001-2009.state.gov/r/pa/ho/frus/nixon/i/21100.htm.

10. Robert I. Rotberg, "Failed States, Collapsed States, Weak States: Causes and Indicators," 2.

11. Gerald Segal, "China and Africa" in *The Annals of the American Academy of Political and Social Science: China Foreign Relations*, Vol. 519 (January 1992): 115–126, 117.

12. Ibid., 118.

13. Donovan Chau, *Exploiting Africa: The Influence of Maoist China in Algeria, Ghana, and Tanzania* (Annapolis, MD: Naval Institute Press, 2014).

14. Gregg Brazinsky. *Winning the Third World: Sino-American Rivalry During the Cold War* (Chapel Hill, NC: University of North Carolina Press, 2017), 1–8.

15. David H. Shinn and Joshua Eiseman, *China and Africa: A Century of Engagement.* Philadelphia: University of Pennsylvania Press, 2012.

16. Christopher J. Lee ed., *Making a World After Empire: The Bandung Moment and Its Political Afterlives* (Athens: Ohio University Press, 2010).

17. Ian Taylor, *China in Africa: Engagement and Compromise* (New York: Routledge Press, 2006).

18. Deborah Brautigam, *The Dragon's Gift: The Real Story of China in Africa* (New York: Oxford University Press, 2009), 22–42.

19. Bruce D. Larkin, *China and Africa, 1949-1970: The Foreign Policy of the People's Republic of China* (Berkley: University of California Press, 1971), 14.

20. Jules Archer, *Chou En-lai*, 120.

21. For further information on the "Friendship Delegation" see the "Cable from the Foreign Cultural Liaison Committee, 'Request to Send Culture and Friendship Delegation to Visit Africa," December 29, 1961. History and Public Policy Program Digital Archive, PRC PMA 108-00323-05. Translated by David Cowig. Available from: https://digitalarchive.wilsoncenter.org/document/120322.

22. "Record of Conversation between Premier Zhou Enlai, Vice Premier Chen Yi, and Pakistani Ambassador Raza," August 12, 1963, History and Public Policy Program Digital Archive, PRC FMA 113-00452-05, 18–22. Obtained and translated by Christopher Tang. Available from: https://digitalarchive.wilsoncenter.org/document/121572.

23. "Zhou Enlai's Discussion with a Kenyan African National Federation Delegation (Excerpt)," September 05, 1963, History and Public Policy Program Digital Archive, Dang de Wenxian (Party Historical Documents), no. 3 (1994): 15–16. Translated by Neil Silver. Available from: https://digitalarchive.wilsoncenter.org/document/114355.

24. "Mao Zedong, 'There Are Two Intermediate Zones,'" September 1963, History and Public Policy Program Digital Archive, Translation from the Ministry of Foreign Affairs of the People's Republic of China and the Party Literature Research Center, eds., Mao Zedong on Diplomacy (Beijing: Foreign Languages Press, 1998), 387–389. Available from: https://digitalarchive.wilsoncenter.org/document/121207.

25. Shinn and Eiseman, China and Africa, 229.

26. "Record of Premier Zhou Enlai's Calling on President Nasser," December 20, 1963, History and Public Policy Program Digital Archive, PRC FMA 107-01027-08, 63–80. Translated by Stephen Mercado. Available from: https://digitalarchive.wilsoncenter.org/document/165432; It is not clear as to the exact date of these talks. According to the Wilson Center Archives, the first talks transcript is dated December 20, 1963, yet the second and third meetings between the two leaders are dated December 17 and December 19, respectively.

27. Ibid., 7.

28. As it pertains to the India matter, this particular conversation was of importance due to the recent border clashes between the PRC and India in October 1962. At the center of the dispute was the McMahon Line, which was an arbitrary border devised by the British in 1914. China did not recognize that line as the official line and instead referred to the borders instituted under the Qing Dynasty. Although the border is still a contentious area, trade and economic agreements between the two countries are strong.

29. "Record of Premier Zhou Enlai's Calling on President Nasser," December 20, 1963, History and Public Policy Program Digital Archive, PRC FMA 107-01027-08, 63–80. Translated by Stephen Mercado. Available from: https://digitalarchive.wilsoncenter.org/document/165432.

30. "Record of the Second Meeting between Premier Zhou Enlai and President Nasser," December 17, 1963, History and Public Policy Program Digital Archive, PRC FMA 107-01027-06, 25–39. Translated by Stephen Mercado. Available from: https://digitalarchive.wilsoncenter.org/document/165401.

31. Ibid.

32. For further readings on the Nonaligned movement see George W. Shepard, Jr. *Nonaligned Black Africa* (Lexington: D.C. Heath and Company, 1970); Guy Arnold, *The A to Z of the Nonaligned Movement and the Third World* (Lanham: Scarecrow Press, 2006); Ali Mazuri ed., *General History of Africa: Africa Since 1935 Vol. 8* (Fontenoy, Paris: United Nations Educational, Scientific and Cultural Organization, 1999).

33. "Record of the Second Meeting between Premier Zhou Enlai and President Nasser," December 17, 1963, History and Public Policy Program Digital Archive, PRC FMA 107-01027-06, 25–39. Translated by Stephen Mercado. Available from: https://digitalarchive.wilsoncenter.org/document/165401.

34. Ibid.

35. "Record of the Third Conversation between Premier Zhou Enlai and President Nasser," December 19, 1963, History and Public Policy Program Digital Archive, PRC FMA 107-01027-07, 41–62. Translated by Stephen Mercado. Available from: https://digitalarchive.wilsoncenter.org/document/165430.

36. Ibid.

37. Ibid.

38. Ibid.

39. Ibid.

BIBLIOGRAPHY

Archer, Jules. *Chou En-Lai.* New York: Hawthorn Books, Inc., 1973.

Arnold, Guy. *The A to Z of the Nonaligned Movement and the Third World.* Lanham: Scarecrow Press, 2006.

Brautigam, Deborah. *The Dragon's Gift: The Real Story of China in Africa.* New York: Oxford University Press, 2009.

Brazinsky, Gregg. *Winning the Third World: Sino-American Rivalry During the Cold War.* Chapel Hill, NC: University of North Carolina Press, 2017.

Chau, Donovan. *Exploiting Africa: The Influence of Maoist China in Algeria, Ghana, and Tanzania.* Annapolis, MD: Naval Institute Press, 2014.

"Foreign Relations, 1969–1976, Volume I, Foundations of Foreign Policy, 1969–1972." US Department of State—Office of the Historian. Accessed 29 April 2019. Available from: https://2001-2009.state.gov/r/pa/ho/frus/nixon/i/21100.htm.

Harris-Craig, Lillian. *The Washington Papers/112: China's Foreign Policy Toward the Third World.* New York, NY: Praeger Publishers, 1985.

Larkin, Bruce D. *China and Africa, 1949–1970: The Foreign Policy of the People's Republic of China.* Berkley: University of California Press, 1971.

Lee, Christopher J. Lee ed. *Making a World After Empire: The Bandung Moment and its Political Afterlives* Athens: Ohio University Press, 2010.

Mazuri, Ali ed., *General History of Africa: Africa Since 1935 Vol. 8.* Paris: United Nations Educational, Scientific and Cultural Organization, 1999.

"Nuclear Test Ban Treaty," John F. Kennedy Presidential Library and Museum. Accessed March 23, 2019. Available from: https://www.jfklibrary.org/learn/about-jfk/jfk-in-history/nuclear-test-ban-treaty.

Olson, Mancur. *The Logic of Collective Action: Public Goods and the Theory of Groups.* Cambridge: Harvard University Press, 2012.

Rotberg, Robert I. "Failed States, Collapsed States, Weak States: Causes and Indicators," in *State Failure and State Weakness in a Time of Terror,* ed. Robert I. Rotberg. World Peace Foundation: Brookings Institution Press, 2003.

Segal, Gerald. "China and Africa," in *The Annals of the American Academy of Political and Social Science: China Foreign Relations* 519 (January 1992): 115–126.

Shepard, George W, Jr. *Nonaligned Black Africa.* Lexington: D.C. Heath and Company, 1970.

Shinn, David H. and Joshua Eiseman. *China and Africa: A Century of Engagement.* Philadelphia: University of Pennsylvania Press, 2012.

Taylor, Ian. *China in Africa: Engagement and Compromise.* New York: Routledge Press, 2006.

"Treaty Banning Nuclear Weapons Test in the Atmosphere, in Outer Space, and Under Water." U.S. Department of State—Bureau of Arms Control, Verification, and Compliance. Accessed March 23, 2019. Available from: https://www.state.gov/t/isn/4797.htm.

Walt, Stephen M. "Alliances: Balancing and Bandwagoning," in *International Politics: Enduring Concepts and Contemporary Issues 13th Edition,* ed. Robert J. Art and Robert Jervis. Boston: Pearson Publishers, 2017.

Waltz, Kenneth. *Theory of International Politics.* Reading, MA: Waveland Press, 2010.

Wilson Center. "Cable from the Foreign Cultural Liaison Committee, 'Request to Send Culture and Friendship Delegation to Visit Africa." December 29, 1961. History and Public Policy Program Digital Archive, PRC PMA 108-00323-05.

Translated by David Cowig. Available from: https://digitalarchive.wilsoncenter
.org/document/120322.

———. "Mao Zedong, 'There Are Two Intermediate Zones'." September 1963, History and Public Policy Program Digital Archive. Translation from the Ministry of Foreign Affairs of the People's Republic of China and the Party Literature Research Center, eds., Mao Zedong on Diplomacy. Beijing: Foreign Languages Press, 1998. Available from: https://digitalarchive.wilsoncenter.org/document/1 21207.

———. "Record of Conversation between Premier Zhou Enlai, Vice premier Chen Yi, and Pakistani Ambassador Raza." August 12, 1963. History and Public Policy Program Digital Archive, PRC FMA 113-00452-05, 18–22. Obtained and translated by Christopher Tang. Available from: https://digitalarchive.wilsoncenter.org/document/121572.

———. "Record of the Second Meeting between Premier Zhou Enlai and President Nasser." December 17, 1963. History and Public Policy Program Digital Archive, PRC FMA 107-01027-06, 25–39. Translated by Stephen Mercado. Available from: https://digitalarchive.wilsoncenter.org/document/165401.

———. "Record of the Third Conversation between Premier Zhou Enlai and President Nasser." December 19, 1963. History and Public Policy Program Digital Archive, PRC FMA 107-01027-07, 41–62. Translated by Stephen Mercado. Available from: https://digitalarchive.wilsoncenter.org/document/165430.

———. "Record of Premier Zhou Enlai's Calling on President Nasser." December 20, 1963. History and Public Policy Program Digital Archive, PRC FMA 107-01027-08, 63–80. Translated by Stephen Mercado. Available from: https://digital archive.wilsoncenter.org/document/165432.

———. "Zhou Enlai's Discussion with a Kenyan African National Federation Delegation (Excerpt)." September 05, 1963, History and Public Policy Program Digital Archive. Dang de Wenxian (Party Historical Documents), no. 3 (1994): 15–16. Translated by Neil Silver. Available from: https://digitalarchive.wilsonc enter.org/document/114355.

Chapter 2

The Policy Framework of Sino-African Relations from the Chinese Perspective

A Review of Selected Policy Papers and Agreements

Wei Ye

INTRODUCTION

The relations between the People's Republic of China (China) and Africa could be divided into three chronological periods with different patterns and priorities, respectively[1]. During 1949–1979, starting with the establishment of diplomatic ties between China and Egypt in 1956, China successively began bilateral ties with several African states based on the Five Principles of Peaceful Coexistence and the Eight Principles for Economic Aid and Technical Assistance to Other Countries announced by Premier Zhou Enlai during his visit to Ghana in 1964. These two documentations laid the foundation for Sino-African relations in this period when bilateral economic aids without conditionality served the political and diplomatic interests of China. During 1979–2000, the changing international relations and the domestic reform and opening policy in China drove Sino-African relations into a more economic-oriented direction though the political ties also strengthened with the frequent high-level visits. With the signing of bilateral agreements on concessional loans between China and Sudan in 1995, China started to provide concessional loans to African countries. Since 2000 when the Forum on China-Africa Cooperation (FOCAC) inaugurated, China has addressed Sino-African relations with a collective pattern by dealing with Africa as a whole and announced its African Policy Paper in 2006 and 2015, respectively. The closer economic tie, marked by the fact that China has become the largest trading partner of Africa in 2009, has driven Sino-African relations into a comprehensive strategic partnership with emphasizing a win-win situation.

However, the way how a win-win situation can be realized will rely largely on the initiative of African countries.

1949–1979: FROM THE FIVE PRINCIPLES OF PEACEFUL COEXISTENCE TO THE EIGHT PRINCIPLES FOR ECONOMIC AID AND TECHNICAL ASSISTANCE TO OTHER COUNTRIES

Although there were a few party-to-party meetings and visits between China and Africa,[2] diplomatic ties between China and African countries started in the late 1950s after the Asian-African Conference in 1955. The Five Principles of Peaceful Coexistence consisted of the political base for China to build those diplomatic ties, giving the fact that the newly built communist regime in China adopted the "leaning to one side" (yi bian dao) policy[3] by emphasizing building diplomatic relations with the communist bloc. With the establishment of diplomatic ties between China and Egypt in 1956, China successively began bilateral ties with several African states. Mutual political support and economic aid were the themes of Sino-African relations during 1949–1979.[4] These themes were mainly driven by the changing international relations during the Cold War, especially the decolonialization in Asia and Africa and the deterioration of Sino-Soviet relations. Ideology played a major role in China's policy toward Africa during this period[5]. More precisely, the Communist Party of China (CPC) leadership perception of international relations, especially the fear of war, in this period influenced its policy toward Africa.

With the establishment of the People's Republic of China in 1949, the newly founded regime established its diplomatic relations with the Soviet Union, the communist countries in Eastern Europe, and several nationalist neighboring countries in Asia based on the "leaning to one side" (yi bian dao) policy.[6] However, the new regime did not necessarily refuse official relations with noncommunist regimes. On the one hand, breaking out the isolation of the West to win international support and influence, especially from Asian and African countries who share similar experiences of struggling for national independence and fighting against colonialism, was considered as a strategy to prevent China from the danger of U.S. attack.[7] On the other hand, the CPC leadership also emphasized the importance of national independence of the Soviet Union.[8]

According to the Joint Program passed by the Chinese People's Political Consultative Conference (CPPCC) in 1949, the guidelines for the foreign policy of China was to ensure national independence, freedom, and sovereignty, to promote sustainable peace internationally and cooperation among nations, and to fight against imperialist invasion and war. It opened to build diplomatic relations based on equality, mutual benefit, and mutual respect for territorial integrity and sovereignty with foreign governments that discontinue official relations with the Kuomintang (KMT) regime and showed positive attitudes to the communist regime.[9]

Equality, mutual benefit, and mutual respect for territorial integrity and sovereignty proposed in the Joint Program of the CPPCC in 1949 consisted of the base for the Five Principles of Peaceful Coexistence that were initially proposed to address China's relation with India. During his meeting with the India delegation in 1953, China's Premier Zhou Enlai proposed the Five Principles of Peaceful Coexistence, including mutual respect for territorial integrity and sovereignty, mutual nonaggression, noninterference in each other's internal affairs, equality and mutual benefit, and peaceful coexistence, for the first time to address the issue of Tibet. The Five Principles of Peaceful Coexistence was formally incorporated into the Agreement on Trade and Intercourse between the Tibet Region of China and India in 1954.[10] In the joint statements between Premier Zhou Enlai and India's Prime Minister Jawaharlal Nehru in June 1954 during Premier Zhou Enlai's visit to India, the Five Principles of Peaceful Coexistence were acknowledged as the base for bilateral relations between the two governments.[11] Later during Premier Zhou Enlai's visit to Burma after India, the Five Principles of Peaceful Coexistence were also adopted in the joint statement between prime ministers of China and Burma as the guidelines for the relation between the two countries. In this joint statement, they claimed that obedience to those five principles would ensure the peaceful coexistence of countries with different regimes and replace the fear of threats of invasion and interference with security and trust.[12]

The contacts and consensus between China and India, based on the Five Principles of Peaceful Coexistence, on achieving peace laid the foundation for Prime Minister Jawaharlal Nehru's support toward China's participation in the Asian-African Conference (also known as the Bandung Conference) in 1955.[13] Despite the hostility toward communism, the potential Chinese influence on unaffected Africa and Arab was also one of the major concerns of the West for opposing China's participation in the Conference.[14] But on the contrary, China's participation in the Asian-African Conference, with anti-colonialism, anti-imperialism, and anti-racism as the major political agenda,[15] appeared as a turning point for initiating diplomatic ties between China and African countries.[16] According to the drafted scheme for participating in the Asian-African Conference, Primer Zhou Enlai met Egypt's incumbent Prime Minister Gamal Abdul Nasser and Sudan's incumbent Prime Minister Ismail al-Azhari in person during the Conference. The personal meetings laid the foundation for the following cooperation and bilateral relations between

China and the two countries, as well as other African countries.[17] The Five Principles of Peaceful Coexistence was eventually incorporated into the final Communique of the Asian-African Conference and remain as a cornerstone of the policy stance of China toward Africa.[18]

Egypt appeared to be the first African country to build a diplomatic tie with China. Before the diplomatic tie, the two countries already had trade relations based on the signed trade agreement. Based on the spirit of the Asian-African Conference, the two countries signed the cultural agreement and Communique on diplomatic relations in 1956. In addition to the expanded trade and economic relations after the Asian-African Conference between China and Africa,[19] supporting the independence and liberation movements in Africa through political support and economic aid consisted of a significant part of China's policy toward Africa.

In return, Beijing insisted that upholding the one-China policy by recognizing China as the only legitimate regime of China should be the precondition for diplomatic recognition between China and African countries.[20] In the late 1950s and early 1960s, Africa had increasingly become a hot place for the Soviet Union and the United States to compete for influence. Taiwan was also actively involved in Africa to obtain political recognition[21]. With the deterioration of Sino-Soviet relations in the late 1950s, China faced diplomatic containment from both the United States and the Soviet Union. As a result, to win support from the "intermediate zone" was seemingly of greater importance. Military and economic aid appeared as a significant role to strengthen the united front against imperialism and to win diplomatic supports.[22] After 1963, Africa and the Middle East replaced Asia as the major region China's economic aid went to.[23]

During December 1963 and Feburary1964, Primer Zhou Enlai visited ten African countries to show support for the struggle against colonialism and imperialism in Africa and to strengthen the ties with African countries to break out diplomatic isolation from the two great powers.[24] China's support expressed by Primer Zhou Enlai was both rhetorical in terms of the morality of the liberation and independence movement against imperialism and material in terms of economic and technical support to African countries. In terms of the morality of the independence movement in Africa, Primer Zhou Enlai's proposed five principles, consistent with the Five Principles of Peaceful Coexistence, specifically regarding China's stance toward African and Arab countries in 1963. The five principles were the following[25]:

- China supports the fight against imperialism and the struggle for national independence in Arabic and African countries.
- China upholds the non-alignment policy, with peace and neutrality at the center, adopted by Arabic and African countries.

- China supports Arabic and African countries' faith to achieve solidarity and unity in their way.
- China supports peaceful settlements of disputes through consultation among Arabic and African countries; and
- China insists that the sovereignty of Arabic and African countries should be respected by other countries, thus opposing invasion and inference from any party.

Despite divergent audiences and regimes in those ten countries, including Tunisia and Ethiopia who had not established diplomatic ties with China at that time, the rhetoric pragmatically expressed the moral support of China toward Africa.[26] With unequivocal stance against imperialism and colonialism, these five principles for China's policy toward African and Arab countries reflected the ideology-oriented policy stance of China toward Africa at that time[27] and have remained a significant component of the political relations, though with less ideological consideration now, between China and Africa.[28]

In terms of material support, during Primer Zhou Enlai's visit to Ghana in January 1964, he formally outlined the eight principles of the Chinese government in providing economic aid and technical assistance to other countries. These principles were the following [29]:

- The Chinese government always bases itself on the principle of equality and mutual benefit in providing aid to other countries. It never regards such aid as a kind of unilateral alms but as something mutual.
- In providing aid to other countries, the Chinese government strictly respects the sovereignty of the recipient countries and never attaches any conditions or asks for any privileges.
- China provides economic aid in the form of interest-free or low-interest loans and extends the time limit for the repayment when necessary to lighten the burden of the recipient countries as far as possible.
- In providing aid to other countries, the purpose of the Chinese government is not to make the recipient countries dependent on China but to help them embark step by step on the road of self-reliance and independent economic development.
- The Chinese government tries its best to help the recipient countries build projects which require less investment while yielding quicker results so that the recipient governments may increase their income and accumulate capital.
- The Chinese government provides the best-quality equipment and material of its manufacture at international market prices. If the equipment and material provided by the Chinese government are not up to the agreed

specifications and quality, the Chinese government undertakes to replace them.

• In giving any technical assistance, the Chinese government will see to it that the personnel of the recipient country fully master such technique.

• The experts dispatched by China to help in construction in the recipient countries will have the same standard of living as the experts of the recipient country. The Chinese experts are not allowed to make any special demands or enjoy any special amenities.

Although the role of economic aid in Sino-African relations and the way to provide economic aid to Africa is changing with the time, the notions of equality, mutual benefits, noninterference in other countries' internal affairs, and unconditionality advocated in the Eight Principles for Economic Aid and Technical Assistance to Other Countries have long been a feature of Chinese aid to Africa and other countries.[30] In contrast to the international situation during the Cold War, the domestic situation of China seemed to play a relatively insignificant role in China's policy stance toward Africa, although the fervent ideology and the Cultural Revolution (1966–1976) in China during this period did influence Sino-African relations especially in terms of party-to-party relations between nationalist and communist parties in Africa and the CPC.[31] Despite the economic difficulties in China resulted from the Great Leap Forward (1958–1960), China continued to expand its economic aid to Africa.

According to the archive of the Central Intelligence Agency (CIA) of the United States, the economic credits and grants provided by China to Africa were about 176.3 million U.S. dollars in 1963.[32] While in 1964 and 1965, China provided economic aid amounting to about 200 million U.S. dollars and 300 million U.S. dollars to Africa, respectively.[33] The amount of economic aid increased significantly in 1965. Even during the Cultural Revolution, China's support for the liberation and independence movements in Africa and economic aid to certain African countries continued even though its ability for that support was hindered.[34] An example of the continued economic aid to Africa is the financing and constructing for the Tanzania-Zambia railroad project during 1970–1976.

1979–2000: FROM THE FOUR PRINCIPLES FOR SINO-AFRICAN ECONOMIC AND TECHNICAL COOPERATION TO CONCESSIONAL LOANS

With the end of the Cultural Revolution, the domestic situation changed significantly in China. In December 1978, the CPC leadership announced the domestic reform and the opening-up policy with domestic economic development turning to be the priority of China's national policy in the Third Plenary Session of the 11th Central Committee of the CPC.[35] With the changing international relations in the late years of the Cold War, the CPC leadership's perception of the international situation also changed. Despite the turbulence in international relations in the 1980s, the CPC leader Deng Xiaoping believed that it was possible to maintain peace over a longer period.[36] He further argued that peace and development were the themes of the contemporary world. With the new judgment about the international situation, reform and opening-up as a national policy of China were further institutionalized.[37]

Due to the diminishing of perceived threats of war, domestic policy, especially the economic reform and opening-up policy, in China began to play a larger role over international relations on influencing China's policy toward Africa in this period. On the one hand, Africa seemed to play a less important role in China's foreign policy than before since the mid-1980s until the Tiananmen Square Incident in 1989 in terms of the relative lack of high-level visits and the stagnated Chinese aid to Africa because of China's diplomatic relations had diversified with the opening-up policy[38] and China's attention on its domestic economic development. On the other hand, China's domestic development started to create new grounding for cooperation between China and Africa. Sino-Africa relations in this period were featured by the increasing market-oriented economic cooperation with and investment in Africa, compared with economic and technical aid previously, with less ideology.

In December 1982 and January 1983, China's Primer Zhao Ziyang officially visited Egypt, Algeria, Morocco, Guinea, Gabon, Zaire, Congo, Zambia, Zimbabwe, Tanzania, and Kenya and outlined China's policy toward Africa in the new era. This was the second official tour of China's primer to Africa after Primer Zhou Enlai's tour in the 1960s.[39] During Primer Zhao Ziyang's visit to Tanzania on January 13, 1983, he announced the four principles of "equality and mutual benefit, pursuing practical results, adopting various ways and seeking common development" for Sino-African economic and technical cooperation. The detailed principles were[40] the following:

- In conducting economic and technological cooperation with African countries, China follows the principles of unity, friendship, equality, and mutual benefit, respects each other's sovereignty without interfering in internal affairs of African countries, and never attaches any conditions or asks for any privileges.
- China's economic and technological cooperation with African countries starts from the actual needs and possible conditions of the two sides and exerts their respective strengths and potentials, striving for less investment, short construction period, quick results, and good economic returns.

- China's economic and technological cooperation with African countries can be carried out in a variety of ways with the consideration of local conditions in Africa countries. These ways include but not limited to technical services, training of technology and management personnel, scientific and technological exchanges, construction projects, cooperative production, and joint ventures. The Chinese side is responsible for the compliance, quality, and justice of the cooperation projects undertaken. Experts and technicians sent by the Chinese side do not require special treatment.
- China's economic and technological cooperation with African countries aims to complement each other and help each other to enhance the ability of both sides to become self-reliant and promote the development of their respective national economies.

Comparing the new four principles with the Eight Principles for Economic Aid and Technical Assistance to Other Countries announced in the 1960s, the principles of equity, mutual benefits, noninference, and self-reliance remained. However, emphasizing economic and technical cooperation rather than aid appeared as a salient change in the discourse. Also, the principle of mutual benefit emphasized both in the 1950s and 1980s was more seriously considered since the 1980s both in terms of the rhetorical phrases and the intention of the CPC leadership. The new four principles mentioned "mutual needs and conditions," "complementary," and "respective economic growth," exemplifying mutual benefits specifically for economic purposes. In Primer Zhao Ziyang's report to the National People's Congress on his Africa tour, he claimed that "economic and technical cooperation contributes to our domestic development."[41]

However, significant international issues still had a notable influence on China's policy toward Africa. Despite the western sanction toward China in 1989 triggered by the Tiananmen Square Incident, China achieved diplomatic success, in terms of ensuring the opening-up policy, through active educational exchange and cooperation with the Third World countries[42] especially African countries. In 1989, the Ministry of Economics and Trade of the People's Republic of China (now known as the Ministry of Commerce) set a special fund, amounting to 4 million RMB, to support university development in Zaire (now known as the Democratic Republic of the Congo), Cameroon, Tanzania, and Zimbabwe to strengthen foreign aid on intellectuals toward Africa.[43]

In the context of China's policy toward Africa in a new era, China's engagement in the development cooperation of Africa has been diversified since the 1980s. It started to participate in development financing in Africa by joining the Africa Development Bank (ADB) and Africa Development Fund (ADF) in 1985.[44] With the approval of the State Council of China in

1995 for the reform of foreign aid provided to other countries, China started to replace interest-free loans with concessional loans in providing foreign aid. In line with the socialist market economy reform in China in the early 1990s, the concessional loans connected development financing in Africa with the market reform of Chinese enterprises and Chinese international trade and investment in Africa.[45] Africa appeared to be the first region that received the Chinese concessional loans with the signing of the Framework Agreement of Concessional Loan between the Republic of Sudan and the People's Republic of China in 1995 that offered 100 million RMB of concessional loan for the Sudan oil project.[46] Within 1995, The Chinese government signed eleven framework agreements on concessional loans among which all were with African countries.[47] In 1999, the total trade between China and Africa had reached 6.5 billion U.S. dollars.[48]

SINCE 2000: THE FOCAC AND CHINA'S AFRICAN POLICY PAPER

Sino-Africa relations, especially the economic tie, have been strengthened since the 1990s. Compared with the economic aid and technical assistance that served political relations in Sino-Africa relations previously, the economic and trade cooperation between China and Africa since the 1990s is turning back to the essence of economic relations. This trend is related to both China's attention on economic development and Africa's new agenda on development especially since the announcement of the New Partnership for Africa's Development (NEPAD). In 2000, the FOCAC was established as a mechanism of collective dialogue to address Sino-African relations in the era of globalization. Since the establishment of the FOCAC, Sino-African relations have been moving forward to a more comprehensive partnership beyond merely political support and economic cooperation.

The establishment of the FOCAC in 2000 was sparked by multiple factors including the improvement of the political and economic situation in Africa, the adjustment of developed countries' policy toward Africa, and the economic globalization.[49] After the "lost decade" in the 1980s,[50] the recovery of the economy in Africa in the 1990s has made itself a promising land to the international world. In the 1990s, with the multipolarization of international relations, Africa turned out to be a new force in world politics. Developed countries, most notably the United States, France, and Japan, adjusted their policy toward Africa by setting up new mechanisms to strengthen the cooperation with Africa.[51] As a traditional partner with Africa since the 1950s, China has been undergoing the fast process of economic modernization and socialist market-orient economic reform since the 1990s. The complementary needs created by domestic development of each other have made China and Africa development partners, facing economic globalization. Notably, the idea of building a collective mechanism between China and Africa was initiated by African countries several times.[52] Considering the influence of the policy adjustments of developed countries and the complementary needs of each other, China and Africa finally established the FOCAC.

According to the *Beijing Declaration of the Forum on China-Africa Cooperation* announced in the first ministerial conference of the FOCAC in 2000, the two parties position the FOCAC as a platform for Sino-African cooperation at all levels and in all fields, also phrased as a new-type partnership, within the context of South-South Cooperation and value the potential of economic and trade cooperation between them. They also emphasized the pursuit of equity through political coordination in international affairs in terms of the international political economy order especially in the era of globalization. This positioning differentiates the FOCAC from the mechanisms between Africa and developing countries by pointing out the convergent pursue of China and Africa, as members of the global south, for a more fair and just international order. In terms of the situation in Africa, disease, poverty, and debt are identified as the major obstacles in the development of Africa.[53]

In 2006, China announced its first African Policy Paper, advocating a new type of strategic partnership featuring political equality and mutual trust, economic win-win cooperation, and cultural exchange. In line with the Five Principles of Peaceful Coexistence and the four principles for Sino-Africa economic and technical cooperation announced in the 1980s, equity, non-interference, mutual benefits, and common development remain the core principles of China's policy stance toward Africa. In addition, the one-China policy is formally phrased in the policy paper as the precondition for African countries to establish diplomatic relations with China. Within the all-round cooperation between China and China advocated in the policy paper, economic, trade, and social development cooperation are emphasized in the context of common development.[54]

With the announcement of the first China's African Policy Paper, China announced initiatives through the mechanism of the FOCAC to facilitate economic cooperation with investment in Africa. The establishment of the China-Africa Development Fund, special loans for small and medium-sized enterprises in Africa was announced, respectively, in 2006 and 2009 to facilitate development financing.[55] Consistent with the priorities of NEPAD, infrastructures, agriculture, and human resource development are identified as major issue areas for cooperation. Sino-African relations, especially economic relations, have been strengthened since the announcement of the initial China's African Policy Paper and the followed initiatives. In 2009, China turned out to be the first largest trade partner in Africa.[56]

The Chinese government announced its second African Policy Paper in Johannesburg in December 2015. The changing international relations and the new priorities of both China and Africa are identified as the background for Sino-African relations in the new era. The economic complementarity of China and Africa is further emphasized as the base for cooperation. Specifically, China believes that its advantage of development experience, technology, capital, and the market could contribute to the industrialization of Africa through infrastructure and human resource development.[57] As a practical action, in the FOCAC Johannesburg Action Plan (2016–2018), the Chinese government announced to initiate a China-Africa production capacity cooperation fund for the transfer of industrial capacity from China to Africa.[58]

However, despite the intensive Chinese economic cooperation with and investment in Africa driven by complementarity from the perspective of China, the way how could the Chinese trade, investment, and infrastructure building in Africa contributes to the development of Africa will largely rely on the initiative of African countries. For one thing, although China emphasizes its development experience as the advantage over Africa in the second African Policy Paper, whether the development experience is suitable for Africa, especially considering the different state-society relationships in African countries, remain doubtful.[59] Specifically, the Chinese trade, investment, and infrastructure building in Africa are not a guarantee to transfer Africa's advantage of energy, natural, and demographic resource into economic growth and social change. Instead, corresponding political, social, and cultural infrastructure of African countries is needed for that transfer. For another, similar as the situation of African countries' initiative to facilitate the establishment of the FOCAC, maintaining the sustainability of mutual interest and benefit will also need initiatives from Africa's side, giving the fact that China is actively conducting economic cooperation and investment through the Belt and Road Initiative.

CONCLUSION

Sino-African relations after 1949 started with the establishment of diplomatic ties between China and Egypt in 1956 after China's diplomatic success in the Asia-African Conference in 1955. The Five Principles for Peaceful Coexistence, incorporated into the final Communique of the Asian-African Conference, remain as a cornerstone of the policy stance of China toward Africa. Despite the expanded trade and economic relations after the Asian-African Conference between China and Africa,[60] supporting the independence and liberation movements in Africa through political support and economic aid consisted of a significant part of China's policy toward Africa during 1949–1979. This is driven by the CPC leadership perception of international relations, especially the fear of war. Africa was considered as a significant role in the united front against imperialism and one of the major sources for China to obtain political recognition.

The changing international relations during the Cold War, especially the decolonialization in Asia and Africa and the deterioration of Sino-Soviet relations influenced China's policy stance and changes toward Africa during this period. In contrast to the international situation during the Cold War, the domestic situation of China seemed to play a relatively less significant role in China's policy stance toward Africa. China continued to provide economic aid to Africa despite the economic difficulties in China resulted from the Great Leap Forward (1958–1960) and the Cultural Revolution (1966–1976). The notions of equality, mutual benefits, noninterference in other countries' internal affairs, and unconditionality advocated in the Eight Principles for Economic Aid and Technical Assistance to Other Countries announced during Primer Zhou Enlai's African tour in 1964 have long been a feature of Chinese aid to Africa and other countries.[61]

Since the 1980s, the diminish of perceived threats of war, domestic policy, especially the reform and opening-up policy, in China began to play a larger role over international relations on China's policy toward Africa. Increasing market-oriented economic cooperation with and investment in Africa has been the new feature of Sino-African relations. China's engagement in the development cooperation of Africa has been diversified with more of the essence of economics. Compared with economic aid, development financing solutions, including the participating of the ADB and the ADF, the concessional loans, that connected the development of African with the market reform of Chinese enterprises and Chinese international trade and investment in Africa are increasingly conducted by China.

Sino-African relations have entered an era of a new type of strategic partnership with all-round cooperation since the establishment of the FOCAC in 2000. With the improvement of the political and economic situation in Africa, the adjustment of developed countries' policy toward Africa, and the challenge of economic globalization, China and Africa established the FOCAC based on the complementary needs of each other in the context of South-South Cooperation. Since the implementation of the opening-up policy, the economic development of China has increasingly related to the world economy and international relations especially in the era of globalization. China's perception of the complementarity of the economy in China and Africa and the growing position of Africa in world politics consists of the foundation of the expanded Sino-African relations. The two African Policy Papers and action plans of the FOCAC announced by China articulate the development agenda of African countries with Chinese trade, investment, and cooperation with special focus mainly on infrastructure, agriculture, and human resource development. However, the way how could the Chinese trade, investment, and infrastructure building in Africa contributes to the development of Africa will largely rely on the initiative of African countries.

NOTES

1. "A Long-term Stable China-Africa Relationship Of All-round Cooperation," Ministry of Foreign Affairs of the People's Republic of China, last modified November 7, 2000, https://www.fmChina.gov.cn/mfa_eng/ziliao_665539/3602_6 65543/3604_665547/t18036.shtml (accessed February 14, 2019).

2. Shinn, David H., and Joshua Eisenman, *China and Africa: A Century of Engagement* (University of Pennsylvania Press, 2012), 32.

3. Mao Zedong, "lun renmin minzhu zhuanzheng" [On people's democratic dictatorship], *Sino-Soviet Culture* 7 (1949): 1–4.

4. "A Long-term Stable China-Africa Relationship Of All-round Cooperation," Ministry of Foreign Affairs of the People's Republic of China, last modified November 7, 2000, https://www.fmChina.gov.cn/mfa_eng/ziliao_665539/3602_6 65543/3604_665547/t18036.shtml (accessed February 14, 2019).

5. Li Anshan, "Lun zhongguo dui feizhou zhengce de tiaoshi yu zhuanbian" [On the adjustment and change of China's African policy], *West Asia and Africa* 8 (2006): 11–20.

6. Mao, "On people's democratic dictatorship," 1–4.

7. Zhang, Shu Guang. "Constructing 'Peaceful Coexistence': China's Diplomacy toward the Geneva and Bandung Conferences, 1954–55," *Cold War History* 7, no. 4 (2007): 509–28.

8. Zhou Enlai, *Zhou Enlai xuanji* [Selected works of Zhou Enlai] (Beijing: Renmin chubanshe, 1980), 322.

Zhou Enlai, *Zhou Enlai wajiao wenxuan* [Selected works on diplomacy of Zhou Enlai] (Beijing: Zhongyang wenxian chubanshe, 1990), 2.

9. "Xin zhongguo chengli qianxi de waijiao zhengce zhiding" [The making of foreign policy by the establishment of the People's Republic of China], Ministry of Foreign Affairs of the People's Republic of China, last modified November 7, 2000, https://www.fmChina.gov.cn/web/ziliao_674904/wjs_674919/2159_674923/t8977.s html (accessed February 14, 2019).

10. Li Danan, "Zhou Enlai yu heping gongchu wuxiangyuanze" [Zhou Enlai and the Five Principles of Peaceful Coexistence], *Bainianchao* 6 (214): 4–7.

11. "Zhongguo changdao heping gongchu wuxiang yuanze" [China advocates the Five Principles of Peaceful Coexistence], Ministry of Foreign Affairs of the People's Republic of China, last modified November 7, 2000, https://www.fmChina.gov.cn/web/ziliao_674904/wjs_674919/2159_674923/t8987.shtml (accessed February 14, 2019).

12. Li, "Zhou Enlai and the Five Principles of Peaceful Coexistence," 4–7.

13. Arif Dirlik, "The Bandung Legacy and the People's Republic of China in the Perspective of Global Modernity," *Inter-Asia Cultural Studies* 16, no. 4 (2015): 615–30.

14. Sally Percival Wood, "Retrieving the Bandung Conference . . . Moment by Moment," *Journal of Southeast Asian Studies* 43, no. 3 (2012): 523–30.

15. Dirlik, "The Bandung Legacy and the People's Republic of China in the Perspective of Global Modernity," 615–30.

16. Ministry of Foreign Affairs of the People's Republic of China, "China advocates the Five Principles of Peaceful Coexistence."

17. Mu Tao, "Zailun wanlonghuiyi dui xiandai zhongfei guanxi de kaichuang yiyi" [The significance of the Bandung Conference on modern Sino-African relations], *Collected Paper of History Studies* 6 (2015): 24–30.

18. Shinn, David H., and Joshua Eisenman, *China and Africa: A Century of Engagement* (University of Pennsylvania Press, 2012), 33.

19. Mu, "The significance of the Bandung Conference on modern Sino-African relations," 24–30.

20. Shinn and Eisenman, *China and Africa: A Century of Engagement*, 35–36.

21. Jiang Huajie, "Guoji lengzhan, geming waijiao yu duiwai yuanzhu-zhongguo duifei yuanzhu zhengce xingcheng de zai kaocha (1956–1965)" [International Cold War, revolutionary diplomacy and foreign aid: thoughts on the forming of China's foreign aid policy towards Africa (1956-1965)], *Foreign Affairs Review* 5 (2016): 81–108.

22. Jiang, "International Cold War, revolutionary diplomacy and foreign aid: thoughts on the forming of China's foreign aid policy towards Africa (1956–1965)," 81–108.

23. "Zhongguo dui feizhou guojia de yuanzhu" [Chinese foreign aid to Africa], The History of Commerce, http://history.mofcom.gov.cn/?newChina=中国对非洲国家的援助 (accessed February 14, 2019).

24. Yang Fan 杨帆, "waijiao dangan jiemi zhouzongli shoufang feishou" [Declassification of diplomatic files: Primer Zhou's first visit to Africa], *World Knowledge* 5 (2009): 52–54.

25. Lu Miaogeng, "Zhou Enlai fangwen feizhou shiguo" [Zhou Enlai visits ten African countries], *Bainianchao* 2 (2015): 17–23.

26. Julia C. Strauss, "The past in the present: historical and rhetorical lineages in China's relations with Africa," *China Quarterly* 199 (2009): 777–795.

27. Li, "On the adjustment and change of China's African policy," 11–20.

28. Lu, "Zhou Enlai visits ten African countries," 17–23.

29. "The Chinese Government's Eight Principles for Economic Aid and Technical Assistance to Other Countries," January 15, 1964, History and Public Policy Program Digital Archive, Zhonghua renmin gongheguo waijiaobu and Zhonggong zhongyang wenxian yanjiushi, eds., Zhou Enlai waijiao wenxuan (Selected Diplomatic Papers of Zhou Enlai) (Beijing: Zhongyang wenxian chubanshe, 1990), 388. http://digitalarchive.wilsoncenter.org/document/121560.

30. "Zhongguo de duiwai yuanzhu (2014)" [China's foreign aid (2014)], State Council, last modified July 10, 2014, http://www.scio.gov.cn/zfbps/ndhf/2014/Document/1375013/1375013_1.htm (accessed February 14, 2019).

31. Li, "On the adjustment and change of China's African policy," 11–20.

32. "Chinese Communist Activities in Africa," Central Intelligence Agency, last modified December 19, 2016, https://www.cia.gov/library/readingroom/docs/CIA-R DP79-00927A004600030003-8.pdf (accessed February 14, 2019).

33. "Chinese Communist Activities in Africa," Central Intelligence Agency, last modified December 16, 2016, https://www.cia.gov/library/readingroom/docs/CIA-R DP79T00472A000800010012-7.pdf (accessed February 14, 2019).

34. Shinn and Eisenman, *China and Africa: A Century of Engagement*, 39.

35. "Zhongguo gongchandang shijijie sanzhong quanhui" [The Third Plenary Session of the 11th Central Committee of the Communist Party of China], The History of the People's Republic of China, last modified August 20, 2009, http://www.scio.gov.cn/zfbps/ndhf/2014/Document/1375013/1375013_1.htm (accessed February 14, 2019).

36. "Zai zhanzheng yu heping wenti shang zuochu xin de kexue lunduan" [Making new scientific judgement on the issue of war and peace], Ministry of Foreign Affairs of the People's Republic of China, last modified November 7, 2000, https://www.fmC hina.gov.cn/web/ziliao_674904/wjs_674919/2159_674923/t8982.shtml (accessed February 14, 2019).

37. Wen Weidong, "Deng Xiaoping yu 'gaigekaifang' yici de tichu" [Deng Xiaoping and the put forward of "Reform and Opening up"], *Dangjian yanjiu* 10 (2013): 65.

38. Ian Taylor, "China's foreign policy towards Africa in the 1990s," *The Journal of Modern African Studies* 36, no. 3 (1998): 443–460.

39. "Zhongguo gongchandang dashiji 1982 nian" [Memorabilia of the Communist Party of China 1982], CPC News, last modified June 24, 2006, http://theory.people .com.cn/GB/40557/67082/67088/4526522.html (accessed February 14, 2019).

40. "Zhongguo tichu zhongfei jingji jishu hezuo yuanze" [China announced principles for Sino-Africa economic and technical cooperation], People, last modified December 2, 2006, http://world.people.com.cn/GB/8212/72927/73386/4988583.html (accessed February 14, 2019).

41. "Guowuyuan zongli Zhao Ziyang xiangdiwujie quanguorenmin daibiao dahui changwuweiyuanhui diershiliuci huiyi zuo guanyu fangwen feizhou shiyi guo de baogao" [Primer Zhao Ziyang's report on his tour to 11 African countries on the 26th meeting of the 5th Standing Committee of the National People's Congress], National People's Congress, http://www.npc.gov.cn/wxzl/gongbao/1983-02/28/cont ent_1480973.htm (accessed February 14, 2019).

42. *China Education Yearbook*. Beijing: People's Education Press, 1990: 382. Published annually.

43. Ibid., 387.

44. "AfDB he zhongguo" [AfDB and China], African Development Bank Group, accessed February 14, 2019, http://afdb-org.cn.

45. International Department of China Exim Bank, "Yuanwai youhui daikuan: zhongguo qiye kuaguo jingying rongzi xinfangshi" [Concessional loans: the new method of financing for international operation of Chinese enterprises], *International Trade* 7 (1997): 7–9.

46. Gao Ning, "Kaipi heise huangjin: zhongguo jinchukou yinhang duiwai youhui daikuan zhichi sudan shiyou xiangmu" [Exploring black gold: China Exim Bank supports oil projects in Sudan through concessional loans], *International Financing* 5 (2001): 14–15.

47. Huang Meibo, "Zhongguo zhengfu duiwai youhui daikuan de fazhan licheng yu qianjing" [The process of prospects of the development of Chinese government concessional loans], *International Economic Cooperation* 11 (2010): 49–55.

48. Ministry of Foreign Affairs of the People's Republic of China, "A Long-term Stable China-Africa Relationship of All-round Cooperation".

49. Li Anshan, "Lun zhongfei hezuo luntan de qiyuan jiantan dui zhongguo feizhou zhanlue de sikao [On the origin of the FOCAC: thoughts on China's African strategy], *Foreign Affairs Review* (3) 2012: 19–36.

50. Ian Taylor, "China's foreign policy towards Africa in the 1990s," *The Journal of Modern African Studies* 36, no. 3 (1998): 443–460.

51. Li, "On the origin of the FOCAC: thoughts on China's African strategy," 19–36.

52. Li, "On the origin of the FOCAC: thoughts on China's African strategy," 19–36.

53. "Beijing Declaration of the Forum on China-Africa Cooperation," Ministry of Foreign Affairs of the People's Republic of China, last modified September 25, 2009, https://www.focac.org/eng/zywx_1/zywj/t606796.htm (accessed February 14, 2019).

54. "Zhongguo dui feizhou zhengce wenjian" [China's African Policy Paper], Ministry of Foreign Affairs of the People's Republic of China, last modified January 12, 2006, https://www.fmChina.gov.cn/web/ziliao_674904/tytj_674911/zcwj_674 915/t230612.shtml (accessed February 14, 2019).

55. "The Forum on China-Africa Cooperation Johannesburg Action Plan (2016–2018)," Ministry of Foreign Affairs of the People's Republic of China, last modified December 25, 2015, https://www.focac.org/eng/zywx_1/zywj/t1327961.htm (accessed February 14, 2019).

"The Forum on China-Africa Cooperation Sharm El Sheikh Action Plan (2010–2012)," Ministry of Foreign Affairs of the People's Republic of China, last modified November 12, 2009, https://www.focac.org/eng/zywx_1/zywj/t626387.htm (accessed February 14, 2019).

"The Forum on China-Africa Cooperation Johannesburg Action Plan (2007–2009)," Ministry of Foreign Affairs of the People's Republic of China, last modified November 16, 2006, https://www.focac.org/eng/zywx_1/zywj/t280369.htm (accessed February 14, 2019).

56. "Zhongguo dui feizhou zhengce wenjian (quanwen)" [China's African Policy Paper (full text)], Ministry of Foreign Affairs of the People's Republic of China, last modified December 5, 2015, https://www.fmChina.gov.cn/web/ziliao_674904/tytj_674911/zcwj_674915/t1321556.shtml (accessed February 14, 2019).

57. Ministry of Foreign Affairs of the People's Republic of China, "China's African Policy Paper (full text)."

58. Ministry of Foreign Affairs of the People's Republic of China, "The Forum on China-Africa Cooperation Johannesburg Action Plan (2016–2018)."

59. Fei-Ling Wang and Esi A. Elliot, "China in Africa: presence, perceptions and prospects," *Journal of Contemporary China* 23, no. 90 (2014): 1012–1032.

60. Mu, "The significance of the Bandung Conference on modern Sino-African relations," 24–30.

61. State Council, "China's foreign aid (2014)."

BIBLIOGRAPHY

African Development Bank Group. "AfDB he zhongguo" [AfDB and China]. Accessed February 14, 2019. http://afdb-org.cn.

Central Intelligence Agency. "Chinese Communist Activities in Africa." Last modified December 19, 2016. https://www.cia.gov/library/readingroom/docs/CIA-R DP79-00927A004600030003-8.pdf (accessed February 14, 2019).

Central Intelligence Agency. "Chinese Communist Activities in Africa." Last modified December 16, 2016. https://www.cia.gov/library/readingroom/docs/CIA-R DP79T00472A000800010012-7.pdf (accessed February 14, 2019.).

China Education Yearbook. Beijing: People's Education Press, 1990: 382. Published annually.

CPC News. "Zhongguo gongchandang dashiji 1982 nian" [Memorabilia of the Communist Party of China 1982]. Last modified June 24, 2006. http://theory.people .com.cn/GB/40557/67082/67088/4526522.html (accessed February 14, 2019).

Dirlik, Arif. "The Bandung Legacy and the People's Republic of China in the Perspective of Global Modernity." *Inter-Asia Cultural Studies* 16, no. 4 (2015): 615–30.

Gao, Ning. "Kaipi heise huangjin: zhongguo jinchukou yinhang duiwai youhui daikuan zhichi sudan shiyou xiangmu" [Exploring black gold: China Exim Bank supports oil projects in Sudan through concessional loans]. *International Financing* 5 (2001): 14–15.

Huang, Meibo. "Zhongguo zhengfu duiwai youhui daikuan de fazhan licheng yu qianjing" [The process of prospects of the development of Chinese government concessional loans]. *International Economic Cooperation* 11 (2010): 49–55.

International Department of China Exim Bank. "Yuanwai youhui daikuan: zhongguo qiye kuaguo jingying rongzi xinfangshi" [Concessional loans: the new method of financing for international operation of Chinese enterprises]. *International Trade* 7 (1997): 7–9.

Jiang, Huajie. "Guoji lengzhan, geming waijiao yu duiwai yuanzhu-zhongguo duifei yuanzhu Zhengce xingcheng de zai kaocha (1956–1965)" [International Cold War, revolutionary diplomacy and foreign aid: thoughts on the forming of China's foreign aid policy toward Africa (1956-1965)]. *Foreign Affairs Review* 5 (2016): 81–108.

Li, Anshan. "Lun zhongguo dui feizhou zhengce de tiaoshi yu zhuanbian" [On the adjustment and change of China's African policy]. *West Asia and Africa* 8 (2006): 11–20.

Li, Anshan. "Lun zhongfei hezuo luntan de qiyuan jiantan dui zhongguo feizhou zhanlue de sikao" [On the origin of the FOCAC: thoughts on China's African strategy]. *Foreign Affairs Review* (3) 2012: 19–36.

Li, Danan. "Zhou Enlai yu heping gongchu wuxiangyuanze" [Zhou Enlai and the Five Principles of Peaceful Coexistence]. *Bainianchao* 6 (214): 4–7.

Lu, Miaogeng. "Zhou Enlai fangwen feizhou shiguo" [Zhou Enlai visits ten African countries]. *Bainianchao* 2 (2015): 17–23.

Mao, Zedong. "lun renmin minzhu zhuanzheng" [On people's democratic dictatorship]. *Zhongsu wenhua* 7 (1949): 1–4.

Ministry of Foreign Affairs of the People's Republic of China. "A Long-term Stable China Africa Relationship of All-round Cooperation." Last modified November 7, 2000. https://www.fmChina.gov.cn/mfa_eng/ziliao_665539/3602_665543/3604_665547/t18036.shtml (accessed February 14, 2019).

Ministry of Foreign Affairs of the People's Republic of China. "Xin zhongguo chengli qianxi de waijiao zhengce zhiding" [The making of foreign policy by the establishment of the People's Republic of China]. Last modified November 7, 2000.https://www.fmChina.gov.cn/web/ziliao_674904/wjs_674919/2159_674923/t8977.shtml (accessed February 14, 2019).

Ministry of Foreign Affairs of the People's Republic of China. "Zai zhanzheng yu heping wenti shang zuochu xin de kexue lunduan" [Making new scientific judgment on the issue of war and peace]. Last modified November 7, 2000. https://www.fmChina.gov.cn/web/ziliao_674904/wjs_674919/2159_674923/t8982.shtml (accessed February 14, 2019).

Ministry of Foreign Affairs of the People's Republic of China. "Zhongguo changdao heping gongchu wuxiang yuanze" [China advocates the Five Principles of Peaceful Coexistence]. Last modified November 7, 2000. https://www.fmChina.gov.cn/web/ziliao_674904/wjs_674919/2159_674923/t8987.shtml (accessed February 14, 2019).

Ministry of Foreign Affairs of the People's Republic of China. "Zhongguo dui feizhou zhengce wenjian" [China's African Policy Paper]. Last modified January 12, 2006. https://www.fmChina.gov.cn/web/ziliao_674904/tytj_674911/zcwj_674915/t230612.shtml (accessed February 14, 2019).

Ministry of Foreign Affairs of the People's Republic of China. "The Forum on China-Africa Cooperation Johannesburg Action Plan (2007–2009)." Ministry of Foreign Affairs of the People's Republic of China. Last modified November 16, 2006. https://www.focac.org/eng/zywx_1/zywj/t280369.htm (accessed February 14, 2019).

Ministry of Foreign Affairs of the People's Republic of China. "Beijing Declaration of the Forum on China Africa Cooperation." last modified September 25, 2009. https://www.focac.org/eng/zywx_1/zywj/t606796.htm (accessed February 14, 2019).

Ministry of Foreign Affairs of the People's Republic of China. "The Forum on China-Africa Cooperation Johannesburg Action Plan (2016-2018)." Ministry of Foreign Affairs of the People's Republic of China. Last modified December 25, 2015. https://www.focac.org/eng/zywx_1/zywj/t1327961.htm (accessed February 14, 2019).

Ministry of Foreign Affairs of the People's Republic of China. "The Forum on China-Africa Cooperation Sharm El Sheikh Action Plan (2010–2012)." Ministry of Foreign Affairs of the People's Republic of China. Last modified November 12, 2009. https://www.focac.org/eng/zywx_1/zywj/t626387.htm (accessed February 14, 2019).

Ministry of Foreign Affairs of the People's Republic of China. "Zhongguo dui feizhou zhengce wenjian (quanwen)" [China's African Policy Paper (full text)]. Last modified December 5, 2015. https://www.fmChina.gov.cn/web/ziliao_67 4904/tytj_674911/zcwj_674915/t1321556.shtml (accessed February 14, 2019).

Mu, Tao. "Zailun wanlonghuiyi dui xiandai zhongfei guanxi de kaichuang yiyi" [The significance of the Bandung Conference on modern Sino-African relations]. *Collected Papers of History Studies* 6 (2015): 24–30.

National People's Congress. "Guowuyuan zongli Zhao Ziyang xiangdiwujie quanguorenmin daibiao dahui changwuweiyuanhui diershiliuci huiyi zuo guanyu fangwen feizhou shiyi guo de baogao" [Primer Zhao Ziyang's report on his tour to 11 African countries on the 26th meeting of the 5th Standing Committee of the National People's Congress]. http://www.npc.gov.cn/wxzl/gongbao/1983-02/28/content_1480973.htm (accessed February 14, 2019.)

People. "Zhongguo tichu zhongfei jingji jishu hezuo yuanze" [China announced principles for Sino-Africa economic and technical cooperation]. Last modified December 2, 2006. http://world.people.com.cn/GB/8212/72927/73386/4988583.html (accessed February 14, 2019).

Percival Wood, Sally. "Retrieving the Bandung Conference . . . Moment by Moment." *Journal of Southeast Asian Studies* 43, no. 3 (2012): 523–30.

Shinn, David H., and Joshua Eisenman, *China and Africa: A Century of Engagement*. Philadelphia: University of Pennsylvania Press, 2012.

State Council. "Zhongguo de dùiwai yuanzhu (2014)" [China's foreign aid (2014)]. Last modified July 10, 2014. http://www.scio.gov.cn/zfbps/ndhf/2014/Document /1375013/1375013_1.htm (accessed February 14, 2019).

Strauss, Julia C. "The past in the present: historical and rhetorical lineages in China's relations with Africa." *The China Quarterly* 199 (2009): 777–795.

Taylor, Ian. "China's foreign policy toward Africa in the 1990s." *The Journal of Modern African Studies* 36, no. 3 (1998): 443–460.

"The Chinese Government's Eight Principles for Economic Aid and Technical Assistance to Other Countries," January 15, 1964, History and Public Policy Program Digital Archive, Zhonghua renmin gongheguo waijiaobu and Zhonggong zhongyang wenxian yanjiushi, eds., Zhou Enlai waijiao wenxuan (Selected Diplomatic Papers of Zhou Enlai) (Beijing: Zhongyang wenxian chubanshe, 1990), 388. http://digitalarchive.wilsoncenter.org/document/121560.

The History of Commerce. "Zhongguo dui feizhou guojia de yuanzhu" [Chinese foreign aid to Africa]. http://history.mofcom.gov.cn/?newChina=中国对非洲国家的援助 (accessed February 14, 2019).

The History of the People's Republic of China. "Zhongguo gongchandang shijijie sanzhong quanhui" [The Third Plenary Session of the 11th Central Committee of the Communist Party of China]. Last modified August 20, 2009. http://www.scio.gov.cn/zfbps/ndhf/2014/Document/1375013/1375013_1.htm (accessed February 14, 2019).

Wang, Fei-Ling and Esi A. Elliot. "China in Africa: presence, perceptions and prospects." *Journal of Contemporary China* 23, no. 90 (2014): 1012–1032.

Wen, Weidong. "Deng Xiaoping yu 'gaigekaifang' yici de tichu" [Deng Xiaoping and the put forward of "Reform and Opening up"]. *Dangjian yanjiu* 10 (2013): 65.

Yang, Fan. "waijiao dangan jiemi zhouzongli shoufang feishou" [Declassification of diplomatic files: Primer Zhou's first visit to Africa]. *World Knowledge* 5 (2009): 52–54.

Zhang Shu Guang, "Constructing 'Peaceful Coexistence': China's Diplomacy toward the Geneva and Bandung Conferences, 1954–55," *Cold War History* 7, no. 4 (2007): 509–28.

Zhou, Enlai. *Zhou Enlai xuanji* [Selected works of Zhou Enlai]. Beijing: Renmin chubanshe, 1980.

Zhou Enlai, *Zhou Enlai wajiao wenxuan* [Selected works on diplomacy of Zhou Enlai]. Beijing: Zhongyang wenxian chubanshe, 1990.

Chapter 3

Jamie Monson and the Historiography of China-Africa Relations

The Tanzania-Zambia Railway (TAZARA) in Focus

Tokunbo A. Ayoola

INTRODUCTION

China-Africa relations with Africa can be traced as far back to the seventh century or much earlier than that. In the seventh century, Africans started arriving in China by ships and disembarking on the southern coast of the Asian country. Later these visitors started to work in different capacities: traders, laborers, lifeguards, divers, soldiers, government officials, artists, and so on. Of particular interest is the fact that some Africans got to China as slaves, particularly from the eastern region of Africa. It is equally on record that the Ming dynasty in China sought and subsequently achieved its desire to establish diplomatic relations and missions with many African states. The main purpose of this was to establish a strong trade relationship with the continent. Then between 1405 and 1433, no less than seven different naval voyages were undertaken by Chinese officials and traders to Africa; and once again, the purpose was to build up trade with and achieve recognition in Africa. The voyages were led by Zhen He.[1]

Meanwhile, in the eighteenth and nineteenth centuries, Chinese workers were imported into Africa, specifically into Mauritius, Seychelles, Madagascar, and South Africa. They were mainly engaged in sugar production, mining, railway construction and development, and agricultural production in general. In addition to all this, during the late colonial period and up until the 1950s, China established formal diplomatic relations with Egypt, Liberia, and South Africa.[2]

On the other hand, the contemporary relationship between Africa and the People's Republic of China started in earnest in 1949, when the sprawling Asian nation-state underwent the great socialist revolution under the leadership of Chairman Mao, and during the decolonization of many parts of Africa by imperialist European powers: Britain, France, Portugal, and Belgium, in the 1950s and 1960s. The imperialists had earlier in the late nineteenth and early twentieth centuries overran the whole of Africa. This latter stage of the Sino-Africa relationship was greatly influenced by the Cold War—principally between the USA and USSR; the bitter rivalry between China and USSR; the determined liberation struggles by colonized territories in Africa, Asia, and Latin America to overthrow once and for all the yoke of colonial and imperial economic exploitation; and the formation and development of the nonaligned movement that was made up of countries of the Third world.[3]

The Africa-China relationship began its steady climb toward its apogee in 1963–1964, when the Premier of China, Zhou Enlai, visited some African countries and committed his country and peoples to help African people still fiercely engaged with colonial authorities. This was to achieve political and economic independence, noninterference in African countries' internal affairs, mutual peace coexistence, the principle of nonalignment and neutrality, peaceful resolution of disputes, and support for Pan-Africanism and solidarity. From this period onwards, China represented itself to her people, Africans, and the rest of the world as an honest and genuine partner in economic development. This, China insisted, contrasted with the designs of the West and the Soviet Union, whose sole purpose of having a relationship with Africa was unending exploitation of her peoples and resources.[4]

Therefore, from the 1950s and 1960s and well into the new millennium, the cordial relationship between two of the world's greatest human civilizations (African and Chinese) went from strength to strength. This is not, however, to posit that the relationship did not witness many rough patches and critical phases. During this rather momentous period, China assisted Africa greatly economically, financially, and through increased trade. Furthermore, from the 1970s onwards, China became much more involved with the construction of many socioeconomic infrastructural projects on the continent. Without a doubt, the largest of such infrastructures in Africa, even up until recently, is the ambitious $600 million TAZARA that was started in the late 1960s and completed in the mid-1970s. It was wholly financed and constructed by the Asian country.[5] This historical edifice and other engagements on the part of China with Africa over the years have been the subject of many scholarly research and publications. One of the prodigious scholars still engaged in the critical study of China-Africa relation is Professor Jamie Monson, who numbers among the pioneer of what has now become the full-fledged China-Africa Studies. She has written widely on the subject matter of China-Africa relations, particularly on the TAZARA project, which is seen as "emblematic of China's enhanced engagement with Africa." This essay, therefore, seeks to engage some of the work on the Tanzania-Zambia Railroad—of which she is, without doubt, an eminent expert.

JAMIE MONSON: BIOGRAPHICAL NOTE

Jamie Monson began her higher education journey in 1974 when she gained admission to Stanford University in California, USA, to read English. She remained at Stanford till 1978 when she bagged a Bachelor of Arts degree in English. Thereafter, between 1979 and 1981 she volunteered under the U.S. Peace Corp's Rural Women in Development Programme in Kenya, East Africa. It was while she was in Kenya that her interest in and passion for Africa History were stirred up. On her return to the United States, she enrolled at the University of California, Berkeley, where she later earned a master's degree in Africa Studies. From the same institution, in 1991, she earned a PhD in African History. Earlier in 1984, she was a researcher with the UCLA's Food and Agricultural Programme. Jamie served on the Programme till 1986. Between 1986 and 1989, she worked as an assistant director of UCLA's African Studies Centre. Then from 1990 to 1991, she was a Graduate Teaching Assistant at UCLA. It was in 1991 that she earned her PhD in African History.

Her first job after postgraduate studies were as an assistant professor of African History at Carleton College and St. Olaf College in Minnesota, a position she held until 1997 when she was promoted to the rank of associate professor and served until either the twin colleges were separated into two entities, or they were absolved into each other and just simply called Carleton College. Monson remained in the latter institution as an associate professor from 2003 to 2007. During that period and slightly beyond, that is, between 2005 and 2008, she was chair of the History Department. It was while she was still the chair that she was promoted a full professor. In 2009, she moved on to Macalester College, Saint Paul, Minnesota—as a full professor. Then in 2015, she became professor of African History in the Department of History and director of African Studies at the highly regarded Michigan State University.[6]

At the start of her academic and research career, she focused primarily on agricultural and environmental history of East Africa, particularly that of southern Tanzania. From that research agenda have emanated some publications. These include " From Protective Lions to Angry Spirits: Environmental Degradation and Authority of Elders in the Kilombero Valley, Tanzania;" "War of Words: The Narrative Efficacy of Medicine during the Maji

Maji War;" "Memory, Migration and the Authority of History in Southern Tanzania, 1860–1960;" " Rice and Cotton and Colonization and Resistance: Cash Cropping in Colonia Tanganyika;" and Legitimate Trade and Industrial Europe: Rubber Extraction in the Inner Kilombero Valley in Tanzania, 18901941."[7]

In the 1990s, Monson shifted her research focus to the history of the Tanzania- Zambia Railway Authority, which was wholly financed and constructed in the 1970s by the government of the People's Republic of China. This project was part of that country's grand and well-determined program in Africa that was meant to contribute to the genuine economic developments on the continent.[8] This was, in the imagination of the leaders of China, in contradistinction to the United States and USSR's neocolonial and imperialistic designs on Africa and Africans. Again, as in her previous research focus and agenda, Monson would appear to have published more widely than previously in the new research area. The consideration of some of these outputs, as stated earlier, is the subject matter of this chapter.

In recent times, Monson has gone ahead again to engage in new research undertaking. This is the historical study of China-Africa relations. The first aspect is the study of technology transfer in the history of China's development engagement with Africa. The second is the critical examination of gendered diplomacy in China's relations with Africa.[9] But how did the fire of intellectual engagement with everything relating to China in Africa was first lit in the heart of a scholar who had started on a different intellectual trajectory? It was while working at the African Studies Centre, UCLA that Monson, in a rather fortuitous circumstance, became involved in China-African Studies. During her sojourn as a graduate student and as a staff of that institution's African Studies Centre, in May 1983 a delegation of five Africanist scholars from China, who were sponsored by the Ford Foundation of the United States, visited the center where Monson was working. The visit to the USA was part of the exchange program between the United States and Chinese Africanist scholars. Monson was not directly involved in the nitty-gritty of the exchange program beyond merely assisting the then director of the UCLA's African Studies Centre, Professor Michael Lofchie—and in Monson's own words—"with making arrangements for the visit and hosting the Chinese guests. My own special assignment was to offer hospitality and assistance to Ms. Wu (the only woman member of the delegation."[10] Thus it is fair to argue that the seed of her subsequent abiding interest and passion in China-Africa Studies was sown there.

After leaving UCLA on the completion of her PhD program there, Monson's academic interest, however, moved in a different direction: that of a historian and researcher of African history, particularly the East African aspect of it. Even then her work was not removed from China's economic developmental activities in Eastern Africa. In the 1990s, Monson began devoting considerable time, interest, and enormous energy into researching the TAZARA railway, the China-financed and built transportation artery in Eastern and Southern Africa. Arguably, it was the largest single construction project by the Chinese anywhere in the developing world in the 1970s and 1980s. Later in 2003 while on an invitational visit to China to lecture on her research on the TAZARA railway and deriving from series of discussions with Chinese Africanist scholars in there, her interest in China-Africa Studies was further rekindled.[11] Ever since then, Monson has been actively and fully involved in different capacities and at different levels developing and extending the coverage of the fast-developing academic field of China-Africa Studies.[12] It is therefore not an exaggeration to state that Monson is one of the leading exponents and pioneers of this ever dynamic academic field. Although Monson has written extensively on the history of East Africa, particularly on Tanzania, this current essay seeks to examine her expansive corpus on the history TAZARA railway in East Africa and the crucial involvement of the Chinese with it.

ORIGINS OF THE TAZARA'S RAILROAD

The very idea of constructing a southern-east Africa railroad had been on from the late nineteenth century. It was first conceived and openly canvassed for by the German imperialists when they had started exploring East Africa with a view to establishing a foothold, particularly in Tanganyika. From this seemingly unremarkable start and well up to the 1960s, when many European colonies in Africa became independent, many officials—colonial and postcolonial—had dreamed up many visions of railroad developments in East Africa.[13] Most of these visions had been undergirded by both economic and political considerations. In the German vision, railroads would serve as an important tool for agricultural production by white colonial settlers in Tanganyika's highlands. Yet another vision was to use the same transportation mode to assist African peasant farmers' subsistence agriculture in the plains of Tanganyika. The third aspect of the German vision was even more ambitious: it sought to construct *Mittelafrica*, an empire, whose various parts would be linked by railroads built across a large segment of the African continent: from the Indian Ocean to the Atlantic Ocean.[14]

It was not only the Germans, however, that saw railroads as a tool of empire building and capitalist exploitation in East Africa. Under British colonial rule and hegemony in Kenya, the white settlers there and their counterparts in Tanganyika, which by the 1920s had come under British colonial exploitation as well, lobbied the colonial governments in both territories to join hands with them to construct an ambitious imperial railroad link that would not only connect all European settler colonies in Eastern and Southern Africa physically but would enhance and consolidate their economic and political interests. The envisioned imperial railroad would link Nairobi in Kenya (East Africa) to Cape Town in South Africa (southern Africa).[15] Interesting enough, it was a version of this envisioned southern railroad that would become in the postcolonial era *the* railroad project that ultimately freed the eastern and southern African countries from dependence on the white supremacist regimes in Rhodesia, South Africa, Angola, Mozambique, and Namibia. That is the "Freedom Railway."[16] Thus, what started as competing for European imperialist railroad visions and projects during the era of European exploration of Africa and the colonial period would continue during the postcolonial times, but more complicated by the start of the Cold War in Africa.

For instance, whereas China was keen to assist both Tanzania and Zambia in constructing a new railroad that would be far removed from the stranglehold of the Southern Africa railroad system so that both countries could be independent in the management of their economies, she equally desired to be involved in the new railroad project to use the opportunity offered to restrict, if not remove the influence of USSR in Africa. China had been locked in a bitter ideological rivalry with her Asian neighbor since the early 1950s—just about the time the Cold War started. What the Chinese therefore sought to gain in East Africa was to set themselves up "through the Tazara railway as a regional player competing against not only USSR's designs on Africa, but also against the capitalist interests of Western Europe and North America."[17]

On the other hand, as far as Presidents Nyerere of Tanzania and Kenneth Kaunda of Zambia were concerned the new railroad would be independent of the southern railroads and would free landlocked Zambia from the stranglehold of white settlers in exercising hegemony over Southern Rhodesia. Furthermore, Jamie Monson believes that the railroad between copper-rich Zambia and Dar es Salaam "was to be materially and symbolically liberating . . . and would end the division of Africa into competing spheres of influence."[18] For Tanzania, the new railroad linking her Indian Ocean port of Dar es Salaam to Zambia would help change for good, several decades of colonial neglect of the southern region of that country and would serve as a catalyst for the socioeconomic transformation of the region.[19] In general, for the Eastern and Southern Africa, the new railroad was envisaged to be a potent instrument for their genuine and radical liberation. First, it would help Zambia to be completely free from the control of the Southern African and international mining interests. Second, Tanzania and Zambia would be well placed to assist and influence various liberation movements engaged in armed struggles with white settlers in Rhodesia, South Africa, Namibia, and Portuguese colonialists in Angola and Mozambique.[20] Thus, the various liberation movements would freely import all they needed including military hardware, by using the new railroad passing through the two countries to transport their materials into the hinterland. The implication of this is that Zambia would no longer be subjected to a constant barrage of sanctions and border blockades because she supported the liberation movements.[21]

As if all the above were not enough cogent reasons for the urgent construction of the TAZARA railroad, according to Monson, in 1965 Zambian transportation problems became even more compounded. In that year, the minority white settlers in Rhodesia led by Ian Smith forcefully took control of the colonial territory and unilaterally declared independence from Britain. This development demonstrated that Zambia could no longer strongly rely on the southern African railroad network for her import and export trade.[22] Furthermore, when in 1966 the international community imposed sanctions, including oil embargo against the new regime in Rhodesia, Zambia was in deep trouble. Her transportation system and supply of basic necessities came to standstill. Indeed, such was the dire situation that Zambia found herself in that some Western countries had to airlift oil into the country.[23] This was a temporary measure; more permanent solutions had to be found.

As a first measure, Zambia sought to improve her road network to the port city of Dar es Salaam in Tanzania. And to achieve this, in 1966, it established a transport company. This was followed in 1968 by the laying of the Tazama oil pipeline from Dar es Salaam to Ndola in Zambia. This was to have a direct and uninterrupted supply of oil, thereby becoming completely independent of the southern African routes.[24] But all these measures notwithstanding, up until the second half of the 1960s Zambia still depended for at least 30 percent of her import and export commodities—including her greatest foreign exchange earner, copper—on passage through Rhodesia and South Africa.[25] Yet Zambia was determined to completely erase this dependence as soon as possible. Apart from trying to improve her road connectivity to Tanzania, which in the end proved rather unworkable, she also considered transporting her goods through an alternative southwest rail route via the Benguela railroad in Angola. Under this arrangement, Zambian goods would be transported by train through Katanga in the Congo Republic, through Lobito in Angola and then on to the Atlantic Ocean port. This proposal in the end also proved infeasible because of the war of liberation by African liberation movements in Angola against Portugal's colonial rule in the territory, and the apartheid South Africa's illegal rule in Namibia, and the South West African People's Organization's (SWAPO) liberation struggle against this arrangement.[26]

In Monson's view, it was as a result of the foregoing factors that Presidents Julius Nyerere and Kenneth Kaunda focused their attention on a Tanzania-Zambia railroad, and to achieve this, the African countries set up a joint committee to study the feasibility or otherwise of the proposed railroad.

In September 1965, the report was submitted to the World Bank, United Nations, and the governments of the United States, Japan, China, Canada, France, and Germany, to assist in the provision of capital for the project.[27] Whereas the Chinese government did not reject the project outright, neither did she initially commit herself to it. For the World Bank and Western countries, there was no such vacillation. They simply rejected the new railroad project as unrealistic and uneconomical and refused to offer any financial support.[28]

It was in the midst of this dilemma on the part of the governments of Tanzania and Zambia that China in 1965 started to show interest in the TAZARA railroad. Even then at this time China was noncommittal on the issue of finance and building the railroad. But two years later in 1967, she changed her stance and signed an agreement with Tanzania and Zambia to support the railroad construction.[29] The announcement of this breakthrough with the project was met with condemnation by the USSR and West; and they accused China, Tanzania, and Zambia of operating in secrecy, bad faith, and deliberately excluding them from participating in the financing and construction of the railroad.[30]

In the agreement, China agreed to grant a yet to be specified amount as an interest-free loan to the governments of Tanzania and Zambia, but subject to the successful completion of a comprehensive survey of the proposed railroad routes, which would determine the specific financing scheme and the construction details of the "Freedom Railway."[31] Soon after, the preliminary survey report was ready, and in 1969, the Chinese agreed to finance the TAZARA railroad with a thirty-year interest-free loan—to the tune of $400 million.[32] Almost immediately after the signing of the agreement, formal surveying, and the construction the railroad started and lasted for almost two years. The actual construction started in 1970 and was completed in 1975—two years ahead of schedule.[33] The railroad, which until the 1990s was China's "largest international development project and the third-largest infrastructure development project in Africa" was officially opened and handed over to the governments of Tanzania and Zambia in July 1976. In all, Jamie Monson's estimation, between 20,000 and 30,000 Chinese and 40,000 Tanzanians and Zambians constructed the 1,865 kilometer (1,060 miles) railroad.[34]

CHINA'S CONCEPTUALIZATION OF DEVELOPMENT, AND THE CONSTRUCTION OF TAZARA

The construction and financing of the TAZARA were conceived and executed against the backdrop of China's definition and understanding of the particular form development should take, especially in Africa from the 1960s to the late

1980s, when she embraced aspects of free-market capitalism and neoliberalism. This new ideological embrace in the 1980s would later inform the Asian country's economic and political relationship with the continent and the rest of the world. However, it is to China's conceptualization of development assistance in Africa in the pre-1980s that we shall now turn to, to provide the background to contemporary China's activities in Africa. In her book, *Africa's Freedom Railway*,[35] Monson, quoting Chinese Premier Zou Enlai, who visited Tanzania in 1963–1964, states that China was of the view that right from the first contacts between it and East Africa, which was pioneered by Chinese Admiral Zheng He in the fifteenth century, Africa and China, had shared the same history of anticolonial struggle. Further, that Zheng He came to Africa, not intending to colonize it "but rather sought to trade and interact with African people as equals."[36] Thus, China's development assistance from the 1960s onwards had been without preconditions. This thinking was in 1963 reformulated into eight principles of African development assistance and was supposed to be based on solidarity, equality, and friendship. For instance, China's financial help to African countries was to make them self-reliant and economically independent of outsiders.[37]

To demonstrate this thinking expressed in the eight principles in a more practical way, Chinese officials lived and worked in the same environment and locations with Africans and taught them by practical example. This was in sharp contrast to their Western counterparts, especially from the United States and Soviet Union, who would live in very posh accommodation; while sentencing their African workers to shambolic and desperate living and working environment.[38] All these ethical considerations, according to Jamie Monson, indeed have their roots in the eight principles as enunciated by the Chinese:

1. In the provision of aids to other countries, the Chinese government adheres strictly to the principle of equality and mutual benefit. Through such aids, friendly and new countries steadily develop their economies, gain genuine independence from colonialism and thereby strengthening the world's anti-imperialist forces;
2. In the provision of aid to other countries, China respects the independence and sovereignty of nations—without demanding privileges or laying down conditionalities.
3. China provides economic aid as interest-free or low-interest loans and extends the repayment time over a long period, to reduce the financial burden on borrowing nations.
4. In the provision of aids to other countries, China does not make receiving countries dependent on it, but to help them gradually achieve self-reliance;

5. China helps recipient countries build projects with fewer investments but that will bring about quicker results, so that receiving countries may increase income and capital.

6. China provides quality equipment and materials manufactured in China, but at international prices. If they fall short of the agreed specifications and quality, the government of China will replace them.

7. Technical assistance is given to countries in a way that their personnel would fully master techniques available under the assistance.

8. Chinese experts involved in construction projects in other countries will have the same standard of living as experts of the recipient countries. Chinese experts must not make any special demands or enjoy any special amenities.[39]

Earlier in one of Monson's works, "Liberating Labour? Constructing Anti-Hegemony on the TAZARA Railway in Tanzania, 1965–76,"[40] she states that through these principles China sought to underscore those key differences between her way of granting foreign aids and those of United States and Soviet Union. They were anti-colonialism, neocolonialism, imperialism, and hegemony. Therefore, the application of the principles to the construction of the TAZARA was designed to grant genuine freedom, work experience, and liberation to Africans from Western "neo-imperialist exploitation in the post-independence era." Second, they were to liberate Africans from the hierarchical, separatist, and racialist structure under which they labored during Western imperialism and colonialism on the continent. In place of this, Chinese management aimed at "cross-racial friendship and worker solidarity." Third, African workers would earn fair wages and salaries and enjoy good health care. Four, the workers would readily participate in the decision-making process by being engaged in all solidarity meetings. Besides, in the construction of the railroad African workers would be exposed to modernity and technology in the process of acquiring new skills from Chinese railway experts. Furthermore, by teaching and mentoring through teaching by practical example, Zambians and Tanzanians would imbibe new and crucial values: hard work, self-discipline, and acquisition of skills and knowledge through technology transfer. Finally, through the TAZARA, Tanzanians, and Zambians would work together in Pan-African solidarity, partnership, and cooperation in the context of regional and continental joint actions.[41]

But how did theory square with practice? In the assessment of Monson indeed African workers were liberated by the concrete experience they acquired in the process of constructing the railroad with their Chinese counterparts gave them freedom from ignorance, backwardness, poverty, and limited horizon and perspectives—associated with life in the rural areas. Some 200 among them have traveled to China to study railway operations and maintenance. Some other Tanzanian and Zambian workers learned to speak Chinese fluently. Notwithstanding all this, Monson believes that there existed some gaps between the well-articulated Chinese principles and the practical reality that played out in Africa.[42]

To begin with, the Chinese could not square up the demand for hard work and discipline on the one hand and the requirement to train and educate workers for future developmental work in their respective countries. Monson argues that many Tanzanians and Zambians complained endlessly about the fast-paced and back-breaking construction work. They, therefore, abandoned work on the TAZARA in drove and sought work in less crushing vocations. They seem justified by these actions as Monson relates their experience: "The way daily work was organized—on an hourly rather than a task basis—was reminiscent of work struggles in the colonial period."[43] Not only this, but part of the African workers' disenchantment was also caused by the neck-speed way the Chinese set about completing the railway project well before the time set for this. This Chinese attitude derived from the fact that China was under strong pressure to satisfy a patently unimpressed and skeptical Western world which had earlier dismissed the project as a vanity political stunt that was destined to fail calamitously. Indeed, the railway had been tagged "Bamboo Railway."[44] Second, Monson says: "the push to complete the railway ahead of schedule—to show the world what could be accomplished through pan Africa and Third World solidarity—made the goal of skills transfer more difficult to achieve."[45]

There were other contradictions as well. First, in the living camps, which were close to the work-fields, there were segregations between the Chinese officials and ordinary African workers. Thus "Chinese technical experts were nominally friends and brothers, but in practice, they were teachers and supervisors."[46] Second, whereas African workers were very young, with limited education and experience, and whose key qualification for the TAZARA work was their physical strength, their Chinese supervisors were much older, better educated, and experienced and technically more advanced.[47] In between these two broad categories of workers was a new group that emerged in the anvil of TAZARA railway construction. Those among the African workers who showed promise, demonstrated leadership skills, and adapted quickly to the new technology were given further training and subsequently promoted into management. These workers eventually became the favorite of the Chinese while the manual laborers remained somewhat alienated from the Chinese.[48]

But notwithstanding these stratifications, which the Chinese never envisaged in the first instance, certainly not in the principles of development for Africa, in the words of Jamie Monson, African workers counted themselves fortunate and lucky to have worked alongside and hand-in-hand with the

Chinese on a gigantic railroad project on the continent—the first of its kind by China in Africa. Monson states further:

> For many of these younger Africa men building the railway is remembered as coming of age experience, a time of moving into adulthood under the guidance of their Chinese leaders. Many recall the experience of earning a wage learning the Chinese language and mastering railway technology as a liberating entrance into a modern postcolonial world.[49]

African workers saw their entire experience in the TAZARA Railway as an opportunity of achieving freedom and liberation from ignorance, poverty, tradition, and lack of education.[50]

TRANSFORMATION OF TAZARA FROM STATE-OWNED BIG PROJECT TO ORDINARY PEOPLE'S RAILROAD

As it was typical of the era in which the TAZARA railway was conceived and constructed in the 1960s, it was a gigantic, state-owned, and modernization-oriented railway. It was essentially a socialist undertaking that was deliberately conceived as a potent instrument against colonialism, neocolonialism, imperialism, and the West hegemonism on the continent. Also, the inter-state railway, as stated earlier, was to provide an alternative route for Zambia, which could no longer transport her import and export goods—including copper—through Rhodesia, South Africa, and Angola, but via Tanzania to the Indian Ocean port of Dar es Salam. Furthermore, the construction of the railway was to symbolize the strong bond and solidarity, mutual dependence on each other among the developing countries. According to Monson, the TAZARA was not aimed "to promote rural economic development or improve the lives of rural producers by connecting local markets.[51] It was against the backdrop of this grandiose conception of the building of the railroad that conservative and liberal economists in the West evaluated the success or lack of it, of the China-financed and constructed railway. They roundly dismissed the entire project as a white elephant project. Reacting to this dismissal, Monson is of the view that using "large scale, international and transregional indicators rather than small scale, everyday traffic in goods and people are typically unfavorable,"[52] and would not do great justice to how the TAZARA in the face of several and complex operational problems was transformed into a railroad that radically and greatly impacted and transformed the socioeconomic and cultural lives of members of the rural communities in Tanzania and Zambia.[53]

Although this outcome was never envisaged at the beginning of the TAZARA project, as far as Monson is concerned its subsequent and unintended effects in rural Africa may teach some definite lessons about economic development in other similar situations and circumstances. She seems to suggest that gigantic projects in Africa and these would include all of the contemporary ones by China scattered all over the continent, should not only be evaluated in terms of the larger purposes they were/are conceived to serve, but how far they have touched, empowered, and appropriated by ordinary Africans who were/are not supposed to be the direct beneficiaries. But what in the entire TAZARA project made Monson come into this interesting conclusion?

Few years after the completion, opening, and handing-over of the TAZARA to both Tanzania and Zambia in the second half of the 1970s to manage and run, the railroad started experiencing many problems and challenges that seriously undermined its operations and services provided to her customers and users. Monson identifies and discusses several factors responsible. First, there was a general failure of the technology used in the construction of TAZARA. Second, in the rush to complete the project ahead of schedule and to impress a cynical and skeptical West that she had the capacity and the gut to construct a modern, efficient, economical, and enormous project, the Chinese management hardly had the time to train an adequate number of Africans who could have effectively taken over the management of the railroad, beginning from 1976. Therefore, when TAZARA started experiencing many problems in the 1980s onwards, the railroad company had to fall back, once again, on the Chinese experts. Third, the locomotives, wagons, and rolling stock imported by the railroad authority in use in the 1970s and 1980s were breaking down at very fast rates and were subsequently dispatched to railroad workshops for repairs and there they spent an unnecessarily long time. In fact, in 1978, 50 percent of TAZARA locomotives were in the workshops rather than in operations. Further, the ninety-seven hydraulic locomotive engines imported from China were found unsuitable to haul heavy goods up the steep sections of the railroad between Zambia and Tanzania.

Four, there was also mismanagement, inefficiency, ineffectiveness, and corruption in the running of the new railroad infrastructure. All these shortcomings were more so at the Dar es Salaam port. As a result, off-loading and transshipment of goods were delayed in both countries. Five, during the planning stage of the TAZARA, it was envisaged that seventeen trains would be transporting goods and passengers between Kapiri Mposhi and Dar es Salaam daily with a total annual tonnage of 2 million tons carriage. Rather, by early 1979, the railroad could only operate with two trains and an annual total tonnage of 8,65,000 tons per year. As for passenger trains, the instrument of livelihood of traders and people in the rural areas, TAZARA could only run two trains per week, in contrast to the six planned.

Six, the railroad in its early life was plagued with many mudslides and washouts of the bed of its lines during the raining seasons. All these developments often introduced many unplanned delays to the operations of the railroad. Seven was the problem of finance. The Tanzania and Zambia endlessly disagreed on their contributions to the TAZARA. Thus, this situation seriously affected it. Between 1976 and 1980, TAZARA lost up to 200 million shillings.[54]

It was given the foregoing factors and problems that the three countries directly involved with the TAZARA project had to renegotiate the initial TAZARA agreement in 1980. The countries identified the key operational challenge confronting the railroad authority: lack of spare parts, lack of good locomotive engines, need for more railway experts and technical help, and the provision of more capital. Two quick solutions Monson says were immediately decided upon were the purchase of fourteen new diesel-electric engines from West Germany, and that China must continue to provide technical assistance to TAZARA. Notwithstanding these measures, TAZARA's rehabilitation would continue. Between 1987 and 1993, seven Western donor countries and China gave $150 million to the railroad authority. Similarly, in October 1987, USAID gave TAZARA about $46 million to purchase seventeen new diesel locomotives, spare parts, and other equipment, set up a locomotive workshop, and receive technical assistance. Also, China gave $7 million for the purchase of spare parts and the provision of fifty-seven Chinese technical experts to help in the repair and maintenance of railway equipment. Furthermore, Norway and Sweden also contributed to the training and provision of rolling stock.[55]

These additional supports, Monson says, gave a temporary reprieve to TAZARA, as revenue, cargo, and passenger numbers increased. Passenger numbers also increased from below 5,00,000 in the early 1980s to 8,60,000 in 1988 and rose to 9,88,000 by 1990.[56] Nevertheless, by the late 1980s, TAZARA faced yet another set of challenges, especially between 1987 and 1991. These included low traffic, management problems, poor financial performance, and high fuel and maintenance costs. According to Monson, it was while all of these were going on that Tanzania, which was then having serious socioeconomic challenges, approached the International Monetary Fund (IMF) and after negotiations later accepted and implementing the international financial institution's "Structural Adjustment Programme (SAP)" in phases, starting from 1986 on to the early 1990s.[57] Under it, Tanzania would liberalize all aspects of her economy. Meanwhile during this period, as Monson reveals, the economies of Tanzania and Zambia came under severe restraints, just as radical changes were also unfolding in southern Africa that would change regional transportation equation and greatly impacted on TAZARA.[58]

In the 1990s, South Africa and Namibia became independent and democratic nations and as a result, the railroads to the south became available again to meet Zambia's transportation needs and offered a cheaper alternative route to the sea than the TAZARA.[59] This forced the latter's management to be more competitive in its strategy of creating a niche for itself in the now expanded regional market. Thus, in 1994, TAZARA was commercialized and its operations were reorganized and streamlined to compete more effectively against road transport and the southern African railroads.[60] In furtherance of these changes, a third of its workforce of 6,000 workers, that is 2,000 staff, were laid off. Thus, the TAZARA effectively transformed from a political and ideological railroad, which China seemed to have used to showcase herself to the world at the height of the Cold War, into a commercial entity.

The transition, however, was far from smooth sailing. Just as Tanzania and the rest of Africa were undergoing transitions from state-led economies to neoliberal free-market capitalist ones, so was China, and a little time later, by Eastern European and Asian nations. The transition in East Africa (Tanzania and Zambia), and their impact on the ordinary people and rural dwellers in the two countries and TAZARA's workers have attracted the intellectual exploration of Monson. In her journal article, "Defending the People's Railway in the Era of Liberalization: TAZARA in Southern Tanzania," she argues that the transition in East Africa did not follow the "blackboard approach." Relying on the work of Michael Burawoy and Janos Lukacs,[61] she says of the two authors: " [they] cautioned that analysis of this transition [in Eastern Europe] tends to follow a 'blackboard' approach to economic change. Eastern European societies are viewed as a 'blackboard' upon which Marxist-Leninist ideology was first written, then wiped clean and replaced with an ideology of free enterprise and market-orientated capitalism." Furthermore, she agrees with the authors that the approach is problematic in many ways: it focuses only on ideology, blurs the connection between ideology and "lived experience," does not reveal the impact of changes in policy in a specific social and historical environment, because society is a *tabula rasa*, a blank slate.[62] In contradistinction to this position, Monson submits that the approach wrongly "presumes that people are actively and willingly embracing 'the market' rather than seeing the transition as a negotiated and possibly incomplete process."[63] Not only this but agreeing also with Verdery,[64] Monson concludes that "the focus on ideology does not allow us to be attentive to the local meaning of concepts such as 'privatization,' 'free markets,' and 'democracy' and how meaning is debated and contested.[65] Set against this backdrop, how then did the people, local leaders, and workers react and negotiated the transition?

From the start of the construction to the completion of the TAZARA project, mobilization of Chinese and African workers and the people, particularly
those that had been resettled in the rural areas and along the railroad corridor,
to take advantage of the new mode of transportation, had been a constant
follow of specific soundbites. That the railroad was a 'people railway,'
'freedom railway,' built on socialist principles of international solidarity and
brotherhood, and the workers who built it were part of a national and regional
political liberation force. When therefore in the 1980s and 1990s, the rural
dwellers in Tanzania started to experience the negative impact of liberalization and privatization of TAZARA operations through "cutting costs and
increasing revenues" the people were aghast. "Efficiency was to be achieved
. . . by reducing the services provided to the smallest railway stations and
village level communities."[66] Further, "management decisions affecting the
communities along the railway line would be further guided by profit-seeking
rather than nation-building priorities."[67]

In response to TAZARA management's efficiency-induced rationalization,
local leaders decided to pay back the Chinese, Tanzanian, and Zambian governments, and the management of TAZARA by deploying the same language
and exhortations used to justify TAZARA in the beginning. They used them
to argue that the state must continue to provide them with the same level of
services TAZARA was providing before the liberalization of its operations.[68]
After all, the railroad was theirs; it was built for their use and not for profits
and did not belong to the World Bank and the IMF—tools of capitalist exploitation—that was now calling the shots.[69] But notwithstanding their trenchant
criticisms of the liberalized TAZARA and its impact, the people did not
call for the abolition of the privatization and liberalization program. Rather,
they decided to appropriate for themselves changes they had brought about
in ways that ultimately profited them in trade and small-scale enterprises.[70]
Using the works of the three authors mentioned above as the theoretical
framework, Monson gives insight into changes that took place in TAZARA
and rural Tanzania and Zambia.

In the 1990s, economic liberalization was extended to the agricultural
sector and this had a lot of implications for TAZARA. Monson gives a background to this radical development.

After the opening of the railroad, rural people who had settled along it were
deliberately and compulsorily resettled into *ujamaa* villages, where governments established agricultural marketing schemes under the village coopera-
tives and marketing boards. Through these two institutions, the government
purchased agricultural products from farmers at reduced and controlled
prices. In the late 1980s and 1990s under liberalization, these government
price mechanisms were dismantled, and agricultural products were now sold
openly and without restrictions in local and regional markets. This opening

up of the rural economy gave great impetus to traders and farmers to actively participate in the production, commerce, and transportation of their products far and near—using the TAZARA. This was where TAZARA became very important in the lives of rural folks and was transformed, according to Monson, from a state-owned grandiose project specifically purposed for international trade into an empowering and connecting instrument for ordinary Tanzanians and Zambians.[71]

Meanwhile, as this "revolution" in the agriculture sector was going on; many workers in the urban areas were losing their jobs as a result of economic liberalization and SAP, just as wages of those in employment were contracting. Consequently, many people were pushed into the informal trade sector, and for them to be successful, they needed to move their products around, and this in the circumstance they found themselves at the time had to be through the TAZARA. Equally, in the "highland maize production areas" in Tanzania and along the TAZARA line, economic liberalization also set the people free in their thinking. As a result of arable land shortage, unproductive landholdings, costly fertilizers, and other essential commodities, many farmers abandoned the maize economy in the hinterland and traveled by TAZARA to the railroad corridor. There they planted maize, wetland rice, vegetables, and other food crops that did not cost much in investments and could easily be taken to markets for sale.[72]

Therefore, crucially, in the second half of the 1990s, TAZARA was an important transportation resource that was empowering traders, farmers, fishermen, jobless, and frustrated urbanites, and others living along its corridor—to be able to move about to carry out their entrepreneurial activities. Thus "[t]he railway . . . made it possible for traders to switch among products by linking different types of settlements, markets, and producing zones."[73] Furthermore, through it:

> "Peddlers hawking consumer items such as plastic buckets, used clothing, and aluminum cooking pots frequent the smaller [railway] stations and most isolated villages. They acquire their goods on consignment from wholesale merchants in the larger town then carry them on train into the countryside. Here the peddlers bicycle from settlements to settlement . . . [selling their wares]. When they have sold enough to repay the wholesaler and keep something for themselves, they take the train back to town.[74]

In essence, TAZARA became an important resource and platform for assisting small-scale business persons to transport their goods packaged in Monson's words in small "parcels" on the trains, to make little profits which were later invested in farming.[75] Apart from TAZARA linking markets, Monson believes that it was also able to marry trading activities with those of farming and industrial work. Such interlinkages made it possible for workers in the Kilombero Sugar Company (KSC) in Tanzania and its sugarcane out-growers living in the TAZARA corridor to farm in places that were several kilometers away from the company and at times near it. This was because as Monson observed, there was a shortage of fertile land near or around the KSC.[76] In the third place, Monson argues that TAZARA was able to connect cultural and linguistic communities. As new migrants came into the TAZARA corridor through the railroad, they settled among their people with whom they shared languages and cultures. And as people blend in this manner, there developed new linguistic and cultural communities.[77] The railroad also facilitated, on a greater scale, the culture of sending young children—from outside of the railroad corridor—to go and stay with relatives who were perceived to be living in *el-dorado*. The railroad also made it possible for migrants to travel back to their homes of origin when they were needed on special occasions. Conclusively, Monson submits that in the context of East Africa at the time, the railroad became "the connective tissue" of the rural world. "It makes socio-cultural connections possible as well as economic ones."[78]

CONCLUSION

This chapter has examined some of Jamie Monson's historical writings on China's first great infrastructural project in Africa, the TAZARA railroad project. It was conceived as a grand national railway owned by the state, pan-Africanist, anti-colonialist, anti-neocolonialist, anti-imperialist, socialist, and a symbol of south-south cooperation. It was also meant to provide an important transportation outlet to the sea for landlocked Zambia via Tanzania and to break free from its reliance on Rhodesian (Zimbabwean), Angolan, and South African railroads and ports. In the 1980s and 1990s, TAZARA faced many operational challenges that necessitated its commercialization and privatization, which forced it to streamline its services and lay off many workers. These reforms strongly affected the ordinary people living along the railroad corridor, who then employed much the same language that the governments of China, Tanzania, and Zambia used at the start of the project to mobilize them in the construction, defense, working for and supporting it, such as TAZARA was a "freedom railway," "people railway," "liberation railway" and so forth—to criticize and extract many concessions from the TAZARA management.

Monson unique contribution to the understanding of China's engagements with Africa from the 1950s to date is to show in sharp relief how a multimillion dollar Chinese supported, financed, and constructed gigantic project which never reached its envisaged performance levels, but greatly affected, in a positive manner, the socioeconomic and cultural lives of ordinary people living along the TAZARA corridor. These people—and what happened to them—were never factored in the conception of the project as direct beneficiaries. Monson would like to see this kind of analysis, of how ordinary people of Africa benefit from big and great projects, particularly those sponsored by China, be used in the critical assessment big projects on the continent.

TAZARA became an important tool that greatly aided the diversification of livelihood strategies in Tanzania and Zambia. Monson was able to show—through the skillful use of oral history and personal testimonies and life histories[79]—how TAZARA made it possible and easy for the ordinary people of Tanzania and Zambia to move about and transport their small goods in "small parcels" from places to places. Second, it also encouraged the migration of many people, particularly rural folks and urbanites that were hard on their luck to the railroad corridor. Monson's work on TAZARA, however, has some shortcomings: inability to offer the actual numbers of Africans in Tanzania and Zambia impacted by the railroad; inability to determine the total number of people that migrated on account of TAZARA; inability to show whether the original purpose and objectives of TAZARA were realized and if so, to what extent; most of the discussions on the TAZARA have been limited to Tanzania; and finally, how relevant have these large Chinese project(s) been to the genuine economic development of Africa or are they just white elephants in the sun? Ultimately, time will tell.

NOTES

1. Paul Tiyambe Zeleza, "The Africa-China Relationship: Challenges and Opportunities," *Canadian Journal of African Studies/ La Revue canadienne des etudes africaines,* 48:1, 146.

2. Ibid.

3. Ibid, 147.

4. Ibid.

5. Ibid, 148.

6. This section draws on Jamie Monson's Curriculum Vitae posted on Macalester College's website—accessed 16 April 2015. See also Michigan State University website and its History Department's web page https://history.msu.edu/people/faculty/Jamie_monson/ (accessed 15 June 2019).

7. Ibid.

8. Michigan State University website and its History Department's web page: https://history.msu.edu/people/faculty/Jamie_monson/ (accessed 15 June 2019).

9. Ibid.

10. Jamie Monson, "Global African Studies and Locating China," in Chris Alden and Daniel Large (eds.) *New Directions in Africa-China Studies* (Oxford: Routledge, 2019), 133.

11. Ibid.

12. For instance, see Jamie Monson and Stephanie Rupp (Guest Editors), African Studies Review (ASR) Forum on Africa and China—"Introduction: Africa and China, New Engagements, New Research," *Africa Studies Review*; and Jamie Monson, "Researching the China-East Africa Cold War Relationship: Archives, Institutions and Personal Collections," *The PRC History Review* 2(3) June 2017, 1–26.

13. Jamie Monson, *Africa's Freedom Railway* (Bloomington: Indiana University Press, 2009), 16.

14. Ibid.

15. Ibid, 19–20.

16. Ibid, 21–22.

17. Ibid, 28–29.

18. Ibid, 21.

19. Ibid, 22.

20. Ibid.

21. Ibid.

22. Ibid, 23.

23. Ibid.

24. Ibid.

25. Ibid.

26. Ibid.

27. Ibid, 23–24.

28. Ibid, 3 and 24.

29. Ibid, 24.

30. Ibid.

31. Ibid.

32. Jamie Monson, "Freedom Railway: The unexpected successes of a Cold War development project." *Boston Review*, December 2004/January 2005, 3.

33. Ibid.

34. Ibid, 2.

35. Jamie Monson, *Africa's Freedom Railway* (Bloomington: Indiana University Press, 2009).

36. Ibid, 6.

37. Ibid.

38. Ibid.

39. Ibid, 6 and Appendix 1 on pages 155–156.

40. Jamie Monson, "Liberating Labour? Constructing Anti-Hegemony on the TAZARA Railway in Tanzania, 1965–76," in Chris Alden, Daniel Large et al (eds.), China Returns to Africa, A Rising Power and a Continent Embrace (London: Hurst Publishers Ltd., 2008).

41. Ibid, 201–202.

42. Ibid, 203.

43. Ibid, 202–203.

44. Jamie Monson, *Africa's Freedom Railway*, 7–8.

45. Jamie Monson, "Liberating Labour? Constructing Anti-Hegemony on the TAZARA Railway, 203.

46. Ibid.

47. Ibid.

48. Ibid.

49. Ibid, 204.

50. Ibid.

51. Jamie Monson, *Africa's Freedom Railway*, 1; and "Working Ahead of Time: Labour and Modernization during the Construction of the TAZARA Railway, 1968–86," in Christopher Lee *Making a World after Empire the Bandung Moment and It's Political Afterlives* (Athens, OH: Center for International Studies, Ohio University, 2010), 243.

52. Jamie Monson, "Freedom Railway: The unexpected successes of a Cold War development project . . . " 1 and 3.

53. Jamie Monson, *Africa's Freedom Railway,* 151–153.

54. Ibid, 100–103 cf "Freedom Railway . . . " 3–4.

55. Ibid.

56. Jamie Monson, *Africa's Freedom Railway...*102.

57. Jamie Monson, "Freedom Railway . . . " 3; idem "Defending the People's Railway in the Era of Liberalization: TAZARA in Southern Tanzania," *Africa* 76 (1), 2006, 122.

58. Jamie Monson, *Africa's Freedom Railway . . .* 104.

59. Ibid.

60. Ibid.

61. M. Burawoy and J Lukacs, *The Radiant Past: Ideology and Reality in Hungary's Road to Capitalism* (Chicago: University of Chicago Press, 1992).

62. Jamie Monson, "Defending the People's Railway in the Era of Liberalization... *Africa* 76 (1), 2006, 114.

63. Ibid.

64. K. Verdery, *What was Socialism, and What Comes Next?* (New Jersey: Princeton University Press, 1996).

65. Monson, "Defending the People's Railway in the Era of Liberalization . . . *Africa* 76 (1), 2006, 114.

66. Ibid, 113.

67. Ibid.

68. Ibid, 113–114 and 128.

69. Ibid, 114 and 128–129.

70. Ibid, 129.

71. Jamie Monson, *Africa's Freedom Railway . . .* 103 and 104.

72. Ibid, 103–106.

73. Monson, "Freedom Railway..." 5.

74. Ibid.

75. Ibid, 105–111.

76. Monson, "Freedom Railway . . ." 4; Africa's *Freedom Railway* . . . 120–121.
77. Monson, "Freedom Railway . . ." 7.
78. Ibid, 8.
79. Jamie Monson, "*Maisha:* Life History and History of Livelihood along the TAZARA Railway in Tanzania," in Toyin Falola and Christian Jennings, Sources and Methods in African History: Spoken, Written, Unearthed (Rochester: The University of Rochester University Press, 2003); "Making Men, Making History: railway work in Cold War Afro-Asian solidarity," *Clio* (38) 2013, 120–147.

BIBLIOGRAPHY

Burawoy, Michael, and János Lukács. *The Radiant Past: Ideology and Reality in Hungary's Road to Capitalism*. Chicago: Univ. of Chicago P., 1994.

Monson, Jamie. "Defending the Peoples Railway in the Era of Liberalization: TAZARA in Southern Tanzania." *Africa* 76, no. 1 (2006): 113–30.

Monson, Jamie. "Defending the Peoples Railway in the Era of Liberalization: TAZARA in Southern Tanzania." *Africa* 76, no. 1 (2006): 113–30.

Monson, Jamie. *Africa's Freedom Railway: How a Chinese Development Project Changed Lives and Livelihoods in Tanzania*. Bloomington, IN: Indiana University Press, 2011.

Monson, Jamie. "Making Men, Making History: Remembering Railway Work in Cold War Afro-Asian Solidarity." *Clio*, no. 38 (2014): 120–47.

Monson, Jamie. "Global African Studies and Locating China," in Chris Alden and Daniel Large (eds.) *New Directions in Africa-China Studies* (Oxford: Routledge, 2019), 133.

Monson, Jamie and Stephanie Rupp (Guest Editors), African Studies Review (ASR) Forum on Africa and China - "Introduction: Africa and China, New Engagements, New Research," *Africa Studies Review* 56, no. 1 (January 2013): 21–44.

Monson, Jamie. "Researching the China-East Africa Cold War Relationship: Archives, Institutions and Personal Collections," *The PRC History Review* 2, no. 3 (June 2017): 1–26.

Monson, Jamie. "Freedom Railway: The unexpected successes of a Cold War development project." *Boston Review*, December 2004/January 2005, 3.

Monson, Jamie. "Liberating Labour? Constructing Anti-Hegemony on the TAZARA Railway in Tanzania, 1965-76," in Chris Alden, Daniel Large et al. (eds.), *China Returns to Africa, A Rising Power and a Continent Embrace* (London: Hurst Publishers Ltd., 2008).

Monson, Jamie. *Africa's Freedom Railway*, 1; and "Working Ahead of Time: Labour and Modernization during the Construction of the TAZARA Railway, 1968-86," in Christopher Lee *Making a World after Empire the Bandung Moment and It's Political Afterlives* (Athens, OH: Center for International Studies, Ohio University, 2010), 243.

Monson, Jamie. "*Maisha:* Life History and History of Livelihood along the TAZARA Railway in Tanzania," in Toyin Falola and Christian Jennings (eds.), *Sources and Methods in African History: Spoken, Written, Unearthed* (Rochester: The University of Rochester University Press, 2003).

Verdery, Katherine. *What Was Socialism, and What Comes next?* Princeton: Princeton University Press, 2010.

Zeleza, Paul Tiyambe. "The Africa-China Relationship: Challenges and Opportunities," *Canadian Journal of African Studies / Revue Canadienne Des Études Africaines* 48, no. 1 (2014): 145–169.

Chapter 4

Alliance Systems Redefined

Toward an Alternative Perspective of China's Hands-off Approach to African Politics

Lawrence Mhandara

INTRODUCTION

China's economic interface with Africa has exponentially grown over the past decades. China is now Africa's largest trading, investment, and aid partner. The evolution of the economic partnership may be reinvigorated as the implementation of projects under China's Belt and Road initiative takes shape. However, what the future holds for this partnership remains subject to conjectures, but China is certainly a major actor on the African continent to the extent that its policies cannot be spurned. A robust debate among stakeholders and academics has often centered on delineating the nature and intent of China's imposing presence on the continent, that is, whether China has cornered Africa into a new spell of exploitation (emerging pattern of imperialism/a rising neocolonial actor) or Africa has discovered a benign economic power keen on developing the continent on mutually acceptable terms. The hands-off approach is a synonym of China's noninterference policy usually expressed in the "no strings" attached principle employed in its trade, investment and aid relations with Africa and the rest of the global south.[1] The hands-off approach is also in harmony with China's principle that international relations for all and domestic politics is reserved for a sovereign state. This approach or noninterference policy is part of China's long-term strategy to rival the Washington Consensus pivoted on conditional aid and investment from Western countries, primarily America. On its part, Africa has warmly embraced, and rejoiced in, the policy given its resentment with Western interference.

Over the years, eclectic views on the policy have emerged such that there is a lack of consensus among scholars as to its nature or the benefits that accrue to China. In some instances, noninterference is dismissed as a nebulous strand of Chinese foreign policy, whose implementation has been calibrated depending on the host's economic and political conditions.[2] China is also reportedly shifting toward a mixture of noninterference and conditional intervention. It is neither simply maintaining the principle, without taking action against conflict and crises in other countries, nor abandoning the principle to become a fully engaged actor.[3] Recent studies have also concluded that China's foreign policy attitude toward other countries, especially in Africa, has transmuted to the extent that it is gradually abandoning the hands-off approach on the back of Western pressure to intervene,[4] or in competition with the United States as part of its "flexigemony" that has forced it to establish a military base in Africa.[5] However, my argument is that even if China's noninterference has ceased to be classical,[6] this cardinal motif of its post-1949 diplomacy remains alive in Africa. Indeed, despite the observed shifts, there has been no fundamental change to the application of the policy,[7] vindicating further research on China's intentions in employing the instrument in Africa. Although China pursued the opening-up policy from the 1970s, its foreign policy continues to be etched in the mantra of peaceful coexistence, which includes the notion of mutual noninterference.[8]

In terms of the teleology of the noninterference policy, the juggernaut of the Western narrative is discernible in literature. It perceives the policy as an opportunistic and gluttonous pretext used by China to exploit Africa's vast natural resources and markets in support of its economic modernization. The hands-off approach is seen as integral to its resource diplomacy that is a key feature of China's modernization diplomacy.[9] As China's economy continues to grow, the argument goes, it wants to expand its markets and secure reliable supplies of resources in support of its economic development. This is considered as the main contributing factor to China's relative economic success and China sees no reason to simply abandon noninterference.[10] In this chapter, I present a revisionist perspective by departing from the prevailing wisdom on how China uses the hands-off approach in its relations with Africa. I propose that the approach has a broader strategic intent that makes sense when one situates it at the systemic level insofar as shifts in power relations among great powers are concerned. Within that framework, China's hands-off approach, taking advantage of its economic advantages, is an attempt to forge a soft alliance with Africa to constrain the power and influence of the United States. I propose that China's relations with Africa have less to do with Africa but the United States in a broader global power game. China is in competition with the United States for Africa's loyalty, hence, it was imprudent on its part to create the means (hands-off approach) with which to win Africa.

The first part of the chapter attempts to locate China's hands-off approach in its foreign policy. This will foreground the study in the right context to understand the instrumental value of the hands-off approach in China's quest to constrain the current hegemony, the United States. The second part presents the argument that the hands-off approach is part of the strategic calculation by China to form a nontraditional alliance with Africa as part of its soft balancing strategy against U.S. policies. The subsequent section explores China's aspirations beyond its soft alliance with Africa in as far as it seeks to supplant the United States as the leader of the globe. The last section concludes the chapter.

SITUATING THE HANDS-OFF APPROACH IN CHINA'S FOREIGN POLICY DISCOURSE

China has been the fastest-growing economy in the world since the 1980s and by 2010 it assumed the second position as the world's largest economy. On the strength of its economic power, China has expanded its global reach beyond East Asia into Africa and Latin America. It has grown its partnership with Africa and a major investor and provider of economic aid to the continent.[11] After decades of Western countries applying the prescriptions laid out in the Washington Consensus, doubts have been raised about the effectiveness of Western conditional support as a remedy to Africa's development maladies. American economic support to Africa has been excessively selective, stringent, sporadic, and generally weak. Moreover, even when cooperation occurred, it has usually been insufficient to overcome the malevolent effects of U.S. hegemony.[12] Thus when forging relationships in Africa and elsewhere in the developing world, Beijing has emphasized its role as a fellow member of the South, its history free of imperialism or colonialism in foreign lands, and its willingness to provide aid, assistance, and economic opportunities based on equality—without the paternalistic prescriptions or conditions often demanded by Western donors and international financial institutions. Parenthetically, Western powers and their international financial have been less supportive in extricating African countries from their subdued economic situation, further accruing image gains for the PRC. In any case, the Chinese economic and political relationship with Africa has scored high diplomatic points while lifting China's relationship with the rest of the Third World to a new level.[13]

The evolution of China-Africa cooperation can be divided into three stages: 1949 to 1979, 1979 to 1999, and from 2000 to the present.[14] Nonetheless, in all the periods, China has largely stuck to the noninterference policy when dealing with African issues. Noninterference has emerged as an important pivot of Third World solidarity in China's foreign policy for more than six decades. The roots of the policy can be situated within the five principles of peaceful coexistence—noninterference, mutual respect for sovereignty and territorial integrity, equality and mutual benefit, mutual nonaggression, and peaceful coexistence—jointly adopted by China and India in 1954 during discussions to end their border dispute.[15] The principles were further reinforced at the first major Afro-Asia summit held in 1955 in Bandung, Indonesia. The adoption of the principles by the Nonaligned Movement (NAM) and the declarations made by developing countries within the framework of the United Nations (UN) in the 1960s and 1970s elevated the five principles to a position of global prominence. The spirit driving the adoption of the principles by relatively weaker countries in the global south was informed by the Cold War context where there was a strategic calculation to steer away from the U.S.-Soviet Union politics and in the process minimize their interference in their internal politics. For China, the end of the Cold War did not justify the shift from the noninterference policy to interference, which has served to leverage China against Western interference not only in its domestic policies but also in the rest of the developing countries.[16]

China's noninterference policy, in general, and Africa, in particular, is associated with the inviolability of the basic pillars of statehood protected by international law whose key reference point is the UN Charter. At the center of the approach is the respect of the internal and external sovereignty, abstaining from interference in the internal affairs of other sovereign states, respect for the independence of other states, and eschewing coercive diplomacy as a means to project or protect its interests abroad. The stance serves as a guarantee that China is respectful of the diversity in ideas, views, and principles of other countries.[17] China has seen regular changes of leadership, the policy of noninterference has been consolidated and it is one area of convergence among all leaders from 1949 to 2019. In the 1970s, Deng Xiaoping set the foundation of the policy through the "Guiding Principle of Twenty-four Characters, where China "must not act as the head. Hegemony have a bad reputation, so acting as the head of the Third World will also be ill-reputed. Even though we are powerful in the future . . . never interfere in the internal affairs of other countries."[18] In 2000, the Chinese diplomat assured Africa on China's commitment to the policy: "China has no intention to undermine Africa's democracy. I doubt there is any tiny political gain China can get by doing such things against the historical trend and the common wish of the people."[19] With Xi Jinping, China enunciated a "five no" stance toward Africa:[20]

- No interference in the development paths of individual countries.
- No interference in their internal affairs.

- No imposition of China's will.
- No attachment of political strings regarding assistance.
- No seeking of selfish political gains in investment and financing cooperation.

The motifs have been central in China's diplomacy and international strategy. Noninterference has served as a guidepost for China's actions/reactions or lack thereof in African and global affairs. Noninterference is underpinned by a respectful tone in China's diplomacy that both dovetails with and reinforces its bilateral ties with individual states and its global position as a whole.[21] Even in situations that would ordinarily invite censure from other big powers, China has pursued an ambivalent line. Sudan, Zimbabwe, Angola, Lesotho, and Democratic Republic Congo (DRC) have had difficult patches in their internal politics, but China resists the temptation to condemn actions of the governments in power. Incidentally, its noninterference policy has assisted China to penetrate Africa and score diplomatic victories compared to the interfering West. In Africa, China is now regarded as an all-weather friend by most states.

Mutual accommodation, in which China uses its power softly (gentler diplomacy) fits nicely with the African style of diplomacy, potentially generating a new form of alliance unprecedented in international relations. China basis its relations with Africa on peaceful coexistence and foreign aid without strings, thereby contrasting with aid from Western countries that were/are given with preconditions. China's aid policies also help it garner the support of African leaders—who were most attracted to the idea that economic assistance could be given without strings attached. Africa has been able to define its strategies while China renders assistance without dictating terms (interference), giving space to pan-African initiatives such as the "African Solutions to African Problems."[22] Africa has found in China's noninterference policy a supportive instrument that all African countries appreciate. China aims at providing support for Africa to pursue its home-made priorities and to attain its objectives. Coming from a background of colonialism and external interference by Western powers in Africa's affairs, it is natural for African countries to recognize the positive essence of Chinese noninterference.[23]

Since the 1980s, and especially since the end of the Cold War, China's foreign policy changed from its focus from exporting revolution to being fundamentally economic. As an inevitable result of this change, China completely embraced the noninterference principle. Keen to secure a better international environment for its economic development China realized that, in a globalized world, noninterference should be at the heart of its foreign policy.[24] Indeed, beyond the economic interests, there is a strategic necessity in sticking to noninterference in the context of global politics.

THE SYSTEMIC POWER CONFIGURATION
AND THE U.S. HEGEMONY

Major powers shape international politics and focusing on them as units of analysis that allows an understanding of the rules by which international relations are played.[25] In that regard, the locus of power at the systemic level is important in as far as it reveals a global hegemony at any given time. Global hegemony is a state with capabilities to create and maintain international or global rules and order in cooperation with its allies using means of its choice.[26] Hegemony is thus identified by its essential traits:

- Its hard power (preponderate military and economic capabilities) has no match among existing powers.[27]
- Consistent with classical realism, a hegemon is driven by self-centeredness in its security, economic, and ideological interests.[28]
- Hegemon can impose rules that govern international relations.[29]
- Hegemony is a theoretical counter to international anarchy; it has a dominant leader who assumes the position of a global leader.

While there are doubts over the sustainability of a unipolar world,[30] the United States is still the hegemony given its predominant power in the international system, measured in terms of that state's share of world Gross Domestic Product (GDP) or other material resources.[31] The United States is the world's leading economy followed by China. It also possesses by far the most powerful military. The United States also enjoys considerable influence in key international institutions and its dominance defines the structure of the current international system. Unipolarity means that the unipole has greater freedom of action than other states. It enjoys greater freedom in its policies in the absence of a power equaling its mammoth capabilities.[32] In nearly every measure of resources, from Gross National Product (GNP) to armed services, the United States overshadows all other states in the post–Cold War period. It has the largest navy and air force, which gives it an unequaled ability to project power around the globe and the collapse of the Soviet military machine made these advantages more obvious. The United States is an essential player in monetary affairs, and the dollar is still the major reserve currency.

For all these reasons, most states await American decisions before making their own. No state can afford to ignore the vast concentration of power in the hands of the United States,[33] because it does what it wants most of the time,[34] a situation in which the strong do as they wish and the weak do as they must. China like Africa sees the United States as a malevolent hegemony. It is perceived as creating, defending, and sustaining rules and regimes that strengthen and perpetuate its dominance. The United States has the military, industrial, and financial capacity to impose its will on the world, but it has not adequately played the part of the international economic hegemon and used its position to support Africa's development. And with the United States rejoicing in this position of prominence, rising states can only aim to exploit the disgruntlement of Africa to take over space from the United States and hope for the hegemony decline. This is why China has become Africa's most embraced great power. The pinnacle of excellence for China's relations with Africa is that it has strategically employed its noninterference policy in a manner that exploits the Africa-U.S. tension and intensified those tensions to its benefit and advantage.

China's worry is how the United States abuses its status which creates concerns about the imbalance of power against itself. This is a concern which emanates from the structural defects of unipolarity where the United States has forced its way on key international issues with utter disregard of the majority opinion to act on the contrary. China and Russia have been able to resist U.S. actions in some cases—its exercise of the veto power in the UN Security Council, but they have not succeeded where salient U.S. interests were concerned. The result is that even bigger powers are worried about the status of the United States in as far as they are unsure of how the hegemony might act and in the process how it might impinge on their interests.[35] Thus, China is unsettled by the concentration of power in the United States. The imbalance of power creates anxiety. The response that is predicted by the classical balance of power theory based on hard balancing to contain the strongest state. But because of the fluidity in statecraft, what is important is to ultimately achieve the objectives of balancing whether one chooses soft or hard means. Faced with the imperative of balancing, states may choose internal or external instruments to do so.[36] China's strategy has been to explore soft ways of constraining the United States in lieu of confrontation. For China, soft alliances are part of this U.S. challenge. This is the context within which the essential tenets of noninterference have been articulated in its foreign policy. This draws us closer to understand China's attempts to form an alliance with Africa using the "hands-off carrot."

CHINA'S HANDS-OFF APPROACH IN AFRICA: IN SEARCH OF AN ALLIANCE AGAINST A PREDATORY HEGEMONY

Alliances play a central role in international relations because they are an integral part of statecraft. Alliances are formed between two or more countries to counter a common adversary. Morgenthau's proposition is that alliance is a process for manipulating equilibrium, that is, a means of maintaining equilibrium. Other states have found it costly to attempt a hard-power balance against United States' overwhelming hard-power capabilities.[37] There is a good reason to fear an unbalanced United States, hence, the continuous search for balancing tools against it.

Balancing takes two forms—soft and hard forms. Efforts to join forces to counter U.S. power or limit U.S. influence have generally taken the form of soft balancing. These actions have been directed against specific U.S. policies than U.S. hard-power capabilities.[38] Hard balancing is based on the belief that a countervailing alliance must be formed to keep the dominant power under control and is not targeted at policies of the hegemony. By contrast, soft balancing works within the status quo but seeks to constrain independent action by the hegemony through establishing alliances that undermine the dominant power's policies. "In the current era of US dominance, therefore, soft balancing is the conscious coordination of diplomatic action to obtain outcomes contrary to US preferences, outcomes that could not be gained if the balancers did not give each other some degree of mutual support. Instead of combining military forces or conducting joint operations, soft balancers combine their diplomatic assets in order to defend their interests."[39] The essence of soft balancing by China is seeking to limit the ability of the United States to impose its preferences on others at the expense of its own. International institutions, economic statecraft, and diplomatic coordination have been tools used by states attempting to balance the United States through nontraditional means. The hands-off approach is thus regarded as a tool to establish a soft alliance with Africa that seeks to soft balance the United States.

Beijing pursues a strategic course which consists of "soft balancing," that is, "actions that do not directly challenge US military preponderance but that use non-military tools to deny, frustrate and undermine US self-serving policies."[40] China's late top leader Deng Xiaoping (1904–1997), the architect of China's opening up and modernization, conceived a doctrine for China's post–Cold War diplomacy, which included not only the *Tao Guang Yang Hui* (low-key) but also the more aggressive *You Suo Zuo Wei* (do something) approach, and has respected the former more than the latter.[41] In this strategy, China is careful not to provoke the United States in a typical Cold War power game.

The key to China's consideration is that its rising power has the potential to generate tensions that may be resolved through war.[42] China recognizes that attempts to balance through hard means may be catastrophic. The examples of Spain, France, Germany, and the Soviet Union who attempted hard-power balancing all lost to the hegemonies.[43] China's awareness of its international status is characterized by an acute awareness of this potential strategy. Part of its self-consciousness would then embrace soft balancing behavior that includes soft alliance formation with countries that perceive the United States as a malevolent hegemony. China is calculative and understands the risk of confronting the United States. China finds it imprudent to unsettle the current hegemony by flaunting its hard power. The soft approach to China's international approach has been echoed by a different Chinese official. China is convinced that confrontational resistance to the U.S. order is futile and counterproductive. From Deng Xiaoping, Jiang Zemin, Hu Jintao to Xi Jingping, nonconfrontation has been a fundamental policy toward the United States: "China will not, repeat, not repeat the old practice of a strong country seeking hegemony,"[44] Under Hu Jintao, who took the reins of power in 2002, "peaceful development" became the phrase of the moment.[45]

Internationally, the U.S.-led global order is structured such that a confrontational hard-power strategy is prohibitively costly, while at the same time a softer approach appears plausible in achieving both the Chinese leadership's domestic agenda and international aspirations.[46] The Chinese strategy conforms to the traditional Chinese statecraft based on the exploitation of the enemy's weaknesses than confronting its strong points. Sun Tsu famously encouraged, "attaining one hundred victories in one hundred battles is not the highest achievement; subjugating the enemy without having to fight is the true pinnacle of excellence."[47] The emphasis of Chinese strategy is political acumen, rather than the contest of physical prowess. Beijing is building a soft alliance with Africa by using its hands-off approach to undermine U.S. influence on the continent which hosts the largest number of developing countries than any other continent. Indeed, Deng Xiaoping's strategy is still alive in China's relations with the United States: "observe calmly; secure our position; cope with affairs calmly; hide our capacities and bide our time; be good at manipulating low profile; never claim leadership."[48] This is part of the behavioral adjustment to dispel the notion that China's hard power poses a threat to the United States. The use of noninterference policy is to pursue a soft alliance by appealing to issues that contradict the foundation of U.S. power.

Soft balancing has a long history dating back to the end of the Cold War. With Soviet disappearance, the Western constructions of rising threat began to gravitate toward China, essentially expressing fears of China as an aggressive revisionist power that needed to be confronted. This narrative has been successfully preempted, at least for now, as China's international strategy is rooted in the soft use of its power in its foreign policy which has endeared it to the majority of developing countries especially Africa. In the process and in line with its nuanced attitude, China appears to be succeeding to achieve its aims without confronting the United States. The argument is that China wants to balance U.S. power to open a window for a possible change of global leadership without risking confrontation with the hegemony. Against the background that most African countries perceive the exercise of power by the United States as disrespectful, they have accepted the carrot dangled by China not to interfere in the politics and development priorities. It is using its economic power to articulate a world vision designed to showcase its leadership as more appealing than that of the United States and in the process of building alliances without provoking a countervailing response from the United States. Thus, as its economy grows, its trade, investment, and aid have cemented ties with the rest of the world while strengthening its strategy to entice developing countries to resist U.S. power.[49] In the process, China has succeeded in currying favors from African countries who feel obligated to denounce U.S. coercive policies and side with China's positions on key international issues. The exercise of hard power by a corky and imprudent United States has damaged its image in Africa, while the exercise of hard power in a gentler way by China has improved its reputation within the same continent. The pendulum of influence in the competition for allies is swinging in China's way owing to its noninterference policy.

China has used its hands-off approach to hold political ground in Africa directly constraining U.S. domination. Its approach typifies a containment impulse in great-power politics that is based on an orderly mechanism hospitable to China's aspirations.[50] China has pursued a foreign policy designed to soften competitive power politics. Many scholars are certain China is designing or working toward a new global order and will ultimately challenge American world domination.[51] China is undermining U.S. primacy using nontraditional means. China is working to contain and weaken the U.S. position. Indeed, China's hands-off approach to African countries may be insensible if detached from current international politics. Its behavior in Africa is consistent with the argument that powerful states may seek to contest the imposition of one set of orders and governance rules in favor of others that may benefit them more than the status quo.[52] In this contest, China has taken measures to deliberately limit power politics in its balancing behavior. China wants to establish the primacy of its power, its international institutions, and normative structures that meet its aspirations and it needs allies to support its cause hence the use of the hands-off approach in its relations with Africa.

In ideological terms, the world is dominated by Western values and standards and for China, its status is not just about recognition of the power it has but also about securing the international environment that makes the power growth possible. China is becoming more involved in Africa to use it as an instrument in its fight against U.S. power and this drives the desire to work toward the strategic objective of building a soft alliance with Africa. Thus, as China becomes more determined to constrain the United States, it views

African countries as natural allies and vice versa. The United States has had traditional political and military ties with Africa, but the latter has been economically gravitating toward China, now Africa's largest trading and aid partner. At the back of its "hands-off" approach, Africa has bandwagoned with China by way of accommodating and joining forces with it against the United States.

The position of Africa is motivated by the desire to be part of a soft coalition that limits the hegemony's global role and shares the benefits of China's position in the future. China's interests and global influence may well coincide with those of Africa, providing opportunities for collaboration. The tendency of Africa to bandwagon with China is likely to become institutionalized in the long-term. Therefore, China's alliance with Africa built out of its hands-off strategy does not seek to balance in the classic sense, that is, it does not try to resist U.S. armed forces directly or send military support in opposition to the U.S. policies but through collective opposition. The result is classic soft balancing: by adopting a unified position, China and its African allies have denied the United States the legitimacy it seeks and thereby impose significantly greater political and economic costs on U.S. decisions, policies, and preferences.

A point to emphasize at this stage is that in a world dominated by the United States, China is adopting innovative alliance formation strategies that balance the U.S. policies in a manner that avoids direct military confrontation.[53] The choice of economic balancing over military balancing is based on the argument that power in ascendancy eschews risk, compared to the one whose power is facing decline who tends to be reckless.[54] Summarizing China's grand strategy, Chan concludes that China is seeking to "enhance its value as an attractive and even indispensable partner on issues critical to other states, and to cultivate its reputation as a responsible member of the international economy."[55] Africa, therefore, is no longer an element of the abstract "Third World" concept in China's diplomacy; it has become a significant political ally in its international strategy.[56] China's strategy is to endear itself to the developing world because its explicit aim is to discredit the United States and undermine its global position and status.[57] China is engaging in covert, tacit, and informal forms of alliance formation with Africa because the United States is most likely to disrupt a formal anti-U.S. alliance, but it is unlikely to do so against the informal alliance emerging out of China's hands-off approach. In nontraditional forms, counterbalancing against the United States is occurring through China's noninterference policy in African affairs. Unlike states engaged in hard balancing, China's soft balancing largely employs nonmilitary instruments of power such as noninterference to build alliances that constrain and delegitimize the actions of a hegemonic United States.[58]

BEYOND THE SINO-AFRICA ALLIANCE:
CHINA'S QUEST FOR GLOBAL LEADERSHIP

China recognizes it needs the alliance with Africa not only to constrain U.S. policies but also to ascend to the prestigious position of a global leader when the balance of power tilts in its favor. To that end, "a state will attempt to change the international system only if it has a relative advantage over the other state, that is if the balance of power in the system is to its advantage."[59] The logic for this aspiration is simple. A dominant power shapes the course of international politics in significant ways. Realists argue that a hegemon can persuade other states to support its interests, benignly or malevolently, in a world of power-seeking states that find themselves in an anarchic international system.[60] Thus, balancing behavior cannot be explained outside the quest for leadership. For Mearsheimer, the world is replete with revisionist powers seeking to restructure the world in its favor.[61]

The competition for status is necessary to set the international rules because great-power dominance and the hierarchy of prestige[62] lie at the heart of international politics. In the aftermath of the Cold War, the hegemony of the United States and its fellow advanced democracies collectively had a firm hold on an international society that cast China to an outlier position. Chinese impulses have been focused on the U.S.-centered hegemony and its corresponding normative order, and to the extent that these components of the international arrangement are perceived to be the biggest drawback to China's status quest. The use of the hands-off approach in its affairs with Africa is part of this power scheme which Chinese president Xi Xinping has described it as a "new type of international relations." It is fair to assume that China sees itself at the center of this new type of international relations. Instead of "working toward", Xi Jingping is now seeking to "lead" the world.[63] Historical patterns reveal that economic changes are major driving forces behind political shifts in the international system. If one economy grows much faster than others for an extended period, it is a significant indication of the rise of a new global power.[64]

As China aspire for global leadership, it has chosen to use soft balancing in which it employs instruments such as noninterference to establish nontraditional alliances with Africa. From a realist point of view, the behavior of all great powers is functionally alike and the injunctions of self-centeredness will compel China to seek global leadership. China's primary strategic option is to cope with U.S. power while downplaying its desire to take over leadership.[65] China is a great power that also harbors hegemonic ambitions. China is not a mindless actor; its rationalism dictates that its intentions to assume global leadership is possible if U.S. power is curtailed through soft balancing. China, like the United States, will continue to maximize its power beyond its current balancing behavior,[66] until it overtakes the United States. This contradicts the common view that China's focus is its economic growth and will support the United States to sustain the system that facilitated its success.[67]

China's ambitions are not distinct from those of any other great power, but the method of execution has unique Chinese characteristics. Xi Jinping's insistence in September 2017 that China "lacks the gene" that drives great powers to seek hegemony should be dismissed when viewed from the perspective. But China has no interest in establishing a web of traditional alliances, sustaining a global military presence, or spreading its system of government abroad. It is using its soft alliance approach to achieve this long-term goal. In Africa, China wants to push out the United States and assume the status of an unchallenged political, economic, and military hegemon. And globally, even though it is happy to leave the United States in the driver's seat, for now, ultimately, it wants to be powerful enough to replace the United States in the position of global leadership. As one Chinese official puts it, "Being a great power means you get to do what you want, and no one can say anything about it."[68] China wants to reorganize the international normative order and wrestle leadership from the United States.[69]

CONCLUSION

The chapter has presented a nuanced position to understand China's hands-off attitude to African politics by employing a strategic lens. Contextualized from systemic relations, China's hands-off approach, a synonym of its noninterference policy, is tied to the changing approach to alliance-building, in an era of U.S. preponderance. From this perspective, it appears China's engagement with Africa is primarily motivated not by imperialism or humanitarian objectives but a subtle strategic calculus; one that seeks to constrain U.S. power and influence through other means except hard balancing. Alliance formation is shifting away from classical forms (hard balancing) to soft approaches hence the choice to pursue a hands-off approach by China where the United States would indicate otherwise. Beyond the establishment of a soft alliance with Africa and other developing countries, the ultimate price for China is global leadership. From a realist point of view, this is a logical choice for China, for it needs to utilize its power to create institutions and normative structures that primarily favor its interests, and later facilitate its ascendance to the position of global leadership.

NOTES

1. Steve Hess and Richard Aidoo. "China's New Dictatorship Diplomacy: Is Beijing Parting with Pariahs?" *Foreign Affairs*, 87, no. 3 (2010): 25.

2. Richard Aidoo and Steve Hess, "Non-interference 2.0: China's Evolving Foreign Policy Towards a Changing Africa," *Journal of Current Chinese Affairs* 1 (2015): 107.

3. Aidoo and Hess. "Non-interference 2.0: China's Evolving Foreign Policy Towards a Changing Africa," 107.

4. Joseph Cheng and Huangao Shi. "China's African Policy in the post-Cold War Era," *Journal of Contemporary Asia* (2009): 46; Harry Verhoeven. "Is Beijing's Non-interference Policy History? How Africa Is Changing China," *The Washington Quarterly* 37, no. 2 (2014): 56.

5. Carmody Padraig and Ian Taylor, "Chinese Interests and Strategies in Africa," in *The New Scramble for Africa*, ed. Padraig Camordy (Cambridge: Polity Press, 2011), 65–67.

6. Admore Mupoki Kambudzi, "Africa and China's Non-interference Policy: Towards Peace enhancement in Afric," in *China-Africa Relations: Governance, Peace and Security,* eds. Berhe, Mulugeta and Hongwu Liu (Institute of Peace and Security Studies: Ethiopia, 2013), 43.

7. Barton Benjamin, "China's Security Policy in Africa: A New or False Dawn for the Evolution of China's Non-interference Policy," *South African Journal of International Affairs* 3 (2018): 415.

8. Zhongying Pang, "The Non-interference Dilemma: Adapting China's Approach to the New Context of African and International Realities," in *China-Africa Relations: Governance, Peace and Security*, ed. Berhe, Mulugeta and Hongwu, Liu (Institute of Peace and Security Studies: Ethiopia, 2013), 47–48. It is also instructive to recognise that China abandoned the rhetoric in the 1960s as it pursued revolution-ary interventionism abroad, in support of international communist and nationalist independence movements.

9. Joseph Cheng and Huangao Shi. "China's African Policy in the post-Cold War Era," 87; Richard Aidoo and Steve Hess. "Non-interference 2.0," 108.

10. Pang. "The Non-interference Dilemma," 48.

11. Ji Young Choi. "Historical and Theoretical Perspectives on the Rise of China: Long Cycles, Power Transitions and China's Ascent," *Asian Perspective* 42 (2018): 67–68.

12. Aidoo and Hess, "Non-interference 2.0," 111–112.

13. Yong Deng, "The New Hard Realities: Soft Power and China in Transition," in *Soft Power: China's Emerging Strategy in International Politics,* ed. Minjiang Li (UK: Lexington Books, 2009), 65.

14. Kambudzi, "Africa and China's Non-interference Policy: Towards Peace enhancement in Africa," p. 30.

15. Hess Steve and Richard Aidoo, "Beyond the Rhetoric: Non-interference in China's African Policy," *African and Asian Studies* 9 (2010): 359.

16. Tull Denis, "China's Engagement in Africa: Scope, Significance, and Consequences," *Journal of Modern African Studies* 44, no. 3 (2006): 462.

17. Martin Davies et al., "How China Delivers Development Assistance to Africa," Centre for Chinese Studies. Stellenbosch: University of Stellenbosch, 2008, 57.

18. Jianfeng Chen. "The Practice of the Mean: China's Soft Power Cultivation," in *Soft Power: China's Emerging Strategy in International Politics,* ed. Minjiang Li (UK: Lexington Books, 2009), 92.

19. Lui Guijin, "China in Africa: A Sincere, Co-operative and Equal Partner," http://www.chinese-embassy.org.za/eng/zfgx/zfhzlt/t277443.htm/.

20. Yun Sun. "The Political Significance of China's latest Commitments to Africa," *Africa in Focus*, September 12, 2018. https://www.brookings.edu/blog/africa-in-focus/2018/09/12/the-political-signifance-of-china's-latest-commitments-to-africa/amp/.

21. Deng, "The New Hard Realities," 67.

22. Verhoeven, "Is Beijing's Non-interference Policy History?," 55.

23. Kambudzi, "Africa and China's Non-interference Policy," 31–32.

24. Pang, "The Non-interference Dilemma," 48.

25. Thomas Volgy, Renato Corbeta, Keith Grant and Ryan Baird, "Major Power Status in International Politics," in *Major Powers and the Quest for Status in International Politics: Global and Regional Perspectives*, ed. Volgy Thomas, Corbeta Renato, Grant Keith and Baird Ryan (New York: Palgrave Macmillan, 2011), 3.

26. Choi, "Historical and Theoretical Perspectives on the Rise of China, 62.

27. Steven Walt, "Alliances in a Unipolar World," *World Politics* 61, no. 1 (2009): 11; John Mearsheimer, *The Tragedy of Great Power Politics* (USA: WW Norton & Company, 2001), 40; Andrew Gamble, "Hegemony and Decline: Britain and the United States," in Patrick Karl O'Brien and Armand Clesse, eds. *Two Hegemonies: Britain, 1846-1914, and the United States, 1941–2001* (Aldershot, UK: Ashgate, 2002), 130.

28. Gilpin, *War and Change in World Politics*, 29–30.

29. Mearsheimer, *The Tragedy of Great Power Politics,* 34.

30. Christopher Layne, "The Unipolar Illusion Revisited: The Coming End of the United States' Unipolar Moment," *International Security* 31, no. 2 (2006): 7–14.

31. Robert Pahre, Leading *Questions: How Hegemony Affects the International Political Economy* (USA: Michigan University Press, 2002), 4.

32. Walt, "Alliances in a Unipolar World," *World Politics,* 91.

33. Walt, "Alliances in a Unipolar World," 93.

34. Walt, "Alliances in a Unipolar World," 11–12.

35. Walt, "Alliances in a Unipolar World," 94–95.

36. Walt, "Alliances in a Unipolar World," 100.

37. Joseph Nye Jr, *The Paradox of American Power: Why the World's Only Superpower Can't Go It Alone* (New York: Oxford University Press, 2005); William Wohlforth, "American Primacy in Perspective," *Foreign Affairs* 81, no. 4 (2002): 20–33 cited in Christopher Layne. "The Unipolar Illusion Revisited," 8.

38. Walt, "Alliances in a Unipolar World," 91.

39. Walt, "Alliances in a Unipolar World," 104.

40. Robert Pape, "Soft Balancing against the United States," *International Security* 30 (2005): 10; Ruben Gonzalez-Vicente, "The limits to China's non-interference foreign policy: pro-state interventionism and the rescaling of economic governance," *Australian Journal of International Affairs* 69, no. 2: 205–208; Steven Brooks and

William Wohlforth, "Hard Times for Soft Balancing," *International Security* 30 (2005), 78.

41. Pang, "The Non-interference Dilemma," 47.

42. Mearsheimer, *The Tragedy of Great Power Politics,"* 51.

43. Chen, "The Practice of the Mean," 96.

44. Wang Yi, China's foreign minister, 2018.

45. Oriana Mastro. "The Stealth Superpower: How China Hids its Global Ambitions," *Foreign Affairs,* January/February Issue (2019). https://www.foreigna ffairs.com/articles/china/china-plan-rule-asia; Chan, Steve. *China, the US and the Power Transition Theory*, 65.

46. Deng. "The New Hard Realities," 65.

47. Ralph Sawyer. *Sun Tsu: Art of War* (Boulder, CO: Westview Press, 2005), 95 cited in Steve. *China, the US and the Power Transition Theory*, 89.

48. Chan, *China, the US and the Power Transition Theory*, 97.

49. Jeffrey Legro, "What China Will Want: The Future Intentions of a Rising Power," *Perspectives on Politics* 5, no. 3 (2007): 518; Deng, "The New Hard Realities," 72.

50. John Ikenberry, "The Rise of China and the Future of the West," *Foreign Affairs* 87, no. 1 (2008): 23–37; Yong Deng and Thomas Moore, "China Views Globalization: Towards a New Great Power Politics?" *Washington Quarterly* 27, no. 3 (2007): 113.

51. Deng, "The New Hard Realities," 75.

52. Volgy et al., "Major Power Status in International Politics," 1.

53. Christopher Layne. "The Unipolar Illusion Revisited," 28.

54. Chan, *China, the US and the Power Transition Theory*, 91.

55. Chan, *China, the US and the Power Transition Theory*, 80.

56. Cheng and Shi, "China's African Policy in the post-Cold War Era," 96.

57. Chan, *China, the US and the Power Transition Theory*, 69.

58. Pape, "Soft Balancing against the United States," 12.

59. Gilpin, *War and Chang in World Politics*, 54.

60. Gilpin, *War and Chang in World Politics*, p. 37.

61. Chen, "The Practice of the Mean," 95.

62. Volgy et al, "Major Power Status in International Politics," 28.

63. Thomas Eder. "China's New Foreign Policy Set Up: How has Xi Jinping remade China's foreign policy apparatus?" *The Diplomat*, August 2018. https://th ediplomat.com/2018/08/chinas-new-foreign-policy-setup/.

64. Kennedy Paul, "Asia's Rise: Rise and Fall." The World Today 66, no. 8/9 (2010): 6–9; Choi. "Historical and Theoretical Perspectives on the Rise of China: Long Cycles, Power Transitions and China's Ascent." *Asian Perspective* 42 (2018): 61; Deng, "The Power and Politics of Recognition," 83.

65. Chen, "The Practice of the Mean," 94.

66. Mearsheimer, *The Tragedy of Great Power Politics*, 76.

67. Robert B. Zoelick, "Whither China: From Membership to Responsibility?" Remarks to National Committee on U.S.-China Relations, September 21, 2005; Zbigniew Brzezinski, "Clash of the Titans," *Foreign Policy*, February 2005. http:// web.rollins.edu/~tlairson/easia/chinaforpol.pdf.

68. Oriana Mastro, "The Stealth Superpower."
69. Deng, "The Power and Politics of Recognition," 77–82.

BIBLIOGRAPHY

Aidoo Richard and Hess Steve. "Non-interference 2.0: China's Evolving Foreign Policy Towards a Changing Africa." *Journal of Current Chinese Affairs* 1 (2015): 107–139.

Benjamin Barton. "China's Security Policy in Africa: A New or False Dawn for the Evolution of China's Non-interference Policy." *South African Journal of International Affairs* 3 (2018): 413–434.

Brooks Steven and Wohlforth Willliam. "Hard Times for Soft Balancing." *International Security* 30 (2005): 72–108.

Brzezinski Zbigniew. "Clash of the Titans." *Foreign Policy*, January 10, 2005.

Chan, Steve. *China, the US and the Power Transition Theory: A Critique.* London and New York: Routledge, 2005.

Chen, Jianfeng. "The Practice of the Mean: China's Soft Power Cultivation". In *Soft Power: China's Emerging Strategy in International Politics,* edited by Minjiang Li, 83–101. UK: Lexington Books, 2009.

Cheng, Joseph and Shi Huangao. "China's African Policy in the post-Cold War Era." *Journal of Contemporary Asia* 31, no. 1 (2009): 87–115.

Choi, Young. "Historical and Theoretical Perspectives on the Rise of China: Long Cycles, Power Transitions and China's Ascent." *Asian Perspective* 42 (2018): 61–84.

Davies Martin, Edinger Hannar, Tay Nastasya and Sunasha Naidu. "How China Delivers Development Assistance to Africa." *Centre for Chinese Studies.* Stellenbosch: University of Stellenbosch, 2008.

Deng, Yong. "The Power and Politics of Recognition: Status in China's Foreign relations." In *Major Powers and the Quest for Status in International Politics: Global and Regional Perspectives*, edited by Volgy Thomas, Corbeta Renato, Grant Keith and Baird Ryan, 77–96. New York: Palgrave Macmillan, 2011.

Deng, Yong and Moore Thomas. "China Views Globalization: Towards a New Great Power Politics?" *Washington Quarterly* 27, no. 3 (2007): 117–36.

Denis, Tull. "China's Engagement in Africa: Scope, Significance, and Consequences." *Journal of Modern African Studies* 44, no. 3 (2006): 459–479.

Eder, Thomas. "China's New Foreign Policy Set Up: How has Xi Jinping remade China's foreign policy apparatus?" *The Diplomat,* November 20, 2018.

Gamble, Andrew, "Hegemony and Decline: Britain and the United States." In *Two Hegemonies: Britain, 1846-1914, and the United States, 1941—2001*, edited by Patrick Karl O'Brien and Armand Clesse, 63–95. Aldershot, UK: Ashgate, 2002.

Gilpin, Robert. *War and Change in World Politics.* Cambridge: Cambridge University Press, 1981.

Gonzalez-Vicente, Ruben. "The Limits to China's Non-interference Foreign Policy: Pro-state Interventionism and the Rescaling of Economic Governance." *Australian Journal of International Affairs* 69, no. 2 (2015): 205–223.

Gu, Jing, Humprey John and Messner Dirk. "Global Governance and Developing Countries: The Implications for the Rise of China." *World Development* 36, no. 2 (2008): 274–292.

John, Ikenberry. "The Rise of China and the Future of the West." *Foreign Affairs* 87, no. 1 (2008): 23–37.

Guijin, Lui. "China in Africa: A Sincere, Co-operative and Equal Partner." December 2, 2018.

Hess, Steve and Aidoo Richard. 2010. "China's New Dictatorship Diplomacy: Is Beijing Parting with Pariahs?" *Foreign Affairs* 87, no. 3 (2010): 23–37.

Hess, Steve, and Richard Aidoo, "Beyond the Rhetoric: Non-interference in China's African Policy." *African and Asian Studies* 9 (2010): 356–383.

Kambudzi, Admore Mupoki. "Africa and China's Non-interference Policy: Towards Peace enhancement in Africa." In *China-Africa Relations: Governance, Peace and Security,* edited by Berhe, Mulugeta and Hongwu, Liu, 29–45. Institute of Peace and Security Studies: Ethiopia, 2013.

Layne, Christopher. "The Unipolar Illusion Revisited: The Coming End of the United States' Unipolar Moment." *International Security* 31, no. 2 (2006): 7–41.

Legro, Jeffrey. "What China Will Want: The Future Intentions of a Rising Power." *Perspectives on Politics* 5, no. 3 (2007): 515–534.

Mastro, Oriana. "The Stealth Superpower: How China Hid its Global Ambitions." *Foreign Affairs,* February 2, 2019.

Nye, Joseph Nye Jr, *The Paradox of American Power: Why the World's Only Superpower Can't Go It Alone.* New York: Oxford University Press, 2005.

Padraig, Carmody and Ian Taylor. "Chinese Interests and Strategies in Africa." In *The New Scramble for Africa,* edited by Padraig Carmody, 65–94. Cambridge: Polity Press, 2011.

Pahre, Robert. *Leading Questions: How Hegemony Affects the International Political Economy.* USA: Michigan University Press, 2002.

Pang, Zhongying. "The Non-interference Dilemma: Adapting China's Approach to the New Context of African and International Realities." In *China-Africa Relations: Governance, Peace and Security,* edited by Berhe, Mulugeta and Hongwu, Liu, 46–54. Institute of Peace and Security Studies: Ethiopia, 2013.

Pape, Robert. "Soft Balancing against the United States." *International Security* 30 (2005): 745.

Kennedy Paul, "Asia's Rise: Rise and Fall." *The World Today* 66, no. 8/9 (2010): 6–9

Ronald Tammen, Jacek Kugler, Lemke Douglas, Stam III Allan, Abdollahian Mark, Alsharabati Carole, Efird Brian, and Organski Abramo Fimo Kenneth. *Power Transitions.* New York: Seven Bridges Press, 2000.

Stephanie, Kleine-Ahlbrandt, and Small Andrew. "China's New Dictatorship Diplomacy: Is Beijing Parting with Pariahs?" *Foreign Affairs* 87, no. 3 (2008): 23–37.

Sun, Yun. "The Political Significance of China's latest Commitments to Africa." *Africa in Focus,* September 12, 2018.

Verhoeven, Harry. "Is Beijing's Non-interference Policy History? How Africa Is Changing China." *The Washington Quarterly* 37, no. 2 (2014): 55–70.

Volgy, Thomas, Corbeta Renato, Grant Keith and Baird Ryan. "Major Power Status in International Politics." In *Major Powers and the Quest for Status in International Politics: Global and Regional Perspectives*, edited by Volgy Thomas, Corbeta Renato, Grant Keith and Baird Ryan, 1–26. New York: Palgrave Macmillan, 2011.

Walt, Steven. "Alliances in a Unipolar World." *World Politics* 61, no. 1 (2016): 86–120.

Xuetong, Yan. "The Age of Unease Peace: Chinese Power in a Divided World." *Foreign Affairs,* January 21, 2019.

Zoellick, Robert. "Whither China: From Membership to Responsibility?" *Remarks to National Committee on U.S.-China Relations*, September 21, 2005.

Chapter 5

The Belt and Road Initiative in Africa

But What Kind of Developmental Power Does China Have?

Kudakwashe Chirambwi

INTRODUCTION

Although China's developmental power has been widely and systematically researched in different parts of the world, what continues to escape scholarly attention is the mutually reinforcing blend of commerce, diplomacy, and military intervention as economic tools central to the Asian giant's phenomenal growth. The triad has all along been studied either as pairs or standalone disciplines of power, ignoring how these are deployed almost contemporaneously as China pursues self-interest and security of assets. With the use of structuralist political economy analysis framework, the chapter examines how the intrinsically linked amalgam dimensions of power have assertively positioned China as a global economic contender. What emerges is that, through the belt and road initiative (BRI) and building a community of shared values, China manipulates other countries to make them believe that common development through trade and infrastructure networks is in their interests when it is not. All combined, the faces of power produce a Foucauldian notion of governmentality characterized by domination and control.

The new economic distress faced by Africa, United States, and Brexit in the European Union (EU) has provided sufficient legroom for China to percolate even down to the village structures of African communities, under the guise of BRI "shared future for mankind and building a better world." As part of the keynote address at the ceremony of The Communist Party of China in Dialogue with World Political Party High-level Meeting in December 2017, President Xi Jinping told delegates that he was excited to "see that the friendly cooperation between China and other countries is increasingly expanding and the concept of a community with a shared future for mankind is gaining support and endorsement from an increasing number of people to build a community with a shared future for mankind and building a better world." Such connectivity and cooperation popularized as BRI have become the organizing principle of China's engagement with Africa.

The arguments will be framed around the warp and weft faces of power—commerce, diplomacy, and hard power, which often swing from being hidden to visible as dictated by the context. The invisible soft power of diplomacy is expressed through befriending pariah-state that are looking for economic options, particularly African states that are shunned for monolithic leadership, corruption, and neopatrimonialism, while visible is conveyed through deploying combat troops in peacekeeping missions in Mali, South Sudan, and Democratic Republic of Congo (DRC). I argue that all the faces of power combine to produce a largely economically and politically distressed Africa and are playing directly into people's mistrust.

CONCEPTUALIZING THE BRI

The BRI is often communicated as a "national vision and foreign strategy, sometimes resembling conceptual propaganda," but it is also mentioned concerning concrete investments and projects. Thus, territorial and functional terms combine to define BRI as "one belt, one road," reflecting the expansion, internationalization, and connectivity of China's economic activities with the rest of the world.[1] China is arguably one of the largest economies globally with an impressive blend of commerce, diplomacy, and hard power as tools to advance economic growth. It has made good use of these through the BRI to penetrate the African market. The metaphor "Belt" refers to mostly land routes (roads, railways, airports, financial structures, and power plants), while "Road" alludes to sea routes (ports and information technology).[2] Both metaphors function as a grandiose scheme to create China-centric socialist economic order and a key pillar of "going global" strategy of promoting its international but amorphous discourse—the "shared future of mankind."[3] The term "Road," was coined in 1877 by a German geographer, Ferdinand von Richthofen to describe "a skein of ancient trading routes which blended commerce, diplomacy, and hard power."[4]

The BRI's globalization of economic expansion is couched in a diplomatic grammar of "many-to-many" and "sunshine initiative" open for all to benefit from[5] or as a "public good.'"[6] The initiative covers a vast area of the geopolitical marketplace. It also connects to fifty-five African countries, which accommodate 17.1 percent of the world's population.[7] This translates to 20 percent of the global economy and close to US$2 trillion infrastructure investment. The BRI commerce is further conceptualized in diplomatic terms as a "gift" of Chinese wisdom to the world's development challenges, as the "project of the century" or the "path of Xi Jinping" or "road of peace." By "road of peace" or peaceful development, China refers to a novel practice of building African institutions without evoking violence, which is in contradistinction to Europeans who aggressively deployed "violence of development" during the scramble for Africa. As such, unlike China, the rise of new powers resulted in drastic violent wars in the name of development.

The uniquely state-centric BRI strategy was established as a joint effort of the National Development and Reform Commission, Ministry of Commerce and Ministry of Foreign Affairs. At the institutional level, the composition mirrors an amalgam of commerce, diplomacy, and hard power which radiate across China's investments in Africa, in what Ramo[8] "the new physics of Chinese Power." The BRI comprises two physical routes, with numerous side-branches and different routes along the way, which ultimately connect China with Europe, Africa, and Southeast Asia.[9] The land route runs from inner China to Southern Europe, while the sea route connects the port of Shanghai via India and Africa. For instance, the sea is increasingly becoming the largest economic ecosystem, where China's blue economy or maritime trade is exponentially growing by an average of 7.5 percent annually and accounts for nearly 10 percent of its GDP. The road "fills connectivity gap in large economically heterogeneous parts of Asia and Africa and has no peers that approximate its scale and speed."[10] While sea transportation is envisaged to reduce the transit time between China and Africa, the land route is expected to be an alternative to more expensive airfreight.

Notwithstanding the overwhelming economic plan, scholars have drawn the comparison between BRI as the "Chinese Marshall Plan" and the post–World War II United States' Marshall Plan of which the latter was deployed to entrench hegemonic control over Europe.[11] However, the comparison has some fault-lines. Unlike the United States' Marshal Plan which excluded other countries, the BRI places emphasis on inclusiveness, win-win, and mutual benefit.

Thus, BRI will run according to market rules and respect international rules. Although this territorial expansion or new world political geography is argued to be achieved through transparency and openness, contrary to this aspiration, evidence from African states shows that Chinese deals are considered not fair and square due to lack of legislation that criminalizes bribes paid overseas in exchange for contracts.[12] China does not have a Foreign Corrupt Practices Act like the United States, for instance, although there is widespread recognition by Chinese companies for the need to meet international best practices on social and environmental safeguards in mining, rubber, and forestry. Subsequent sections will further examine material power, particularly, how it is embedded in China's socialist market economy. The conversation which is not occurring among scholars is how BRI deploys hidden power as a strategic tool to charm Africans.

CHINA'S STRATEGIES IN AFRICA: COMMERCE AND DIPLOMACY

To understand why Africa is wildly enthusiastic about BRI as it feels connected to China's powers—money, infrastructure, expertise, and diplomacy,[13] it is imperative to explore the Chinese complex hidden or soft power schemes central to spreading wealth and prosperity across the globe.[14] China's commercial power emanates from material capability and financial agility. In BRI,

> The Chinese government sees a way to offset part of the existing domestic overcapacity by exporting its well-developed engineering and construction capabilities, materials and equipment and self-developed technology. Apart from China's experience in building world-class infrastructure, it will mostly export excess capacity with low opportunity cost and therefore there isn't necessarily a need to gain quick returns.[15]

It has the capital to spare and export surplus capacity. China is now the single largest bilateral financier of infrastructure in Africa, surpassing the African Development Bank (ADB), the European Commission, the European Investment Bank, the International Finance Corporation, the World Bank, and the Group of Eight (G8) countries combined. This is accounted for by the fact that even China's private companies do not heavily rely on capital from the state but have own adequate cash reserves.

China's soft power is further consolidated and strengthened by the weakening grip of European and U.S. economic and political institutions on Africa. The West's global domination in phenomenally sliding to low ebbs, including the Trump administration which has shown a growing unwillingness to defend the liberal order, creating space for China to implant its socialist market economy in its place. A socialist market economy is increasingly superseding the capitalistic approach based on a neoliberal development model that assumes that welfare is maximized by economic growth through economic liberalization, free market, diversification, and modernization of structures of African economies.[16] Prolific writers such as Henry Kissinger declared "Capitalism has won!," and Francis Fukuyama claimed it was "End of history," as they conceptualized capitalist development to be the only valid basis for modern human society and development. Over the years, neoliberalism and its flagship, Economic Structural Adjustment Programme (ESAP), repudiated the role of African governments in economic growth and development, guided by the organizing principle that states have an irrelevant role in wealth creation. African governments, rather than being agents of development, have been viewed as obstacles because they are corrupt, inefficient, and parasitic, therefore, they should be restricted mainly to creating a conducive environment for foreign and private investment China opportunistically has taken advantage of limitations of capitalism.

The BRI, underpinned by the socialist market economy approach, is emerging as an alternative development paradigm for Global South, which has rolled "the state back in" as a strong economic agent. This development paradigm is prostate. It assumes that state intervention in economic affairs is necessary and that the state's direct control of market outcomes is helpful for economic growth and wealth creation. BRI has, therefore, advocated the "rolling back" of the state as central to market-friendly economies as guided by the dictates of inclusive socialist market economies. Thus, BRI is increasingly challenging the original goals of development and methods of development. However, the philosophy of BRI and neoliberalism is the same, therefore, fundamentally flawed. It appears, at the normative level, there are no contesting paradigms in development in Africa between China and Europe.[17] The promarket development paradigm of neoliberalism singly dominated African economics and investments. Both have the same impact on Africa as retain externally oriented economic investments focusing on expanded exports and increased foreign direct investment (FDI).

Through BRI, China simply endeavors to dislodge the EU's long-standing political and economic hegemony. It is suspected that capitalism is not working as it should; hence, African leaders see in China an alternative. Scholars increasingly see a trade war between China and Europe over Africa and BRI as a political tool deployed to beat back Western influence. While this may be a positive trend, it also precipitates greater militarization of economic institutions in Africa. Comrade Xi Jinping told delegates at the opening ceremony of The Communist Party of China in Dialogue with World Political Party High-level Meeting (December 2, 2017) that he was excited to

> See that the friendly cooperation between China and other countries is increasingly expanding and the concept of a community with a shared future for mankind is gaining support and endorsement from an increasing number of people community with a shared future for mankind and building a better world.

Such connectivity and cooperation popularized as BRI have become the organizing principle to China's engagement with Africa. Sensing BRI's threat to the balance of power, the EU has made moves to frustrate Chinese efforts. EU is currently under pressure to rebuild partnerships in Africa, with the UK and France heads of government making far more visits to Africa from 2010 to date. Britain is opening embassies in Niger, Burkina Faso, Mali, and Morocco. To countervail China's efforts, the President of the European Commission, Jean-Claude Juncker, in his State of the Union Address on September 12, 2018, on EU-Africa Alliance, remarked,

> Africa does not need charity; it needs true and fair partnership. And we, Europeans need this partnership just as much. Today, we are proposing a new Alliance for Sustainable Investment and Jobs between Europe and Africa. This Alliance, as we envision it, would help create up to 10 million jobs in Africa in the next 5 years alone. I believe we should develop the numerous EU-African trade agreements into a continent-to-continent free trade agreement, as an economic partnership between equals.

The competition sets Africa as a stage of global economic wars. Both China and EU relations to Africa are characterized by connections that bring disruptions. But pariah states in Africa prefer China to avoid political and economic conditions needed to attract foreign direct investment from Europe. China's hidden economic power overbears and radiates across Africa because trade between African countries is fragmented, making economies of scale hard to achieve despite the continent being the fastest-growing economy and with the fastest-growing middle class which enables large spending of luxury goods. What does China see in Africa? As argued by Taylor,[18] China sees new markets and investment opportunities in Africa and its strategic blend of commerce, diplomacy, and military power endears to secure resource security from the cheapest continent.

The continent has the potential for 1.4 billion consumers, emerging middle class, and reduced civil and interstate wars.[19] Africa has space for symbolic diplomacy (a space in which global powers are demonstrated), development cooperation, and potential frontier of globalization. China is fully aware that Africans, who constitute 25 percent of the UN membership, are increasingly becoming assertive in UN matters, hence, the need for forging strategic partnerships. Evidentially, embedded in the BRI are several bilateral and multilateral forums that capture and control Africa, including the Tri-annual Forum for China Africa Cooperation, South-South Co-operation, Forum on China-Africa Cooperation (FOCAC), and FDIs. For instance, the pledged sum of US$60bn at the 2018 FOCAC summit will be structured differently to reflect China's shifting priorities. The total amount will be spread over three years as grants, interest-free loans and concessional loans (US$15bn), credit lines (US$20bn), a special fund to deepen China-Africa relations (US$10bn), and projected direct investment by Chinese firms (US$10m). The final US$5bn constitutes a second special fund, geared to boosting China's imports from Africa.

COMMERCIAL POWER AND AID EFFECTIVENESS

China's commercial power, therefore, provides an alternative source of foreign capital through foreign aid.[20] In 2016, the United Kingdom, France, and the United States have been top three in FDI. In 2017, China was nearly top in FDI, especially in the manufacturing industry and energy. The World Investment Report from the UN Conference on Trade and Development (UNCTAD) indicates that China's FDI stock in Africa climbed to US$40bn in 2016, from US$16bn in 2011, placing it in the fourth position behind the United States (US$57bn), the United Kingdom (U$55bn), and France (US$49bn). In Africa, China is emerging as the largest foreign aid in areas such as budget support and project-based lending as evidenced by the establishment of the FOCAC.[21] China is even urging economically weak countries such as Zimbabwe to exploit billions offered by BRI. The acting ambassador to Zimbabwe, Zhao Baogang, claimed that "Beijing's multibillion-dollar opportunities for Zimbabwe under the Belt and Road Initiative and the Forum for China-Africa Co-operation [FOCAC], were not being taken up by Harare."[22]

More generally, scholarly debates on aid effectiveness are less conclusive on the relationship between heavy foreign capital injection and economic growth in Africa. To date, aid effectiveness has passed through three generations, leaving in their wake deleterious economic downturn in most African states. The first of 1960 and early 1970s primarily focused on savings and investment gap (Rostow), guided by the assumption that poor African countries could not get to the level of savings required for investment that would then spur economic growth (Easterly). The second generation, which shared economic nuances with the first, focused on the linkage between aid and growth. The assumption was that aid drives investment, which then results in economic growth. The third and most recent wave is the "North-South" cooperation and "South-South" cooperation which assumes that development assistance can only be effective when there are equality and solidarity between the donor and recipient countries. The focus is on equality and fairness in trade and investments. However, the promise of equality is misleading because of power differentials.[23] China's presence in the "South-South" and FOCAC rhetoric disguises power differentials between and within African countries which make it more difficult to identify exactly which states are benefiting the most, or least.[24]

FOCAC is a matching economic structure to the African Continental Free Trade Area (AFCTA). However, the latter has not galvanized sufficient traction among fifty-five member states. There is no one African market, which is a waste of opportunities for economic integration and ring-fencing against exploitation and predation by China. For example, for the pact to be in force, twenty-two signatory states must first ratify. However, Africa's economic powerhouses, Nigeria and South Africa have not acceded due to heightened fear of flooding their markets with cheap goods which might lead to job losses. As such, this lack of political will, inadvertently, throws asunder the African philosophy of free-trade area which is currently the world's largest by country coverage and with eleven (11) of the world's top twenty fastest-growing economies.[25]. China, riding on its material power, takes advantage of such economic heterogeneity and carves opportunities in Africa's collective GDP which stands at $1.6 trillion and $2.6 trillion by 2020. Africa's combined consumer spending is envisaged to hit 4 trillion by 2025. By 2020, Africa's consumer spending is expected to be $1.4 trillion, supported by a steadily growing population heading toward 2 billion.

Given that China is looking for the cheaper continent for investment with fewer consequences, the above statistics provide sufficient legroom for commercial power to dominate. In subsequent sections, I will attempt to provide an answer to some pesky questions to why China is risking investing in weak/failed states, stateless, moribund economies, terrorist threats, ethnic militias, a mixture of rebels and soldiers, military coups, criminality, and violence against leaders who stay longer in power.[26] In this Afro-pessimism, China sees an opportunity, upholding the belief that problems can be resolved through force or military intervention.

Some argue to the contrary, suggesting that, instead, it is Africa engaging in "global scramble for China" because of the latter's material power. Africa is seen participating in a fierce battle to access China's[27] development funding. For instance, most African states turn to China for help. Zambia is a widely cited example of how former President Kenneth Kaunda turned to China to build the railways to export the copper, a practice that continues today.[28] The political economy analysis of China's material power reveals how BRI rhetoric is divisive among ruling elites. For instance, Michael Sata, the fifth President of Zambia, sees Chinese aid and investments as Trojan horses endeared to exploit and predate local resources without any significant contribution to the development of African economies, while John Magufuli, the fifth President of Tanzania argues that "a lot of people get nervous about China but I am not. I think China is Africa's friend."[29]

Another extreme example of friendship is that of the Ugandan President, Yoweri Museveni who has ordered the military to protect Chinese companies from theft. He has gone further to establish a new civilian militia known as Local Defence Units to protect Chinese businesses from local criminals. It is also not clear why China, despite the long-standing relationship with

Zimbabwe, for example, has not helped to clear part of its total debt of about $16,9bn ($680 million with ADB, $1,3 billion with the World Bank, and $308 million with European Investment Bank). It could be that China has been selling "hot-air" to fragile states such as Zimbabwe as most of the "mega-deals" collapse before taking off. While Magufuli is of the view that Chinese investment is effective because of the strong institutions and policies he has put in place, to Sata, Chinese investment is growth-depressing. It has neither increased investment nor has it benefited poor Zambians. Like Trojan horses, investments have exacerbated rent-seeking, corruption, civil strife, and lack of accountability. Sata fears that Chinese investments are increasing dependency which lowers domestic production and its attendant problems of undermining the quality of local institutions. Local institutions are weakened in the sense that Chinese investments have squeezed off policy space to formulate innovative strategies for trade through a bottom-up integrated approach.

In response to the discord among African leaders, China has applied a "five-no approach" diplomacy in its engagement with them: no interference in the politics and development paths of individual countries; no interference in their internal affairs; no imposition of China's will; no attachment of political strings regarding assistance; and no seeking of selfish political gains in investment and financing cooperation.[30] More importantly, China takes better account of individual states' demands and their need for growth, identifying itself as an all-time weather friend. However, critical questions have been raised on the nature of its strategic partnership with individual states under debt peonage.

Africa must look to China for development and fulfill Chinese criteria to be qualified as "developed." Heavy reliance on China inadvertently undermines traditional and indigenous approaches to development. The difference could be that while the North Bretton Woods dictate policies and political conditionalities to the economic reform policies prescribed by the Structural Adjustment Programs (SAPs), China has the power to promote economic dependence on already indebted African economies.[31] For instance, Chinese loans come with a set of conditions, which include access to natural resources, high-interest payments, use of Chinese labor, and technology.[32] Some scholars argue that neo-BRI have caused economic crisis and massive foreign debt burden and debt service obligations. Africa's total debt burden caused by BRI billion stands at $136bn. Despite losing close to three million of its timber forests, Mozambique is under $2bn Chinese debt peonage. By 2017, China was owed more than $700m in arrears on debt repayments.

The economically distressed Mozambique has never wanted the IMF to know it is under the Chinese debt burden for fear of credit lines to be closed. Angola, despite supplying oil to China in exchange for infrastructural development, still owes $19bn to China. In 2017, the International Monetary Fund has warned that at least 40 percent of African countries are either in debt distress or at high risk, including Chad, Eritrea, Mozambique, Congo Republic, South Sudan, and Zimbabwe. Surprisingly, Zambia and Ethiopia were downgraded to "high risk of debt distress." A smaller degree of risk is attached to Cameroon, Ethiopia, Ghana, Mozambique, Sudan, and Zimbabwe. Moreover, Chinese lending to Africa surged from $30bn to $60bn in 2018, thereby lifting total disbursements to about $90bn since in a space of two years. Despite the debt forgiveness on offer (diplomacy), the inconclusive debate is still on whether China's loans to African countries are designed to give China a strategic hold over them, metaphorically as a "dragon's gift."[33]

The immediate implications are that a huge debt burden means the continent's total export proceeds are devoted to servicing external debts as well as increasing dependence on China's IFIs. The imposition of BRI could be viewed as a deliberate attempt by China to control and marginalize the already at-risk poor African states. BRI, just like ESAP, is likely to compromise economic growth and leave in its wake huge social costs. For instance, most Zambians, Angolans, and Kenyans are already disgruntled on how China has disrupted social services and public sector employment. Chinese aid has contributed to political instability due to large-scale unemployment, increasing poverty, inequality, and deindustrialization. BRI policies have also eroded political, economic, and fiscal sovereignty of Africa yet consolidating China's power, a growing euphemism for "neocolonialism."[34]

Southern Africa, which has risks from military coups, with Zimbabwe and Lesotho and DRC leading the pack, still have China as the all-weather friend, dating back to 1950s for the support rendered to African independence movements and several revolutionary groups—such as the Zimbabwe African National Union (ZANU) and the Mozambique Liberation Front (FRELIMO).[35] Of the top five recipients of Chinese foreign direct investments, four are in Southern Africa, namely Zambia, Zimbabwe, South Africa, and DRC, and only one in West Africa, Nigeria. In Lesotho, for example, the "Chinese are in almost every village—the cornfields of the western lowlands right up to the snow-dusted peaks of the mountainous east. But many quietly acknowledge the entrepreneurial spirit and resourcefulness." China has a strong grip on Africa.

RESILIENCE AND POWER TO NEGOTIATE

Questions have been raised on whether African governments have the power to negotiate, resist, or be resilient against BRI's damaging blend of commerce and diplomacy. Evidence continues to show the asymmetry of power in the negotiations of the transactions between China and Africa, with China having more leverage, couched in justificatory rhetoric of cooperation, coordination, and interaction yielding to "mutual benefit" and "the development of a community with a shared future for mankind," resulting in "win-win arrangements."[36] China is fully aware that Africa is a young continent with no capacity to negotiate on win-win deals. The language of inclusivity, equality, and a "win-win" necessarily preserve China's position and interests and development with Chinese characteristics.[37] In international relations and diplomacy, such promulgations could be considered as perfidious or diplomatic sleights in pursuit of self-interest. As phantom public relations diplomatic tactic, African states are seen giving away security powers and economic rights in exchange for superhighway, bridges, and railway lines. Africa suffers a financial loss of over US$200bn each year due to incompetence and lack of expertise to negotiate contracts beneficial to the state. China's domineering power lies also in its ability to tailor and customize investment projects that align with the regimes' electoral messages. For instance, the Chinese-funded $3.8bn Kenya's Standard Gauge Railway (SGR) and Djibouti–Ethiopia railway were in line with the electoral calendar of each respective country.[38]

HUMAN RIGHTS IN BRI PROJECTS

What continues to dodge scholarly attention is how China has adopted a robust engagement policy anchored on economic diplomacy, through the inclusion of social and economic rights in BRI projects. The Asian giant is assertive including human rights and higher standards on labor and protection of the environment to establish a "gold standard" in BRI projects, given that it is now the second-biggest investor in the world. In line with the international standards, and increasingly so, China is now including both economic and social human rights issues in trade agreements to win the hearts and minds of the local communities. Instancing this is the discourse of human rights, which is very conspicuously evident in China's National Human Rights Action Plan (NHRAP) which is intrinsically aligned to the Chinese Economic and Social Development Plan. Comprehensive human rights training courses are being rolled out to Chinese outbound companies. To reinforce, Chatham House observed that

> Business and human rights in relation to the BRI is a hot topic in China at the moment, with a marked increase in education on the issue. It was noted that in the past three years, the Chinese government has increasingly discussed international development issues using the language of the UN Sustainable Development Goals (SDGs) rather than "international human rights."[39]

China is increasingly engaging with international human rights issues even at the UN level, especially agitating for the strengthening of treaty bodies. On March 23, 2018, the UN Human Rights Council eventually adopted a resolution called by China to bind intergovernmental organizations to engage in "mutually beneficial cooperation" to "build a community of shared future for human beings" that respects human rights. Resolution A/HRC/37/L.36, 37th session of the UNHRC. This is a massive shift from long-held criticism of a poster child ignoring human rights to become an assertive social and economic right underpinning BRI projects. These baby steps in the BRI project are helping China to reinvent and recalibrate into a superpower without blemishes. How does China manage risks and sustain the blend of commerce and diplomacy given the several complex political dynamics in Africa? The next section examines the role of hard power or military intervention plays to wade off risks.

RISK MANAGEMENT STRATEGIES

What has evaded scholarly scrutiny is how China deploys hard power as it takes substantial risks by investing in fragile states which could, inadvertently, affect its economy. All rising powers more often seek to mitigate risks to their supply chains and China is no exception. There are a lot of pesky questions around BRI's capacities to manage insecurities characterized by political dynamics, such as monolithic dictators, terror attacks, and breakdown of governance structures in African states.

Due to expanded investment in fragile regions of Africa, the Chinese military is compelled to protect overseas interests, citizens, and assets. However, this is not peculiar to Africa. China has militarily manned the China-Pakistan Economic corridor to hedge-off India. Scholarly opinion is divided on the spin-off benefits from China's risk management strategies. While poststructuralist writers such as Dellios and Ferguson[40] argue that hard power will help to stabilize states and regions, the political economists strongly feel BRI is a red herring in China's foreign policy that undermines African economies and the liberal order.[41] The purists take a middle ground, arguing that China is not only about cold, hard commerce—it also wants to make friends.[42]

The Politics of Development and Security Nexus

Earlier I have argued that China has a unique risk management strategy central to BRI's economic development through its ability to blend commerce, diplomacy, and hard power. The critical sectors in which BRI investments are established, namely manufacturing and information communications and technology are high-risk areas. One of the long-held perceptions, and increasingly so, is the view that Africa is conflicted largely because of state fragility and ungoverned spaces that increase risks of defaulting on loans, damage to infrastructure, and loss of life. Also, throughout the implementation of BRI projects, there has been a risk of resentment and hostility from disgruntled local communities. An assemblage of terminologies have been coined to express the urgency of fragility in Africa: "anarchic zones," "dangerous chaos," "ungoverned areas," "lawless zones," "predatory state," "garrison state," "no man's lands," "intermittent," "failed states," "weak states," and "collapsed states."[43] All of the fifty-four African states fall in one or several of these descriptively dominant categories.

China has responded discretely to each of the regional risks through commerce, diplomacy, and hard power that allow opening and maintaining trade routes. In response to political instability, China continues to deploy hard power through peacekeeping and peacemaking missions. BRI, in this context, as alluded by Wang[44] is deployed as a conflict management mechanism.

China is fully aware of risks emerging from the impact of the Arab Spring on radical political Islam particularly in oil and gas-rich Tunisia, Libya, and Mali. Jihadist groups emerged after the fall of long-standing Tunisia's leader Ben Ali and Libya's Muammar Qaddafi which resulted even in the creation of armed African Muslim AQIM (Al-Qaeda in the Islamic Maghreb) in northern Mali. China's involvement in Africa security phenomenally grew from 1998 to date, especially exemplified by military attachés and visits. In 1998, there were only nine African Défense Attaches in Beijing. In 2007, the number increased to eighteen, which then jumped to twenty-eight in 2010. Conversely, Chinese Defense Attaches in Africa grew from nine to fourteen between 1985 and 2006. The number increased to sixteen in 2007, with surprisingly few high-level military visits. Six delegations visited nine countries—Egypt, Tanzania, South Africa, Kenya, Ethiopia, Sudan, Algeria, and Zambia.

Before the BRI, China used to send only noncombat troops such as police, logistics, construction, and medical contingents on peacekeeping missions. China now considers peacekeeping as a core activity of the UN.[45] In 2011, China had 1,550 troops, 40 police, and 42 military experts in Africa—to six UN peacekeeping operations, far more than any other permanent member of the Security Council. The largest was Liberia (564 troops, 18 police, and 2 military experts) followed by Southern Sudan (444 troops, 22 police, and 12 military experts). With the advent of BRI and the need to secure increasingly investments, China has contributed 403 combat troops in the UN's Multidimensional Integrated Stabilization Mission in Mali (MINUSMA), 518 in UN Mission in South Sudan (UNMISS) in South Sudan, 374 in United Nations–African Union Mission in Darfur (UNAMID) in Sudan

(Darfur), 232 in The United Nations Organization Stabilization Mission in the Democratic Republic of the Congo (MONUSCO) in the DRC, and 12 in United Nations Mission for the Referendum in Western Sahara(MINURSO) in Western Sahara.

At the UN General Assembly in New York in September 2015, the Chinese President Xi Jinping pledged to create a rapid-deployment standby force and a standing peacekeeping police force of eight thousand troops as well as financial assistance of $100m for the creation of an African Union standby force to effectively respond to continental conflicts. Such vigorous pledges herald China's potential to control, UN's peacekeeping organizationally and financially. Thus, through such missions, China is not only expanding its diplomatic influence and hard power in Africa but contemporaneously aims to train its soldiers and police to acquire experience to work in extremely hostile and dangerous conflict contexts. For instance, in 2017 and as part of a UN Formed Police Unit, the Chinese police have been awarded a UN Medal for their protecting civilians, patrol beats, and information management to the UN and the people of South Sudan.

In more recent times, China has managed risks and secured lines of business from ethnoreligious conflict, civil war, and piracy from bandits and "terrorists," through land and maritime security. China has opened its first military base to secure economic interests in Djibouti, Somalia, Rwanda, Burundi, Eritrea, Ethiopia, Kenya, and Uganda. The People's Liberation Army (PLA) is involved in geopolitics by building a string of military bases at seaports in Africa. It is argued that China has been stampeding to control foreign seaports along strategic transit channels to secure its enterprises.[46] In Djibouti, a military logistical base with the potential capacity to accommodate ten thousand troops has been established. To date, a contingent of two thousand personnel is already stationed there.

More recently, plans are underway to supply approximately 8,000 police for peacekeeping and anti-piracy mission at the UN. To protect its wider strategic interests, Chinese warships are increasingly being used to secure the East African coastline from Somali pirates. China is fully aware of the great need to integrate security and development, as they rise and fall together. Without hard power, there is no development and without development, there is no security to its assets and people. China drew lessons from history that a global power must possess strong maritime power as "weak maritime power leads to a declining nation; strong maritime power leads to a strong nation."[47]

Today, by contrast, China contributes more personnel to UN peacekeeping missions than any other permanent member of the UN Security Council, and China is now the second-largest contributor to the UN Department of Peacekeeping Operations budget (behind the United States, but ahead of Japan). China does not necessarily see this as a violation of her noninterference stance, but as a Responsibility to Protect (R2P) especially when states fail to safeguard civilian populations from acts of war crimes, terrorism, and other human rights abuses. Although her argument is without merit, the use of force and combat troops is part of China's use of hard power to test new weapons, troop readiness, collaborate with peacekeepers from African and European countries to gain knowledge of rough terrains. In early 2010, China's white paper on national Défense stated that it "will never seek hegemony, nor will it adopt the approach of military expansion now or in the future, no matter how its economy develops."

As part of risk management, China is developing a growing footprint in the peacemaking processes. As part of the peace process between warring South Sudan and Sudan, China built the much-needed pipeline that takes oil from South Sudan to Sudan. In South Sudan, which is one of the biggest oil trading partners of China, the latter has deployed, for the first time, hundreds of troops known as a CHN-BATT (Chinese Battalion) to bolster the UN peace mission. Thus, China has not changed its commercial oil deals with South Sudan because of risks but has chosen a corresponding action to avert risks. However, China has been criticized for playing a "double game" by supplying rifles, rockets, and ammunition and anti-tank missiles to South Sudan. Other illustrative examples come from Ethiopia and Djibouti. The Chinese commerce and hard power are witnessed in the assemblage of the first Africa-made smartphone in Ethiopia and the establishment of the largest Chinese-built free trade zone as part of special economic zones in Djibouti. China has won the hearts and minds of the two countries, resulting in the protection and upscale investment interests. China bolsters and boosts its diplomatic image by increasing contacts with local populations through even providing medical support to victims, building schools, sending engineers, transport battalions, and military camps (although galling allegations criticized shifting to arms sale and contracts for military construction and training). Such widened security roles have been applauded during the September 2018 FOCAC summit held in Beijing, under the banner of strengthening and consolidating our relations for mutual benefit.

China could also be aware that Africa is understood only in terms of its strategic interests to the West. Thus, such identified security threats are imperial constructs[48] invented and maintained to consolidate the governmentality of Africans. As cogently captured by the Copenhagen School on securitization theory, "the logic around which the whole issue of security has been framed" is "among strategic actors imbued with intentionality."[49] The result has been what Buzan calls "hypersecuritization" of imagined threats, a tendency to exaggerate threats to justify brutal countermeasures.[50]

Similarly, China has inherited terrorism discourse peddled by the West which has geographically divided Africa into zones, often called "zonenization" of terrorism conflict. For example, China misconstrues Muslim populations as dangerous, and the largely Christian-dominated Southern Africa countries are perceived as less hostile than Central, West, East, and Horn of Africa. The Horn of Africa and East Africa for instance, are distorted as an arch of instability, with countries such as Somalia, Djibouti Kenya, Zanzibar, and Tanzania heavily securitized.

Unexpected and Unintended Consequences

The BRI as a national vision and foreign strategy is bound to face difficulties, as projects go awry, debts go bad, and people grow hostile to China's presence. BRI's threat to the balance of power has provoked the United States, for example, to establish a National Defence Strategy, in line with the "Great Power competition" against China and Russia. The "rise and encroachment of China" in Africa is upsetting the EU and Americans, and this has the potential to ignite global just-short-of-war conflict. For instance, the EU-Africa summit and India-Africa Summit are both a reactionary response to BRI's expansionist program. As nations scramble for Africa, their common interest in energy security, the battle might be in cyberspace—with cyber weapons transforming geopolitics. African states will be vulnerable to crippling attacks, especially on already distressed institutions.

The BRI is going to reconfigure politics of the continent through a new paradigm of development, especially with the shift from neoliberalism[51] to a pluralist socialist economic order constituted by a new "community with a shared future." As observed in Namibia in late 2009s, the new African community will be composed of a new assemblage of the Chinese population as a result of increased mobility, technologies, and resources.[52] The immediate implications are security entanglements and the need to establish extraterritorial security institutions that undermine the sovereignty of local security institutions.

Most of the BRI projects in Africa are not renminbi-financed, but highly dependent on dollar-denominated funding. China does not have an infinite supply of dollars. As such, most of the BRI projects are likely to suffer once China experience "dollar constraint." Even if China anchors its BRI projects on cofinancing with Asian Development Bank, Asian Infrastructure Investment Bank, European Investment Bank, European Bank for Reconstruction and Development, and World Bank, these institutions are strict on business ethics—therefore, less flexible to finance loss-making BRI projects. Zhang (2018, 56) is of the view that if Chinese Yuan devalues because of the economic downturn in China, all goods from Africa priced in dollars are going to be too expensive for Chinese consumers. This results in lower demand for and less trade on African goods.[53] The net effect is felt in

Africa where fewer earnings will result in shrinking economies and governments taking on more debt. Dayo[54] might want to dismiss this observation as weak because Africa is on the rise, and there is increased regional trade between African countries which could neutralize China's damaging powers.

CONCLUSION

Although Africa is increasingly decolonizing by shifting from its traditional Western partners toward China, it might not escape the snare of China's developmental powers: commerce, diplomacy, and military intervention. A group of scholars sees China engaging in a "new scramble for Africa" under the guise of creating a "community with a shared future." Are there any positive spin-offs in terms of development, connectivity, and cooperation between China and Africa as espoused by BRI?

Although President Xi Jinping boasts of being the largest bilateral financier of projects in Africa, there is no sufficient evidence of "mutual benefit" except a systematic rip-off of African resources. Consequently, the continent is now extremely skeptical toward China, particularly the latter's offer to seemingly unconditional capital and contradictions of causing debt distress. The construction of rails, roads, electricity, dams, stadia, and commercial buildings has put African states under debt peonage.[55] The more Africa is under debt burden, the more it brings huge businesses for BRI companies. Therefore, the BRI seems is more of a symbolic portrayal of development than a factual interpretation of genuine African-oriented economic growth. Here, BRI mirrors the politics of development in Africa in particular, domination through a blend of commerce, diplomacy, and hard power. Through the grammar of "mutual benefit," and "shared future of mankind" China is clearly promoting a development discourse that entrenches her political and economic hegemonic powers.

NOTES

1. Callahan, William A. "China's 'Asia Dream': The Belt Road Initiative and the New Regional Order." *Asian Journal of Comparative Politics* 1, no. 3 (2016): 226–243.

2. Zeng, Lingliang. "Conceptual Analysis of China's Belt and Road Initiative: A Road towards a Regional Community of Common Destiny." *Chinese Journal of International Law* 15 no. 3 (2016): 517–541.

3. Tekdal, Veysel. "China's Belt and Road Initiative: At the Crossroads of Challenges and Ambitions." *Pacific Review* 31, no. 3 (2018): 373–390.

4. Chi, He. "The Belt and Road Initiative as Global Public Good: Implications for International Law." In *Normative Readings of the Belt and Road Initiative: Road to*

New Paradigms, edited by Wenhua Shan, Kimmo Nuotio, and Kangle Zhang. Cham: Springer International, 2018.

5. The Economist. "Planet China: What to Make of the Belt and Road Initiative." *The Economist* 428, no. 9102 (2018): 13–16.

6. Ibid, Chi, 2018.

7. United Nations Population Fund. *Africa Fastest Growing Continent*. New York: USA, 2019.

8. Ramo, Joshua Cooper. *The Beijing Consensus: Notes on the New Physics of Chinese Power*. London: Foreign Policy Centre, 2004.

9. Ibid, Callahan, 2016.

10. Ghiasy, Richard, Su, Fei, and Saalman, Lora. "The 21st Century Maritime Silk Road: Security Implications and Ways forward for the European Union." Report by the Stockholm International Peace Research Institute, Solna, Sweden 2018. Accessed July 30, 2020 https://www.sipri.org/sites/default/files/2019-10/the-21st-century-mar itime-silk-road.pdf.

11. Chan, Mary. *China in Africa: A Form of Neo-Colonialism?* Boston: Houghton Mifflin Harcourt, 2018.

12. Langan, Martin. "Emerging Powers and Neo-Colonialism in Africa." In *Neo-Colonialism and the Poverty of 'Development' in Africa*, edited by Martin Langan. Newcastle: Palgarve Macmillan, 2017.

13. Ojakorotu, Victor and David Dan-Woniowei. "African Quest for Development and Chinese Strategic Policy in the Continent: Myth or Reality in a Developmental Path in the 21st Century." *Journal of Reviews on Global Economics* 8, no. 1 (2019): 92–99.

14. Yiwei, Wang. *Public Diplomacy and the Rise of Chinese Soft Power*. London: Sage, 2008.

15. Akter, Sima. *The Chinese One Belt One Road*. Bangladesh: University of Dhaka, 2018.

16. He, Yafei. "Belt & Road vs. Liberal Order." *China-US Focus, 2017.* Accessed 10 December 2018. https://www.chinausfocus.com/foreign-pol icy/-belt–road-vs-liberal-order.

17. Ibid, He, 2017.

18. Taylor, Monique. *The Chinese State, Oil and Energy Security*. London: Palgrave Macmillan, 2014.

19. Radelet, Steven. *Emerging Africa: How 17 Countries Are Leading the Way*. Baltimore, MD: Brookings Institution Press, 2010.

20. Power, Marcus, Mohan Giles, and May Tan-Mullins. *China's Resource Diplomacy in Africa: Powering Development*. London: Palgrave Macmillan, 2012.

21. Woods, Ngaire. "Whose Aid? Whose Influence? China, Emerging Donors and the Silent Revolution in Development Assistance." *International Affairs* 84, no. 6 (2008): 1205–1221.

22. Staff Reporter. Zimbabwe Has Billions it is Not Exploiting, Says China. Zimbabwe. Byo24 News. Accessed 12 November 2018. https://bulawayo24.com/in dex-id-news-sc-national-byo.

23. Chaponnière, Jean-Raphael. *Chinese Aid to Africa, Origins, Forms and Issues. The New Presence of China in Africa*. Paris: Armand Colin, 2009.

24. Morvaridi, Behrooz and Caroline Hughes. "South–South Cooperation and Neoliberal Hegemony in a Post-aid World." *Development and Change* 49, no. 3 (2018): 867–892.

25. The World Bank. *The World Bank in Africa*. Washington D.C. USA, 2013.

26. Celso, Anthony and Nalbandov, Robert, eds. *The Crisis of the African State: Globalization, Tribalism, and Jihadism in the Twenty-first Century*. Quantico: Marine Corps University Press, 2016.

27. Ngonlardje, Kabra Mbaidjol. *African Countries and the Global Scramble for China a Contribution to Africa's Preparedness and Rehearsal*. The Netherlands: Hotei Publishing, 2018.

28. Moyo, Dambisa. *Dead Aid. Why Aid is Not Working and How There is Another Way for Africa*. London: Allen Lane, 2009.

29. Karuri, Kenneth. *Politics. Mired in Western Aid Disputes, Tanzania's Leader Praises China*. Television Bloomberg, November 27, 2018.

30. Ibid, Ngonlardje, 2018.

31. Rolland, Nadège. "China's 'Belt and Road Initiative': Underwhelming or Game-Changer?" *The Washington Quarterly* 40, no. 1 (2017): 127–142.

32. Graf, Arndt and Azirah Hashim. *African–Asian Encounters: New Co-operations and New Dependencies*. The Netherlands: Amsterdam University Press, 2017.

33. Bräutigam, Deborah. *The Dragon's Gift: The Real Story of China in Africa*. Oxford: Oxford University Press, 2009.

34. Chan, Mary. *China in Africa: A Form of Neo-Colonialism?* Boston: Houghton Mifflin Harcourt, 2018; see also; Mbaidjol, Ngonlardje Kabra. "*Chinese 'Neocolonialism': Fact or Fiction?*" In *African Countries and the Global Scramble for China*, edited by Ngonlardje K. Mbaidjol. The Netherlands: BRILL, 2018 and Langan, Martin. "Emerging Powers and Neo-Colonialism in Africa." In *Neo-Colonialism and the Poverty of 'Development' in Africa*, edited by Martin Langan. Newcastle: Palgarve Macmillan, 2017.

35. Muzapu, Rangarirai, Taona Havadi and Kudzai Mandizvidza. *Belt and Road Initiative: Positioning Zimbabwe for Investment Opportunities*. Beijing: University of International Business and Economics, 2018.

36. Simelane, Thokozani Lavhelesani R. Managa. *Belt and Road Initiative: Alternative Development Path for Africa*. South Africa: Africa Institute of South Africa, 2018.

37. Bräutigam, Deborah. "Aid with Chinese Characteristics': Chinese Foreign Aid and Development Finance Meet the OECD-DAC Aid Regime." *Journal of International Development* 23, no. 5 (2011): 752–764.

38. Dossou, Toyo. *The Impact of China's One Belt One Road Initiative in Africa: The Evidence from Kenya*. Texas: South Western University, 2018.

39. Chatham House. *Exploring Public International Law Issues with Chinese Scholars – Part 4*. Chatham House in Collaboration with the China University of Political Science and Law, 2018.

40. Dellios, Rosita, and R James Ferguson. "The Human Security Dimension of China's Belt and Road Initiative." *Journal of Management and Sustainability* 7, no. 3 (2017): 48–62.

41. Lee, Jones. "Does China' Belt and Road Initiative Challenge the Liberal, Rule-Based Order?" *Fudan Journal of the Humanities and Social Sciences* 12, no. 1 (2019): 1–21.

42. Ibid, Zeng, 2016.

43. Celso, Anthony and Nalbandov, Robert, eds. *The Crisis of the African State: Globalization, Tribalism, and Jihadism in the Twenty-first Century.* Quantico: Marine Corps University Press, 2016.

44. Wang, Guiguo. "The Belt and Road Initiative in Quest for a Dispute Resolution Mechanism." *Asia Pacific Law Review* 25, no. 1(2017): 1–16.

45. Ibid, Ngonlardje, 2018.

46. Fanell, James E. "Asia Rising: China's Global Naval Strategy and Expanding Force Structure." Naval War College Review 72, no. 1 (2019): 4–17.

47. Shinn, David. H., Joshua Eisenman. *China and Africa: A Country of Engagement.* Pennsylvania: University of Pennsylvania Press, 2012.

48. Sidaway, James D. and Chih Yuan Woon. "Chinese Narratives on "One Belt, One Road in Geopolitical and Imperial Contexts." *The Professional Geographer* 69, no. 4 (2017): 591–603.

49. Waever, Ole.1995. "Securitization and Desecuritization," in Ronnie Luschutz (ed) *On Security.* New York: Columbia UP.

50. Buzan, Barry. "China in International Society: Is 'Peaceful Rise' Possible?" *Chinese Journal of International Politics* 3, no. 1 (2010): 5–36.

51. Lee, Jones. "Does China' Belt and Road Initiative Challenge the Liberal, Rule-Based Order?" *Fudan Journal of the Humanities and Social Sciences* 12, no. 1 (2019): 1–21.

52. Dobler, Gregor. "Chinese Shops and the Formation of a Chinese Expatriate Community in Namibia." *The China Quarterly* 199 (2009): 707–727.

53. Ookeditse, Lawrence. *Africa Must Cut Trade Deficit with China and Look to Itself.* Opinionista: Daily Maverick. Accessed September 19, 2018. https://www.dailymaverick.co.za/opinionista/2018-09-19.

54. Dayo, Olopade. *The Bright Continent: Breaking Rules and Making Change in Modern Africa.* Boston: Houghton Mifflin Harcourt, 2014.

55. Asongu, Simplice and Gilbert Aminkeng. "The Economic Consequences of China–Africa Relations: Debunking Myths in the Debate." *Journal of Chinese Economic and Business Studies* 11, no. 4 (2013): 261–277.

BIBLIOGRAPHY

Akter, Sima. *The Chinese One Belt One Road.* University of Dhaka: Bangladesh, 2018.

Asongu, Simplice, and Gilbert Aminkeng. "The Economic Consequences of China-Africa Relations: Debunking Myths in the Debate." *Journal of Chinese Economic and Business Studies* 11, no. 4 (2013): 261–277.

Bräutigam, Deborah. *The Dragon's Gift: The Real Story of China in Africa.* Oxford: Oxford University Press, 2009.

Bräutigam, Deborah. "Aid with Chinese Characteristics': Chinese Foreign Aid and Development Finance Meet the OECD-DAC Aid Regime." *Journal of International Development* 23, no. 5 (2011): 752–764.

Buzan, Barry. 2010. "China in International Society: Is 'Peaceful Rise' Possible?" *Chinese Journal of International Politics* 3, no. 1 (2010): 5–36.

Callahan, William A. "China's 'Asia Dream': The Belt Road Initiative and the New Regional Order." *Asian Journal of Comparative Politics* 1, no. 3 (2016): 226–243.

Callahan, William A. *China's Belt and Road Initiative and the New Eurasian Order.* Policy Brief 22. Oslo: Norwegian Institute of International Affairs, 2016.

Celso, Anthony and Nalbandov, Robert, eds. *The Crisis of the African State: Globalization, Tribalism, and Jihadism in the Twenty-first Century.* Quantico: Marine Corps University Press, 2016.

Chan, Mary. *China in Africa: A Form of Neo-Colonialism?* Boston: Houghton Mifflin Harcourt, 2018.

Chaponnière, Jean-Raphael. *Chinese Aid to Africa, Origins, Forms and Issues. The New Presence of China in Africa.* Paris: Armand Colin, 2009.

Chatham House. *Exploring Public International Law Issues with Chinese Scholars— Part 4.* Chatham House in Collaboration with the China University of Political Science and Law, 2018.

Chen, Kai. "China in Africa: A Threat to African Countries?" *Strategic Review for Southern Africa* 38, no. 2 (2016): 100–122.

Chi, He. "The Belt and Road Initiative as Global Public Good: Implications for International Law." In *Normative Readings of the Belt and Road Initiative: Road to New Paradigms*, edited by Wenhua Shan, Kimmo Nuotio, and Kangle Zhang. Cham: Springer International, 2018.

Dellios, Rosita, and R. James Ferguson. "The Human Security Dimension of China's Belt and Road Initiative." *Journal of Management and Sustainability* 7, no. 3 (2017): 48–62.

Dobler, Gregor. "Chinese Shops and the Formation of a Chinese Expatriate Community in Namibia." *The China Quarterly* 199 (2009): 707–727.

Dossou, Toyo. *The Impact of China's One Belt One Road Initiative in Africa: The Evidence from Kenya.* Texas: South Western University, 2018.

Fanell, James E. "Asia Rising: China's Global Naval Strategy and Expanding Force Structure." *Naval War College Review* 72, no. 1 (2019): 4–17.

Ghiasy, Richard, Su, Fei, and Saalman, Lora. "The 21st Century Maritime Silk Road: Security Implications and Ways Forward For The European Union." Report by the Stockholm International Peace Research Institute, Solna, Sweden 2018. Accessed July 30, 2020 https://www.sipri.org/sites/default/files/2019-10/the-21st-century -maritime-silk-road.pdf.

Graf, Arndt and Azirah Hashim. *African–Asian Encounters: New Co-operations and New Dependencies.* The Netherlands: Amsterdam University Press, 2017.

He, Yafei. "Belt & Road vs. Liberal Order." *China-US Focus, 2017.* Accessed 10 December 2018. https://www.chinausfocus.com/foreign-pol icy/-belt–road-vs-liberal-order.

Karuri, Kenneth. *Politics. Mired in Western Aid Disputes, Tanzania's Leader Praises China*. Television Bloomberg, November 27, 2018.

Langan, Martin. "Emerging Powers and Neo-Colonialism in Africa." In *Neo-Colonialism and the Poverty of 'Development' in Africa*, edited by Martin Langan. Newcastle: Palgrave-Macmillan, 2017.

Lee, Jones. "Does China' Belt and Road Initiative Challenge the Liberal, Rule-Based Order?" *Fudan Journal of the Humanities and Social Sciences* 12, no. 1 (2019): 1–21.

Mbaidjol, Ngonlardje Kabra. *"Chinese 'Neocolonialism': Fact or Fiction?"* In *African Countries and the Global Scramble for China*, edited by Ngonlardje K. Mbaidjol. The Netherlands: BRILL, 2018.

McDevitt, Rear Admiral. Becoming a Great "Maritime Power": A Chinese Dream: CAN Strategic Studies: China, 2016.

Mbaidjol, Ngonlardje Kabra. *African Countries and the Global Scramble for China: A Contribution to Africa's Preparedness and Rehearsal*. The Netherlands: BRILL, 2018.

Morvaridi, Behrooz and Caroline Hughes. "South–South Cooperation and Neoliberal Hegemony in a Post-aid World." *Development and Change* 49, no. 3 (2018): 867–892.

Moyo, Dambisa. *Dead Aid. Why Aid is Not Working and How There is Another Way for Africa*. London: Allen Lane, 2009.

Muzapu, Rangarirai, Taona Havadi and Kudzai Mandizvidza. *Belt and Road Initiative: Positioning Zimbabwe for Investment Opportunities*. Beijing. University of International Business and Economics, 2018.

Ngonlardje, Kabra Mbaidjol. *African Countries and the Global Scramble for China a Contribution to Africa's Preparedness and Rehearsal*. The Netherlands: Hotei Publishing, 2018.

Ojakorotu, Victor and David Dan-Woniowei. "African Quest for Development and Chinese Strategic Policy in the Continent: Myth or Reality in a Developmental Path in the 21st Century." *Journal of Reviews on Global Economics* 8, no. 1 (2019): 92–99.

Olopade, Dayo. *The Bright Continent: Breaking Rules and Making*. New York: Houghton Publishing, 2014.

Ookeditse, Lawrence. *Africa Must Cut Trade Deficit with China and Look to Itself*. Opinionista: Daily Maverick. Accessed 19 September 2018. https://www.dailymav erick.co.za/opinionista/2018-09-19.

Power, Marcus, Mohan Giles, and May Tan-Mullins. *China's Resource Diplomacy in Africa: Powering Development*. London: Palgrave Macmillan, 2012.

Radelet, Steven. *Emerging Africa: How 17 Countries Are Leading the Way*. Baltimore, MD: Brookings Institution Press, 2010.

Ramo, Joshua Cooper. *The Beijing Consensus: Notes on the New Physics of Chinese Power*. London: Foreign Policy Centre, 2004.

Rolland, Nadège. "China's 'Belt and Road Initiative': Underwhelming or Game Changer?" *The Washington Quarterly* 40, no. 1 (2017): 127–142.

Shinn, David. H., Joshua Eisenman. *China and Africa: A Country of Engagement.* University of Pennsylvania Press: Pennsylvania, 2012.

Sidaway, James D. and Chih Yuan Woon. "Chinese Narratives on "One Belt, One Road" in Geopolitical and Imperial Contexts." *The Professional Geographer* 69, no. 4 (2017): 591–603.

Simelane, Thokozani Lavhelesani R. Managa. *Belt and Road Initiative: Alternative Development Path for Africa.* South Africa: Africa Institute of South Africa, 2018.

Staff Reporter. Zimbabwe Has Billions it is Not Exploiting, Says China. Zimbabwe. Byo24 News. Accessed 12 November 2018. https://bulawayo24.com/index-id-new s-sc-national-byo.

Taylor, Monique. *The Chinese State, Oil and Energy Security.* London: Palgrave Macmillan, 2014.

Tekdal, Veysel. "China's Belt and Road Initiative: At the Crossroads of Challenges and Ambitions." *Pacific Review* 31, no. 3 (2018): 373–390.

The Economist. "Planet China: What to Make of the Belt and Road Initiative." *The Economist* 428, no. 9102 (2018): 13–16.

The World Bank. 2013. The World Bank in Africa: Washington D.C. USA.

Wang, Guiguo. "The Belt and Road Initiative in Quest for a Dispute Resolution Mechanism." *Asia Pacific Law Review* 25, no. 1(2017): 1–16.

Waever, Ole.1995. "Securitization and Desecuritization," In Ronnie Luschutz (ed) *On Security.* New York: Columbia UP.

Woods, Ngaire. "Whose Aid? Whose Influence? China, Emerging Donors and the Silent Revolution in Development Assistance." *International Affairs* 84, no. 6 (2008): 1205–1221.

Yiwei, Wang. *Public Diplomacy and the Rise of Chinese Soft Power.* London: Sage, 2008.

Zeng, Lingliang. "Conceptual Analysis of China's Belt and Road Initiative: A Road towards a Regional Community of Common Destiny." *Chinese Journal of International Law* 15 no. 3 (2016): 517–541.

Zhang, Han. *The Values of National Development in Contemporary China: Contemporary Value Systems in China.* Singapore: Springer, 2018.

Part II

NEW IMPERIALISM OR
A NEW WORLD ORDER

Chapter 6

China in Africa

The Fifth Wave of Conquest and Plunder?

Sabella Ogbobode Abidde

INTRODUCTION

In its ancient and enduring history, the African continent has undergone four waves of conquest and plunder. The first was the Transatlantic Slave Trade which lasted from the fifteenth to the nineteenth centuries, followed by the Berlin Conference of 1884–1885 which formalized the colonization of the continent. Though the decolonization efforts resulted in independence, it did not bring about the complete freedom of African countries—but instead led to the continuation of European and American control of the continent in the form of neocolonialism. The fourth wave, by way of globalization, has made it possible for Western and non-Western nations, along with many of their multinational corporations (MNCs) to usurp state sovereignty and authority, and in the process acted and conducted their businesses in ways that are, in many instances, inimical to labor laws, environment conditions, and the well-being of the workers—especially those in the margins.

The fifth wave of what some have called the Chinese Imperialism has its early beginning in the vision and efforts of Mao Zedong[1] and Zhou Enlai.[2] Today, and for the last three decades, many African states have been hoping that China would hasten their infrastructural and economic development. In this regard, they are expecting China to do for them what the United States and European countries have failed to do in terms of advancing their growth and development. Successive African governments and leaders have also failed at governance, and in providing of basic human needs.[3] So, in exchange for loans, infrastructures, and other economic and financial possibilities, China is quietly acquiring the power to dictate to African states and societies and solidifying their ability to control the continent's vast resources.

At the basic level, one is not frowning at nor does one disapprove of Africa's engagement with the People's Republic of China (PRC). Fundamentally, one is not against clear-cut loans, trade, foreign direct investments, or other forms of economic and development activities by Beijing, individual Chinese citizens, or private entities that are interested in engaging states and societies on the continent if—if—they do not injuriously hypothecate or contribute to the mortgaging of the lives and prosperity of this and future generations. African leaders and elites must be smart and forward-looking about Chinese activities on the continent. But so far, they have not been. But rather many states and societies have been subservient, timid, obedient, and thankful for crumbs from China, and in many instances, have been overwhelmed by China and Chinese presence.

On the other hand, is China self-restraint and principled enough not to exploit, overpower, and take advantage of a self-interested, self-serving, shady, avaricious, extravagant, and ineffectual leaders and leadership that has come to characterize much of the continent for much of its postindependence years? And while Beijing has a set of principles in the conduct of its foreign policy,[4] the extent to which these principles are strictly adhered to in her dealings with African governments and societies. International commerce has been part of the global system since antiquity. And in a post-Westphalia system, no nation can isolate itself from the global system. Still, no nation must engage in international affairs at the expense of the well-being of its people, institutions, culture, traditions, and sovereignty. This is what we see of African leaders in the Sino-African relations.

The United States and the Europeans may not be comfortable with Beijing's presence and activities in Africa. That may be. But really, that is hypocritical of them. It is hypocritical because, after several decades of engaging Africans, they have not done better; they have not been righteous. But rather, they have been supercilious and exploitative and do not respect Africans and their leaders. The Chinese, as with the Americans and Europeans, disrespects and brutalizes Africans at almost every turn. On the other hand, African leaders and elites must shoulder some of the blames: they kowtow to foreigners but abuse their people; they defend foreign citizens in Africa, but commit political violence and terroristic acts against their people; they steal and then move their ill-gotten wealth to foreign banks, yet go on their knees begging for foreign aids. Their callousness, stupidity, and indifference have caused many Africans to be atrophied by deprivation, poverty, and imaginable and unimaginable physical and mental diseases.

CHINA-AFRICA IN ANTIQUITY
AND IN MODERN TIMES

The documentary evidence of early contacts and connections between China and Africa is neither robust nor voluminous. However, the available evidence is strong enough to categorically assert that the relationship between both regions dates to ancient times. Mesopotamia, Indus Valley, the Incas, and the Mayan, the Osirian along with the Egyptian and Ancient Chinese are some of the oldest ancient civilizations. It is therefore inconceivable that Ancient Egypt and Ancient Chinese Civilization would not have had contact and connections. Both were too advanced for their time to have remained isolated or unaware of one another. Let us fast forward several centuries later where according to Louise Levathes in *When China Ruled the Seas*:

> From the ninth century A.D., there are excellent descriptions of Africa in Chinese sources, suggesting that if indeed Chinese junks never traveled to Africa, the Chinese were at least getting reliable information from Persian and Arab traders. Duan Chengshi, who died in 863 A.D., relates his account of what appears to be an early encounter with African herdsmen in Yuyang za zu (Miscellany of Yuang mountain), a compendium of various kinds of knowledge.[5]

Levathes also asserts that "the Arab word *'ishra,* which al-Idris used to describe the relationship between the Chinese and the Swahili, implies friendship over an extended period and close, sometimes intimate, association. The description certainly opens the possibility that the Chinese did intermarry with the local population and were one of the populations, along with Arabs, Persians, Indians, and later the Portuguese, who contributed to the mélange of coastal peoples on the Swahili coast."[6] And in 1947, at a public lecture given at the University of London, Dr. J. J. L. Duyvendak, a prominent Dutch Sinologist and professor of Chinese at the Leiden University, gave credence to the ancient connections between both regions.[7] What these and other historical accounts tell us is that the contact and connections between China and Africa date far longer and deeper than many historians have been able to verify or probe.

What is not in dispute, however, is the modern account of what has come to be known as the Sino-African relations—a relationship that commenced when Zhou Enlai, between 1963 and 1965, toured several African countries. This was followed by other high-powered state visits by Zhao Ziyang (1982), and Jiang Zemin (1996).[8] It is, however, instructive to note that between 2007 and 2017, China's top leadership (the president, premier, and foreign minister) made a total of seventy-nine official visits to forty-three different African countries—with the most visits to South Africa because she has the largest stock of Chinese foreign direct investment in Africa.[9] Such visits are not likely to end or diminish anytime soon because of China's expanding and deepening tentacles in the continent. Another avenue used by China to strengthen its position and relationship in Africa is the intergovernmental body known as the Forum on China-Africa Cooperation (FOCAC).

The FOCAC "was established in 2000. It is a multilateral platform for exchange and cooperation between China and African countries that have formal diplomatic relationships with China and covers various aspects of politics, trade, economy, society, and culture. All previous FOCAC ministerial conferences and their follow-up actions have had a great impact and deepened bilateral cooperation between China and Africa."[10] The inaugural conference was held in Beijing from October 10 to 12, 2000. All the African countries, except for Eswatini (Swaziland),[11] are members of FOCAC. These countries pledged to and abide by Beijing's declaration that the PRC is the only, rightful, and legitimate representative of China—as opposed to the Republic of China (ROC/Taiwan).

WHAT BOTH SIDES WANT

More than five decades after the commencement of Sino-African relations, almost no one doubts or is confused about China's motives and motivations. If it was not very clear in the 1950s through the 1990s, it has become very clear in the second decade of the twenty-first century. Regarding China's objectives, Yun Sun, writing in *Africa in China's Foreign Policy*, argued that

> China seeks to satisfy four broad national interests in its relations with the continent. Politically, China seeks Africa's support for China's "One China" policy and for its foreign policy agendas in multilateral forums such as the United Nations. Economically, Africa is seen primarily as a source of natural resources and market opportunities to fuel China's domestic growth. From a security standpoint, the rising presence of Chinese commercial interests in Africa has led to growing security challenges for China, as the safety of Chinese investments and personnel come under threats due to political instability and criminal activities on the ground. Last but not least, China also sees an underlying ideological interest in Africa, as the success of the "China model" in non-democratic African countries offers indirect support for China's own political ideology and offers evidence that Western democratic ideals are not universal.[12]

In terms of its political interest vis-a-vis the "One China" policy, China has been able to achieve this as fifty-three of the fifty-four states on the continent currently adheres to the policy. In this regard, Taiwan—the once dominant of the two on the continent decades earlier—has only one ally: Swaziland. What is more, African countries hardly deviate from China's policy dictates. Economically, a section of the continent is, in many regards, China's cotton and cocoa field as she can and does roam the continent picking and plucking whatever she wants. And in the other section—with a shovel and pale in hand—she can dig deep and extract whatever she wants. China has been able to, in two or so decades, achieved what attendees at the Berlin Conference of 1884–1885 attained with pain and in much longer a period. China's role, position, achievements, drive, and intention is a source of anxiety in many Western capitals—especially in the United States, Britain, and France. The suspicions and hostility run deep. The allegations are many and they include

1. That investment in infrastructures follows or mimic European colonial-patterns.
2. That China's predatory lending will undoubtedly entrap African nations.
3. That China is engaged in land grabs.
4. That Chinese companies rarely employ African workers (save at the menial level).
5. That China does not encourage democracy and is indifferent to illiberalism.
6. That China, individual Chinese, and their MNCs does not pay attention to local cultures.
7. Chinese workers and immigrants abuse and dehumanize Africans in ways that are not different from the cruelty of colonial-Europe.

On April 12, 2018, the *Washington Post* published an op-ed in which Professor Deborah Brautigam, of the Johns Hopkins University's School of Advanced International Studies, challenged and attempts to put to rest the common rhetoric and misconception of China's engagement in Africa. She was especially taken aback because "Just before he visited Africa, former secretary of state Rex Tillerson accused China of using 'predatory loan practices,' undermining growth and creating 'few if any jobs' on the continent. In Ethiopia, Tillerson charged the Chinese with providing 'opaque' project loans that boost debt without providing significant training. As secretary of state, Hillary Clinton sang the same tune, warning Africans to beware of this 'new colonialism.' China, we are often told, is bringing in its workers or 'grabbing' African land to grow food to send back to feed China. But researchers who have explored China's role in Africa suggest that many of the things our politicians believe about Chinese engagement are not true."[13] The truth, according to Brautigam, is that

We found a story of globalization, not colonization; a story of African agency, rather than Chinese rapacity . . . To be sure, increased Chinese engagement comes with significant and very real challenges for many Africans. Traders complain about competition from Chinese migrants . . . Chinese demand for African ivory, abalone, rhinoceros tusk and materials from other endangered species has taken a significant toll on conservation efforts. And Chinese President Xi Jinping's recent lifting of his own term limits is bound to embolden African leaders who are reluctant to leave their comfortable presidential posts... Chinese loans are powering Africa, and Chinese firms are creating jobs...China may boost Africa's economic transformation, or they may get it wrong—just as American development efforts often go awry.[14]

In the early parts of the twenty-first century, "China became an important source of finance for African development. The continent's infrastructure was in disrepair; it had crumpled after decades of abject neglect and destruction from senseless civil wars. A substantial investment was—and still—needed to rebuild this infrastructure. To close the infrastructure gap, annual spending of $93 billion would be required. Africa must spend US$360 billion on infrastructure by 2040. Africa, however, does not have the funds but had natural resources, which China needed to feed its economic machine. So, China went looking for resources in Africa and elsewhere, wooing African leaders with diplomatic platitudes about "equal terms" and lofty promises of foreign aid without conditions."[15] And while there have been some queries, quarrels, and displeasures,[16] many African governments are happy with China's involvement in their respective countries.

Therefore, some governments see Beijing's involvement as an opportunity for growth and development. And indeed, with China comes offerings for infrastructural development, the chance to borrow at an acceptable rate, the possibility for technology and skills transfer; and a government, they believe, that will not interfere in their domestic affairs. According to Mehari Maru, "For Africans, China has four major attractions: Unconditional soft loans and access to capital; quick delivery of services and cheap goods; funding of peacekeeping; and an alternative development model."[17] In order words, "China's unconditional cooperation has allowed African governments to enjoy access to finance, expertise, and development aid. China has aided African governments to meet their growing demands for services and infrastructure more quickly. China is also engaged in peace and security projects in Africa. China's history of fast and successful economic growth is a model from which many lessons could be learned in Africa."[18]

The reality is that whatever the drawbacks may be—terrible terms of trade, loans, investments, and so forth—African governments bear the responsibility of whatever the downsides might be. They entered a partnership where they are the junior partners, were insultingly deferential to Beijing, went on their knees begging for loans and other economic packages. These leaders remained on their knees while at once kowtowing to the Chinese government and companies. Previous loans, FDIs, grants, and aid packages from Europe, Asia, the United States, and Canada have not made a dent in the pitiable economic and political conditions on the continent precisely because the majority of African leaders have been poor and ineffective managers of resources. In the years since independence, not much has changed about leadership and governing institutions on the continent. With China and Chinese firms, they simply found willing partners—partners who are willing to give a little but take much more in return.

CONDITIONS IN AFRICA

One of the epoch-making events of the twentieth century was the decolonization of Africa. But as great as independence was, many African leaders inherited weak and fragmenting states. The fragility of their inheritance aside, the condition in many of these states were exacerbated by the inadequacies and excesses of their nationalist leaders—many of whom personalized the rule of law and did little to promote and strengthen democracy, democratic culture, and its institutions. Many states were administered as if they were personal fiefdoms with power concentrated in the hands of these leaders and their cronies and surrogates. The abuse and misuse of state power contributed to the spate of upheavals, military coups, secessionist fervor, and wars that engulfed many of these states.

From Tunisia to South Africa, from Nigeria to Djibouti, and from Mauritania to Uganda, the reality of the continent is similar in all aspects and sectors: lacking in economic and political power, lacking in technological know-how, and lacking the political will to transform and modernize its societies. What we have here, then, is the failure of Africans to overcome what other states and societies with similar history and experiences have overcome. There are, for instance, the oil-rich countries of the Middle East most of whom have gone from economic backwardness to decent economies within six decades—so have countries in Asia that seem set to catch up with the West in terms of growth and development. But not so in Africa, where preliterate conditions, disintegration, sweltering poverty, and grave deficiency in basic human needs reign supreme. Walter Rodney, in his enduring and seminal work, *How Europe Underdeveloped Africa*, states that

> Western Europe and Africa had a relationship which ensured the transfer of wealth from Africa to Europe. The transfer was possible only after trade became

truly international; and that takes one back to the fifteenth century when Africa and Europe were drawn into common relations for the first time—along with Asia and the Americas. The developed and underdeveloped parts of the present capitalist section of the world have been in continuous contact for four and a half centuries. The contention here is that over that period Africa helped to develop Western Europe in the same proportion as Western Europe helped to underdevelop Africa.[19]

Certainly, Europe is complicit in African condition. From the Trans-Atlantic Slavery Trade to Colonialism and down to their neocolonial actions, they have, in no small measure mightily contributed to the problems and challenges the continent faces today. Nonetheless, Africans are not blameless. Many Nationalist leaders were complicit, and so have many of the men and women who have overseen their respective countries, private and public institutions, and the direction their countries have taken since the independence years. And while Walter Rodney analysis was irrefutable, the quality of leadership has also been a burden on the continent: it is the dearth of quality leadership and good governance that's responsible for its weak and fragmenting institutions; makes it possible for endogenous and exogenous forces to exploit the continent; and for the continent's inability to provide life's necessities.

That the government of China and Chinese companies are fully engaged in Africa's economic and political space is fully acceptable. That is the reality of the international system—a system that allows for meaningful engagement and connections with other countries. The Chinese are in Latin America and the Caribbean, so are the German and the Dutch and the French. Brazil, Australia, Italy, and Portugal are also busy in Africa and elsewhere in the world. That, essentially, is the nature of globalism and globalization. In this regard, therefore, Africa cannot, should not, and must not close its doors to China or any other country. In return, there must be reciprocity: other countries must also open their doors to African governments and businesses. Reciprocal engagement, however, is not and cannot be a substitute for personal responsibility, the rule of law, self-discipline, and the well-being and welfare of the state and society. This is where most African governments gave and gotten it wrong. They and they alone are responsible for the growth and development of their states and societies—not the Europeans, not the Americans, not the Japanese and, certainly, not the Chinese.

Several decades after independence, and two decades into the twenty-first century, what we have in Sub-Saharan Africa is continuity—the continuity of the old—instead of change and progress. The consensus among many Western governments and institutions is that *Africa is Rising*. They cite, for instance, GDP numbers and the seeming prevalence of democratic regimes. And that Africa, as with the rest of the Global South, is changing politically and economically in ways that advance progress. That is an illusion, and that is not the everyday reality. The supposed growth and development are insignificant because the everyday reality shows that much of the continent has stagnated; many governments have reintroduced treacheries and vile survival strategies that contributed to human suffering and the underdevelopment of the continent. Take, for instance, the political phenomenon known as *Tenure Elongation.*

Tenure elongation, sometimes referred to as *Sit Tight Syndrome*[20] is as old as Africa's postcolonial history. It was mostly associated with one-party states and military regimes. It is a political tactic whereby the sitting president, colluding mostly with members of the Parliament, manipulates the electoral laws and the constitution to enable him/her to serve beyond the original term limit outlined in the law. Many of these leaders ended up being *President-for-Life.*[21] This was one of the characteristics of Africa's nationalist leaders. This practice usually ends if (a) there is a military coup; (b) a palace-coup occurs; (c) the president dies in office, or (d) internal dynamics forces the president to hold meaningful elections. Or, in rare cases, he is forced out and exiled or jailed as was the case with Omar Hassan Ahmad al-Bashir of Sudan. But as African countries began to embrace democracy, tenure elongation began to fizzle. Evidence of this could be found in countries such as Zambia, Nigeria, Senegal, Benin, and Togo, where there was an orderly transition of government.[22]

In the second decade of the twenty-first century, however, some leaders reverted to tenure elongation—as in Burundi, Rwanda, and Uganda. The attempt by President Yahya Jammeh (The Gambia) to affect tenure elongation in 2016/2017 was foiled by regional and international forces—forcing the former president to go into exile in Equatorial Guinea. This reemerging practice has the potential to void many of the gains made by emerging democracies. Unless the perpetrators of tenure elongation are made to bear the cost for their extralegal acts, it is likely to overshadow many of the democratic gains of the previous decades. Whatever gain they make, they destroy, and are also good at encouraging others to destroy states and societies on the continent.

In China's contacts with Africa, therefore, it is the Africans—African political leaders and elites—that are likely to betray their countries. They will make it possible for China and Chinese companies to overrun and colonize them even if that was not the intention. For many African leaders and the elite, their thirst for monetary and material possession far outweighs their love for country or national interest.

IS CHINA COLONIZING OR CAPABLE
OF COLONIZING AFRICA?

Is China colonizing Africa? The data is not there, yet. Or, put another way: the observable indicators are not yet persuasive. Furthermore, unlike the Europeans who partook in the Berlin Conference of 1884–1885, China, to one's knowledge, did not engage in a formal conference to strategize the takeover of the continent. Nonetheless, that an open conference had not taken place or that Beijing's intentions have not been made public does not mean that colonization has not begun or that it will not formally begin sometimes in this century. And even if we put aside the question of colonization, the other possibility would be the dependency[23] of African nations on China, which would make Chinese domination possible. So, let us segue, not so much with the definition of colonization and neocolonization, but with a very instructive enunciation and how they relate to Sino-African relations. According to Jian Junbo, an associate professor at the Institute of International Studies, Fudan University, China,

> It is clear there are two contradictory opinions on China's image and actions in Africa: colonizing power or capitalist benefactor? Classic colonialism beginning in the 15th century commonly consisted of foreigners occupying distant lands, controlling their economic and political affairs and exploiting their material resources through unfair or one-sided trade practices or simply by force. By that definition European states acted as colonizing powers in Africa and Asia, but they went far beyond colonialism through the slave trade, proxy wars and imposing cultural norms . . .[24]

Jian Junbo went further to say that

> Unfortunately, a new colonialism paradigm subsequently emerged and quickly grew in the 1960s . . . This neocolonialism embraces all aspects of classic colonialism except for occupying foreign lands, since all states in Africa remain technically independent. In this neocolonialism, the exploiting power controls weaker states' economic resources and political systems and exploits their wealth under the name of liberal capitalism. So where does China fall? Is it a colonizing power or not when it engages Africa, especially as more and more Chinese began to arrive on the continent at the beginning of the 21st century?[25]

Here is the zinger

> Of course, we cannot be blind to the possibility of China becoming a colonizing power someday. The day might come when African national economic systems

have become so dependent on Chinese investments and export commodities that their domestic and foreign policies would in effect be decided by Beijing. With its increasing investments in Africa, there is the possibility that Chinese business people will push African national industries aside and bankrupt national economic systems; meanwhile, more and more companies from China are entering Africa, but they simply focus on profits regardless of their harmful influences on African society, such as environmental pollution, excessive development and exploitation of local labor.[26]

China does not need to be a colonial state (in the classical sense) to be a colonialist at a future date. It does not need to employ the tactics and strategy employed by the fourteen European countries that ventured into the continent in search of land and resources. China has the power to do whatever it wants to do without resorting to force. Hedrick Smith in *The Power Game* posits that "power is the ability to make something happen or to keep it from happening. It can spring from tactical ingenuity and jugular timing, or simply from knowing more than anyone else at the critical moment of decision."[27] This is what China knows best and Africans know very little of. As a result, Chinese leaders, without resorting to brute force, may lord over African states. At the current rate of its involvement—an involvement that continues to deepen, broaden, and intensify—it will take or be given the power to dictate to states and societies on the African continent.

Africa, as Akol Dok and Bradley Thayer tell us, is on the cusp of a new period in its history. Freed from centuries of colonialism and neoimperialism, states and societies on the continent can grow and develop. But unfortunately, the continent faces a new danger: Sino-imperialism. Akol Dok and Bradley Thayer also assert that "China is in Africa now not to advance Maoism, but to control its resources, people, and potential. The Chinese superficially appear to maintain a mutually beneficial relationship with Africa by providing financial and technical assistance to Africa's pressing developmental needs. China's activities and behavior in Africa may only be described as neocolonial and exploitative of African peoples and the environment."[28]

The more China invests in Africa, the more of Africa it will own and control. What is true of colonial states, is also true of neocolonial states. From 1880 to1914—and especially between 1914 to two decades after the independence years, Europeans controlled 90 percent or more of Africa—with the dominant power being Great Britain, closely followed by France. And while it took France, Germany, Belgium, and Britain more than one hundred and twenty-five years to achieve hegemonic status on the continent; China is likely to achieve the same in less than fifty years. By 2045, therefore, China is likely to be the Primus inter pares among colonial and neocolonialist not just in Africa but also in much of the Global South. The near-total control of

Africa's economic space may be such that the European countries, along with the United States and Canada, would seek permission for entry or seek joint ventures arrangement with the Chinese.[29]

In addition to the economic ventures, China would continue to build schools and Chinese language centers for Africans—compelling Africans who want an inroad into the Chinese market or who want to engage Chinese companies to learn mandarin and/or other Chinese languages. Also, China would continue giving scholarships to Africans to attend universities in China. It is not outside of the realm of possibilities that China would build primary and secondary schools for Africans in Africa thereby "catching them young and early." It is also not inconceivable that China—while it is one of the most irreligious countries in the world—would support and help fund religious houses and centers. These are some of the indicators of a country wanting to colonize—even if not in the traditional sense of colonization.

Sanusi Lamido Sanusi, the former Emir of Kano, a one-time banker and governor of the Central Bank of Nigeria, writing for the *Financial Times of London*, asserts that Africa's relationship with China carries with it a whiff of colonialism and that it was time for Africans to wake up to the realities of their romance with China. "The Chinese," according to Sanusi, "have set up huge mining operations. They have also built infrastructure. But, with exceptions, they have done so using equipment and labor imported from home, without transferring skills to local communities. So, China takes our primary goods and sells us manufactured ones. This was also the essence of colonialism. The British went to Africa and India to secure raw materials and markets. Africa is now willingly opening itself up to a new form of imperialism capable of the same forms of exploitation as the west. It is a significant contributor to Africa's deindustrialization and underdevelopment."[30] Sanusi went on to say that

> We cannot blame the Chinese, or any other foreign power, for our country's problems. African nations will not develop by selling commodities to Europe, America and China . . . Africa must recognize that China—like the US, Russia, Britain, Brazil and the rest—is in Africa not for African interests but its own. The romance must be replaced by hard-nosed economic thinking. Engagement must be on terms that allow the Chinese to make money while developing the continent, such as incentives to set up manufacturing on African soil and policies to ensure the employment of Africans.[31]

The impression that China has exploited resources without building up local economies has triggered fierce criticism from some leaders. In 2011, for example, Michael Sata won Zambia's presidency in part by tapping into anti-Chinese sentiment after Chinese managers shot protesters at a large coal mine in southern Zambia. Furthermore, African workers have also begun to fault Chinese companies for unfair labor practices, including disputes over wages and working conditions, thus undermining China's official stance promoting Chinese investment in Africa as "win-win."[32]

To be sure, China has insisted again and again and again that she is not interested in colonizing Africa. And some African leaders have backed Beijing's assertion—insisting that the ongoing relationship benefits both sides. "As a country with a deep historical memory of being colonized by Western powers," says Jian Junbo, "China does not want to control Africa's economic and political systems. The Chinese government neither appoints military consultants to African governments nor constructs military bases on the continent. Moreover, China has not used deceitful means to steal and exploit African resources. Relations between China and African countries are grounded on reciprocal benefits, which is not just a slogan but a fact. China is not now and will not likely become a colonizing power."[33]

Rwandan President Paul Kagame, one of the most please borrowers and enthusiastic supports of China's involvement in Africa, termed Chinese aid and investment strategy in Africa "as deeply transformational and respect-ful of the continent's global position,"[34] insisting that "our growing ties with China do not come at anyone's expense. The gains are enjoyed by all who do business with us. Building the capacity of African institutions to transact and monitor more effectively is what will make the biggest difference."[35] Kagame went to say that "The relationship between Africa and China is based on equality, mutual respect and a commitment to a shared well-being."[36] Kagame, as with most leaders on the continent, does not see or foresee China as a colonial or colonizing force but instead he "view China's role in Africa positively, welcoming China's heavy emphasis on government-to-govern-ment contracts with few, if any, strings attached. These leaders believe that as a fellow developing country, China has more philanthropic motives than Western governments and corporations do. As a result, they praise China's contributions to their nations' growth and development."[37]

AFRICA DOES NOT NEED CHINA OR ANYONE ELSE

The fourteen European countries whose injurious and inhumane activities led to the partitioning, the subjugation, and exploitation of the continent all contributed to the underdevelopment of states and societies in Africa. These Europeans did not go to Africa simply because they were curious, needed to establish trade links, or engage in diplomacy. And neither were they in Africa in search of humanitarian development or equal partnership. Even their evan-gelizing activities were a pretext to steal and dehumanize Africans. Even after decolonizing activities led to independence, politically and economically, Africans have remained under the control of the Europeans in an arrangement known as neo-colonization. Not long after independence, the United States of America (USA) joined in the gory festivity.

It is asinine to think that the West is a friend of Africa. Their objective is simple: take, take, and take some more from Africa. Since the tail end of the twentieth century, the PRC has increased its presence on the continent. Two decades into the twenty-first century, she is on her way to becoming the single most dominant country on the continent. She is today seen by many—especially within the continent—as a friend and a partner in search of humanitarian development, while others see her as an emerging imperialist. And even if the tactics and strategies are different, Beijing's motives and motivations could not be any different from the Europeans and the Americans. And indeed, no one should be under the illusion that the Chinese see the Africans as equals. They probably see people needing guidance and assistance.

Even if they wanted to, neither the West nor the East sees Africa as a resource-poor continent. If Africa were a poor a continent, they and others would not be on the continent outdoing each other, struggling for supremacy. But they see a continent that can be taken advantage of. Especially since the independence years, African leaders made it possible, or easy, for others to take advantage of their respective countries. Not then, not now: No country or region in the world is doing Africa a favor; but rather Africa has, ironically, been doing the world a huge favor by immolatingly engaged in unequal relationships that have led to its bleeding and asphyxiation. Africa was not poor. It is still not a poor continent. But for the criminal actions, despicable attitude, and detrimental pronouncement of many of its leaders, which has resulted in the mismanagement of human and natural resources, Africa would be feeding and giving to much of the world.

According to the China Africa Research Initiative at the Johns Hopkins University School of Advanced International Studies (SAIS-CARI),

China-Africa bilateral trade has been steadily increasing for the past 16 years. The value of the China-Africa trade in 2018 was $185 bn, up from $155 bn in 2017. In 2018, the largest exporter to China from Africa was Angola, followed by South Africa and The Republic of Congo. In 2018, South Africa was the largest buyer of Chinese goods, followed by Nigeria and Egypt. Chinese FDI annual flows to Africa, also known as OFDI ("Overseas Foreign Direct Investment") in Chinese official reports, have been increasing steadily since 2003. From 2003 to 2018, the number has surged from US$75 million in 2003 to US$5.4 billion in 2018. In terms of foreign aid, Chinese foreign aid expenditures increased steadily from 2003 to 2015, growing from USD 631 million in 2003 to nearly USD 3 billion in 2015. Foreign aid expenditures dropped sharply to USD 2.3

billion in 2016 but rebounded to a new high of USD 3.3 billion in 2018. And from 2000 to 2017, the Chinese government, banks and contractors extended the US $143 billion in loans to African governments and their state-owned enterprises (SOEs).[38]

Whatever the amount China has given to Africa in terms of loans, grants, foreign direct investment, aid, and so forth, it is insignificant when compared to the amount of money and other quantifiable resources that have been stolen or forcefully taken from the continent by China and others. For instance, African governments received a combined $32.8bn in loans in 2015 but paid $18bn in debt interest and principal payments, with the overall level of debt to the global community rising rapidly. And an estimated $29bn a year is being stolen from Africa in illegal logging, fishing, and the trade in wildlife and plants. The reality is that Africa is not poor; however, the key problem is that the rest of the world, particularly Western countries, are extracting far more than they send back. Meanwhile, they are pushing economic models that fuel poverty and inequality, often in alliance with African elites.[39] That is the reality of the African condition.

The other realities are simply that African governments are sourcing for loans they are not able to repay within a reasonable amount of time. In instances where such loans are repaid, it may take several decades and several generations to accomplish. Essentially, therefore, the loan trap accusation is plausible. After all, there are countries in Africa still trapped by loans from two to four decades ago.[40] Today many African countries are pleased with the infrastructures China is providing. In many ways, that seem right, but in many other ways, it is another avenue to trap African governments because some of these so-called "infrastructures" are nothing but White Elephant Projects—projects that do not add value to the lives of the people. They may look beautiful and may command instant gratification, but in the long run, they become a drag on the landscape and the economy. What is more, many countries do not have maintenance culture or the expertise to manage gigantic and sometimes complex edifices. Thus, they will be compelled to seek more loans to pay Chinese and or other foreign experts to fix and manage them.

During the colonial era, many African cities had secluded residential areas that were meant for the whites who mostly worked for the colonial administration either directly or indirectly. In Lagos (Nigeria), they had what was and is still Ikoyi—a residential reservation area meant exclusively for the whites and their families. Indeed, Government Reservation Areas (GRA) or European Quarters (EQ) can be found in places such as Benin, Sapele, Wari, Jos, Kaduna, and elsewhere in Nigeria where you had colonial officers. Along with these exclusive residential areas comes reserved/exclusive amenities such as schools, clinics, and hospitals, supermarkets, in which Africans were not allowed access—except perhaps as laborers. The next big thing in many African cities would be similar arrangements: The Chinese Reservation Areas. This would be another form of apartheid, but this time sanctioned by African governments.

CONCLUSION AND SUGGESTIONS

The PRC, as of 2019, is the dominant power in Africa's economic space. In addition to the Chinese government, an estimated 10,000 Chinese-owned firms are operating in Africa as of the summer of 2017.[41] Adding to this mix are individual Chinese who set out on their own in search of the golden fleece. And why are they in Africa? The evidence suggests a gradual move toward hegemonic status and, eventually, the colonization of the continent. And while China has a favorable view in many parts of the continent, especially among current African leaders like Kagame of Rwanda, others see China's involvement as rapacious. Long before he became the President of Zambia (September 23, 2011–October 28, 2014), Michael Charles Sata, asserted that "European colonial exploitation in comparison to Chinese exploitation appears benign, because even though the commercial exploitation was just as bad, the colonial agents also invested in social and economic infrastructure services Chinese investment, on the other hand, is focused on taking out of Africa as much as can be taken out, without any regard to the welfare of the local people."[42]

Nonetheless, Africa has reaped some benefits by way of the provision of infrastructures, loans, trade agreements, and foreign direct investments. What is more—for now at least—Beijing is said to have stayed out of the domestic politics of individual African country. Whether this is true or not is hard to tell (because rare is the African government that would publicly admit to Chinese interference in their domestic affairs). In the words of Elizabeth Manero, "however one characterizes the relationship, there is no question that both China and African nations stand to benefit. There is much reason to hope for continued economic benefits to both parties and growing infrastructural improvement throughout Africa. China's investments have already begun to change how the West approaches development deals—causing a shift from a focus on pure lump aid to new systems like *Aid for Trade*, where developing countries receive focused trade capacity and infrastructure building assistance."[43]

One of the most frequently asked questions by scholars, commentators, journalists, diplomats, and those with a broad interest in Sino-African relations is whether China is colonizing Africa, or, if the relationship is evidence of China's benevolence toward Africa. The evidence to support either proposition is not yet available. At least not incontrovertibly. But there are indications that within the next one or three decades, there would be enough evidence to this answer one way or another. Even so, we know the followings facts: First, China is a hegemon within the African economic space, and with that come political influence to the point where, for instance, she was able to convince fifty-three of fifty-four African nations to excommunicate the Republic of China/Taiwan.

Second, while China has not publicly expressed her intention to colonize, one of the resultant consequences of her economic and political power would be that with time, she will privately and public chastise and penalize governments that do not adhere to her dictates. Third, Africa has a history of third-rate leadership—leaders who kowtow to foreign governments and entities. Many of these leaders are obedient and subservient to foreigners because, instead of worrying about their nation's national interest and the interest and well-being of their people, they mostly look out for themselves and the interest of their family and associates. In the end, therefore, most African leaders would bow to the wishes of Beijing.

Fourth, there would come a time when, in the interest of the *hegemonic bloc*—China, Russia, and the West—they would meet to *discuss the affairs of Africa* and come to an agreement on how *not to step on each other's toe.* They all speak for Africa while the so-called "African" leaders act mute. While these governments are having those negotiations, MNCs and powerful individuals and organization—all in the name of globalization and WTO rules that allows for unfettered access to global markets would join in subverting and exploiting Africa. However, at the top of the pyramid would be China. The aforementioned, of course, would be the third round of the *Scramble for Africa* which may lead to a complete enslavement of the continent.

To avoid this, the African electorates must rethink three things: the types of men and women they elect/select as leaders. And the intelligentsia must be fully involved in the economic and political space to put to an end the ascension of scoundrels, robbers, and those suffering from Dissociative Identity Disorder. The younger generations must be actively and genuinely involved in the affairs of their immediate and wider community. To leave the leadership space for men and women with brittle bones and degenerating mind and intellect, would be a disservice to the continent. To allow this is to hasten the fall and takeover of the continent by external powers and entities. And finally, Africans in the Diaspora must, beyond being transnational migrants who dutifully send remittances home, engage their countries.

Every single African country has an untold number of its citizens living in Europe, the United States, Canada, and elsewhere. The majority are well-educated and sophisticated. They understand how the international system works and therefore can checkmate endogenous and exogenous forces bent on subjugating and exploiting their countries. In concert with the home-based intelligentsias, they could steady and reposition their various countries for the challenges, prospects, and possibilities of the twenty-first century. Unless Africans, at home and abroad, recommit to their countries and the continent, they will be fighting a losing battle now and in the future in which case the events leading to 1619 and 1884/1885 would be a child's play.

NOTES

1. Mao Zedong (December 26, 1893–September 9, 1976) was the Chairman of the Central Committee of the Communist Party of China and was also the head of the Communist Party of China (CPC). It was during his administration that the current economic and political relations with African began.

2. Zhou Enlai (March 5, 1898–January 8, 1976), was the first Premier of the PRC. He was the head of government from October 1949 until his death in January 1976. As a diplomat, he was point man for the Sino-African relations embarking on a ten-country tour of Africa between December 1963 and January 1964.

3. In this instance, Basic Human Needs refers to the unfettered access of the masses to: gainful employment and participation in the economic arena; access to nutritious food and potable water; access to quality healthcare and education; a clean and healthy environment; personal security and the safety of the community; access to good roads and other infrastructure; and good governance.

4. China's five principle of peaceful co-existence are (1) Mutual respect for sovereignty and territorial integrity (2) mutual nonaggression (3) noninterference in each other's internal affairs (4) equality and mutual benefit and (5) peaceful coexistence. Please see: China's Initiation of the Five Principles of Peaceful Co-Existence (2000), Published: Nov 17, 2000. (This was cited in Jerker Hellström. China's emerging role in Africa—A strategic overview. FOI Studies in African Security. Swedish Defense Research Agency 164 90 Stockholm, Sweden. Accessed May 2009. www.foi.se/africa; And China's eight principles for foreign aid (1964) are (1) Assistance to foreign countries according to the principle of equality and mutual benefit (2) respect for the sovereignty of recipient countries, no strings attached and no privilege required (3) providing interest-free or low interest loans (4) help recipients of aid to enter the path of self-reliance and independent economic development (5) achieve quick results through small investments (6) provide top quality Chinese equipment, goods and materials (7) help recipient countries to master the technology (8) experts (who are dispatched by Chinese government) should receive the same treatment as experts of recipient countries. Please see: 1964 nian duiwai yuanzhu ba xiang yuanze [The 'Eight Principles of Foreign Aid' of 1964] (2008), People's Daily online, Published: Jan 16, 2008; He, Wenping, (2003), China-Africa Relations Facing the 21st Century Published: May 27, 2003 (This was cited in Jerker Hellström. China's emerging role

in Africa - A strategic overview. FOI Studies in African Security. Swedish Defence Research Agency 164 90 Stockholm, Sweden. Accessed May 2009. www.foi.se/africa.

5. Louise Levathes. *When China Ruled the Seas: The Treasure Fleet of the Dragon Throne, 1405–1433*. New York: Oxford University Press, 1996.

6. Ibid, Levathes, p. 201.

7. Jan Julius Lodewijk Duyvendak. *Chinas Discovery of Africa: Lectures given at the University of London on January 22 and 23, 1947*. London: Arthur Probsthain, 1949.

8. Julia C. Strauss. "The Past in the Present: Historical and Rhetorical Lineages in Chinas Relations with Africa." *The China Quarterly* 199 (2009): 777–795.

9. Lijadu, Kemi. "Chinese Leaders Visit Africa More Often than You Think, and Not Always the Places You Expect." Quartz Africa. Quartz, July 26, 2018. https://qz .com/africa/1335418/chinese-leaders-visit-africa-more-often-than-you-think-and-not -always-the-places-you-expect/.

10. Li Anshan, Liu Haifang, Pan Huaqiong, Zeng Aiping and He Wenping. "FOCAC Twelve Years Later achievements, challenges and the Way Forward." Discussion Paper 74. Peking University, School of International Studies in Cooperation with The Nordic Africa Institute Uppsala, 2012.

11. eSwatini, formerly known as Swaziland, chose to maintain relations with Taiwan after a diplomatic tussle between Taiwan and China. As of Spring of 2020, eSwatini is Taiwan's last only ally in Africa. Please see: "ESwatini Stands by Taiwan despite Chinese Overtures." BBC News. BBC, August 22, 2018. https://www.bbc .com/news/world-africa-45271974.

12. Sun, Yun. *Africa in Chinas Foreign Policy*. Washington, DC: Brookings, 2014.

13. Deborah Brautigam "U.S. Politicians Get China in Africa All Wrong." The Washington Post. WP Company, April 12, 2018. https://www.washingtonpost.com/ news/theworldpost/wp/2018/04/12/china-africa/.

14. Ibid, Deborah Brautigam.

15. George B. N. Ayittey. "Chinese Investments in Africa: 'Chopsticks Mercantilism.'" Al Mariam's Commentaries, September 27, 2017. http://almariam .com/2017/09/27/chinese-investments-in-africa-chopsticks-mercantilism/.

16. Patey, Luke. "The Chinese Model Is Failing Africa." Subscribe to read | Financial Times. Financial Times, August 26, 2018. https://www.ft.com/content/ca4 072f6-a79f-11e8-a1b6-f368d365bf0e; See also: "Mamamah Airport: Sierra Leone Cancels China-Funded Project." BBC News. BBC, October 10, 2018. https://www .bbc.com/news/world-africa-45809810.

17. Maru, Mehari Taddele. "Why Africa Loves China." Poverty & Development | Al Jazeera. Al Jazeera, January 6, 2019. https://www.aljazeera.com/indepth/opinion/ africa-loves-china-190103121552367.html.

18. Ibid

19. Walter Rodney. *How Europe Underdeveloped Africa*. Washington, DC: Howard University Press, 1974.

20. Daniel N. Posner., and Daniel J. Young. "The Institutionalization of Political Power in Africa." *Journal of Democracy* 18, no. 3 (2007): 126–140; see also Ayodeji.

Olukoju. "Sit-tight Syndrome and Tenure Elongation in African Politics." *Lagos Historical Review: A Journal of the Department of History,* University of Lagos, vol. 14, p. 117–134.

21. The longest serving African presidents include: Teodoro Obiang Nguema Mbasogo (Equatorial Guinea, 1979–till date) Paul Biya (Cameroon, 1982–till date); Yoweri Museveni (Uganda, 1986–till date); Idrissa Deby (Chad, 1990–till date); Isaias Afwerki (Eritrea, 1993–till date); Denis Sassou Nguesso (Republic of the Congo, 1979–1992; 1997–till date); and Paul Kagame (Rwanda, 2000–till date).

22. Senegal and Botswana remain two of the few African countries where, since their independence, there has been a peaceful and orderly change of government.

23. Osvaldo Sunkel, "National Development Policy and External Dependence in Latin America," *The Journal of Development Studies,* Vol. 6, no. 1, October 1969, p. 23; Theotonio Dos Santos, "The Structure of Dependence," in K.T. Fann and Donald C. Hodges, eds. *Readings in U.S. Imperialism.* Boston: Porter Sargent, 1971, p. 226; See also Andre Gunder Frank, "The Development of Underdevelopment," in James D. Cockcroft, Andre Gunder Frank, and Dale Johnson, eds. *Dependence and Underdevelopment.* Garden City, New York: Anchor Books, 1972, p. 3.

24. Jian Junbo. China in Africa: From capitalism to colonialism? China-African Relations. Beijing Review, February 8, 2007. http://www.beijingreview.com.cn/lia nghui/txt/2007-02/05/content_57281.htm.

25. Ibid.

26. Ibid.

27. Hedrick Smith. *The Power Game: How Washington Works.* (New York: Random House, 1988).

28. Dok, Akol Nyok, and Bradley A Thayer. "Takeover Trap: Why Imperialist China Is Invading Africa." The National Interest, July 10, 2019. https://nationalinte rest.org/feature/takeover-trap-why-imperialist-china-invading-africa-66421.

29. The evidence of this can be gleaned from how their agreements with other countries isolated the Republic of China (Taiwan).

30. Lamido, Sanusi. "Africa Must Get Real about Chinese Ties." Financial Times (London), March 11, 2013. https://www.ft.com/content/562692b0-898c-11e2-ad3f -00144feabdc0.

31. Ibid, Sanusi Lamido.

32. Eleanor Albert, Christopher Alessi, and Beina Xu. "China in Africa." Council on Foreign Relations, July 12, 2017. https://www.cfr.org/backgrounder/china-africa.

33. Ibid, Jian Junbo.

34. Mugisha, Ivan R. "Rwanda's Kagame Endorses Chinese Investment in Africa." The East African, September 4, 2018. https://www.theeastafrican.co.ke/news/ea/ Rwanda-Paul-Kagame-endorses-Chinese-investment-Africa/4552908-4742800-5bru alz/index.html.

35. Ibid, Mugisha.

36. Ibid, Mugisha.

37. Larry Hanauer, and Lyle J Morris. "China in Africa Implications of a Deepening Relationship." RAND Corporation - Research Briefs - Document Number: RB-9760-OSD, 2014.

38. "Other China-Africa Data." The China Africa Research Initiative at the Johns Hopkins University School of Advanced International Studies (SAIS-CARI), 2020. http://www.sais-cari.org/other-data.

39. Curtis, Mark, and Tim Jones. "How the World Profits from Africa's Wealth." Honest Accounts 2017 $203 billion OUT How the world profits from Africa's wealth. Global Justice Now, May 2017.

40. Ndikumana, Léonce, and James K Boyce. *Africa's Odious Debts: How Foreign Loans and Capital Flight Bled a Continent.* London: Zed Books, 2012; See also Ajayi, S Ibi, and Mohsin S Khan. *External Debt and Capital Flight in Sub-Saharan Africa.* Washington DC: International Monetary Fund, 2000.

41. Sun, Irene Yuan, Kartik Jayaram, and Omid Kassiri. "Dance of the Lions and Dragons: How Are Africa and China Engaging, and How Will the Partnership Evolve?" McKinsey & Company, New York, June 2017.

42. Quoted in Scott D. Taylor's "The Nature of Chinese Capital in Africa," *Current History* 117, no. 799 (May 2018), p. 197.

43. Manero, Elizabeth. "China's Investment in Africa: The New Colonialism?" Harvard Political Review, February 3, 2017. http://harvardpolitics.com/author/e manero/.

BIBLIOGRAPHY

Ajayi, S. Ibi, and Mohsin S Khan. *External Debt and Capital Flight in Sub-Saharan Africa.* Washington DC: International Monetary Fund, 2000.

Albert, Eleanor, Christopher Alessi, and Beina Xu. "China in Africa." Council on Foreign Relations, July 12, 2017. https://www.cfr.org/backgrounder/china-africa.

Ayittey, George B. N., and Related Posts. "Chinese Investments in Africa: 'Chopsticks Mercantilism.'" Al Mariam's Commentaries, September 27, 2017. http://almariam .com/2017/09/27/chinese-investments-in-africa-chopsticks-mercantilism/.

Brautigam, Deborah. "U.S. Politicians Get China in Africa All Wrong." The Washington Post. WP Company, April 12, 2018. https://www.washingtonpost.com /news/theworldpost/wp/2018/04/12/china-africa/.

Curtis, Mark, and Tim Jones. "How the World Profits from Africa's Wealth." Honest Accounts 2017 $203 billion OUT How the world profits from Africa's wealth. Global Justice Now, May 2017. https://www.globaljustice.org.uk/.

Dok, Akol Nyok, and Bradley A Thayer. "Takeover Trap: Why Imperialist China Is Invading Africa." The National Interest, July 10, 2019. https://nationalinterest.org/ feature/takeover-trap-why-imperialist-china-invading-africa-66421.

Duyvendak, J. J. L. *Chinas Discovery of Africa: Lectures given at the University of London on January 22 and 23, 1947.* London: Arthur Probsthain, 1949.

"eSwatini Stands by Taiwan despite Chinese Overtures." BBC News. BBC, August 22, 2018. https://www.bbc.com/news/world-africa-45271974.

Frank, Andre Gunther. "The Development of Underdevelopment." In *Dependence and Underdevelopment*, edited by James D Cockcroft and Andre Gunther Frank, 3. Garden City, New York: Anchor Books, 1972.

Hanauer, Larry, and Lyle J Morris. "China in Africa Implications of a Deepening Relationship." RAND Corporation—Research Briefs—Document Number: RB-9760-OSD, 2014.

Hellström, Jerker. "China's Emerging Role in Africa—A Strategic Overview." Swedish Defense Research Agency, 2009. https://www.foi.se/download/18.7fd3 5d7f166c56ebe0bc16c/1542369070783/Chinas_emerging_role_in_Africa_IB-171 _1-2009.pdf.

Junbo, Jian. "China's Role in Africa." China-African Relations. Beijing Review, February 8, 2007. http://www.beijingreview.com.cn/lianghui/txt/2007-02/05/cont ent_57281.htm.

Lamido, Sanusi. "Africa Must Get Real about Chinese Ties." Financial Times (London), March 11, 2013. https://www.ft.com/content/562692b0-898c-11e2-ad3f -00144feabdc0.

Levathes, Louise. *When China Ruled the Seas: The Treasure Fleet of the Dragon Throne, 1405-1433*. New York: Oxford University Press, 1996.

Lijadu, Kemi. "Chinese Leaders Visit Africa More Often Than You Think and Not Always the Places You Expect." Quartz Africa. Quartz, July 26, 2018. https://qz .com/africa/1335418/chinese-leaders-visit-africa-more-often-than-you-think-and-n ot-always-the-places-you-expect/.

"Mamamah Airport: Sierra Leone Cancels China-funded Project." BBC News. BBC, October 10, 2018. https://www.bbc.com/news/world-africa-45809810.

Manero, Elizabeth. "China's Investment in Africa: The New Colonialism?" Harvard Political Review, February 3, 2017. http://harvardpolitics.com/author/emanero/.

Maru, Mehari Taddele. "Why Africa Loves China." Poverty & Development | Al Jazeera. Al Jazeera, January 6, 2019. https://www.aljazeera.com/indepth/opinion/ africa-loves-china-190103121552367.html.

Mugisha, Ivan R. "Rwanda's Kagame Endorses Chinese Investment in Africa." The East African, September 4, 2018. https://www.theeastafrican.co.ke/news/ea/Rwan da-Paul-Kagame-endorses-Chinese-investment-Africa/4552908-4742800-5brualz /index.html.

Ndikumana, Léonce, and James K Boyce. *Africa's Odious Debts: How Foreign Loans and Capital Flight Bled a Continent*. London: Zed Books, 2012.

"Other China-Africa Data." The China Africa Research Initiative at the Johns Hopkins University School of Advanced International Studies (SAIS-CARI), 2020. http://www.sais-cari.org/other-data.

Patey, Luke. "The Chinese Model Is Failing Africa." Subscribe to read | Financial Times. Financial Times, August 26, 2018. https://www.ft.com/content/ca4072f6 -a79f-11e8-a1b6-f368d365bf0e.

Rodney, Walter. *How Europe Underdeveloped Africa*. Washington, DC: Howard University Press, 1974.

Santos, Theotonio Dos. "The Structure of Dependence." In *Readings in U.S. Imperialism*, edited by K.T Fann and Donald C Hodges, 226. Boston: Porter Sargent, 1971.

Smith, Hedrick. *The Power Game: How Washington Works*. New York: Random House, 1988.

Strauss, Julia C. "The Past in the Present: Historical and Rhetorical Lineages in Chinas Relations with Africa." *The China Quarterly* 199 (2009): 777–795.

Sun, Irene Yuan, Kartik Jayaram, and Omid Kassiri. "Dance of the Lions and Dragons: How Are Africa and China Engaging, and How Will the Partnership Evolve?" McKinsey & Company, New York, June 2017.

Sun, Yun. *Africa in Chinas Foreign Policy*. Washington, DC: Brookings, 2014.

Sunkel, Osvaldo. "National Development Policy and External Dependence in Latin America." *Journal of Development Studies* 6, no. 1 (1969): 23–48.

Chapter 7

Changing Africa-China Relations—Colonialism or Partnership?

Simbo Olorunfemi

INTRODUCTION

The relationship between Africa and China, strengthening by the day, is one that has generated more than a cursory interest in different quarters, in and out of Africa. The more noticeable presence of China in Africa, an increase in high-level engagement between political leadership and business between the two, and the interest it has elicited is so high that Professor Ian Taylor cites it as arguably the most important development for the continent since the end of the Cold War.[1] It is one relationship wherein the parties involved do not enjoy the luxury of privacy as much as they might like to, with probing eyes and questions from all over, especially outside Africa, would make one conclude, without interrogation that the relationship is an illicit affair, one neither in the interest of Africa nor the world.

The unease or what might be called apprehension on the part of the West on the growing relationship between Africa and China is particularly striking. In March 2018, just before he visited Africa, which eventually ended abruptly following his sack, former American Secretary of State Rex Tillerson accused China of "predatory loan practices" in Africa, which, to him, was undermining growth and creating "few if any jobs" on the continent. While in Ethiopia, the American Secretary of State accused the Chinese of providing "opaque" project loans which only boost African debt without providing significant training to them. Indeed, that accusation is neither new nor was it coming from a high-ranking American Official for the first time. Tillerson's predecessor in office, Hillary Clinton was of the same voice. She sternly warned Africans to be careful of what she tagged "new colonialism."[2]

The question is—Why is the Africa-China relationship of so much interest to the West that it would be issuing a FATWA against its consummation? What is the nature of the relationship? Could it be that Africa is so carried away on the wings of love that she is no longer able to see clearly as she is being led down the path of exploitation and abuse? Is the growing relationship between Africa and China one of mutual consent? Is it a symbiotic or parasitic relationship? These questions are of prime interest, concern, and interrogation, in light of the recent history of Africa.

THEORETICAL FRAMEWORK

The nature and peculiarities of the rising profile of China in Africa is not just a difficulty for international actors to appropriately situate and contextualize, finding a suitable theoretical framework within which explanation can be made is also daunting. That is evident in the review of the literature on the subject. While there are elements in the relationship that might lead one into going in a particular direction for theoretical guidance, on further consideration, the shortcomings of the theory in properly capturing and successfully explaining all the dimensions of the relationship strikes one. It becomes even more difficult in that Africa has been largely overlooked in international relations scholarship as a valid unit of analysis. That, in part, can be explained on the back of the dominance of realism within the field of international relations and the primacy it places on power, which Africa does not have much of, making it largely irrelevant in a global arena dominated by self-interested actors jostling for power. With that comes limited relevance of power-based theoretical postulations, which makes it inevitably difficult for them to find the right teeth with which to deal with the peculiarities of the African context.

That perhaps explains why scholarship which has engaged with the subject of Africa-China relations employs the same well-known, even if different theoretical tools to explain the situation. Scholars have engaged the Africa-China geopolitics from the prism of the different theoretical constructs deemed most suitable. In the case of Mohan and Power, they opted for a political economy perspective—arguing that "there are other ways of approaching the development/international politics nexus and that China-Africa relations offer the opportunity for de-centering the West from accounts of global politics and looking more closely at the 'entwining' of knowledge as many post-colonial theorists have urged."[3]

Botha employed realism and economic nationalism as tools in situating the crux of China's engagement with Africa as primarily about securing self-interest founded around guaranteeing energy security and advancing its economic agenda.[4] Matambo settles for a constructivist interpretation in engaging with the relationship between South Africa and China. He argues that unlike the proposition by realists that cooperation among actors all consumed by the pursuit of self-interest, with cooperation difficult, if not impossible to achieve, "the current international system reinforces the constructivist claim that when identities and interests between actors in the international system correlate, the formation of genuine cooperation, community, and international interests becomes possible."[5]

In opting for constructivism, he acknowledges that the concession that actors and their structures in the international system are mutually constitutive and that an analysis of the complexities of international relations requires a theory that acknowledges that states are not bound by unchanging structures and interests in the international system. Unlike realism and liberalism with claim to some form of predictability over international politics, constructivism argues that events in the international system occur because they are germane to a certain context and not because they are unavoidable effects of predetermined conditions. Motolani Agbebi and Petri Virtanen employ the "Dependency theory" as a tool for engaging China's contemporary presence in Africa, interrogate the nature of it and explore if it is likely to end in the manner that had been submitted by Dependency theorists. They conclude that the theory cannot apply wholesale as a 'straightforward deployment' in seeking to understand the Africa-China relationship, arguing that the engagement is more suggestive of "a case of growing interdependency."[6]

Then, there is the theory of complex interdependence which was put forward by Robert Keohane and Joseph Nye. It was a response to neorealism and its emphasis on states as the dominant actors in international relations, the primacy of force as an instrument of policy and the assumption of hierarchy in international relations. At the heart of Keohane and Nye's argument is that there are in existence multiple channels that connect societies outside of the conventional Westphalian system of states. They argue that the decline of military force as a tool of policy and the increase in economic and other forms of interdependence should increase the probability of cooperation among states. They argue that "states and their fortunes are inextricably tied together . . . and that the various and complex transnational connections and interdependencies between states and societies were increasing, while the use of military force and power balancing is decreasing but remain important. (Of interest, especially concerning Africa-China relations, is the argument that) there is not, in fact, a hierarchy among issues, meaning that not only is the martial arm of foreign policy, not the supreme tool by which to carry out a state's agenda but that there is a multitude of different agendas that come to the forefront."[7]

The argument by the theory of complex interdependence offers a tool for interrogating the relationship between Africa and China. The reality of international relations is that it is a web of complex interdependence with varied actors jostling for the realization of their interests through multiple points of contact and channels for engagement. A successful analysis of the complexities, in the light of dynamism therein, one does require a theory that acknowledges that states are not tied down by fixed structures and interests in the international system. Having reviewed the different theories above, this work sets its theoretical framework within the ambit of the theory of complex interdependence.

HISTORICAL RELATIONS

The impression often painted is that the Africa-China affair is a recent one, but evidence from literature indicates otherwise. It might be waxing stronger today than it had ever been, but then, there have been flings in the past. The relationship has been traced as far back as 202 BC and AD 220 with Africa reported to have been mentioned in the *Yu-yang-tsa-tsu*, a compendium of general knowledge where he wrote about the *land of Po-pa-li* (referring to Somalia) by Tuan Ch'eng-shih who died in AD 863. The Somalis from the Ajuran Empire are believed the first Africans to have contact with the Chinese. [8]

Archaeological excavations at Mogadishu in Ajura Empire and Kilwa, Tanzania have recovered many coins from China. The majority of the Chinese coins date to the Song Dynasty, although the Ming Dynasty and Qing Dynasty are also represented, according to Richard Pankhurst. The Chinese explorer, Admiral Zheng He, is reported to have reached the eastern coast of Africa in October 1415, the same year some accounts have it that some Chinese ships sank near Lamu Island in Kenya with the survivors said to have settled in the island and married local women. [9] There are believed to be only six descendants left there. In 2002, DNA tests conducted on one of the women confirmed that she was of Chinese descent. [10]

To prove this record, Chinese and Kenyan archaeologists have been searching the African coast for the fabled wreck of a junk and have recently identified several shipwrecks of interest off the Kenyan coast. Archaeologists have found Chinese porcelains made during the Tang dynasty (AD 618–907) in Kenyan villages which were believed to have been brought over by Zheng He during his ocean voyages. [11] Ceramics found in Zimbabwe and South Africa dated back to Song dynasty China. Some tribes to Cape Town's north claimed descent from Chinese sailors during the thirteenth century. Their physical appearance is said to be similar to the Chinese with paler skin and their language having tonal similarities with Mandarin. In Awatwa, their language, the name they have for themselves means "abandoned people."

According to Melanie Yap and Daniel Leong Man in their book *Colour, Confusions and Concessions: the History of Chinese in South Africa*, Chu Ssu-pen, a Chinese mapmaker, in 1320 had southern Africa drawn on one of his maps.[12] It was also not a one-way journey. "On 2/2/1421, Kings and Envoys from the length and breadth of Asia, Arabia and Africa and the Indian Ocean assembled amid the splendor of Beijing to pay homage to Emperor Zhu Di, the son of Heaven."[13]

CONTEMPORARY RELATIONS

Following the Communist revolution of 1949, the Chinese began another round of engagement with Africa. This became strengthened by the role the Chinese played in the liberation struggle and push against colonial forces in Africa, as they subtly sold their socialist manifesto as opposed to that of the Soviet Union. The Chinese strategy for the minds of Africans was two-pronged—political and economic. They supported the liberation struggle and following independence, rendered economic assistance to some of the countries.

The defining contribution by the Chinese to economic development in Africa in the 1970s was its decision to build the Tanzam railway which linked land-locked Zambia's copper belt with the Tanzanian coast 1,100 miles away. The project which started with Surveying and design in 1968 and construction in 1970 was necessitated by the need to help Zambia overcome its dependence on Rhodesia and South Africa, which at the time was under the control of white-minority governments. The Tanzam Railway which runs 1,860.5 kilometers between Dar es Salaam in Tanzania and Kapiri Mposhi in Zambia was constructed at the cost of $406m thirty-year interest-free credit from China, the equivalent of $2.56bn today was completed in 1976[14] (global security.org 2008). A year before the assistance from China, Western funding was not forthcoming. Britain, Japan, West Germany, World Bank, the United States, and the United Nations all turned down the proposal, declining to fund the project.[15]

The significance of the project even went beyond the possible economic gains. Its political and strategic importance, at the time, was even more tell-ing. "Zambia and Tanzania had been by far the leading supporters of the liberation movements directed against southern Africa. The completed road gave Zambia access to the sea through a friendly country, in place of the tra-ditional routes through Rhodesia and Mozambique or Angola. By thus reduc-ing Zambia's vulnerability to economic retaliation for its aid to guerrillas operating in the south, the project was expected to contribute directly to the revolutionary anti-imperialist struggle."[16] Also, there is a growing community of over 100,000 African traders and merchants working and living in a sort of ethnic enclave in the southern Chinese metropolis of Guangzhou (Canton)—a historical trading enclave in and gateway to China after 1760 while the number of Chinese living in Africa has grown from a few thousand years back to between one and two million, mostly businesspeople, across the continent today. [17]

Over time, China and the different peoples of Africa have, in varied ways, found points of convergence around trade and commerce, as the basis for a relationship. But it is the economic turnaround in China that has lent itself as a model and basis for the possible partnership for the African countries burdened by the challenge of poverty in the face of limited resources. Professor H.E. Wenping of the Institute of West African and Asian Studies of the Chinese Academy of Social Sciences captured what it was like, only forty years ago, thus: "China, which is now the world's second-biggest economy, used to be very poor. Before you could get married as a man then, you must get three things; a bicycle, which you would ride with your wife, a television set (a whole community may have just one, which they would all gather to watch in an open place), and a sewing machine. That would be used to sew clothes worn by the family."[18]

The 1979 reform begun by Deng Xiaoping changed all that. According to Professor Li Ping of the Institute of Quantitative and Technical Economics, Chinese Academy of Social Sciences, "since the reform and opening up, we have carried out large-scale poverty alleviation and development policies, and have successfully lifted 700 million rural people out of poverty."[19]

Beyond the domestic successes which triggered a high growth rate, the reforms not only enhance the global standing of China but turned it into a major global trading power. Its energy needs for driving the tremendous development was so high that it accounted for about 40 percent of the growth of global energy demand for oil in the early 2000s, with that need rising as much as 9 percent annually before the recent dip. China has the largest foreign reserves in the world and remains the world's largest energy consumer, accounting for 23.2 percent of global energy consumption and contributing 33.6 percent of global energy demand growth in 2017, the largest contributor to global growth for the seventeenth consecutive year.[20]

Alli explains the evolution of China-Africa relations through what he calls the push and pull factors. For the "push," "as the economy expanded, there was a need for more markets for the products of the very productive Chinese manufacturing sector. And equally important, there was a need for more access to all manner of raw materials from solid minerals, to oil and gas and even timber and agricultural products."[21] The "pull" factors have to do with the huge endowment of solid mineral resources, oil and gas, and agricultural products in Africa and the 'relatively huge market of potential consumers of products." China's gas consumption increased by 15 percent in 2017, accounting for 32.6 percent of global gas consumption net growth which, in part, might explain China's interest in Africa, with countries like Nigeria and Angola sitting on abundant reserves of oil and gas, with the Gulf of Guinea estimated to hold a minimum of 15 billion barrels of oil in deep waters.[22] Apart from the presence of natural resources being a pull, African countries have put in place different incentive packages in a bid to attract foreign investment, which is a further source of interest for investors from other countries. It is the coincidence of all these factors that have prompted renewed Chinese interest in Africa with President Hu Jintao affirming Africa as the natural partner of China.

CHARACTERISTICS OF THE CHINA-AFRICA RELATIONS

The debate that surrounds the China-Africa relations has been energized by what is perceived as enthusiasm on the part of the African power elite for a handshake with the Chinese and warm embrace with "Chinese investments and development aid, leading to speculation in some quarters about the prospects of Africa's rejection of the 'Washington consensus' in favor of a 'Beijing consensus' based on the Chinese model of state-guided capitalism. Linked to this is the issue of what China represents for Africa: an opportunity/ partner for an (alternative model of) mutual development or (neo) colonialism by invitation."[23]

Efem Ubi sits this debate around two schools of thought. One group is made of "Sinophobes" and "Sinoskeptics" who argue that by "China's energy needs and craving for strategic raw materials, its main drive into Africa, as well as a push factor for its gifts to Africa, and more so, by its presence in Africa, it seems China is inadvertently tilting towards colonizing the continent."[24] But the other group argues that "China's presence in Africa is positively affecting Africa's economy, by driving up commodity prices and thus, heightening economic investment and trade growth to countries with or without resources. And at the same time, there has also been a steady increase in China's share of trade as well as access to raw materials that are needed to build the Chinese domestic economy."[25]

TRADE AND INVESTMENT

The increasingly dominant position of China in Africa is evident in the volume of trade between the two. Whereas in 1980, the trade volume between

China and Africa was only US$1bn and US$10bn by 2000, according to statistics by China Customs, it amounted to US$170bn in 2017. It was up 14.1 percent year on year, 2.7 percentage points higher than the general increase of foreign trade from 2016 to 2017. Among these, China's exports to Africa reached US$94.74bn, up 2.7 percent; while China's imports from Africa reached US$75.26bn, up 32.8 percent with a trade surplus in favor of China of US$19.48bn, down 45.2 percent year on year.[26]

China meets a significant portion of its oil need through imports from Africa, mainly from Angola. Benin, Burkina Faso, and Mali supply China with cotton, with Cocoa coming from Côte d'Ivoire, coffee imported from Kenya, while Namibia is one of the main sources for fish products. "A 2017 McKinsey study reports that more than 10,000 Chinese-owned firms are operating in Africa today, about a third of whom are involved in manufacturing. Notably, French academic Tierry Pairault points out that the overwhelming majority of these enterprises are small and micro-businesses. McKinsey also reports that Chinese investment in Africa increasingly contributes to job creation, skills development, and the transfer of new technologies, practices more generally associated with Western business norms."[27] China is not only the biggest partner that Africa has but also the biggest investor on the African market, having overtaken the United States and the former colonial powers who had been traditional largest economic partners to Africa. The trade volume between China and Africa has grown significantly over the last decade.

"China's role on the African continent has been defined by the financing of more than 3,000, largely critical, infrastructure projects, according to the AidData Project. China has extended more than $86 billion in commercial loans to African governments and state-owned entities between 2000 and 2014, an average of about $6 billion a year . . . As a result, China has become the region's largest creditor, accounting for 14 percent of sub-Saharan Africa's total debt stock, according to Foresight Africa 2018."[28] China extends unconditional and low-rate credit lines (rates at 1.5 percent over fifteen years to twenty years) which have now taken the place of the more restricted and conditional loans from the West. Of note is the fact that since 2000, China has canceled more than $10bn in debt owed by African nations. During the sixth Forum on China-Africa Cooperation (FOCAC) meeting in Johannesburg, South Africa, in December 2015, Chinese President Xi Jinping pledged $60bn over a three-year deal in loans and assistance to the continent to help with manufacturing and development of infrastructure.[29] The extent to which China has delivered on the FOCAC commitment cannot be fully determined, but the Chinese vice foreign minister is reported by the Chinese People's Daily to have said that 243 cooperation agreements were signed between December 2015 and July 2016, with a total amount of $50.7bn, including $46bn for direct investments and commercial loans by Chinese companies.[30]

However, "what percentage of the $50.7billion came from the $60 billion official commitment of financing from the Chinese government. Instead, the official explanation is that the $60 billion commitment by the Chinese government had achieved a multiplier effect by inspiring private capital and commercial financiers."[31] From this report, it does appear that China is on track concerning meeting the financing promised under the Johannesburg commitment.

Chen and Nord are of the position that "this rapid growth in trade and project financing has served both Africa and China well. For Africa, trade has boosted economic development in many countries, and the financing of infrastructure projects, for which little concessional financing is available, has helped address crucial bottlenecks to industrial development and structural transformation. For China, while trade with Africa remains a small part of its total foreign trade, many of its project loans are tied to Chinese suppliers, and, as a result, about a quarter of all Chinese engineering contracts worldwide by 2013 on a stock basis went to sub-Saharan Africa, with most of these contracts being awarded in energy (hydropower) and transport (roads, railways, ports, or aviation)."[32]

Nevertheless, these synergies are coming under severe strain. On the trade side, China's growth is rebalancing away from investment toward relying increasingly on domestic consumption. The resulting drop in China's imports of commodities has hit Africa's commodity exporters hard, especially the oil producers, through sharp declines in both the volume and prices of major commodities.[33] Africa's almost decade-old trade surplus with China has now turned into a trade deficit as lower growth in Africa curbs import demand.[34]

FOREIGN AID

The relationship between Africa and China is also characterized by assistance to Africa by China in the form of aid. It is an instrument of policy engagement for China. Officially, China provides eight types of foreign aid: complete projects, goods and materials, technical cooperation, human resource development cooperation, medical assistance, emergency humanitarian aid, volunteer programs, and debt relief. Africa has been a major recipient of Chinese aid with seven of the top ten recipients of all-out concessional aid by China in Africa.[35] By the end of 2009, Africa had received 45.7 percent of the RMB 256.29 billion cumulative foreign aid of China. This covers a wide array of fields, such as agriculture, education, transportation, energy, communications, and health.[36]

According to Brookings Institution, between 2000 and 2012, China funded 1,666 official assistance projects in fifty-one African countries, which accounted for 69 percent of all Chinese public and private projects. Among these projects, 1,110 qualified as Official Development Assistance (ODA)—defined by the Organisation for Economic Co-operation and Development (OECD) as flows of concessional, official financing administered to promote the economic development and welfare of developing countries. The remaining 556 projects could be categorized, also according to the OECD, as Other Official Flow (OOF)—transactions by the state sector that are not "development-motivated or concessional (such as export credits, official sector equity and portfolio investment, and debt reorganization."[37]

Again, there are two sides to the issue of Chinese aid to Africa. While one school sees China's aid and development financing as filling the void left by the West and promoting the development of African countries, helping to take care of large projects with long-term payback period which traditional donors are not keen to support, the other side argues that "these short-term benefits should not form a cover-up for the potential long-term negative consequences associated with neglecting issues of governance, fairness, and sustainability. For example, when the 'tied aid' is linked to the profitability of Chinese companies, it becomes questionable whether China would prioritize Africa's interests or its own."[38] Even within China, Yun Sun draws our attention to a debate about the place of aid between foreign policy bureaucrats and trade promoters. While one sees foreign aid as largely a political instrument for China to strengthen bilateral ties and facilitate the development of African countries with economic benefits associated with aid projects, such as profitability, resource extraction, or the acquisition of service contracts for Chinese vendors being secondary, trade promoters see things differently. For them, all aspects of aid decisions should reflect broad economic considerations.

"Under this logic, the inclination is to allocate the aid budget to countries that offer China the greatest number of commercial opportunities and benefits. Since China's top economic interest is Africa's natural resources, aid decisions are inevitably skewed toward resource-rich countries while others receive less favorable consideration. This practice is problematic in that many of the resource-rich African countries with which China works also suffer from serious political problems, such as authoritarianism, poor governance, and corruption. When the Ministry of Commerce pursues economic gains and associates aid projects with resource extraction, it uses aid packages to promote business relations. This directly contributes to the negative perception that China is pouring aid, funding, and infrastructure projects to prop up corrupt governments in exchange for natural resources."[39]

CONCERNS BY THE WEST

Despite the apparent gains and economic development that China's increased presence in Africa has triggered, or perhaps because of it, the West has been concerned. But rather than the concerns be expressed around the fear that there is an obvious move from "Washington Consensus' towards 'Beijing Consensus,' rather it is presented as one about the interests of Africa. But Professor Deborah Bräutigam argues that the concerns are generally misplaced. With respect to the effect of the Chinese presence on jobs and training opportunities in Africa, she says "Surveys of employment on Chinese projects in Africa repeatedly find that three-quarters or more of the workers are, in fact, local. This makes business sense. In China, textile workers now earn about $500 a month—an amount that far exceeds what workers in most African countries earn. Chinese investors flocking to set up factories in low-cost countries like Ethiopia are not thinking about importing Chinese workers. Like U.S. and European factory owners who moved their factories to China in past decades, Chinese firms are now outsourcing manufacturing to cheaper countries."[40]

On the allegation of predatory lending by China, she cites research findings, one being the work of Scholars at Boston University and Johns Hopkins University who have been assembling databases of Chinese loans provided since 2000. It was found that China had lent at least $95.5bn between 2000 and 2015 to Africa, which is a lot over such a short period. But it was found "by and large, the Chinese loans in our database were performing a useful service: financing Africa's serious infrastructure gap. On a continent where over 600 million Africans have no access to electricity, 40 percent of the Chinese loans paid for power generation and transmission. Another 30 percent went to modernizing Africa's crumbling transport infrastructure. Some of these were no doubt pork barrel projects and white elephants: airports with few passengers, or bridges to nowhere. African presidents, like others, love to cut ribbons and leave legacies of big buildings. Chinese companies will receive nearly all of the contracts to build this Chinese-financed infrastructure. Questions have been raised about its quality. Yet, on the whole, power and transport are investments that boost economic growth. And we found that Chinese loans generally have comparatively low-interest rates and long repayment periods."[41]

China has also been accused of land grab in Africa. This became a particularly widespread concern with the spate of reports in the Western media. However, Prof. Deborah Bräutigam's findings do not agree with the apprehension. "Our team at the International Food Policy Research Institute and at Johns Hopkins University collected a database of 57 cases where Chinese firms (or the government) were alleged to have acquired or negotiated large (over 500 hectares) amounts of African farmland. If all of these media reports had been real news, this would have amounted to a very alarming 6 million hectares—1 percent of all the farmland in Africa. We spent three years tracking down every single case. We traveled from Madagascar to Mozambique, Zimbabwe to Zambia. We confirmed that nearly a third of these stories, including the three above, were literally false. In the remaining cases, we found real Chinese investments. But the total amount of land actually acquired by Chinese firms was only about 240,000 hectares: 4 percent of the reported amount. The stories of large-scale land grabbing and Chinese peasants being shipped to Africa to grow food for China turned out to be mostly myths. As researchers at the Center for International Forestry Research concluded after their own rigorous research, 'China is not a dominant investor in plantation agriculture in Africa, in contrast to how it is often portrayed.' We found a story of globalization, not colonization; a story of African agency, rather than Chinese rapacity."[42]

A FAIRY TALE RELATIONSHIP?

The Africa-China relationship has not been a mirage; nonetheless, it has not been without cause for concern. There are reports of what Xiangming Chen and Garth Myers sum up as "highly negative outcomes of Chinese investments."[43] In Zambia in particular, they cite "low wages, poor working conditions, horrible health and safety conditions, exacerbating inequalities, importation of low-skilled workers and a failure to build backward and forward linkages in Zambia's economic interest"[44] as a drawback to the Africa-China relations.

There have been complaints about the dumping of products by Chinese companies who have the benefit of local subsidy and cheaper cost of production as an aid in delivering cheap products with which they flood the markets in Africa. Apart from being detrimental to local manufacturing, it also worsens the unemployment situation in Africa. But beyond that is the matter of poor-quality Chinese products and knock-off items which are below standard and cannot be exported to Europe and America but are brought into Africa thus short-changing consumers in the continent. Indeed, some challenges have come with increased engagement on the part of the Chinese with Africa. There is the place of low-level Chinese workers brought in as technical expatriates to take the place of locals, but this is not peculiar to the Chinese companies but other foreign companies in Africa. But then there is also the Chinese demand for African ivory, abalone, rhinoceros' tusk and materials from other endangered species which over time has taken a toll on conservation efforts in Africa.[45]

IS CHINA GOOD FOR AFRICA?

There is no clear-cut answer to this, but given evidence of China's level of engagement in only such as short period and the direct impact it is making in the development of infrastructure, the balance does appear to be more in the affirmative. Relative to its early years of providing official foreign aid to Africa almost half a century ago, China now has a much more diversified presence and influence in Africa through both government and private channels or their combination. In helping Africa set up special economic zones, China has transplanted its relatively successful developmental strategy with market-based decisions and investment by its private companies in these zones. Retaining an old focus on infrastructure, China has scaled it up by rehabilitating the 840-mile Benguela railway line that now connects Angola's Atlantic coast with the Democratic Republic of Congo and Zambia. This kind of large-scale infrastructure, which would not have been built without China, has won it some praises.[46]

In Nigeria, China is not only a major trading partner, providing funding for several infrastructure projects from roads, airport renovation, as well as the reconstruction and rehabilitation of the railway system, apart from partnering with the Lagos state government on the Lekki Free Trade Zone and Light Rail projects. It has increased its oil imports from Nigeria as well as investment in the sector, both upstream and downstream, having signed an agreement to construct a refinery at a time. But the latest major development in the Nigeria-China bilateral engagement is the historic Currency Swap Deal entered into by both countries, following President Muhammadu Buhari's visit to China in April 2016. The deal valued at US$2.5bn is aimed at easing foreign exchange liquidity, reducing dollar dependency for transactions involving Nigerians and the Chinese, providing the Naira (the official currency of Nigeria) liquidity to Chinese businesses, and the Renminbi (the official currency of China) liquidity to Nigerian businesses. The question of diversification of Nigeria's foreign reserves has been up for consideration for a while, with the Central Bank of Nigeria announcing a switch in 2011 of "between 5 and 10 percent of its dollar buffers into Yuan as part of plans to diversify the reserves away from the dollar."[47] The extent to which the currency swap will hasten a move in the direction of greater diversification of foreign reserves is a matter of interest.

The question of China's cozy relationship with some African countries, irrespective of human rights abuse and weak democratic credentials, has been a recurring question, especially with Sudan when the world was counting on China to help with the resolution of the crisis in Darfur and act as a responsible power. Even though China itself is high on the rhetoric of peace, citing it as a central feature in its official presentation of its purpose in international affairs even proceeding to place peace-orientation as "the first and foremost characteristic of China-Africa relations"[48] and the Chinese President Hu promising, on his visit to Tanzania in 2009, to "play a constructive role of settling conflicts and maintaining peace and security in Africa."[49]

With nonintervention as a cornerstone of its foreign policy, "China does not present itself to the developing countries as a dominant power, but rather, as a developing country and partner from the South similar interest to that of other developing countries. Its foreign policy is driven by principles of sovereignty, win-win objective, non-interference in the affairs of other states."[50] Of late, China has been paying more attention to finding its place in the peace and security architecture of Africa, aligning itself more with the multilateral vehicles of the United Nations and African Union, while taking bit roles in some peace-keeping missions in different conflict regions in Africa, as it seeks to enhance its role as a more engaged actor in the international arena.

CONCLUSION

China is often lambasted as a nefarious actor in its African dealings, but the evidence tells a more complicated story. Chinese loans are powering Africa, and Chinese firms are creating jobs. China's agricultural investment is far more modest than reported and welcomed by some Africans. China may boost Africa's economic transformation, or they may get it wrong—just as American development efforts often go awry.[51] The fact that Western powers and institutions are being forced to take a second look at their relations with Africa and find means for a better partnership, given increase Chinese engagement, is enough gain for Africa. Both China and the United States of America now host African Heads of States to Summits from time to time. Even if it is yet to hold under President Trump, he hosted African leaders to a working luncheon in September 2017, while they were there for the United Nations meeting, even if the U.S. approach toward Africa seems less embracing and largely unclear under the Trump Administration.

Africa and China had set up the FOCAC as a platform "to give teeth to the new strategic partnership that will take into consideration political equality and mutual trust, economic win-win cooperation and cultural exchanges. Thus, the new strategic partnership which is more inclusive and holistic in approach provides a structure for the establishment of a long-term and stable partnership, a partnership to facilitate the sharing of China's development experiences with countries in the continent, irrespective of the political, economic and ideological system in operation."[52] To some, China's intentions in Africa may not be "completely altruistic, they are also not completely exploitative,"[53] but one of mutual reinforcement, even if both parties might not be completely satisfied.

But that is the nature of international relations. It is all about interests, which are dynamic in form and content, with trade-offs always a part of the bargain. It is up to each party to ensure that its interests are secured and find the means to maximize benefits from the relationship. Africa-China relations leans more in the direction of a partnership with prospects than one of colonialism.

NOTES

1. Ian Taylor. "China's Challenges: Africa." The Diplomat, November 29, 2013. https://thediplomat.com/2011/02/africa.

2. Deborah Bräutigam. "U.S. politicians get China in Africa all wrong," April 12, 2018, accessed from https://www.washingtonpost.com/news/theworldpost/wp/2018/04/12/china-africa/?utm_term=.94b5993d4574, 17th June 2018.

3. Power, Marcus and Giles Mohan. "The Geopolitics of China's Engagement with African Development." The Open University. Paper presented at the POLIS and BISA supported workshop, July 9, 2008. https://www.open.ac.uk/socialsciences/bisa-africa/workshop/mohan_and_ power.pdf.

4. Botha Ilana. China in Africa: Friend or Foe? China's contemporary political and economic relations with Africa, University of Stellenbosch, 2006.

5. Emmanuel Matambo. "The Evolution of China-South Africa Relations: A Constructivist Interpretation," University of KwaZulu-Natal, Pietermaritzburg, South Africa, June 2014.

6. Agbebi, Motolani, and Petri Virtanen. "Dependency Theory—A Conceptual Lens to Understand China's Presence in Africa?" *Forum for Development Studies* 44, no. 3 (2017): 429–451.

7. Robert Keohane and Joseph Nye. "Interdependence in World Politics." In Crane, G.T. & Amawi, A., *The Theoretical Evolution of International Political Economy: A Reader.* New York: Oxford University Press, 1997.

8. Geoffrey York. "Revisiting the History of the High Seas," *The Globe and Mail*, retrieved 2009-03-30.

9. People's Daily, "Children of the master voyager?" November 3, 2006 in *Is China an Empire*, Toh Han Shih, World Scientific, 2017 at Google Books.

10. "Is this young Kenyan Chinese descendant?, China Daily, 2005-07-11, retrieved June 22, 2018.

11. Xiangming Chen & Garth Myers. "China and Africa: The Crucial Urban Connection," December 28, 2013 accessed from http://www.europeanfinancialreview.com/?p=557.

12. Alex Perry. "A Chinese Color War." *TIME.* Retrieved June 17, 2018.

13. Ariyo Adegboyega. "The New Scramble for Africa: Africa-china Engagement," Osita C. Eze and Chike A. Anigbo (eds.), *New Scramble for Africa*, Lagos, NIIA, 2010, p. 132.

14. Tanzania—TANZAM Railway, https://www.globalsecurity.org/military/world/tanzania/tanzam.htm.

15. Jamie Monson. "The unexpected successes of a Cold War development project." December 1, 2004, accessed from http://bostonreview.net/jamie-monson-fre edom-railway-tazara-tanzania.

16. Ibid, Tanzania—TANZAM Railway.

17. Ibid, Xiangming Chen, and Garth Myers.

18. Femi Adesina. "Femi Adesina Reveals How China Took 700 Million People out of Poverty." Vanguard News, June 4, 2018. https://www.vanguardngr.com/2018 /06/femi-adesina-reveals-china-took-700-million-people-poverty/.

19. Ibid.

20. Statistical Review of World Energy, accessed on June 17, 2018 from https ://www.bp.com/en/global/corporate/energy-economics/statistical-review-of-world-e nergy/country-and-regional-insights/china.html.

21. Alli W.O. (2010), "China-African Relations and the Increasing Competition for Access to Africa's Natural Resources," Osita C. Eze and Chike A. Anigbo (eds.), *New Scramble for Africa*, Lagos, NIIA, p. 107.

22. Ibid, Statistical Review of World Energy.

23. Cheru, Fantu and Cyril Obi (2011) De-coding China-Africa Relations: Partnership for development or "(neo) colonialism by invitation"? The World Financial Review September—October 2011, p. 72.

24. Ubi N. Efem (2013), "China and Africa's Development," Bola A. Akinterinwa and Ogaba D. Oche (eds.), *Nigeria-China Dialogue Series: Issues in Contemporary China-Africa Relations*, Lagos, NIIA, p. 123.

25. Ibid.

26. Wenjie Chen and Roger Nord, "China and Africa: Crouching lion, retreating dragon?" Chapter 6, Reassessing Africa's Global Partnerships. Archived from the original (PDF). Retrieved on June 12, 2018.

27. Witney Schneidman and Joel Wiegert. "Competing in Africa: China, the European Union, and the United States." Brookings. Brookings, April 18, 2018. https ://www.brookings.edu/blog/africa-in-focus/2018/04/16/competing-in-africa-china-t he-european-union-and-the-united-states/.

28. Ibid.

29. Ibid.

30. Yun Sun. "China's engagement in Africa: What can we learn in 2018 from the $60 billion commitment?" Chapter 6, Reassessing Africa's Global Partnerships. Archived from the original (PDF). Retrieved on June 12, 2018.

31. Ibid.

32. Ibid.

33. Ibid.

34. Ibid, Xiangming Chen and Garth Myers.

35. Junyi Zhang. "ORDER FROM CHAOS—Chinese foreign assistance, explained," July 19, 2016 retrieved June 19, 2018 from https://www.brookings.edu/ blog/order-from-chaos/2016/07/19/chinese-foreign-assistance-explained/.

36. Ralph Jennings. "China is giving more foreign aid that it gets" accessed on June 24, 2018 from https://www.forbes.com/sites/ralphjennings/2017/12/22/china-is -giving-more-foreign-aid-than-it-gets/#722eca874f35.

37. Ibid.

38. Yun Sun, (February 7, 2014) "China's Aid to Africa: Monster of Messiah?" accessed on June 24, 2018 from https://www.brookings.edu/opinions/chinas-aid-to-africa-monster-or-messiah/.

39. Ibid.

40. Deborah Bräutigam. "U.S. politicians get China in Africa all wrong," April 12, 2018, accessed from https://www.washingtonpost.com/news/theworldpost/wp/2018 /04/12/china-africa/?utm_term=.94b5993d4574, June 17, 2018.

41. Ibid.

42. Ibid.

43. Ibid, Xiangming Chen & Garth Myers.

44. Ibid.

45. Ibid, Deborah Bräutigam.

46. Ibid, Wenjie Chen &Roger Nord.

47. Daily Trust, May 14, 2018 retrieved on June 22, 2018.

48. Charles Dokubo. "China's Role in Conflict Resolution and Management in Africa," Bola A. Akinterinwa and Ogaba D. Oche (eds.), *Nigeria-China Dialogue Series: Issues in Contemporary China-Africa Relations*, Lagos, NIIA, 2013, p. 56.

49. Ibid.

50. Ibid.

51. Ibid, Bräutigam, Deborah, 2018.

52. Ibid.

53. Ibid, Ubi N. Efem.

BIBLIOGRAPHY

Adesina, Femi. "Femi Adesina Reveals How China Took 700 Million People out of Poverty." Vanguard News, June 4, 2018. https://www.vanguardngr.com/2018/06/ femi-adesina-reveals-china-took-700-million-people-poverty/.

"Africa, China Trade," *Financial Times*. Archived from the original (PDF) on 2009-03-11. Retrieved June 19, 2018.

Agbebi, Motolani, and Petri Virtanen. "Dependency Theory—A Conceptual Lens to Understand China's Presence in Africa?" *Forum for Development Studies* 44, no. 3 (2017): 429–51.

Alli, W.O. "China-African Relations and the Increasing Competition for Access to Africa's Natural Resources," Osita C. Eze and Chike A. Anigbo (eds.), *New Scramble for Africa*, Lagos, NIIA. 2010. p.107

Ariyo, Adegboyega. "The New Scramble for Africa: Africa-china Engagement," Osita C. Eze and Chike A. Anigbo (eds.), *New Scramble for Africa*, Lagos, NIIA, 2010, p.132.

Bräutigam, Deborah. *The Dragons Gift: The Real Story of China in Africa*. Oxford: Oxford University Press, 2011.

Bräutigam, Deborah. "U.S. Politicians Get China in Africa All Wrong." The Washington Post. WP Company, April 12, 2018. https://www.washingtonpost.com /news/theworldpost/wp/2018/04/12/china-africa/.

Bräutigam, Deborah. "Opinion | U.S. Politicians Get China in Africa All Wrong." *The Washington Post*. WP Company, April 12, 2018. https://www.washingtonpost.com/news/theworldpost/wp/2018/04/12/china-africa/.

Botha, Ilana. "China in Africa: friend or foe? China's contemporary political and economic relations with Africa." Thesis (MPhil (Political Science), University of Stellenbosch, Western Cape province of South Africa, 2006.

Chen, Wenjie, and Roger Nord. "Reassessing Africa's Global Partnerships." Brookings. Brookings, April 30, 2018. https://www.brookings.edu/research/reassessing-africas-global-partnerships/.

Chen, Xiangming, and Garth Myers. "China and Africa: The Crucial Urban Connection." *The European Financial Review*, December 28, 2013. https://digitalrepository.trincoll.edu/cgi/viewcontent.cgi?article=1100&context=facpub.

Cheru, Fantu, and Cyril Obi. "De-Coding China-Africa Relations: Partnership for Development or '(Neo) Colonialism by Invitation'?" *The World Financial Review*, 2011. https://pdfs.semanticscholar.org/473e/b69b86a11a0bdbd1991a86568c984df31826.pdf.

"Country Insight—China: Energy Economics: Home." BP global. Accessed March 23, 2020. https://www.bp.com/en/global/corporate/energy-economics/statistical-review-of-world-energy/country-and-regional-insights/china.html.

Dokubo, Charles. "China's Role in Conflict Resolution and Management in Africa," Bola A. Akinterinwa and Ogaba D. Oche (eds.), *Nigeria-China Dialogue Series: Issues in Contemporary China-Africa Relations*, Lagos, NIIA, 2013, p. 56.

Hall, Richard, and Hugh Peyman. *The Great Uhuru Railway. Chinas Showpiece in Africa*. London: Gollancz, 1977.

"Is This Young Kenyan Chinese Descendant?" China Daily. Accessed June 22, 2018. http://www.chinadaily.com.cn/english/doc/2005-07/11/content_459090.htm.

Jennings, Ralph. "China Is Giving More Foreign Aid Than It Gets." Forbes. Forbes Magazine, December 22, 2017. https://www.forbes.com/sites/ralphjennings/2017/12/22/china-is-giving-more-foreign-aid-than-it-gets/.

Keohane, Robert O, and Joseph S Nye. "Interdependence in World Politics." In *the Theoretical Evolution of International Political Economy: A Reader*, edited by G T Crane and A. Amawi. New York: Oxford University Press, 1997.

Marcus, Power, and Giles Mohan. "The Geopolitics of China's Engagement with African Development" *New Directions in IR and Africa*, The Open University, Johannesburg, July 9, 2008.

Monson, Jamie. "Freedom Railway: The Unexpected Successes of a Cold War Development Project." *Boston Review*, May 1, 2004. http://bostonreview.net/jamie-monson-freedom-railway-tazara-tanzania.

Matambo, Emmanuel. "The Evolution of China-South Africa Relations: A Constructivist Interpretation," University of KwaZulu-Natal, Pietermaritzburg, South Africa, June 2014.

People's Daily, "Children of the master voyager?" In *Is China an Empire?* Toh Han Shih, World Scientific, 2017.

Perry, Alex. "A Chinese Color War." Time. Time Inc., August 1, 2008. http://content. time.com/time/world/article/0,8599,1828432,00.html.

Power, Marcus, and Giles Mohan. "The Geopolitics of China's Engagement with African Development." The Open University. Paper presented at the POLIS and BISA supported workshop, July 9, 2008. https://www.open.ac.uk/socialsciences/bi sa-africa/workshop/mohan_and_ power.pdf.

Schneidman, Witney, and Joel Wiegert. "Competing in Africa: China, the European Union, and the United States." Brookings. Brookings, April 18, 2018. https://www .brookings.edu/blog/africa-in-focus/2018/04/16/competing-in-africa-china-the-eu ropean-union-and-the-united-states/.

Statistical Review of World Energy, accessed on June 17, 2018 from https://www .bp.com/en/global/corporate/energy-economics/statistical-review-of-world-energy /country-and-regional-insights/china.html.

Sun, Yun. "China's Aid to Africa: Monster or Messiah?" Brookings. Brookings, July 28, 2016. https://www.brookings.edu/opinions/chinas-aid-to-africa-monster -or-messiah/.

Sun, Yun. "China's engagement in Africa: What can we learn in 2018 from the $60 billion commitment?" Chapter 6, Reassessing Africa's Global Partnerships. Archived from the original (PDF). Retrieved on June 12, 2018.

Taylor, Ian. "China's Challenges: Africa." The Diplomat, November 29, 2013. https://thediplomat.com/2011/02/africa.

Ubi N. Efem. "China and Africa's Development," Bola A. Akinterinwa and Ogaba D. Oche (eds.), *Nigeria-China Dialogue Series: Issues in Contemporary China-Africa Relations*, Lagos, NIIA, 2013, p. 123.

Zhang, Junyi. "Chinese Foreign Assistance, Explained." Brookings. Brookings, August 1, 2016. https://www.brookings.edu/blog/order-from-chaos/2016/07/19/c hinese-foreign-assistance-explained/.

Chapter 8

China and Africa

The Beginning of a New World Order or A New Form of Colonialism

Priye S. Torulagha

INTRODUCTION

Since the epic landing of Christopher Columbus in the Americas in 1492 which ushered in the European age of conquest, colonization, and domination, the world has never been the same. As a result, all the modern states in Africa, Latin America, Middle East, and some in Asia are products of European creations. Hence, international relations are primarily influenced by Euro-centric conceptualizations and rationalizations of how the world should operate. Eurocentrism resulted in the predominance of the principle of realism, based on Machiavelli's model of power politics, the reason of state, and expediency, as the basis for international intercourse.[1] It is not by accident that all international economic and financial organizations, including the United Nations (UN), International Monetary Fund (IMF), World Bank (WB), and World Trade Organization (WTO) are dominated by Western nations.

The frustration and anger emanating from the West's capitalistic economic system spawned counter-Western theories of communism, dependency, and neocolonialism. It also led to the hatred of the WB and the IMF by many in the developing countries. The non-Western countries maintain that the global economic and financial systems are designed to exploit and render them underdeveloped and dependent.[2] Then, out of the blue, a sleeping China rose and developed its economy to the extent that it is now the second-largest economy in the world, after the United States of America.[3] As if it is driven by an unknown force to change the economic status quo, China has steadily built economic relationships with African, Latin American, Middle Eastern,

and some European countries to the point, whereby, many developing countries now prefer to do business with it rather than with the West.

The purpose here is to explore the increasing economic and political relationship between China and Africa by accomplishing the following goals:
(1) identify the factors that motivate them to work; together; (2) determine
the nature and characteristics of Chinese investments in Africa: (3) find out
whether African countries are trying to cut their umbilical colonial cord by
moving away from the European/Western sphere of influence; (4) determine
whether China is attempting to effect a paradigm change in international
economic and political relations; (5) find out whether China and African
countries are attempting to create a new world order based on reciprocity
and reject Machiavellian power politics model; and (6) determine whether
Chinese business generosity which includes tremendous loans and major
infrastructural investments is intended to liberate African countries from
Western control or create a dependency that could spawn a new form of
colonialism in the future.

MOTIVATING FACTORS IN POLITICAL
AND ECONOMIC COOPERATION

The increasing economic and political relationship between China and Africa
seems to be motivated by several historical factors that have affected them
both. It might be necessary to identify and analyze them here.

The African Experience in Dealing with the West

First, African contact with the European world started when the Greeks
invaded ancient Egypt. The Greeks conquered and colonized Egypt. In doing
so, they looted, destroyed, and imposed their leaders on Egypt. George James
noted that the numerous written works attributed to many Greek philosophers
and scholars were captured Egyptian writings. Thus, the power struggle
between Africa and Europe began with the Greek colonization of Egypt.[4]
The colonization resulted in the defacement of black African contributions to
Egyptian civilization.

The second major encounter between Africa and Europe by way of the
Atlantic slave trade which resulted in the forceful capture and shipment of
millions of African people to the Americas and parts of Europe. The slave
trade lasted for three centuries, starting from the sixteenth century and ending in the nineteenth century. The Trans-Atlantic Slave Trade Database
showed that about 12. 5 million Africans were transported to the Americas.[5]
However, UNESCO estimated the total number to be twenty-five to thirty

million people.⁶ Major European political leaders and institutions supported the Atlantic slave trade since it was considered as a business investment intended to boost the financial wherewithal of slave tycoons and the economies of their home countries. Hence, the leadership of the Roman Catholic Church issued papal bulls which authorized the Spanish and Portuguese to import slaves from Africa. Likewise, the Treaty of Tordesillas of 1494 led to the demarcation of the globe into the Portuguese and Spanish spheres of influence. This enabled Portugal to gain control of an area stretching from West Africa, starting from Cape Verde in the Atlantic Ocean and extending to the Indian Ocean and Brazil in the Americas. Spain gained the right to control the Mediterranean region, East Africa, and the entire Americas, except Brazil.⁷

Third, the Christian Church contributed greatly in laying the intellectual, religious, and strategic justification for European colonization of the Americas, Africa, the Middle East, and parts of Asia since the Treaty of Tordesillas of 1494 legitimized the Portuguese and Spanish colonization of the non-Christian world. The treaty enabled Spain to become the colonial master of the territory stretching from the tip of the USA to the tip of South America, except Brazil, which colonized by Portugal. Fourth, after the Treaty of Tordesillas of 1494 justified the right of colonial imposition, European powers, during the Berlin Conference (also known as the Congo Conference or West African Conference) of 1884–1885, divided Africa among themselves. Portugal conveyed the conference, but Chancellor Otto von Bismarck of united Germany led the conference. Belgium, Britain, France, Germany, Netherlands, Portugal, and Spain attended the conference. Eventually, Great Britain ended up having to control 30 percent, France 15 percent, Portugal 11 percent, Germany 9 percent, Belgium 7 percent and Italy 1 percent of the African population. However, France had the largest number of colonies, followed by Britain, Portugal, Germany, Belgium, Spain, and later Italy. Germany gave up its colonial possessions after the World War I.⁸ Almost all modern African states, except for Ethiopia and Liberia, were established by European countries.

Fifth, the exploitation of Africa started immediately following colonization since the European powers needed "raw materials to feed the industrial factories of Europe and markets to sell manufactured goods." In many colonies, lands were expropriated and given to Europeans to set up farms, plantations, and mining companies to exploit the resources. African indigenous political systems were trampled, and Eurocentric systems were instituted. The Europeans practiced compulsory labor and forced the indigenes to work in the plantations and mining companies set up to explore and exploit the resources.

To ensure a steady flow of certain raw materials, African farmers were compelled to concentrate on cash crop farming and production of cotton, cocoa, sisal, palm oil, groundnuts, rubber, timber, and so forth. In the Congo, the Belgians were particularly vicious in maltreating the indigenes who did not meet their agricultural production quotas. The price of raw materials was determined by the monopolistic European companies which the colonial authorities permitted to do business in the colonies. This meant that the prices of goods and services were not based on demand and supply but dictated by the buyers and the producers had no choice but to sell at those prices. Likewise, African traders were not allowed to trade their goods directly in foreign markets since they were compelled to sell their products to the monopolistic companies.[9]

Sixth, to finance economic activities in the colonies, expatriate banks were set up by the citizens of the colonial powers. Generally, the banks discriminated against African businesses, thereby, making it difficult for them to compete with the Europeans. Also, Africans were not allowed to engage in mining. Only the expatriates and their companies could. Due to the intolerable nature of the colonial system, indigenous opposition started to take root. The African people rebelled against the colonial system in five stages. The first stage involved the period starting from the 1890s to 1918, the second stage of rebellion started from 1919 to 1935, the third stage took place from 1935 to 1960, the fourth stage started from the 1960s to the 1980s, and the fifth stage started from the 1980s to the present,[10] whereby, African countries are attempting to reduce their volume of business engagement with Western nations while increasing business activities with China and other Third World countries.

Seventh, the Cold War which existed from 1945 to 1990 between the United States and the Soviet Union was fought at the backs of Africans, Asians, and Latin Americans. The Cold War resulted in the staging of military coups, the instigation of separatist and irredentist movements, and armed rebellions that retarded political and economic development in the continent. Thus, leaders such as Kwame Nkrumah of Ghana, Patrice Lumumba of the Democratic Republic of the Congo, Sylvanus Olympio of Togo, Milton Obote of Uganda, and a host of other African leaders were either overthrown or killed through external instigation.

Eighth, perhaps, for strategic reasons, Western nations have been unwilling to create an enabling economic environment that allows African countries to move from being mere producers of raw materials to become the producers of finished industrial goods. For instance, when Ghana gained independence in 1957. President Kwame Nkrumah wanted to develop the economy. Hence, Ghana looked for Western assistance in building the Volta Dam. Through the efforts of the U.S. government, in 1958, Kaiser Industries accepted to build a smelter that would rely on electricity generated by the Volta Dam. Ghana obtained a $30m loan from the WB in 1960 to finance the dam. However, the conditions stipulated for executing the project and Cold War politics resulted in mismanagement, cost-overruns, and corruption, so much so that the project became a political albatross for President Nkrumah.[11] Another example is Nigeria which wanted to build a steel mill to jump-start the industrialization of the country. Nigeria sought assistance in building the mill from Britain, the United States, Germany, and Canada without succeeding. It was a company in the Soviet Union named TYAZHPROMEXPORT (TPE) which did the feasibility study and helped in constructing the Ajaokuta Steel Mill.[12]

Likewise, throughout the continent, many African countries were ill-advised by Western nations to build capital-intensive industrial projects that ended up mired in corruption and mismanagement. The failed industrial projects contributed to the massive debt that many African countries incurred in the 1970s and 1980s. The debt enabled the IMF to institute Structural Adjustment Programs (SAP) which further sapped away the financial resources of the continent.[13] In particular, France seems unwilling to let go and continues to have a considerable influence on Francophone Africa. As a result, it continues to maintain its seventy-four-year old two currency policy where eight African countries are placed under the West African Economic and Monetary Union while six others are placed under the Central African Economic and Monetary Community. Through this mechanism, France imposes its currency on the fourteen African countries and expect them to deposit 50 percent of its foreign exchange reserves with the Bank of France.[14]

The Italian Deputy Prime Minister Luigi Di Maio made a very revealing statement when he criticized French policy in Africa for causing underdevelopment and poverty, thereby, forcing many Africans to migrate to Europe as economic refugees. He called upon the European Union to address the issue of decolonization of Africa.[15] Ninth Sub-Saharan Africans (blacks) seem to suffer the most from racism in the world. Therefore, racism could be partially responsible for the lukewarm attitude in the West toward assisting the industrialization and modernization of African economies. Perhaps, the need to avoid racism might be a motivating factor in compelling African states to do more business with China, due to a growing belief that the Chinese are more likely to work cooperatively with African countries to develop and modernize the continent.

CHINA'S EXPERIENCE IN DEALING WITH THE WEST

China's desire to do business with Africa, the Middle East, and Latin America seems to have been motivated by nine circumstances, as indicated below: First, China's painful experience in dealing with European/Western nations continues to haunt the soul of the Chinese nation. It should be recalled that China was a proud empire that contributed to human civilization in so many ways and dominated the South East region of Asia for centuries. Then, in the eighteenth century, European nations led by Britain encouraged and supported the opium trade. Due to the profitability of the trade, traders from Portugal, France, and the United States also got involved. Between 1790 and 1832, thousands, if not millions of Chinese got addicted to the drug. The Chinese emperor decided to stop the epidemic of addiction by banning the selling and buying of opium in the country in 1836. Britain reacted militarily, resulting in the First Opium War (1839 to 1842). China suffered defeat and had to sign the Treaty of Nanjing on August 29, 1842, which opened ports in Guangzhou, Xiamen, Fuzhou, Ningbo, and Shanghai to Western trading. It allowed Hong Kong to become a British colony. Distrust, disagreements and missteps led to the seizure of a British ship (Arrow) in 1856. This led to the Second Opium War in which the British captured Guangzhou, Dagu forts, and Tianjin. This forced China to sign the Tianjin Treaty in June 1858, which opened ten more ports to foreign traders and allowed Christian missionaries to go into the interior of the country. China also signed treaties with France, the United States, and Russia. Russia took a large chunk of territory from China.[16]

Second, it should also be noted that while China was grappling with the opium situation, in 1848, Mr. Robert Fortune, a Briton working for the British India Company, was sent to steal the secrets of tea production.[17] He succeeded in doing so and helped to establish the tea industry in British India, thereby, undercutting the Chinese monopoly of the industry. Third, the tide of history changed when Japan emerged as a regional military and technological power after it defeated Russia in 1905. Thereafter, Japan transformed itself as an imperial nation and invaded Manchuria in September 1931 on the pretext that the Chinese army had wrecked a railway line and killed a Japanese. The other explanation was that Japan invaded Manchuria because it needed territorial expansion to accommodate its burgeoning population and to acquire resources to feed its industrial machines. The Chinese viewed Japanese occupation and maltreatment during the World War II as a humiliation. Therefore, it is inferable that China's rapid development of the economy, science, and technology is a product of the desire to catch up and become a dominant force in the world.

Fourth, China too suffered from the effects of the Cold War which was fought by the United States and the Soviet Union after the World War II. China became a victim of the Cold War because Mao Zedong and his communist comrades fought a revolutionary war against the Nationalist Government of General Chiang Kai Shek. The Nationalist Government was supported by the United States and the Chinese communists were supported by the Soviet Union. The communists prevailed over the nationalists in 1949.

General Chiang Kai Shek and his supporters fled to Taiwan and established the Republic of China (ROC) and the communist took over mainland China and established the Peoples Republic of China (PRC). Communist China and the Soviet Union signed an alliance treaty in 1950. The United States and its Western allies refused to recognize the Communist Government of China and continued to treat the government of Chiang Kai Shek as the legitimate government of China.[18] On the other hand, the Soviet Union and its allies recognized the PRC as the authentic government of China. Thus, throughout the 1950s, 1960s, and 1970s, there were two Chinas—the People's Republic of China and the ROC in Taiwan.

Fifth, China felt humiliated and treated disrespectfully even at the UN since the United States and its Western allies refused to allow the PRC to replace the ROC (Taiwan) at the UN. It should be noted that the ROC was a founding member of the UN and served as a permanent member of the Security Council since October 24, 1945. However, having won the civil war against the nationalists, the communists expected the People's Republic of China to replace the Republic of China. This did not take place until 1971 when Communist China finally replaced the ROC in the UN. Today, the ROC is no longer a member of the UN. Sixth, after successfully overthrowing a regime that was supported by the United States, the United States and its allies used the UN to intervene in the Korean War which began in 1950, after North Korea had invaded South Korea. The United States and its allies supported South Korea and China and the Soviet Union supported North Korea. The Korean conflict enabled the United States to maintain troops in South Korea, thereby, compelling China and North Korea to build up their military forces.

Seventh, having succeeded beyond bounds in massively transforming its economy into the modern age, China now needs inexhaustible amounts of raw materials to feed its industries. Since Africa is endowed with vast natural resources, China has made a strategic decision to establish a political and economic relationship with African countries. Eighth, like Black Africans and blacks in general, the Chinese too suffered from racism perpetrated by the West. It should be noted that many Chinese who worked in various parts of the Western world were treated like slaves even though they were indentured servants. The Chinese were made to do menial back-breaking jobs that whites would not do. This was particularly the case in the United States during the building of railway lines in the West. Likewise, the Chinese were discriminated against and forced to live in China towns just like blacks were forced to live in black towns. Chinese rights were easily violated just as black rights in the Americas. These factors seem to provide the impetus for China and Africa to eagerly establish a mutual relationship. They share humiliating experiences in dealing with the West, even though Africans had the worst of it with the slave trade, colonialism, and neocolonialism.

THE NATURE OF CHINA'S INVESTMENT IN AFRICA

Chinese and African political and economic relationship seems particularly propelled by the need to fill a void left by European/Western nations. China's business relationship with African countries tends to focus on fundamental economic areas that European/Western powers declined to focus upon in their economic relationship with African states. In other words, Western nations have been very strategic and tactical in dealing with African countries. They have never been eager to invest in areas that are essential for turning African countries into producers of finished goods. The *US Congressional Research Service* noted, "China often promotes economic projects in countries, areas, and sectors that developed country governments and multinational corporations have avoided because they have determined them to be unfriendly, too arduous, or infeasible."[19]

As a result, China's approach to foreign development assistance is markedly different from the traditional Western approach which is typical of the Official Development Assistance (ODA) program, as defined by the Organization for Economic Co-operation and Development. China's foreign assistance program is less focused on military and security-related items as the traditional ODA format.[20] Similarly, Western nations, have never been sincerely interested in investing in substantive infrastructural development projects that are capable of enabling African countries to provide accessible mass transportation system to the teaming African population, as well as provide a means to move goods from various parts of the countries to markets at a reduced time and cost. The reason is that most roads and railway lines that the former colonial powers built were directed at transporting raw materials and not necessarily at easing public transportation.[21]

Apparently, after decades of bitter experiences dealing with the West, many African leaders decided to look toward China as an alternative to the capitalistic system. It appears that China too has been eager to establish relations with Africa to counteract Western dominance of the world's economic system. Therefore, areas of African and Chinese economic cooperation can be broken down into the following: (1) infrastructural development, ((2) industrial projects, (30 financial investments in the form of loans, (4) trade, and (5) Chinese aid.

Infrastructural Development

African countries wanted more than merely serving as agricultural plantations to feed the industrial machines of Western countries. Hence, African leaders have found an alternative partner in China. Owei Lakemfa explained the African experience:

They turned to the European countries beginning with Britain to assist with the railway construction. They were turned down as did then Soviet Union. Then, China was also an underdeveloped country, but out of frustration, Nyerere during his February 1965 visit to China, raised the issue and surprisingly, China committed itself. In a follow up visit by Kaunda. In June 1967, China agreed to the construction. Then, Chinese leader, Mao Tse-Tung said given the need for total African liberation and African development, China would build the railway even it meant his country suspending some of its own development projects.[22]

Eventually, China, Tanzania, and Zambia signed an agreement for the construction of the 1,860-kilometer transnational railway line that connects Dar es Salaam, the capital of Tanzania with Kapri Mposhi in Zambia in July 1976. The railway project was completed in 1969 and involved an interest-free loan of 988 million RMB Yuan from China. Since that fateful railway project, China and African countries have signed numerous contracts for major infrastructural development projects. On January 1, 2018, the Chinese constructed 754-kilometer Addis Ababa to Djibouti standard gauge railway line was opened. The rail line is helping to facilitate the movement of Ethiopian goods from the interior to the coast much faster, thereby, increasing trade. The Chinese built Abuja Rail Mass Transit system in Nigeria was opened in July 2018. The Chinese also built the Abuja- to Kaduna railway line, while the Lagos to Ibadan railway line is under construction. The Chinese are also building the Ajaokuta-Kaduna-Kano pipeline project that would enable Nigeria to move gas easily across the country.[23] It is doubtful whether any Western country would have agreed to build a major infrastructural development project in Africa with an interest-free loan.

Industrial Development

China's industrial engagement in Africa is focused on energy, mining, telecommunications industries, road and railway construction, technical assistance, public health, public works, and scholarships for African students to study in China. Other industrial activities include industrial parks, power plants, optical cable networks, port facilities, hydropower, dam construction, offshore oil development, medical training, public buildings, and light industry.[24]

Financial Investments

In terms of financial investment, China is providing loans to African countries at a much-reduced rate than Western countries. Chinese loans are very attractive to African leaders because they are devoid of the torturous bureaucratic processes and high-interest rates that are typical of Western loans. This means that an African country can obtain a Chinese loan without having to wait endlessly and surmount political and legal impediments that. The Chinese eagerness to do business with Africa was demonstrated in December 2015 during the China-Africa summit in Johannesburg in South Africa when China announced a $60bn funding for infrastructural development projects in Africa.[25] After the declaration, many African countries have been able to obtain more loans from China.

Eleanor Albert of the U.S. *Council of Foreign Relations* noted that "Between 2000 and 2014, Chinese banks, contractors, and the government loaned more than $86 billion to Africa, according to the China Africa Research Initiative at the Johns Hopkins University School of Advanced International Studies (SAIS-CARI). Angola, the Democratic Republic of Congo (DRC), Ethiopia, Kenya, and Sudan were the top recipients."[26] China's major financial banks that provide loans and investment funds include the People's Bank of China, the China Development Bank, the Export–Import Bank of China, and the China-Africa Development Fund.[27]

Trade for Resources and Goods

Trade between Africa and China is booming as both seek to satisfy their mutual needs. Africa needs investment loans, technical assistance for infra-structural and industrial development while China needs resources to feed its vast economic stomach. As a result, 15 to 16 percent of Sub-Saharan African exports now go to China. In return, 14 to 21 percent of the region's imports now come from China. Africa exports minerals, raw materials, food, and agricultural products while China exports machinery, transportation, com-munication equipment, and manufactured goods. Due to increasing trade, China has surpassed the United States as Africa's largest trading partner.[28] The General Administration of Customs of China noted that between January and August 2018, the total volume of trade between China and Africa was US$134.15bn. During the period, China's total exports were worth US$68.54bn, while its total imports from Africa were US$65.62 bn. Thus, between January and August 2018, China's trade with Africa was the highest in the world.[29] Thus, for nine years now, China has been the greatest trading partner with Africa.[30]

China's Aid to Africa

China offers development and humanitarian aid to Africa also. Aid comes in the form of the building of schools and hospitals, the provision of medical training, debt cancellations, grants, technical assistance, food aid, disaster assistance, concessional loans, and export credits. In the 2002–2007 period, the estimated value of aid amounted to about US33$bn.[31]

SEVERING COLONIAL CORD, THE NEED FOR BENEFICIAL RELATIONS

It appears that African countries are trying very hard to cut their umbilical cord from their former colonial masters. The reason is that their European creators seem to treat them like vassals that must be kept as prisoners of war. Hence, they do not see the need for African countries to develop industrially and become producers of finished goods. First, during the 1960s, 1970s, and 1980s, Western countries routinely overthrew progressive African leaders who were bent on developing and modernizing their countries. Some of the saddest experiences of the African states included the killing of Patrice Lumumba of DRC, the overthrow of Kwame Nkrumah, the French hostile attitude toward Guinea for refusing to join the French community, the assassination of Dr. Eduardo Chivambo Mondlane, President Samora Machel, and the sudden death of Capt. Thomas Sankara. The most recent being the killing of Muammar Gaddafi and the destabilization of Libya, thereby, turning a once prosperous oil-producing state into a failed state. Sadly, the DRC has not recovered from the killing of Lumumba, as armed insurrection has become part of the political culture, even though the Congo basin is one of the richest regions of the world.

Second, human rights violations are often used tactically to intervene in the continent. Generally, when a leader is viewed as being antagonistic to the strategic interest of the former colonial power, human rights violations are leveled against him to remove him from power. On the other hand, an African leader who is friendly to the former colonial power is rarely overthrown or condemned for human rights violations. Similarly, human rights violations have been used on numerous occasions to drag African leaders or political leaders to face charges at the International Criminal Court (ICC). Thus, since the creation of the ICC, more Africans have been dragged to that court than from any other region of the world. On the other hand, despite the atrocities that have been perpetrated in Afghanistan, Iraq, Syria, and Yemen, not a single individual has been arrested and taken to the ICC to stand trial for war crimes or human rights violations.

Third, another common tool for intervening in the continent is through election monitoring. There is no part of the world in which elections are monitored as much as in Africa. Quite often, leaders who are favorable to the former colonial powers remain untouched, regardless of the degree of election rigging. On the other hand, African leaders who are not favorable to the former colonial leaders are constantly criticized and often compelled to vacate their positions. Thus, leaders such as Paul Biya of Cameroon, Teodoro Obiang Nguema of Equatorial Guinea, and Idris Deby of Chad are rarely criticized for remaining in power endlessly while leaders like Robert Mugabe, Muammar Gaddafi were constantly criticized. Eventually, Muammar Gaddafi was forced out through a staged rebellion and he lost his life. Mugabe was replaced in an internal bloodless coup in November 2017.

Fourth, the unspoken word is that Africa is the ground for testing and dumping of biochemical products. The first such case was France's testing of its atomic bombs in Algeria in 1960, thereby, spreading radiation and causing severe medical problems in Africa.[32] It is speculated that HIV/AIDS and Ebola viruses are by-products of research experiments carried out by the industrialized countries and tested in Africa to determine their effects on human beings. The rumor was intensified by the speediness in which Africa was attributed as the source of the HIV/AIDS virus by Western scientists, even without corroborating evidence to show a direct linkage.[33]

Almost all African countries experience foreign intervention in one form or another that makes them incapable of rising economically. In particular, the Francophone countries seemed to be the most severely affected because many of them have their currencies tied to the French franc and the Bank of France. Thus, there is a perception that if the continent is to rise as expected, the leaders must seek alternative economic arrangements that would allow them to grow. Therefore, many African leaders are eager to do business with China while tactically moving away from the Western economic orbit. Former Senegalese President Abdoulaye wrote "China, which has fought its own battles to modernize, has a much greater sense of the present urgency of development in Africa than many western nations."[34]

Also, the Western media have been particularly hostile to Africa. As if there is a secret agreement that nothing good should be reported about Africa, positive developments in the continent are rarely reported while negative developments are constantly spread. Therefore, most Western citizens, including a considerable number of political and educated elites, know very little about Africa. Due to the negativity, many Africans in the diaspora try to respond to the extreme Western negativity by saying that there are two Africas; the one that is portrayed in the West and the real Africa. The real Africa is moving ahead while the one portrayed in the West never changes and is embedded in Tarzanic typecasting. Africa is often portrayed as a continent of squalor, pestilence, and sorrow, yet, history shows that the bloodiest and most destructive wars have taken place in Europe and not in Africa. Europe had a period in history known as the "Dark Ages." The Bubonic Plague took millions of lives in Europe and not in Africa, yet, historical facts are turned upside down. This accounts for why African leaders seem to be moving away from the West.

EFFECTING PARADIGM SHIFT

China seems determined to change the world economic system. It wants to create an economic order in which the European/Western world is no longer the most dominant force in international relations. To do so, it is redefining economic relationships in a manner that is removed from the Machiavellian style where the buyer determines the price of raw materials while the seller determines the price of finished goods. China is consciously applying a communalistic model to woo and create friendship by informing the world that business can be mutually beneficial. As a result, it makes friends with other nations readily and responds to their economic needs by being easily accessible for negotiations.

China is willing to provide loans with little or no condition attached and sign contracts to carry out major construction projects in a short duration. On the other hand, it generally takes much longer to complete business negotiations with Western nations. Likewise, while the United States and its Western allies prefer to provide transfer of "cash and materiel," China prefers to provide export credits and loans for infrastructure development with little or no interest. Western nations tend to attach many conditions with high interests that seemed exploitative.[35] Due to its business practices, it is inferable that China is determined to affect a paradigm change in international economic and political relations. For instance, in Latin America, China is providing loans and engaging in infrastructure development that can enhance the economies of the region. Hence, Ariel Armony and Enrique D. Peters stated:

> Thanks to Beijing's loans, Chinese corporations are building dams and hydro-electric power plants in the Amazon and Patagonia. They are laying thousands of kilometers of rail to reduce freight transportation costs and connect populations in Brazil, Peru and Venezuela. China's development banks are even financing a state-of-the-art nuclear energy plant in Argentina.[36]

China's active involvement in the development and modernization of the economies of Latin America and the Caribbean (LAC) began in the 1990s. China became greatly involved in financing direct investments in LAC. As a result, in January 2018, Chinese Foreign Minister Wang Yi met with thirty-three representatives of the two regions and invited them to join the Belt and Road Initiative (BRI). The BRI is an infrastructural development plan which is intended to connect China with its Asian neighbors.[37]

Likewise, Middle Eastern countries are also strategically aligning with China since it has veto power at the UN. The view in the Arab world is that China could help to tip the balance, thereby, increasing the political value of the Arab world in the UN. The Arab strategy is to use China as an alternative ally to the United States and Russia, thereby, compelling the United States and Russia to work much harder in establishing strategic alliances in the region. Saudi Arabia and China are already working cooperatively in many economic and technology-related areas, including space exploration.[38] The rapid rate of Chinese development, coupled with the China-Africa Forum and the BRI is intended on changing the world dramatically, away from the West and toward the East.

It is also arguable that a paradigm shift is taking place, hence, the U.S. Secretary of Commerce Wilbur Ross teamed up with U.S. Senator Chris Coons to write an opinion piece, in which they acknowledged the inroads China is making in Africa. They seem to view China's successes as a threat to the national security of the United States. As a result, they urged the United States to be more proactive in ensuring its leadership in promoting economic growth and prosperity in the world.[39] The U.S. Congressman, Gerald Connally also views China's active role in Africa as a threat to the U.S. national interest.[40]

THE REJECTION OF MACHIAVELLIAN POWER

While there are no concrete facts to support the view that China and African countries want to create a new world order, their intentions and actions seem to go in that direction. These countries have dealt with the Western-oriented international economic system for decades. Throughout the decades, their economies did not see any remarkable growth because of the inhibitive structures that hinder their development. The tactical roadblocks led many countries to opt for socialist and communist systems to move away from the Western orbit in 1960, the 1970s, and 1980s. It also led to the view that developing countries would never move forward because their economies are designed to depend upon the advanced countries rather than encouraging economic independence.[41] The following circumstances and actions indicate a trend toward a new global economic direction.

First, it could be said that African countries and China are determined to change the pattern of economic relationships in the world. For instance, between 2001 and 2011, the United States promised about US$90bn in aid to African countries, but the Africans preferred Chinese aid instead. Hence, China committed US$75bn in aid to the African continent during the same period.[42] Second, it seems that African countries are determined to reduce their business ties with the West, in the hope of changing the dog-eat-dog power politics. Perhaps, this accounted for why African countries encourage Chinese businesses to thrive in the continent. As a result, by April 2018, Nigeria had 404 projects that were being carried out by 240 Chinese companies, South Africa had 280 projects being carried out by 152 Chinese companies, Zambia had 273 projects involving 125 Chinese companies, Ethiopia had 258 projects being executed by 114 Chinese companies, Egypt had 197 projects being executed by 99 Chinese firms, the Democratic Republic of the Congo had 193 projects being carried out by 80 Chinese firms, Ghana had 192 projects that were executed by 90 Chines companies, Angola had 189 projects that 80 Chinese firms were executing, Zimbabwe had 167 ongoing projects being executed by 68 Chinese companies, and Tanzania had 149 projects that Chinese firms were working on.[43]

Third and interestingly, even Francophone African countries that generally have a special relationship with France are also consciously developing a relationship with China. In April 2018, Algeria had 123 projects that were being carried out by seventy-five Chinese firms, Cameroon had sixty projects with Chinese affiliations, Gabon had seventy-one projects being carried out by twenty-three Chinese companies, Mali had sixty-eight projects that were being executed by thirty-three Chinese firms, and Mauritius had sixty-five projects that were being executed by forty Chinese companies.[44]

Fourth, it is inferable, based on the increasing economic relationship between African and China that new world order is gradually taking place, from a power-politics-driven form of a free-market enterprise system to one of mutual sharing based on a mixed economic system. It seems that a communal relationship is taking place between China and Africa because both societies have communal cultural systems where working together, sharing, and planning together are encouraged. The Chinese are communalistic because they have an ancestral-based family system of societal arrangement that is like African communalism. Therefore, there is cultural compatibility between the way Chinese and Africans think about economic and political relationships. On the other hand, Europeans/Westerners do not seem very comfortable with a communal system of social and economic arrangement since they are more oriented toward the rational-legal model of economic and political relationships based on individualism.

Fifth, China and Africa, using the communal cultural system, are introducing into the world the view that an economic relationship with mutual benefits can take place simultaneously between economic partners without one partner attempting to exploit the other in the characteristic Western-driven system which is always intended to result in a win/loss formula. As a result, for the first time, African countries are getting what they want in terms of infrastructural development that might help to transform their economies fundamentally. This is why the vice chairman of China Council for the Promotion of International Trade, Chen Zhou explained: "China and African countries are highly complementary in resources and technology and new cooperation platforms such as the Forum on China-Africa Cooperation (FOCAC) have Injected impetus into bilateral economic collaboration."[45]

Sixth, it is also arguable that the power-politics-driven Western international economic system was designed to encourage the nonindustrialization of the African economy. This is buttressed by the fact that even Western Transnational Corporations (TNC) that would have helped to transform Africa have been primarily interested in only exploiting the resources and recycling wealth back to the West. Their business practices are inimical to domestic industries and agricultural enterprises.[46] Seventh, colonialism was foisted upon Africa by European powers. However, it was communist and socialist countries that assisted some colonies to gain independence. The communists supported African liberation movements to gain independence in Algeria, Angola, Guinea-Bissau, Mozambique, Namibia, South Africa, and Zimbabwe (former Rhodesia). China was part of the groups of communist nations that supported African liberation, while the Western tactically supported the status quo.

Eighth, to usher a new economic order, China and African countries have established the FOCAC. The forum has held two meetings, one in South Africa and the other in China. Most African countries attended the second forum which took place in China from September 3 to 4, 2018. The Forum is expected to increase political and business cooperation between Africa and China. Ninth, China, and other Asian countries have the China-Northeast Asia Expo. This conference has taken place eleven times since it was inaugurated.[47] Thus, the FOCAC is based on the China-Northeast Asia Expo model. Both are designed to ensure economic cooperation.

Tenth, the fact that China is not only interested in changing the paradigm in political and economic relations but also wants to lead the world as evidenced by its massive scientific and technological development.[48] Consequently, it is building, updating, and expanding its military technology to the point where it would be able to defend its geopolitical interest anywhere in the world. Perhaps, to match and probably outpace the United States and Russia in space exploration, it successfully landed a craft on the moon. The most outstanding part of this landing was that China decided to land its spacecraft on the moon's far side.[49]

Eleventh, the strongest indication that China wants to be the foremost world power soon is the fact that it is building the world's largest telescope[50] to facilitate a better understanding of the universe. It probably wants to be the leader in space exploration. Sensing the possibility that China could become the world's leading superpower, Finian Cunningham wrote: "China has not just made an historic landing on the moon, it has also given notice that the country is set to become a global leader in technology and science."[51] Indeed, Chinese industrial development is comprehensive, involving manufacturing, military build-up, space technology, computer technology, agriculture, and science.

GENEROSITY AND THE DANGER OF INDEBTEDNESS AND DEPENDENCY

To comprehend the concerns being expressed over China's generosity toward granting loans to African countries, it is necessary to define "politics." Politics is generally defined as "deciding who gets what when and how?"[52] It is obvious from the definition that politics connotes a struggle for power over the control and distribution of government, resources, goods, and services. This happens because resources are always scarce, while the demand for them is always high. States are like people, in the sense that they compete in the global arena to maximize their self-interest and ensure their existence. Therefore, international politics is generally characterized as being anarchic.[53] Since international politics is chaotic and competitive, why does China seem so generous to African countries by providing massive financial loans and engaging in major infrastructural projects? Is China doing so because it is a generous nation or is there other motives behind the perceived generosity? Indeed, some critics are increasingly worried that there is an ulterior motive behind China's generosity since international politics has never been known to be altruistic or philanthropic.

POTENTIAL INDEBTEDNESS

Sensing a potential debt problem, the IMF noted that in 2012, 12 percent of Sub-Saharan Africa's total debt was owed to China.[54] McKinsey & Co. estimated that in 2015, a third of debt owned by African countries was to China. Djibouti, a country of barely one million people, took a loan of $1.4bn from China within two years. China used that opportunity to establish a military base in the country.[55] Djibouti is now providing military bases to the United States of America and China.

China's foreign aid seems to be tied to its development in the form of exchanging assistance for raw materials. The *U.S. Congressional Research Service* noted that "China's aid projects to a large extent serve its own development needs, facilitating the export of raw materials to China, and requiring that 50% of project materials and services are to be sourced in the PRC.[56] This approach is different since Western nations generally do not tie assistance programs directly with their economies. Worried by the unprecedented debt that African countries are owing to China, the Emir of Kano, Lamido Sanusi, the former governor of the Central Bank of Nigeria, expressed concern that China's presence in Africa could result in a new form of imperialism.[57]

Indeed, Chinese generosity seems to arouse suspicion that it is designed to trap and render African countries dependent upon China in the foreseeable future.

Consequently, some observers view the relationship as a new form of imperialism, whereby, China will eventually become the colonial master of the continent. The *China Daily* inadvertently described the enormity of the loans when it noted: "Over the past decade China has become an important investor in Africa, with a total investment of more than $100 billion, ranging from infrastructure, mining, telecommunications to agriculture and manu-facturing."[58] The ease with which China doles out loans to African countries raises an alarm bell. For instance, during the China-Africa summit in Beijing, Chinese President Xi Jinping offered an additional sum of $60bn to Africa. To douse suspicion, he stated that Chinese loans and other financial assis-tance to African countries are intended to yield mutual benefits to both sides. He explained:

China does not interfere in Africa's internal affairs and does not impose its will on Africa. What we value is the sharing of development experience and the sup-port we can offer to Africa's national rejuvenation and prosperity.[59]

However, African leaders do not seem bothered by the fact that they are taking on too much loan in a rush without thinking about the consequences. In 2017 alone, African countries engaged Chinese companies to execute projects totaling $76.5bn, according to Jeremy Stevens of the Standard Bank in China.[60] It is estimated that about 40 percent of low-income countries in the continent, including Chad, Eritrea, Mozambique, Congo Republic, South Sudan, and Zimbabwe are already in debt distress while Zambia and Ethiopia are of a high risk of debt distress. Even Nigerians are worried that their coun-try is becoming a debtor nation as the country continues to borrow. During the 2018 China-Africa Forum, President Muhammadu Buhari of Nigeria signed agreements and Memorandum of Understanding with Chinese com-panies involving thirteen projects that worth $10bn.[61]

Despite the increasing African debt to China, Rwandan President Paul Kagame and President Cyril Ramaphosa of South Africa disagreed with the notion that African countries might suffer from the debt trap.[62] Nigeria's director-general of Debt Management Office (DMO), Ms. Patience Oniha, confidently informed journalists that the Federal Government of Nigeria "is on top of the situation in the borrowing plans." She added that Nigeria does not experience "inability to service debt."[63] Nevertheless, the IMF listed "vulnerability to foreign debt as one of the major threats to economic growth amongst African countries, especially in the Sub-Saharan group which includes Nigeria."[64] Concerned about over-borrowing and high cost-led Sierra Leone to suspend the construction of the Mamamah International Airport that was initiated by former President Ernest Bai Koroma and financed by China Exim Bank.[65] Joining the chorus of African personalities who have raised concerns about the possibility of African indebtedness to China, a notable Nigerian lawyer, Femi Falana, argued that it was unnecessary for African leaders who attended the China-Africa Forum in Beijing to seek $60bn loans from China. Instead, he suggested that they should stop the illegal transferring of $100bn annually from Africa to other parts of the world.[66]

A POTENTIAL NEW WORLD ORDER

Overall, it is inferable that Africa's relationship with China is different from Africa's relationship with the West. European nations came to Africa to conquer and colonize to exploit the people and the resources while China came to Africa to establish a mutual economic relationship. Thus, African leaders are voluntarily establishing a relationship with China while African leaders did not voluntarily sign any contract to allow European colonization. However, there is a great danger that the continent could be trapped by indebtedness, thereby, resulting in Chinese colonization. Apart from indebtedness, cultural and racial differences could generate animosity. Already, tension is rising in some countries as some Chinese workers have been alleged to display racist attitudes toward Africans, as had happened in Kenya.[67] If African leaders fail to use this great opportunity to carry out substantive economic development, the continent would be doomed. It is essential to stop the looting of public funds by public officials.

Indeed, China's supposed financial generosity, not only to Africa but also to Latin American and other Asian countries can lead to indebtedness. Such a development could have a boomerang effect that negatively impacts the world economy. Venezuela's political and economic problems are a reminder of what could happen in any developing country. China must exercise caution in rushing to outspend and outpace the West so that it does not repeat the mistakes of the Great Leap Forward which ended disastrously. Indeed, just as there is a great danger in massive African borrowing from

China, there is also a great danger in China's rush to outpace the world. Whether for good or bad, a new economic order is taking place in the world. Regardless, a new world order is emerging. The emerging world is shifting the pendulum from the West toward an Afro-Asiatic one with China at the center.

NOTES

1. James H. Wolfe. *Modern International Law: An Introduction to the Law of Nations.* Upper Saddle River, NJ: Prentice Hall, 2008.

2. James Lee Ray, and Juliet Kaarbo. *Global Politics.* Boston: Houghton Mifflin, 2005.

3. Albert Eleanor. "China in Africa." Council on Foreign Relations. Council on Foreign Relations, July 12, 2017. https://www.cfr.org/backgrounder/china-africa.

4. George James G. M. *Stolen Legacy: Greek Philosophy Is Stolen Egyptian Philosophy.* Drewryville, VA: Khalifahs Booksellers & Associates, 2005, 1–5

5. Henry Louis Gates, Jr., "The African Americans: Many Rivers to Cross." PBS. Public Broadcasting Service, May 1, 2017. https://www.pbs.org/show/african-am ericans-many-rivers-cross/.

6. "Transatlantic Slave Trade: United Nations Educational, Scientific and Cultural Organization." Social and Human Sciences. March 21, 2017. http://www.unesco.org/ new/en/social-and-human-sciences/themes/slave-route/transatlantic-slave-trade/.

7. Nazeer Ahmed. "The Atlantic Slave Trade." History of Islam, March 22, 2017. http://historyofislam.com/contents/onset-of-the-colonial-age//the-atlantic-slave -trade/.

8. Ateki Seta Caxton. "The Anglophone Dilemma in Cameroon: The Need for Comprehensive Dialogue and Reform." ACCORD. The African Centre for the constructive Resolution of Disputes, July 21, 2017. https://www.accord.org.za/conf lict-trends/anglophone-dilemma-cameroon/.

9. Albert Adu Boahen. *African Perspectives on Colonialism.* Baltimore, MD: Johns Hopkins Univ. Press, 1987.

10. Ibid.

11. Peter Calvert. *Politics and Society in the Developing World.* London: Routledge, 2016.

12. Francisca Oluyole. "Ajaokuta: How Nigeria's Largest Industrial Project Failed." Premium Times Nigeria, December 26, 2017. https://www.premiumtimesng .com/news/headlines/253680-analysis-ajaokuta-nigerias-largest-industrial-project-fai led.html.

13. Peter Calvert. *Politics and Society in the Developing World.* London: Routledge, 2016.

14. Owei Lakemfa. "Africa: Italy Tells France the Truth, but Africa Isn't Listening." allAfrica.com, February 15, 2019. https://allafrica.com/stories/20190 2150165.html.

15. Gavin Jones and Crispan Balmer, "Italy's Di Maio Repeats Attacks on French Policies in Africa,*" Reuters,* January 22, 2018, https://af.reuters.com/articles/idA FKCNIPGOKK-OZATP (accessed February 16, 2019).

16. Roberts, J. A. G. *Concise History of China.* Cambridge: Harvard University Press, 2001, p. 165–173.

17. Sarah Rose. "The Great British Tea Heist." Smithsonian Institution, March 9, 2010. https://www.smithsonianmag.com/history/the-great-british-tea-heist-9866709/.

18. Ibid, James Ray, and Juliet Kaarbo, 2005.

19. Thomas Lum, Hannah Fischer, Julissa Gomez Granger, and Anne Leland. "China's Foreign Aid Activities in Africa, Latin America, and Southeast Asia." Congressional Research Service, February 25, 2009. https://fas.org/sgp/crs/row/ R40361.pdf.

20. Ibid, Thomas Lum, Hannah Fischer, Julissa Gomez Granger, and Anne Leland, 2009.

21. Ibid, Boahen, A. A, 1987.

22. Owei Lakemfa. "Opinion: The African Road to China." African Examiner, August 24, 2018. https://www.africanexaminer.com/opinion-the-african-road-to-china-by-owei-lakemfa/.

23. Ibid, Owei Lakemfa, 2018.

24. Ibid, Thomas Lum, Hannah Fischer, Julissa Gomez Granger, and Anne Leland, 2009, p. 6.

25. Inwalomhe Daniel. "Africa-China's Debt Diplomacy." Vanguard News, September 10, 2018. https://www.vanguardngr.com/2018/09/africa-chinas-debt-diplo macy/.

26. Albert Eleanor. "China in Africa." Council on Foreign Relations. Council on Foreign Relations, July 12, 2017. https://www.cfr.org/backgrounder/china-africa.

27. Ibid, Albert Eleanor, 2017.

28. Ibid, Albert Eleanor, 2017 p. 4.

29. "Statistics on China-Africa Trade in January–August, 2018." Ministry of Commerce People's Republic of China, September 27, 2018. http://english.mofcom .gov.cn/article/statistic/lanmubb/AsiaAfrica/201811/20181102804578.shtml.

30. "China Continues to Develop Africa Trade Ties." The Telegraph, September 4, 2018. https://www.telegraph.co.uk/news/world/china-watch/business/business/chi na-africa-trade/.

31. Ibid, Albert Eleanor, 2017.

32. Ibid, Owei Lakemfa, 2019.

33. "Where Did HIV Come from?" The AIDS Institute, February 27, 2019. https ://www.theaidsinstitute.org/education/aids-101/where-did-hiv-come-0.

34. Ibid, Albert Eleanor, 2017 p. 6.

35. "African Countries Hope to Attract More Chinese Investment." China Daily, May 9, 2017. https://www.chinadaily.com.cn/business/2017-09/05/content_3157798 2.htm.

36. Armony, Ariel, and Enrique Dussel Peters. "The Pros and Cons of Chinese Investment in Latin America." The News Lens International Edition, August 14, 2018. https://international.thenewslens.com/article/101850.

37. Fabian Cambero and Dave Sherwood, "China invites Latin America to take part in One Belt, One Road," Reuters, January 22, 2018, https://www.reuters.com/articcle/us-china/china-invites-latin-america-to-take-part-in-one-belt-one-road-i dUSKBN1FB2CN (accessed March 4, 2019).

38. Tony Nash and Jay Heister. 2018, "China's Latest Conquest: Middle East Power Broker.," *CNBC*, June 27. 2018, https://www..cnbc.com/2018/06/28/chinas-latest-con quest-middle=-east-power-broker-commentary.html (accessed October 4, 2018).

39. Wilbur Ross and Chris Coons. "How the US Can Level the Playing Field as China Pours Money into Africa." CNBC. CNBC, August 2, 2018. https://www.cnbc .com/2018/08/02/china-is-pouring-money-into-in-africa-heres-why-the-us-must-com pete.html.

40. Chijioke Jannah. "Nigeria's Election a Sham, Not Credible—US Lawmaker." Daily Post Nigeria, March 9, 2019. https://dailypost.ng/2019/03/09/nigerias-election-sham-not-credible-us-lawmaker/.

41. Ibid, Peter Calvert. 2016.

42. Pham, J. Peter, Abdoul Salam Bello, and Boubacar-Sid Barry. "Chinese Aid and Investment Are Good for Africa." Foreign Policy, August 31, 2018. https://fo reignpolicy.com/2018/08/31/chinese-aid-and-investment-are-good-for-africa/.

43. "20 African Countries with the Most Chinese Investment Projects." Bulawayo24 News, April 5, 2018. https://bulawayo24.com/index-id-news-sc-natio nal-byo-132300.html.

44. Ibid, Bulawayo24 News.

45. "African Countries hope to Attract more Chinese Investment," China Daily, September 5, 2017, http://www.chinadaily.com.cn/business/2007-09/05/content-315 77982.htm (accessed September 10, 2018).

46. Ibid, Peter Calvert 2016 p. 55.

47. "African Countries Hope to Attract More Chinese Investment." China Daily, May 9, 2017. https://www.chinadaily.com.cn/business/2017-09/05/content_3157798 2.htm.

48. Finian Cunningham. "Why China's Over the Moon." TheAltWorld, January 5, 2019. http://thealtworld.com/finian_cunningham/why-chinas-over-the-moon.

49. Mike Wall. "China Just Landed on the Moon's Far Side—and Will Probably Send Astronauts on Lunar Trips." Space, January 5, 2019. https://www.space.com /42914-china-far-side-moon-landing-crewed-lunar-plans.html.

50. Ibid, Mike Wall 2019.

51. Ibid, Cunningham 2019.

52. Thomas R. Dye. *Politics in America*. Upper Saddle River, NJ: Prentice-Hall, 1999.

53. John T. Rourke and Mark A. Boyer. *International Politics on the World Stage*. Boston: McGraw-Hill Higher Education, 2010.

54. Anaeto, Emeka, Emma Uja, and Babajide Komolafe. "Foreign Debt: Nigeria, Other African Countries Vulnerable—IMF." Vanguard News, October 12, 2018. https://www.vanguardngr.com/2018/10/foreign-debt-nigeria-other-african-countries -vulnerable-imf/.

55. Pham, J. Peter, Abdoul Salam Bello, and Boubacar-Sid Barry. "Chinese Aid and Investment Are Good for Africa." Foreign Policy, August 31, 2018. https://fo reignpolicy.com/2018/08/31/chinese-aid-and-investment-are-good-for-africa/.

56. Lum, Thomas, Hannah Fischer, Julissa Gomez Granger, and Anne Leland. "China's Foreign Aid Activities in Africa, Latin America, and Southeast Asia." Congressional Research Service, February 25, 2009. https://fas.org/sgp/crs/row/ R40361.pdf.

57. Ibid, Peter Pham, Abdoul Salam Bello, and Boubacar-Sid Barry, 2018.

58. Ibid, *China Daily*, September 5, 2017.

59. "Why Is China Pouring Money into Africa?" BBC, September 2, 2018. https ://www.bbc.com/news/av/world-africa-45361053/why-is-china-pouring-money-into -africa.

60. Ibid, Emeka Anaeto, Emma Uja, and Babajide Komolafe, 2018.

61. Adesomoju, Ade. "Nigeria Signs $10bn Agreements in China—Presidency." Punch Newspapers, September 9, 2018. https://punchng.com/nigeria-signs-10bn-a greements-in-china-presidency/.

62. Ibid, Why Is China Pouring Money into Africa?" BBC, September 2, 2018.

63. Ibid, Emeka Anaeto, Emma Uja, and Babajide Komolafe, 2018.

64. Ibid, Emeka Anaeto, Emma Uja, and Babajide Komolafe, 2018.

65. "China Defends $318 Million Airport Project after Sierra Leone Halts Construction." Premium Times Nigeria, October 11, 2018. https://www.premiumt imesng.com/foreign/west-africa-foreign/289902-china-defends-318-million-airport-project-after-sierra-leone-halts-construction.html.

66. Chijioke Jannah. "Chinese Loan: How Buhari, 51 Other Presidents Exposed Africa to Ridicule—Falana." Daily Post Nigeria, October 28, 2018. https://dailypost .ng/2018/10/28/chinese-loan-buhari-51-presidents-exposed-africa-ridicule-falana/.

67. Joseph Goldstein. "Kenyans Say Chinese Investment Brings Racism and Discrimination." The New York Times, October 15, 2018. https://www.nytimes.com /2018/10/15/world/africa/kenya-china-racism.html.

BIBLIOGRAPHY

Adesomoju, Ade. "Nigeria Signs $10bn Agreements in China—Presidency." Punch Newspapers, September 9, 2018. https://punchng.com/nigeria-signs-10bn-agreem ents-in-china-presidency/.

"African Countries Hope to Attract More Chinese Investment." China Daily, May 9, 2017. https://www.chinadaily.com.cn/business/2017-09/05/content_31577982 .htm.

Ahmed, Nazeer. "The Atlantic Slave Trade." History of Islam, March 22, 2017. http: //historyofislam.com/contents/onset-of-the-colonial-age//the-atlantic-slave-trade/.

Albert, Eleanor. "China in Africa." Council on Foreign Relations. Council on Foreign Relations, July 12, 2017. https://www.cfr.org/backgrounder/china-africa.

Anaeto, Emeka, Emma Uja, and Babajide Komolafe. "Foreign Debt: Nigeria, Other African Countries Vulnerable - IMF." Vanguard News, October 12, 2018. https://www.vanguardngr.com/2018/10/foreign-debt-nigeria-other-african-countries-vulnerable-imf/.

Armony, Ariel, and Enrique Dussel Peters. "The Pros and Cons of Chinese Investment in Latin America." The News Lens International Edition, August 14, 2018. https://international.thenewslens.com/article/101850.

Art, Robert J., and Robert Jervis. *International Politics: Enduring Concepts and Contemporary Issues*. Boston: Pearson, 2017.

Boahen, Albert Adu. *African Perspectives on Colonialism*. Baltimore, MD: Johns Hopkins Univ. Press, 1987.

Calamur, Krishnadev. "Tillerson to Latin America: Beware of China." The Atlantic, February 3, 2018.

Calvert, Peter. *Politics and Society in the Developing World*. London: Routledge, 2016.

Cambero, Fabian. "China Invites Latin America to Take Part in One Belt, One Road." Reuters. Thomson Reuters, January 22, 2018. https://www.reuters.com/article/us-chile-china/china-invites-latin-america-to-take-part-in-one-belt-one-road-idUSKBN1FB2CN.

Caxton, Ateki Seta. "The Anglophone Dilemma in Cameroon: The Need for Comprehensive Dialogue and Reform." ACCORD. The African Centre for the constructive Resolution of Disputes, July 21, 2017. https://www.accord.org.za/conflict-trends/anglophone-dilemma-cameroon/.

"China Continues to Develop Africa Trade Ties." The Telegraph, September 4, 2018. https://www.telegraph.co.uk/news/world/china-watch/business/business/china-africa-trade/

"China Defends $318 Million Airport Project after Sierra Leone Halts Construction." Premium Times Nigeria, October 11, 2018. https://www.premiumtimesng.com/foreign/west-africa-foreign/289902-china-defends-318-million-airport-project-after-sierra-leone-halts-construction.html.

Cunningham, Finian. "Why China's Over the Moon." TheAltWorld, January 5, 2019. http://thealtworld.com/finian_cunningham/why-chinas-over-the-moon.

Donald, Inwalomhe. "Africa-China's Debt Diplomacy." Vanguard News, September 10, 2018. https://www.vanguardngr.com/2018/09/africa-chinas-debt-diplomacy/.

Dye, Thomas R. *Politics in America*. Upper Saddle River, NJ: Prentice-Hall, 1999.

"20 African Countries with the Most Chinese Investment Projects." Bulawayo24 News, April 5, 2018. https://bulawayo24.com/index-id-news-sc-national-byo-132300.html.

Gates, Jr., Henry Louis. "The African Americans: Many Rivers to Cross." PBS. Public Broadcasting Service, May 1, 2017. https://www.pbs.org/show/african-americans-many-rivers-cross/.

Gavin Jones and Crispan Balmer, "Italy's Di Maio Repeats Attacks on French Policies in Africa," *Reuters*, January 22, 2018, https://af.reuters.com/articles/idAFKCNIPGOKK-OZATP (accessed February 16, 2019).

Goldstein, Joseph. "Kenyans Say Chinese Investment Brings Racism and Discrimination." The New York Times, October 15, 2018. https://www.nytimes.com/2018/10/15/world/africa/kenya-china-racism.html.

Heisler, Tony Nash and Jay. "China's Latest Conquest: Middle East Power Broker." CNBC. CNBC, June 28, 2018. https://www.cnbc.com/2018/06/28/chinas-latest-conquest-middle-east-power-broker---commentary.html.

"Italy's Di Maio Repeats Attack on French Policies in Africa." Reuters. Thomson Reuters, January 21, 2019. https://www.reuters.com/article/us-france-italy-dimaio/italys-di-maio-repeats-attack-on-french-policies-in-africa-idUSKCN1PF1YG.

James, George G. M. *Stolen Legacy: "Greek Philosophy Is Stolen Egyptian Philosophy."* Drewryville, VA: Khalifahs Booksellers & Associates, 2005.

Jannah, Chijioke, and Chijioke Jannah. "Chinese Loan: How Buhari, 51 Other Presidents Exposed Africa to Ridicule—Falana." Daily Post Nigeria, October 28, 2018. https://dailypost.ng/2018/10/28/chinese-loan-buhari-51-presidents-exposed-africa-ridicule-falana/.

Jannah, Chijioke, and Chijioke Jannah. "Nigeria's Election a Sham, Not Credible—US Lawmaker." Daily Post Nigeria, March 9, 2019. https://dailypost.ng/2019/03/09/nigerias-election-sham-not-credible-us-lawmaker/.

Lakemfa, Owei. "Opinion: The African Road to China." African Examiner, August 24, 2018. https://www.africanexaminer.com/opinion-the-african-road-to-china-by-owei-lakemfa/.

Lakemfa, Owei. "Africa: Italy Tells France the Truth, but Africa Isn't Listening." allAfrica.com, February 15, 2019. https://allafrica.com/stories/201902150165.html.

Lum, Thomas, Hannah Fischer, Julissa Gomez Granger, and Anne Leland. "China's Foreign Aid Activities in Africa, Latin America, and Southeast Asia." Congressional Research Service, February 25, 2009. https://fas.org/sgp/crs/row/R40361.pdf.

Oluyole, Francisca. "Ajaokuta: How Nigeria's Largest Industrial Project Failed." Premium Times Nigeria, December 26, 2017. https://www.premiumtimesng.com/news/headlines/253680-analysis-ajaokuta-nigerias-largest-industrial-project-failed.html.

Pham, J. Peter, Abdoul Salam Bello, and Boubacar-Sid Barry. "Chinese Aid and Investment Are Good for Africa." Foreign Policy, August 31, 2018. https://foreignpolicy.com/2018/08/31/chinese-aid-and-investment-are-good-for-africa/.

Ray, James Lee., and Juliet Kaarbo. *Global Politics*. Boston: Houghton Mifflin, 2005.

Roberts, J. A. G. *A Concise History of China*. Cambridge: Harvard University Press, 2001.

Rose, Sarah. "The Great British Tea Heist." Smithsonian Institution, March 9, 2010. https://www.smithsonianmag.com/history/the-great-british-tea-heist-9866709/.

Ross, Wilbur, and Chris Coons. "How the US Can Level the Playing Field as China Pours Money into Africa." CNBC. CNBC, August 2, 2018. https://www.cnbc.com

/2018/08/02/china-is-pouring-money-into-in-africa-heres-why-the-us-must-com
pete.html.

Rourke, John T., and Mark A. Boyer. *International Politics on the World Stage.*
Boston: McGraw-Hill Higher Education, 2010.

"Statistics on China-Africa Trade in January-August 2018." Ministry of Commerce
People's Republic of China, September 27, 2018. http://english.mofcom.gov.cn/a
rticle/statistic/lanmubb/AsiaAfrica/201811/20181102804578.shtml.

"Transatlantic Slave Trade: United Nations Educational, Scientific and Cultural
Organization." Social and Human Sciences. United Nations Educational, Scientific
and Cultural Organization, March 21, 2017. http://www.unesco.org/new/en/social
-and-human-sciences/themes/slave-route/transatlantic-slave-trade/.

Wall, Mike. "China Just Landed on the Moon's Far Side—and Will Probably Send
Astronauts on Lunar Trips." Space, January 5, 2019. https://www.space.com/429
14-china-far-side-moon-landing-crewed-lunar-plans.html.

"Where Did HIV Come from?" The AIDS Institute, February 27, 2019. https://www
.theaidsinstitute.org/education/aids-101/where-did-hiv-come-0.

"Why Is China Pouring Money into Africa?" BBC, September 2, 2018. https://
www.bbc.com/news/av/world-africa-45361053/why-is-china-pouring-money-int
o-africa.

Wolfe, James H. *Modern International Law: An Introduction to the Law of Nations.*
Upper Saddle River, NJ: Prentice-Hall, 2008.

Chapter 9

China's Cultural Rapprochement

The Uses of Soft Power as a Form of Building Alliances in Africa

Alecia D. Hoffman and Regina Moorer

INTRODUCTION AND OVERVIEW

Sino-African relations can be traced as far back as Zhang He, when the first explorations and cultural exchanges took place with Africa during the Ming Dynasty. Over the years Sino-African relations have waxed and waned due to the changing dynamics of the international landscape, domestic policy directives, and the varying shifts of cultural diplomacy. However, in the latter part of the twentieth century a pivot toward reigniting relations, particularly as it pertains to China's cultural footprint in Africa. To date, there has been much research conducted on Sino-African relations, and within this research, the debates ensue about the true motives behind China's role in Africa. Whether it is the development of special economic processing zones (SPZ), the extraction of raw materials in exchange for infrastructure, low to no interest loans, the influx of Chinese expatriates, or the spread of Chinese culture and language; the conversations amongst policymakers, scholars, and lay-persons around the globe has piqued in recent years around this renewed relationship. Of interest in this seemingly never-ending set of topics, is the export of Chinese culture and language, particularly through the ever-growing number of Confucius Institutes and classrooms that operate in approximately forty-one countries in Africa.

METHODOLOGY

To understand the export of Chinese culture using Confucius Institutes (CIs), an examination of soft power as an appropriate theory will be employed throughout this study. Joseph Nye's conceptualization of soft power was first employed during the 1990s, and since the origins of this theory, its applicability and use in the study of foreign policy in a globalized world has increased exponentially. The concept, although initially used in the study of Western governments, has now become the watchword of Chinese foreign policy. Through this exporting of culture, China has employed soft-power to achieve its domestic policy objectives and also increase its presence, likability, and posturing with the international community. For this study, the authors will examine this stance in each of the African countries that have CIs or Confucius classrooms in operation.

Data are collected on the dependent variables and the key explanatory variables. Secondary source and archival data are collected for all of the countries. The data for the independent variable is collected from the English translation HANBAN website databases. Data are collected on the number of CIs and CI classrooms in each country. The HANBAN website indicates that there are fifty-nine CIs and CI classrooms in Africa. However, our count found that HANBAN lists locations for sixty-one CIs and CI classrooms. The HANBAN website also lists counts for CIs and CI classrooms, but the website does not provide physical location information for the institutes and classrooms. As such, this research only considers those institutes and classrooms that have location information listed. For example, the HANBAN website indicates that there are six CIs and five CI classrooms in South Africa. However, location information is only given for five CIs and three CI classrooms. In these instances, we only count CIs and CI classrooms.

This research asserts that the use of Confucius institutes in African countries has increased the spread of Chinese culture, that is, customs, values, and language, to other people not of Chinese origin. As such, cultural influence is measured based on the level of China/Africa's cultural goods imports and exports. In the 2009 UNESCO Framework for Cultural Statistics (FCS), cultural goods are defined as goods "conveying ideas, symbols and ways of life, some of which may be subject to copyrights." Cultural goods are "experience goods meaning that consumers can determine their value only after they have been consumed." They are thus different from other products by their system of valorization, inherent in which is an irreproducible characteristic that is intrinsically linked to its appreciation by consumers. Measuring the trade in cultural goods provides insight into the dynamism of Chinese cultural industries and the interest for such goods, as indicated by their supply and demand by African countries.

The data for the categorical dependent variables are collected by conducting a content analysis of archival materials found on news websites. This study purports that the use of Confucius Institutes in African countries has led to an increase of African people with the necessary knowledge, skills, and abilities (KSAs) to live and work in harmonious relations with Chinese expatriates and settlers in African countries. We test this hypothesis by examining the number of Confucius Institute-sponsored job fairs held in each country. These data are measured using quantitative content analysis. Content analysis is described as the scientific study of the content of the communication. Content analysis is defined as a research technique for making replicable and valid inferences from data to their context.[1] Content analysis is a research methodology that utilizes a set of procedures to make valid inferences from the text.[2] Content analysis is defined as "a method of studying and analyzing communication in a systematic, objective, and quantitative manner to measure variables."[3] The specific content analysis techniques used in this study are categorized as news website observation and analysis.

THEORETICAL FRAMEWORK

Since Joseph S. Nye, Jr. first utilized the term soft power in the 1990s, numerous scholars have taken the time to opine on the theory and also apply it in varied contexts. As it pertains to the contexts of the use of soft power, scholars have studied the theory and used it to examine the foreign policy objectives and goals of many of the developed Western nations and as of more recent, have used it to deconstruct and analyze the ambitions of some countries that had once, not long ago, designated themselves as Least Developed Nations (LDC), but now may be considered second-world nations. The PRC is one such country that has moved to this status after long being seen as part of the developing world and labeled as an LDC. Although Nye himself did not directly apply the theory of soft power to the country of China during its early usage, it is now commonly known by foreign policy scholars, practitioners, and researchers as the watchword in studying Chinese foreign policy.

Hard Power versus Soft Power

The use of hard power is as old as the study of human interaction and state-to-state relations and is usually measured in the form of military might and economic prowess. Invariably grounded in the realist school of thought, many proponents of the hard power theoretical paradigm believe strongly in the use of militaristic or economic means as a form of coercion to get others to do what you want. This use of hard power has been used for quite some time in international relations and many of the developed nations of the world today have employed this technique as a sine qua non component of their international relations and foreign policy strategies. Some of the early scholars that have thoroughly covered hard power include Hans Morgenthau, George Kennan, Robert Dahl, Max Weber, Talcott Parsons, E.H. Carr, John Mearsheimer, and Harold Laswell.

Typically, when one thinks of the concept of hard power, a zero-sum game invariably comes to mind. The idea that one party must lose something if the other one gains. This concept of power, however old its practice, has taken on several meanings and different conjectures of the term "hard power" have been proffered by the different practitioners and scholars of international relations and foreign policy. However, during the later portion of the twentieth century, a novel approach to the age-old concept of power emerged. The notion of power began to take a decidedly different view; one that can still be considered power nonetheless, but not one that emphasized the "carrot-and-sticks" dimension that became the foundation of hard power. The new approach was called soft power, and this conceptualization of power took a more genteel approach toward getting others to adhere, follow, and or adopt one's approach.

The concept of soft power was first discussed by Joseph S. Nye in 1990 in his article published in the *Foreign Policy* magazine.[4] Since that time, Nye went on to provide more meaning to this concept in his book entitled *Soft Power: The Means to Success in World Politics.* As noted by Nye, "soft power rests on the ability to shape the preferences of others."[5] When examining this concept, it must be noted that although "hard power" became the synonymous watchword in foreign policy circles of the Western world, "soft power" was also being exercised. The inducement to get others to do what one wants or to get others to think along the same lines has indeed long been a part of Western foreign policy. One need only think of payments made or foreign aid given by one country to another. This can also rightfully be called the "carrots," which make up the better half of the "sticks" practice of foreign policy. However, when we delve further into the use of "soft power," we find that it also "appeals to a sense of attraction, love, or duty in our shared relationship and appeal to our shared values about the justness of contributing to those shared values and purposes."[6] More importantly, Nye notes that if the desires of an intangible attraction can cause one's behavior to conform, then soft power has indeed been employed.[7]

When examining Sino-African relations, this observable attraction is seen throughout the continent of Africa. To date, the "one-China" principle is in full effect for all the independent nation-states on the continent. The date as to when the "one-China" principle took effect can vary from a situational point of view. For some, it is believed to have taken place when the United

Nations employed Resolution 2758 in 1971 when the government of Taiwan was supplanted by the PRC in the United Nations. For others, the *Shanghai Communique* of 1972 when the U.S. normalized relations with the PRC is viewed as the true date of the "one-China" principle. Whether it is 1971 or 1972, the policy that the PRC is the official government of China and Taiwan as an extension of the PRC has fully taken hold on the African continent. Although each independent African country did not accept this principle, over time, the world has witnessed countries, one by one, sever ties with Taiwan and establish relations with the PRC. To date, there is only one country in Africa that maintains ties with Taiwan, Eswatini (formerly Swaziland).

With Joseph S. Nye, Jr's idea regarding desires of intangible attractions being the basis for soft power, then one would have to question the need for aid with no strings attached if there is an overarching desire for Chinese culture? It is indeed true that part of the draw to China is the inducements of aid and infrastructure, but how does Chinese culture and language fit within this overall equation? It is believed that this is the crux of the PRC's soft power initiative. The increase of infrastructure projects; goods and services, in the form of commodities, financial institutions, military support, and even healthcare is a likely impetus for the importation of Chinese culture.[8] With the increase of Chinese Foreign Direct Investment (FDI) into African countries, this brings an increase of Chinese nationals into the countries to work in the varied sectors. This increase of people from a foreign nation also brings with it cultural and language barriers. There are two main Chinese languages; Cantonese and Mandarin, and several different dialects based on region. Although there are varied dialects, the lingua franca of the PRC is Mandarin Chinese. However, in Africa, there are over 1,500 languages, yet there are three main languages, and at least ten widely spoken languages across fifty-four different countries. One would cautiously surmise that by gently encouraging the spread of Chinese language and culture in the countries that have witnessed a large increase of Chinese FDI, this would likely foster the development of stronger business relationships in the hopes of building "win-win relationships" and facilitate understanding. If Chinese enterprises are operating in Africa, there will be a need for workers, and to foster these relationships and build some form of trust, communication, understanding, and cultural exchange is not unfathomable for the PRC, which can be seen as an independent variable in this discussion and the African countries seen as a dependent variable; the giver and the receiver. However, this does not mean that the exchange is not reciprocal, because indeed it is. There are innumerable examples of Chinese expatriates also receiving African culture and language skills, however, this is not the exact focus of this chapter.

The relationship between Africa and the PRC is as old as the Ming Dynasty. It is believed that during this dynasty, which lasted until the end of dynastic rule in 1911 and the commencement of the modern-day Communist system under the auspices of Mao Tse Tung, which began in 1949, the PRC fomented relationships with countries of the Western classified "third world." This is believed to be the case because the PRC was sympathetic to those countries that were mired by the forces of imperialism. After all, it too endured the subjugation of colonialism and outside invaders. To show the PRC's support of the colonized and semicolonized areas of the world, vice-chairman of the PRC, Liu Shao-Chi "presented China's revolution as a model for all under-developed and semi-colonized nations."[9] The idea that the PRC could serve as a model for all other underdeveloped countries of the world, particularly those located in the "global south," was highlighted in the opening speech entitled "Working Class in the Struggle for National Liberation" delivered by Liu Shao-Chi at the Trade Union Conference of Asian and Australasian countries. This relationship with African countries has continued to develop, albeit there have been times of a lull due to the PRC's domestic political-economic, and social issues. However, after the Tiananmen Square incident of the later part of the twentieth century, the PRC began to reestablish relationships with Africa, and reinstitute its policy of "going global." It is during this time that an influx of culture and language began to permeate the African continent by way of educational opportunities for Africans, indeed an aspect of soft power as defined by Nye.

REVIEW OF THE LITERATURE

Sino-African relations are not of new origin and have ebbed and flowed at varied levels and depths for centuries. Of particular interest to this study are the relationships that have been established between the PRC and African nations with the commencement of the Forum on China African Cooperation commencing in 2000 and how with each subsequent conference, the strengthening of ties between the two regions has continued to deepen. Although there was a time where the PRC retracted to handle its internal affairs after the incidents of Tiananmen Square of 1989, the PRC reopened to the world and began the push toward fomenting stronger relations with African nations. As a part of the "going global" strategy which commenced around 2000, the CCP and the PRCs Ministry of Education has worked toward developing stronger ties to the African continent as part of the South-South strategy of foreign policy. Of particular interest is the role of education and the export of culture from the PRC to Africa by way of CIs. With the export of education and Chinese language skills, the question arises as to what, if any, positive implications do this new knowledge offer the students that enroll in the CIs/

classrooms regularly? Furthermore, how does the export of Chinese culture strengthen ties in the Sino-African international dynamic?

The role that the PRC has taken in the export of culture and language has grown exponentially in the twentieth-first century and a host of foreign policy practitioners, researchers, and students have explored this topic from the perspective of cultural and educational exports to the African continent to augment the increasing economic ties between the two regions.

The strengthening of Sino-African relations in the areas of cultural and educational exchanges has received a great deal of attention. Li Baoping and Luo Jian Bo provide background analysis regarding this strengthening of ties between both regions at the Forum on China/Africa Cooperation IV and V.[10] At both of these events, held in 2009 and 2012, respectively, Li and Luo illustrate the commitments made toward education. Although agreements for strengthening education occurred at the first meeting in 2000, it was at the V ministerial meeting where new measures were implemented. According to Li and Luo's research, the new measures instituted during the FOCAC Summit consisted of:

> The two sides will continue to implement the 20+20 Cooperation Plan for Chinese and African Institutions of Higher Education, improve the cooperation mechanism between Chinese and African Institutions of higher education, encourage Chinese and African Universities to increase cooperation in regional and country studies, and support African Universities in establishing China Research Centers.[11]

Furthermore, the PRC committed to providing two million USD annually under the auspices of the United Nations Educational, Scientific, and Cultural Organization (UNESCO) in support of education development. This support of education as envisioned by the PRC through UNESCO is one where the country would commit to providing more scholarships and building long-term educational facilities. However, the continued push for CIs would remain from a cultural perspective.[12]

Although there is a great deal of positive press surrounding the establishment of CIs in Africa, Li and Luo identify several negatives. The authors of this manuscript note that the Sino-African educational arrangements are not living up to their full potential due to skewed processes. From this perspective, the authors note that there is little to no African expertise and the lack of the use of African indigenous knowledge. On the second drawback, the authors highlight the lack of coordination between the respective ministries, that is, Ministry of Commerce, Ministry of Education, and the Ministry of Foreign Affairs from the Beijing perspective. And for the third and fourth criticism of the Sino-African exchanges, the authors note the use of cultural counselors who do not focus very much on education, but culture, and lastly, the waste or improper management of resources. Lastly, the fifth criticism of the educational agreements between the PRC and several African countries centers around the lack of volunteers to leave the PRC and go to Africa to teach.[13]

Kenneth King offers insight into the PRCs education engagement in Africa and provides some case study analyses, particularly on the country of South Africa as it pertains to the CIs/classrooms. King offers insight into human resource development in Africa by the PRC through the training of people in both a short-term stance and a long-term stance. Just as the 20 +20 scheme was discussed by Li and Luo, King also discusses this in his writings in conjunction with the CIs and other autonomous projects. However, the important approach that King takes is one of comparative analysis. He discusses the difference between the traditional institutions such as the Organization for Economic Cooperation and Development versus that of the PRC to obtain a better understanding of how the Sino-African partnership works.[14]

King also provides a case study analysis of the PRC's role in South Africa with a specific examination of the role of the FOCAC in the development of human resources on the continent. Just as King provided the rationale of examining the CIs on the entire continent in his later writing, which was previously discussed, in this particular manuscript, he examines enterprise-based training within Chinese firms, and how this differs from what is offered by the traditional Western-backed donors.[15]

In Maddalena Procopio's article, an examination is provided of the role of the PRCs CIs in through the employment of the country's foreign policy objectives, more importantly, the export of the Chinese foreign language and how this is conducted through the CIs. The thesis of Procopio's article centers on the use of CIs to export Chinese culture to utilize a soft power framework to achieve its foreign policy objectives. Just as King examined the role of CIs and the goals of FOCAC in South Africa, Procopio research also centers on this country. Her analysis is timely, as it discusses the attraction to CIs at the executive and student levels and provides a summation which insinuates that although there is a great promotion of CIs and incursion of Chinse soft power, soft power being utilized effectively by the Chinese is tenuous at best through the use of CIs.[16]

James F. Paradise discusses the role of CIs and how these entities bolster Beijing's soft power. Of particular interest in Paradise's article, is the supposition that although these institutes are promoted benignly, anxiety exists as to whether or not the PRC is unleashing a "Trojan horse."[17] Paradise concludes that the use of soft power may not be winning as many hearts and minds through the use of CIs; however, these entities are at the very least able to increase their educational contacts with other regions of the world which will, in turn, buttress their scientific capabilities and economic advancement, all of which are a part of their opening up to the world.[18]

As James Paradise's article concludes with the point that the utilization of soft power is not winning as many hearts and minds, others have surmised the same point. Individuals such as Frank Youngman examines the Botswana-Sino relationship and notes that there is a multidimensional approach to this relationship and that each level must be analyzed.[19] Of particular interest in Youngman's article is the number of cultural visits that are made to Botswana from the PRC and the relatively small number of visits of the people of Botswana to the PRC. Furthermore, his study highlights that many Chinese expatriates reside in Botswana, however, the relationships between African and Chinese communities within Botswana has received very little analysis. Additionally, Youngman cites a few studies which indicate that relations at worksites have not been very amicable.[20]

An examination of the cultural exchanges between African and the PRC was conducted by Bertha Z. Osei-Hwedie. As previously noted, FOCAC IV was instrumental in the strengthening of cultural activities between Africa and the PRC. During this particular iteration of FOCAC, a three-year action plan ushered in the deepening of cultural activities between the two regions. Osei-Hwedie highlights the deepening of cultural relations through the mutual exchange of cultural arts, movies, music books, and human resource training.[21] Through the strengthening of ties in the cultural sector, it is believed that several misconceptions that are shared by both the Chinese and Africans can be rectified which will lead to stronger relationships.

When discussing the role of Chinese media in Africa, the editors of *Evolving Media Interactions Between China and Africa* provide timely analysis from many authors who discuss the role of the PRCs media campaign in Africa from both a Chinese and African perspective.[22] Several contributors to this edited work provide timely analysis of the media dynamic and the implications it has for Africa. Ran Jijun examines the growth of media relations between Africa and the PRC utilizing two theoretical frameworks. Both the media intervention and media exchange frameworks are utilized to highlight how both Africa and China are taking steps to enhance bilateral alignment in media.[23]

Within the same text, Dani Madrid-Morales provides a historical preview of the PRCs outward media expansion in Africa and other countries when other western nations, particularly North America, have been withdrawing attention from Africa. His main focus centers on the question of, why are the Chinese media in Africa?[24]

The last contributor to this edited work, Jacinta Mwende Maweu examines the perceptions of Sino-African relations from the journalists and public audience viewpoints with a specific analysis of Chinese media in Africa.[25]

In conclusion, the literature reviewed for this chapter provides a nuanced examination of Sino-African relations. The literature provides an overview of some of the writings about the two major hypotheses addressed in this chapter, the implications of CIs in the spread of Chinese culture, customs, values, and language and the role that CIs play in the transfer of language skills and knowledge that would, in turn, assist Chinese expatriates and Africans to live and work in harmonious relations. The literature provided in this brief overview is not exhaustive yet provides a catalyst for further discussion and analysis of the role of CIs in the role of the PRC's cultural rapprochement.

AN EXAMINATION AND ANALYSIS OF THE USES OF SOFT POWER THROUGH CIS AND CULTURAL EXPORTS

The impetus to begin CIs in Africa is a part of the PRCs going global strategy and to understand how these institutions operate, it is necessary to examine the structure of the PRC's educational system in the twenty-first century. It also should be noted that the CIs in Africa do not operate independently of the PRC, for there is a great deal of oversight of the CIs that are operating around the globe through The Office of Chinese Language Council International, most commonly known as HABAN. This entity is an arm of the Chinese Ministry of Education. According to Haban, "the Haban/Confucius Institute Headquarters, as a public institution affiliated with the Chinese Ministry of Education, is committed to providing Chinese language and cultural teaching resources and services worldwide, it goes all out in meeting the demands of foreign Chinese learners and contributing to the development of multiculturalism and the building of a harmonious world."[26] Xioahe Cheng notes that the impetus to export the Chinese language and culture began in 2002.[27] Before the move to open institutions overseas to "promote Chinese culture and language," the 1999 meeting of the Teaching Chinese as a Foreign Language (TCFL) announced by Vice-Premier Qian Qichen. The Vice-Premier "pointed out that teaching the Chinese language was 'a national cause' and had 'important and far-reaching' meaning in expanding China's influence."[28] This announcement led to the implementation of "going global" for the Chinese education system. For years, the PRC practiced the "bring-in strategy" through the provision of educational opportunities for foreigners wishing to study in China, but to increase the country's international footprint, it was necessary to export more than just expatriates, money, commodities, and projects.

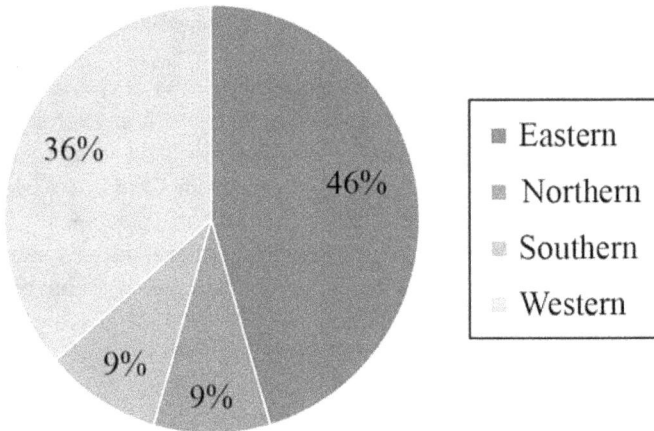

Figure 9.1 Job Fairs by Region. Data Compiled and Aggregated by Hoffman and Moorer. The employment fairs were gleaned from news articles published by African universities that host Confucius Institutes, data and news articles compiled by Haban, and news articles from the China People's Daily. An entire listing of these sources is provided in the bibliography of this chapter.

The findings that this chapter presents highlights the role that CIs and CI classrooms have played on the African continent through the export of language, culture, and promoting harmonious "win-win" relationships for both regions. Both hypotheses are analyzed; the first being the impact that the presence of CIs in African countries have on the ability of African people to live and work in harmonious relations with Chinese expatriates and settlers, and second, how China uses cultural encroachment by way of soft power exertion to increase the spread of Chinese culture.

The first examination provided pertains to the number of job fairs hosted by CIs in the respective regions that house CIs and classrooms. Job fairs may have multiple effects on those who attend. The main aim is for attendees to be recruited by participating employers. Content analysis research reveals that, since 2004, there have been eleven job fairs held at CI sites in Africa. Egypt, Nigeria, South Africa, and Zambia have each hosted one job fair. Kenya and Tanzania have hosted two, and Ghana has hosted three job fairs. As shown in figure 9.1, most of the job fairs have been held in the Eastern and Northern Regions.

CIs and Classrooms in North Africa

This examination of CIs/classrooms in Africa will commence with the region designated by the UNs Statistical Division as North Africa. In this region, four countries house CIs at the respective universities and educational systems that operate within each country. As illustrated in the chart below, one can find the countries of Egypt, Morocco, Tunisia, and Sudan housing CIs/ classrooms.

Another focus of this chapter is to examine an area of Sino-African relations that has not been fully researched—that is, how China exercises cultural encroachment by way of soft power exertion using the import of printed materials to Africa and the outbound tourism from China to Africa. More specifically, this chapter analyzes the impact that the placement of CIs has on the Sino-African interactions with regards to cultural imports and tourism. China setting up CIs around the world allows the country to have access to platforms and spaces that can be used to spread its language and culture. The institutes could increase China's soft power and help it project an image of itself as a benign country. However, this project seeks to explore the impact of CIs as a mechanism for cultural encroachment. Personal interests, as well as institutional factors incorporating political and commercial interests, are driving forces behind this increase in Chinese outbound tourism to Africa. For example, the Beijing Action Plan (2019–2021) of the Forum on China-Africa Cooperation (FOCAC) encourages tourism to Africa. Beijing has also granted more and more countries the Approved Destination Status (ADS), which is designed to encourage outbound Chinese tourism. The ADS policy permits citizens to take overseas leisure trips on group package tours to countries that have negotiated an ADS agreement. Usually, an ADS agreement will allow a Chinese travel agency to apply to the destination country's government for visas for all members of a tour group. By reducing the cost of obtaining an individual visa and providing for destination tour packages, ADS agreements opened up the opportunity for large increases in overseas Chinese travel. In 2015, China was ranked number one in international outbound tourism expenditures.[29] China is now Asia's largest source of international outbound tourists.

While Beijing considers many factors before giving ADS to a country, typically the country will already have a politically symbiotic relationship with China. Table 9.1 provides a list of countries receiving and implementing ADS agreements with China each year through 2014. The bolded African countries indicate that those countries also have a CI/CI Classroom. Every African country with an ADS agreement with China houses at least one CI/ CI Classroom. There are sixty-one CIs/CI classrooms in Africa; forty-two are housed in countries with ADS agreements with China. In other words, China encourages tourism to the countries that house about 70 percent of the CIs/ CI classrooms in Africa.

There are nineteen institutes and classrooms in countries that do not have an ADS agreement with China. Table 9.2 lists the countries that have a CI/ CI classroom, but do not have ADS. As shown in table 9.2, there eighteen countries that do not have an ADS agreement with China but have a CI/CI classroom.

Table 9.1   ADS Agreements with All Countries by Year

Year	Recipient	Cumulative Total
1983	Hong Kong, Macau	2
1988	Thailand	3
1990	Malaysia, Singapore	5
1992	Philippines	6
1998	South Korea	7
1999	Australia, New Zealand	9
2000	Brunei, Cambodia, Japan, Myanmar, Vietnam	14
2002	**Egypt**, Indonesia, Malta, Nepal, Turkey	19
2003	Croatia, Cuba, Germany, Hungary, India, Maldives, Pakistan, **South Africa**, Sri Lanka	28
2004	Austria, Belgium, Cyprus, Czech Republic, Denmark, Estonia, **Ethiopia**, Finland, France, Greece, Iceland, Ireland, Italy, Jordan, **Kenya**, Latvia, Liechtenstein, Lithuania, Luxembourg, **Mauritius**, Netherlands, Norway, Poland, Portugal, Romania, **Seychelles**, Slovenia, Slovakia, Spain, Sweden, Switzerland, **Tanzania, Tunisia, Zambia, Zimbabwe**	63
2005	Antigua and Barbuda, Barbados, Brazil, Chile, Fiji, Jamaica, Lao PDR, Mexico, Northern Mariana Islands, Peru, Russia, United Kingdom, Vanuatu	76
2006	Bahamas, Grenada, Mongolia, Tonga	80
2007	Andorra, Argentina, Bangladesh, Bulgaria, **Uganda**, **Morocco**, Monaco, **Namibia**, Venezuela, Oman, Syria	91
2008	French Polynesia, Israel, Taiwan, United States	95
2009	**Cape Verde**, Dominican Republic, Ecuador, **Ghana**, Guyana, **Mali**, Montenegro, Papua New Guinea, United Arab Emirates	104
2010	Canada, Lebanon, Federated States of Micronesia, North Korea, Uzbekistan, Serbia	110
2011	Iran	111
2012	**Madagascar**, Columbia, Samoa, **Cameroon**	115
2013	**Rwanda**	116
2014	Ukraine	117

* *African countries marked in bold have at least one CI or CI Classroom.*
Source: China National Tourism Administration. Available from: http://www.cnta.gov.cn/. Data compiled and aggregated by Alecia D. Hoffman and Regina Moorer.

Despite the ADS agreements, data from the Ministry of Culture and Tourism of the People's Republic of China show that there are no African countries among the top ten Chinese outbound tourist destinations. Every two years, the World Economic Forum produces the Travel and Tourism Competitiveness Index (TTCI). This index gives each country competitiveness in travel and tourism score and rank based on several factors such as infrastructure, safety and security, environmental sustainability, and health and hygiene. There were 136 countries analyzed in the 2017 TTCI Report. The data in table 9.3 show that the eighteen countries that do not have ADS agreements with China but have CIs tend to have low TTCI rankings.

Table 9.2   Countries with CI/CI Classrooms But No Ads with China

Country	Number of CIs/CI Classrooms
Angola	1
Benin	1
Botswana	1
Burundi	1
Comoros	1
Congo	1
Cote de Ivoire	1
Equatorial Guinea	1
Eritrea	1
Lesotho	1
Liberia	1
Malawi	1
Mozambique	1
Nigeria	2
Senegal	1
Sierra Leonne	1
Sudan	1
Togo	1

Sources: China National Tourism Administration. Available from: http://www.cnta.gov.cn/ztwz/cjyzt/gltl /201507/t20150708_723265.shtml. Data compiled and aggregated by Alecia D. Hoffman and Regina Moorer.

Confucius Institute Classroom/About Confucius Institute Classroom. Accessed March 24, 2020. Available from: http://english.hanban.org/node_10971.htm. Data compiled and aggregated by Alecia D. Hoffman and Regina Moorer.

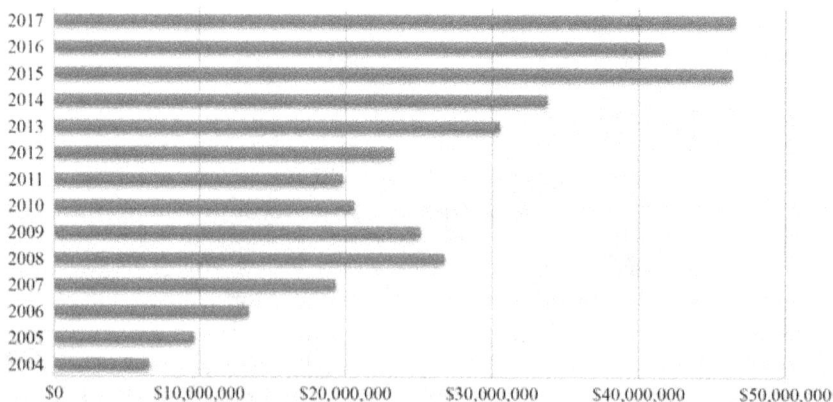

Figure 9.2   Chinese Printed Materials Exports to Africa. United Nations Comtrade Database. Accessed March 25, 2020. Available from: https://comtrade.un.org/data. Data compiled and aggregated by Alecia D. Hoffman and Regina Moorer.

Table 9.3   Travel and Tourism Competitiveness Index for Countries with CI/CI Classrooms but no ADS with China, 2017

Country	Global Rank
Angola	No data
Benin	127
Botswana	85
Burundi	134
Comoros	No data
Congo	No data
Cote de Ivoire	109
Equatorial Guinea	No data
Eritrea	No data
Lesotho	128
Liberia	No data
Malawi	123
Mozambique	122
Nigeria	129
Senegal	111
Sierra Leonne	131
Sudan	No data
Togo	No data

Source: Travel & Tourism Competitiveness Report. Accessed March 24, 2020. Available from: http://www3 .weforum.org/docs/WEF_TTCR_2017_web_0401.pdf. Data compiled and aggregated by Alecia D. Hoffman and Regina Moorer.

According to the TTCI, Europe tends to attract more inbound tourists than other regions of the world. African countries, on the other hand, tend to have a more difficult time attracting inbound tourists. This seems to suggest that the placement of CIs has had little impact on African countries' ability to attract Chinese tourists.

In addition to tourism, the FOCAC outlines China's cultural reach in Africa in several other areas of cultural significance: education; press; and publishing and media.[30] The trade in cultural goods has become an emerging and transformative force behind sociocultural encroachment. However, the literature on the trade potential of cultural goods has remained largely unexplored. It is not uncommon for countries with common cultural and historical attributes and ties to engage in trade in cultural goods. Since trade in Chinese cultural goods in Africa is increasing, we also consider printed materials exports as a proxy for cultural encroachment. However, there are some limitations to using these data. Printed material exports from China do not necessarily represent Chinese-only content. These exports can also, for example, include books by foreign authors printed by Chinese publishers.

For the export trade analysis, we use UN Comtrade data with China as the reporter and each African country as the partner for export flows. China has been Africa's largest trading partner since 2009 when it surpassed the United States. With a few exceptions, Chinese printed material exports to Africa have continued to grow at a steady rate, reaching a little over $46 billion in 2017. Figure 9.2 shows the trend in printed material exports to Africa. All figures are shown in U.S. dollars. Since 2012, South Africa, Egypt, and Ethiopia have ranked in the top five importers of Chinese printed materials.

As shown in table 9.4, Nigeria and Kenya replaced Benin and Tanzania in 2015 as top importers of printed materials from China. The Confucius Institutes and classrooms in the top five ranked countries house roughly 45 percent of the institutes and classrooms in Africa.

China's influence on African economies extends beyond the direct effects of trade by way of printed material exports. The trade between China and Africa has grown fast over the past few years, and exports from China now saturate the markets in most African countries. This deepening of the trade networks that import goods from China and export them in Africa are key drivers for the growth in Sino-African trade. As a rising power, seeking increasing influence in the international community, China has dedicated even more effort to strengthen its cultural and economic ties with African countries. The intensified ties between China and Africa have generated vigorous debates about the long-term effects of China's economic relationship and engagement in Africa. Sino-African trade has implications for Africa that extend beyond the import-export of printed materials. As a continent, Africa is currently China's third-biggest trading partner, after the United States and France. As China continues to increase its global cultural influence, the increase in printed material exports to Africa may be one tool that China is using to strengthen its soft power reach into Africa.

As previously stated, thirty-seven countries have CIs or Confucius classrooms in Africa. As of 2018, there are approximately sixty-one CIs/classrooms within these thirty-seven countries, with some countries having a substantial number of CIs or classrooms in their jurisdictions. For this research, Africa is divided into five regions. The methodology for devising the regions is based on the United Nations' geoscheme, a process devised by the UN Statistical Division as a means of dividing the varied continents into regions for statistical purposes and is commonly known as the M49 standard.[31] Figure 9.3 shows the number of institutes and classrooms in each region.

Commencing with the central region of Africa, the countries of Angola, Cameroon, Congo, Democratic Republic of Congo Equatorial Guinea, and Madagascar house CI classrooms. Table 9.5 highlights the names of the CIs, the Chinse partner institutions, and the date that each CI became operational.[32]

East Africa has the largest contingency of CIs on the continent. One of the major factors that may contribute to a host of CIs being located in this

Table 9.4 Top Five African recipients of Chinese printed materials, 2012–2017 (US $/millions)

Rank	*2012*		*2013*		*2014*		*2015*		*2016*		*2017*	
1	Egypt	4.1	South Africa	6.8	South Africa	8.0	Nigeria	10.7	South Africa	10.3	South Africa	12.5
2	South Africa	3.3	Egypt	5.6	Egypt	7.1	Egypt	9.5	Egypt	8.7	Egypt	9.2
3	Ethiopia	2.4	Ethiopia	3.3	Ethiopia	3.1	South Africa	8.8	Nigeria	7.6	Nigeria	8.3
4	Benin	1.5	Tanzania	2.4	Benin	2.0	Ethiopia	3.6	Ethiopia	3.0	Ethiopia	4.0
5	Tanzania	1.5	Benin	2.1	Tanzania	1.5	Kenya	1.5	Kenya	1.9	Kenya	1.7

Source: United Nations Comtrade Database. Accessed March 25, 2020. Available from: https://comtrade.un.org/data. Data compiled and aggregated by Alecia D. Hoffman and Regina Moorer.

	Central	Eastern	Northern	Southern	Western
▪ Institutes	6	18	7	8	11
▪ Classrooms	0	4	2	4	1

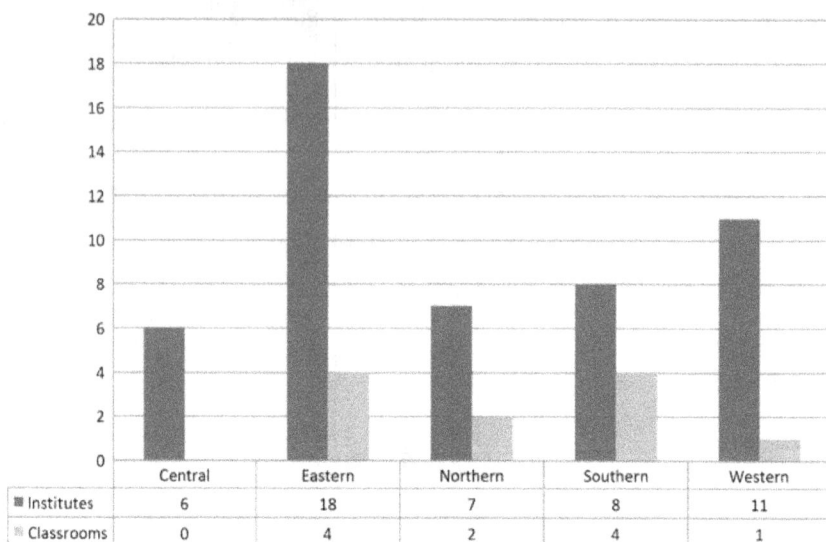

Figure 9.3 Institute and Classroom Location by United Nations Geoscheme Region. Confucius Institute Classroom/About Confucius Institute Classroom. Accessed March 24, 2020. Available from: http://english.hanban.org/node_10971.htm. Data compiled and aggregated by Alecia D. Hoffman and Regina Moorer.

Table 9.5 CIs in Central Africa

Country	CI Host Institute	CI Classroom	PRC Partner	Operational
Angola	Agostino Neto University	—	Harbin Normal University	2/6/2015
Cameroon	University of Yaounde II	—	Zhejiang Normal University	11/9/2007
Congo	University of Marien NGOUABI	—	University of Jinan	3/1/2013
Democratic Republic of Congo	Congolese Diplomatic Academy	—	Central South University of China	8/21/2018
Equatorial Guinea	National University of Equatorial Guinea	—	Zhejiang International Studies University	1/25/2016
Madagascar	Antananarivo University Toamasina University	—	Jiangxi Normal University Ningbo University	11/13/2008 9/19/2014

Source: Confucius Institute Classroom/About Confucius Institute Classroom. Accessed March 24, 2020. Available from: http://english.hanban.org/node_10971.htm. Data compiled and aggregated by Alecia D. Hoffman and Regina Moorer.

region of the continent may be correlated to the One Belt One Road Initiative, which has already commenced major projects in this part of Africa. The countries with CIs are Burundi, Comoros, Eritrea, Ethiopia, Kenya, Malawi, Mauritius, Mozambique, Rwanda, Seychelles, Tanzania, Uganda, Zambia, and Zimbabwe. Table 9.6 provides the names, partner institutions, and dates for operational commencement.[33]

Northern Africa has seven countries that house CIs and classrooms. Egypt, Morocco, Sudan, and Tunisia are represented in table 9.7. The names of the host institutes, partner institutions, and dates of operation are provided.

Southern Africa houses eight CIs and four classrooms, with the majority of the CIs and classrooms located in the country of South Africa. South Africa alone has five CIs and three classrooms. The countries of Botswana, Lesotho, and Namibia all have operational CIs/classrooms. Table 9.8 highlights the host institutions and partner institutions in China to the host institute in Southern Africa, along with the dates that each of the CIs became operational.

The last area of the continent that hosts the second largest number of CIs/classrooms is the western region of Africa. The countries of Benin, Cape Verde, Ivory Coast, Ghana, Liberia, Mali, Nigeria, Senegal, Sierra Leonne, and Togo are all home to CIs or classrooms. Table 9.9 provides the names of the host institutions, the Chinse partner institutions, and the year the CI became operational for each country.[34]

CONCLUSION

The PRCs "going out" strategy, with the emphasis on spreading Chinese culture and language, was one of the major goals of the FOCAC VI summit and to date, the PRC has held constant to its commitment to meeting this goal. Although this objective is occurring across the globe in several regions, the role that China is undertaking toward winning the hearts and minds in Africa using soft power has been the focus of this chapter. Furthermore, CIs have not only operated to extend the language and culture of the PRC with the benign goal of winning the hearts and minds of people in foreign lands, but the motive is directly related to the country's own foreign policy objectives.

As a part of the "going global" strategy, which became the watchword for earlier FOCAC summits and also a part of Deng Xiaoping's "opening up" of the Chinese economy in the later 1970s, the need to extend ties that go beyond infrastructure agreements, low-interest loans, economic processing zones (EPZs), and resource extraction is of paramount importance. With the PRCs growing presence in Africa, a connection must be made on the human level, and the exchange of cultural practices must take place on both sides to

Table 9.6 CIs in East Africa

Country	CI Host Institute	CI Classroom	PRC Partner	Operational
Burundi	University of Burundi	—	BOHAI University	9/6/2012
Comoros	University of Comoros	—	Dalian University	6/1/2014
Eritrea	National Board of Higher Education	—	Guizhou University	6/5/2013
Ethiopia	Technical Vocational Education and Training Institute	(Mekelle University)	Tianjin University of Technology and Education	5/12/2010
	Addis Ababa University	(Hawassa University)	Tianjin Vocational Technology Normal University	11/26/2013
Malawi		—	University of International Business and Economics	8/12/2013
Mauritius	University of Mauritius	—	Zhejiang Sci-Tech University	12/14/2016
Mozambique	Eduardo Mondlane University	—	Zhejiang Normal University	04/16/2012
Rwanda	University of Rwanda-College of Education	—	Chong Qing Normal University	04/01/2009
Seychelles	University of Seychelles	—	Dalian University	06/2014
Tanzania	University of Dodoma	(Zanzibar)	Zhengzhou Institute of Aeronautical Industry	04/28/2013
	University of Dar es Salaam		Zhejiang Normal University	10/9/2013
Uganda	Makerere University	—	Xiangtan University	12/19/2014
Zambia	University of Zambia	—	Hebebi University of Economics and Business	9/01/2010
Kenya	University of Nairobi	(CRI Nairobi)	Tianjin Normal University	12/19/2005
	Kenyatta University		Shandong Normal University	6/5/2009
	Egerton University		Nanjong Agricultural University	10/21/2012
	Moi University		Donghua University	03/01/2015
Zimbabwe	University of Zimbabwe	—	RENMIN University of China	03/05/2007

Source: Confucius Institute Classroom/About Confucius Institute Classroom. Accessed March 24, 2020. Available from: http://english.hanban.org/node_10971.htm. Data compiled and aggregated by Alecia D. Hoffman and Regina Moorer.

Table 9.7 CIs in North Africa

Country	CI Host Institute	CI Classroom	PRC Partner	Operational
Egypt	Cairo University	(Ain Shams	Peking University	3/18/2008
	Suez Canal University	University)	Beijing Language and Culture University	4/01/2008
Morocco	University Mohammed V Agdal University of Hassan II Abdelmalek Essaadi University	—	Beijing International Studies University Shanghai International Studies University Jiangxi Science and Technology Normal University	10/19/2009 10/10/2012 09/22/2017
Sudan	University of Khartoum	—	Northwest Normal University	12/17/2009
Tunisia	University of Carthage	(SFAX)	Dalian University of Foreign Languages	5/14/2018

Source: Confucius Institute Classroom/About Confucius Institute Classroom. Accessed March 24, 2020. Available from: http://english.hanban.org/node_10971.htm. Data compiled and aggregated by Alecia D. Hoffman and Regina Moorer.

Table 9.8 CIs in Southern Africa

Country	CI Host Institute	CI Classroom	PRC Partner	Operational
Botswana	University of Botswana	—	Shanghai Normal University	9/6/2009
Lesotho	—	Machabeng College International School of Lesotho	—	—
Namibia	University of Namibia	—	China University of Geosciences (Beijing)	08/23/2013
South Africa	Stellenbosch University University of Capetown Rhodes University Institute of Durban University of Technology University of Johannesburg	(Cape Academy of Mathematics, Science, and Technology) (Westerford High) (Chinese Cultural and International Education Exchange Center)	Xiamen University Sun Yat-sen University Jinan University Fujian Agricultural and Forestry University Nanjing University of Technology	1/01/2009 07/01/2010 08/20/2008 2/20/2014 07/04/2014

Source: Confucius Institute Classroom/About Confucius Institute Classroom. Accessed March 24, 2020. Available from: http://english.hanban.org/node_10971.htm. Data compiled and aggregated by Alecia D. Hoffman and Regina Moorer.

Table 9.9 CIs in West Africa

Country	CI Host Institute	CI Classroom	PRC Partner	Operational
Benin	University of Abomey Calavi	—	Chongqing Jiaotong University	10/21/2009
Cape Verde	University of Cabo Verde	—	Guangdong University of Foreign Studies	09/2015
Cote de' Ivoire	University of Felix Houphouette Boigny	—	Tianjin University of Technology	05/28/2015
Ghana	University of Ghana University of Cape Coast	—	Zhejaing University of Technology Hunan City University	05/2013 09/2016
Liberia	University of Liberia	—	Changsha University of Science and Technology	12/18/2008
Mali	—	Lycee Mohamed Asikia Mohamed School	—	—
Nigeria	University of Lagos Nnamdi Azikwe University	—	Beijing Institute of Technology Xiamen University	05/2009 02/2009
Senegal	University of Dakar	—	Liaoning University	12/03/2012
Sierra Leonne	University of Sierra Leonne	—	Gannan Normal University	9/2012
Togo	University of Lome	—	Sichuan International Studies University	10/30/2009

Source: Confucius Institute Classroom/About Confucius Institute Classroom. Accessed March 24, 2020. Available from: http://english.hanban.org/node_10971.htm. Data compiled and aggregated by Alecia D. Hoffman and Regina Moorer.

build win-win relationships. Additionally, the use of Chinese culture through CIs/classrooms, media, books, movies, and so forth, operates twofold: (1) The sharing of language and culture builds bridges which assist in obtaining jobs with Chinese firms that operate in Africa; (2) the sharing of culture and language through CIs have also helped African students further their education through study abroad programs at host universities in the PRC. Although an examination of the data on the number of African students studying abroad in China after completing initial studies at CIs in Africa was not a variable or hypotheses covered in this research, it is of extreme importance for the entire continent. When these graduates return to Africa, the knowledge, skills, and abilities learned by way of earlier enrollment in CIs and the study abroad programs at the Chinese host institutions will lead to new opportunities for

African people to not only work in companies owned by Chinese firms but to become the managers and voices of authority within these firms and even those that have African genesis which leads to the development and economic forward progression of Africa.

NOTES

1. Klaus Krippendorff. *Content Analysis: An Introduction to Its Methodology* (London: Sage, 1980).

2. Robert PhillipWeber. *Basic Content Analysis* (New Delhi: Sage, 1985).

3. Fred N. Kerlinger. *Foundations of Behavioural Research* (3rd ed). (New York: Holt, Rinehart and Winston, 1986).

4. Joseph S. Nye, Jr., "Think Again: Soft Power," *Foreign Policy* 23 February 2006, accessed 17 December 2018, https://foreignpolicy.com/2006/02/23/think-ag ain-soft-power/.

5. Joseph S. Nye, Jr. *Soft Power: The Means to Success in World Politics* (Cambridge, MA: Perseus Books, 2004), 5.

6. Ibid., 7. Nye paraphrases Jane S. Mansbridge's work entitled *Beyond Self Interest.* (Chicago: University of Chicago Press, 1990).

7. Ibid.

8. "Chinese Medical Services Boost Healthcare in Africa," *Global Times: Discover China, Discover the World*, August 21, 2018, Accessed December 17, 2018, http://www.globaltimes.cn/content/1116386.shtml.

9. Jean Kachiga, *China in Africa: Articulating China's Africa Policy* (Trenton, NJ: Africa World Press, 2013), 3. Also see John Cooley, *East Wind over Africa: Red China's African Offensive* (New York: Walker Books, 1965).

10. Li Baoping and Luo Jianbo, "Dissecting Soft Power and Sino-Africa Relations in Education and Exchanges Cooperation," in *Forum on China-Africa Cooperation: The Politics of Human Resource Development,* ed. Li Anshan and Funeka Yazini April (South Africa: Africa Institute of South Africa, 2013), 28–29.

11. Ibid., 28.

12. Ibid., 29.

13. Ibid., 35–37.

14. Kenneth King, "Higher Education Engagement with Africa: A Different Partnership and Cooperation Model?" in *Education, Learning, Training: Critical Issues for Development.* Gilles Carbonnier Michael Carton, and Kenneth King eds. (Leiden—Boston, MA: Brill Publications, 2014), 151–173.

15. Kenneth King, "China's Cooperation with Africa, and Especially South Africa, in Education and Training: A Special Relationship and Different Approach to Aid," *Journal of International Cooperation in Education* Vol. 13, no. 2 (2010): 73–87.

16. Maddalena Procopio, "The Effectiveness of Confucius Institutes as a Tool of China's soft power in South Africa," *Africa East-Asian Affairs* no. 2 (June 2015): 98–124.

17. James F. Paradise, "China and International Harmony," *Asian Survey* Vol. 49, no. 4 (July/August 2009): 647.

18. Ibid., 665.

19. Frank Youngblood, "Strengthening Africa-China Relations: A Perspective from Botswana" *Centre for Chinese Studies at Stellenbosch University* (November 2013): 1–20.

20. Ibid., 8–10.

21. Bertha Z. Osei-Hwedie, "The Dynamics of China-Africa Cooperation," *Afro-Asian Journal of Social Sciences* Vol. 3 no. 3.1 (Quarter 1 2012): 8.

22. Xiaoling Zhang, Herman Wasserman and Winston Mano eds., *Evolving Media Interactions Between China and Africa* (New York: Palgrave MacMillan, 2016).

23. Ran Jijun, "Examining Media Interactions Between China and Africa," in *Evolving Media Interactions Between China and Africa*, eds. Xiaoling Zhang, Herman Wasserman, and Winston Mano, 47–61. Palgrave Series in Asia and Pacific Studies (New York: Palgrave MacMillan, 2016).

24. Dani Madrid-Morales, "Why are the Chinese Media in Africa," in *Evolving Media Interactions Between China and Africa*, eds. Xiaoling Zhang, Herman Wasserman, and Winston Mano, 79–92. Palgrave Series in Asia and Pacific Studies (New York: Palgrave MacMillan, 2016).

25. Jacinta Mwende Maweu, "Journalists and Public Perceptions of the Politics of China's Soft Power in Kenya Under the 'Look East' Foreign Policy," in *Evolving Media Interactions Between China and Africa*, eds. Xiaoling Zhang, Herman Wasserman, and Winston Mano, 123–134. Palgrave Series in Asia and Pacific Studies (New York: Palgrave MacMillan, 2016).

26. "About Us—Haban" 2014. Accessed December 20, 2018, http://english.hanban.org/node_7719.htm.

27. Xiohe Cheng, "Education: The Intellectual Base of China's Soft Power" in *Soft Power: China's Emerging Strategy in International Politics*, ed. Mingjiang Li (Lanham, MD: Lexington Books, 2009), 103–123, 114.

28. Ibid.

29. World Tourism Organization [UNWTO]. *UNWTO Tourism Highlights, 2016 Edition*. Madrid: UNWTO, 2016. Available from: http://www.unwto.org/facts/eng/highlights.htm. Last access on April 12, 2019.

30. "Forum on China-Africa Cooperation Beijing Action Plan (2019-2021)," 2018 Beijing Summit of the Forum on China-Africa Cooperation, Accessed March 31, 2019, https://focacsummit.mfa.gov.cn/eng/hyqk_1/t1594297.htm.

31. "Methodology—Geographic Regions," United Nations, accessed December 13, 2018, https://unstats.un.org/unsd/methodology/m49/.

32. Much of the data pertaining to the Chinese partner institutions for the countries of Central Africa can be accessed through Haban. Available from: http://english.hanban.org/node_10971.htm. However, the countries of The Democratic Republic of Congo and Equatorial Guinea lacked specific data via Haban. Additional information was found via Haban news articles. For more information pertaining to the countries see "The First Confucius Institute of the Democratic Republic of the Congo Holds Unveiling Ceremony" *Xinhuanet.com* August 29, 2018. Available from: http://english.hanban.org/article/2018-08/29/content_742888.htm; "The First Confucius Institute Opens in Equatorial Guinea" Confucius Institute Headquarters (Haban)

January 29, 2016, Available from http://english.hanban.org/article/2016-01/29/conte
nt_630631.htm. All data from the each of the five regions was obtained from Haban
"Confucius Institute Classroom/About Confucius Institute Classroom. Available
from: http://english.hanban.org/node_10971.htm.

33. Haban does not offer complete data for the countries of Comoros, Malawi,
and Seychelles. Cross referencing of news articles was completed to obtain dates
of inaugural opening of the CIs in the countries. See "President Xi Jinping Witness
Signing Ceremony of Agreement on Establishing Confucius Institute at University of
Comoros," *Haban News* September 5, 2018 available from: http://english.hanban.org/
article/2018-09/05/content_743300.htm; "Confucius Institute at University of Malawi
Officially Inaugurated," *Haban News* August 26, 2016 available from: http://eng
lish.hanban.org/article/2016-08/26/content_654616.htm; "Students of the Confucius
Institute Receive Chinese Course Certificates," News—University of Seychelles
September 26, 2014 available from: https://www.unisey.ac.sc/index.php/media-content
/news/item/92-students-of-the-confucius-institute-receive-chinese-course-certificates.
The countries that house Confucius classrooms are not associated to the PRC partner
institution nor are they associated with the host institution of the country. Furthermore,
the dates of establishment are not provided for the CI classrooms in the table.

34. There is a lack of information pertaining to the start date for the Confucius
Institute in Cape Verde. According to the Permanent Secretariat of Forum for
Economic and Trade-Cooperation Between China and Portuguese Speaking
Countries, the CI opened its doors in Cape Verde in September 2015. For more
information see "Confucius Institute Opening Cape Verde Branch in September,"
Permanent Secretariat of Forum for Economic and Trade-Cooperation Between
China and Portuguese Speaking Countries—News July 28, 2015. Accessed April
4, 2019. Available from: http://www.forumchinaplp.org.mo/cabo-verde-2/; As it
pertains to the Ivory Coast, see "First Confucius Institute in Côte d'Ivoire Officially
Inaugurated," *Haban News* June 12, 2015. Accessed April 14, 2019. Available from:
http://english.hanban.org/article/2015-06/12/content_604336.htm.

BIBLIOGRAPHY

"2018 Campus Recruitment Hosted by the Confucius Institute at the University of
Ghana." The University of Ghana. March 2, 2018. http://www.ug.edu.gh/conf
ucius-institute/news/2018-campus-recruitment-hosted-confucius-institute-universi
ty-ghana.
"About Us—Haban." 2014. http://english.haban.org/node_7719.htm.
Cheng, Xiohe. "Education: The Intellectual Base of China's Soft Power," *In Soft
Power: China's Emerging Strategy in International Politics*, edited by Mingjiang
Li, 103–123. Lanham: Lexington Books, 2009.
"China Business Job Fair Attracts Egypt University Students." *China Daily*. May 2,
2017. http://www.chinadaily.com.cn/business/2017-05/02/content_29164593.htm.
China National Tourism Administration. Available from: www.cnta.gov.cn.

"China-Tanzania Job Fair Kicks Off in Dar es Salaam." *Xinhuanet News.* June 17, 2007. http://www.xinhuanet.com//english/2017-06/17/c_136373605.htm.

"Chinese Campus Recruitment Fair Yields Employment for Several Ghanaians." *The Finder Online.* March 2, 2018. https://thefinderonline.com/news/item/12014 -chinese-campus-recruitment-fair-yields-employment-for-several-ghanaians?tmpl =component&print=1.

"Chinese Medical Services Boost Healthcare in Africa." *Global Times: Discover China, Discover the World.* August 21, 2018. http://www.globaltimes.cn/content /1116386.shtml.

"Chinese Serves as Bridge for Exchanges and Cooperation (Consultation, Contribution, and Shared Benefits: Fifth Anniversary of Belt and Road Initiative)." *People's Daily* October 12, 2018. https://webcache.googleusercontent.com/search?q=cache :http://english.hanban.org/article/2018-10/12/content_747014.htm.

"Confucius Institute Classroom/About Confucius Institute Classroom." Haban. http:/ /english.hanban.org/node_10971.htm.

"Confucius Institute Holds Graduation, Alumni Inauguration, and Job Fair, July 31." TheUniversity of Lagos. July 26, 2018. https://unilag.edu.ng/confucius-institute -holds-graduation-alumni-inauguration-and-job-fair-july-31/.

"Confucius Institute at University of Malawi Officially Inaugurated." *Haban News.* August 26, 2016. http://english.haban.org/article/2016-08/26/content_654616.htm.

"Confucius Institute Opening Cape Verde Branch in September." Permanent Secretariat of Forum for Economic and Trade-Cooperation Between China and Portuguese Speaking Countries—News. July 28, 2015. http://www.forumchin aaplp.org.mo/cabo-verde-2/.

Cooley, John. *East Wind Over Africa: Red China's African Offensive.* New York: Walker Books, 1965.

"First Confucius Institute in Côte d'Ivoire Officially Inaugurated." *Haban News.* June 12, 2015. http://english.haban.org/article/2015-06/12/content_604336.htm.

"First Confucius Institute of the Democratic Republic of the Congo Holds Unveiling Ceremony." *Xinhuanet.com.* August 29, 2018. http:english.haban.org/article/2018 -8/29/content_742888.htm.

"First Confucius Institute Opens in Equatorial Guinea." Confucius Institute Headquarters (Haban). January 29, 2016. http://english.haban.org/article/2016-01 /29/content_630631.htm.

"Forum on China-Africa Cooperation Beijing Action Plan (2019-2021)." 2018 Beijing Summit of the Forum on China-Africa Cooperation. https://focacsummit. mfa.gov.cn/eng/hyqk_1/t1594297.htm.

Haban. http://english.haban.org/node_10971.htm.

———. "Confucius Institute Classroom/About Confucius Institute Classroom." http://english.haban.org/node_10971.htm.

Huaxia. "Ghanaian Graduates Bank on Chinese Firms for Jobs." *Xinhua News.* March 19, 2017. https://webcache.googleusercontent.com/search?q=cache:http://news .xinhuanet.com/english/2017-03/19/c_136140542.htm.

———. Huaxia. "Zambia's Confucius Institute Host Job Expo to Help Chinese Firms Attract Local Talent." *Xinhua.* October 27, 2018. https://webcache.googleusercon

tent.com/search?q=cache:http://www.xinhuanet.com/english/2018-10/27/c_13756 2639.htm.

Jijun, Ran. "Examining Media Interactions Between China and Africa." *In Evolving Media Interactions Between China and Africa,* edited by Xiaoling Zhang, Herman Wasserman, and Winston Mano, 47–61. Palgrave Series in Asia and Pacific Studies. New York: Palgrave MacMillan, 2016.

Kachiga, Jean. *China in Africa: Articulating China's Africa Policy.* Trenton: Africa World Press, 2013.

Kargbo, Abu Bakar. "China Facilitates First Job Fair and International Company Exhibition." *People's Daily Online.* May 3, 2018. https://webcache.googleus ercontent.com/search?q=cache:http://en.people.cn/n3/2018/0503/c90000-945598 3.html.

Kazoka, Ludovic. "Tanzania: Chinese Companies to Recruit En Masse at Job Fair in Dar." *AllAfrica.com News.* June 16, 2016. https://allafrica.com/stories/20160 6160394.html.

Kerlinger, Fred N. *Foundations of Behavioral Research 3rd Edition.* New York: Holt, Rinehart and Winston, 1986.

King, Kenneth. "China's Cooperation with Africa and Especially South Africa, In Educational Training: A Special Relationship and Different Approach to Aid." *Journal of International Cooperation in Education.* Vol. 13, no. 2 (2010): 73–87.

———. "Higher Education Engagement in Africa: A Different Partnership and Cooperation Model?" In *Education, Learning, Training: Critical Issues for Development* edited by Giles Carbonnier, Michael Carton, and Kenneth King, 151–173. Leiden—Boston: Brill Publications, 2014.

Krippendorff, Klaus. *Content Analysis: An Introduction to Its Methodology.* London: Sage Publications, 1980.

Lanka. "2018 Confucius Institute at the University Job Fair." Confucius Institute-University of Nairobi. January 11, 2019. http://confucius.uonbi.ac.ke/print/68327.

———. "Job Fair for Kenyan Students in 2017 Held at Confucius Institute at University of Nairobi." December 20, 2017. Available from: http://confucius.uon bi.ac.ke/content/job-fair-kenyan-students-2017-held-confucius-institute-university -nairobi-0.

Liben, Habtamu and Wang Shoubao. "Feature: Ethiopian Professionals Learn Chinese Language to Boost Career Opportunities." *China.org.cn.* January 20, 2019. http:// www.china.org.cn/world/Off_the_Wire/2019-01/20/content_74391477.htm.

Li, Bioping and Luo Jianbo. "Dissecting Soft Power and Sino-African Relations in Education and Exchanges Cooperation." In *Forum on China-Africa Cooperation: The Politics of Human Resource Development,* edited by Li Anshan and Feneka Yazini April 28–29. South Africa: Africa Institute of South Africa, 2013.

Madrid-Morales, Dani. "Why are the Chinese Media in Africa." *In Evolving Media Interactions Between China and Africa,* edited by Xiaoling Zhang, Herman Wasserman, and Winston Mano, 79–92. Palgrave Series in Asia and Pacific Studies. New York: Palgrave MacMillan, 2016.

Masiyiwa, Gamuchirai. "Knowledge of Mandarin Chinese Opens Doors for Zimbabwe's Young Job Seekers." *Global Press Journal.* [nd].https://globalp

ressjournal.com/africa/zimbabwe/knowledge-mandarin-chinese-opens-doors-zimb abwes-young-job-seekers/.

Maweu, Jacinto Mwende. "Journalist and Public Perceptions of the Politics of China's Soft Power in Kenya Under the 'Look East' Foreign Policy." In *Evolving Media Interactions Between China and Africa,* edited by Xiaoling Zhang, Herman Wasserman, and Winston Mano, 123–134. Palgrave Series in Asia and Pacific Studies. New York: Palgrave MacMillan, 2016.

"Methodology—Geographic Regions." United Nations. https://unstats.un.org/unsd/ methodology/m49/.

Iddriss, Mussa Iddriss. "CIUCC Organizes a Maiden Chinese Enterprise Job Fair for UCC Students." Confucius University Cape Coast Ghana. February 5, 2018. https:/ /confuciusucc.com/2018/05/02/ciucc-organizes-maiden-chinese-enterprise-job-fai r-ucc-students/.

Nye, Joseph S. *Soft Power: The Means to Success in World Politics.* Cambridge: Perseus Books, 2004.

———. "Think Again: Soft Power," *Foreign Policy* 23 February 2006, accessed 17 December 2018. https://foreignpolicy.com/2006/02/23/think-again-soft-power/.

Osei-Hwedie, Bertha. "The Dynamics of China-Africa Cooperation." *Afro-Asian Journal of Social Sciences.* Vol. 3, no. 3.1 (Quarter 1 2012): 1–25.

Paradise, James F. "China and International Harmony." *Asian Survey.* Vol. 49, no. 4 (July/August 2009): 647.

"President Xi Jinping Witness Signing Ceremony of Agreement on Establishing Confucius Institute at University of Comoros." *Haban News.* September 5, 2018. Available from: http://english.haban.org/article/2018-09/05/content_743300.htm.

Procopio, Maddalena, "The Effectiveness of Confucius Institutes as a Tool of China's Soft Power in South Africa." *Africa East-Asian Affairs.* no. 2 (June 2015): 98–124.

"Students of the Confucius Institute Receive Chinese Course Certificates." News— University of Seychelles. September 26, 2014. Available from: https://www.uni sey.ac.sc/index.php/media-content/news/item/92-students-of-the-confucius-institu te-receive-chinese-course-certificates.

United Nations. United Nations ComTrade Database. Available from: https://com-trade.un.org/data.

"Universities Collaborate with Business Establishments." *Business Ghana.* March 22, 2017. https://www.businessghana.com/site/news/general/143298/Universities-co llaborate-with-business-establishments.

"University of Ghana Hosts Chinese Enterprises Campus Recruitment." *New China.* [nd]. http://www.xinhuanet.com/english/2017-03/21/c_136145747.htm.

Weber, Robert Phillip. *Basic Content Analysis.* New Delhi: Sage Publications, 1985.

World Economic Forum. *The Travel and Tourism Competitiveness Report 2017.* Available from: http://www3.weforum.org/docs/WEF_TTCR_2017_web_0401.pdf.

World Tourism Organization [UNWTO]. *UNWTO Tourism Highlights, 2016 Edition.* Madrid: UNWTO, 2016. Available from: http://www.unwto.org/facts/eng/highlig hts.htm.

Yan, He. "Students Explore Employment Opportunities in China-Tanzania Job Fair." *CGTN News.* June 20, 2017. https://news.cgtn.com/news/3d49444f324d444e/s hare_p.html.

"You are Wanted: Confucius Institute at Durban University of Technology Organizes Chinese Enterprises to Job Fair for the First Time." *Haban News*. September 6, 2018. https://webcache.googleusercontent.com/search?q=cache:http://english.h anban.org/article/2018-09/06/content_745763.htm.

Youngblood, Frank. "Strengthening Africa-China Relations: A Perspective from Botswana." *Centre for Chinse Studies at Stellenbosch University* (November 2013): 1–20.

Yue, Wang. "Chinese Firms Resonate with Kenyan Youth in Search of Career Mobility." All- China Women's Federation. December 19, 2018. http://www .womenofchina.cn/womenofchina/html1/news/international/1812/5857-1.htm.

Chapter 10

Politics and Governance

*China's Hands-Off Approach
to African Politics*

Charles Mutasa

INTRODUCTION

China's foreign policy is premised on the principle of sovereignty and equality, which is very appealing to many African countries that have suffered a lot from Western conditionalities for development aid. By placing equality at the forefront of cooperation, the Chinese managed to win the hearts of many African leaders. Based on this principle, China's hands-off approach, which is dubbed "the non-intervention and no strings attached" foreign policy has dominated the relations between China and African countries. The Forum on China-Africa Cooperation (FOCAC) was set up in 2000 as a way of strengthening China-Africa political and economic relations.[1] China for most African leaders offers a completely different model of human development, a model very different than Europe and the United States. China's hands-off approach to African politics has been viewed as undermining initiatives by Western countries to use development aid as a carrot and stick approach to compel African countries to embrace good governance and respect the promotion and protection of human rights. The noninterference approach in the internal affairs of African countries as a key tenet of Chinese foreign policy calls for more rigorous academic scrutiny than any other developmental phenomenon in the twenty-first century.

Many scholars recognize the potential and importance of China's presence, in opening up new opportunities for sub-Saharan Africa's development. Most African leaders, contrary to what their citizens think, have praised Chinese presence and investment to support growth in their countries. However, most scholars and human rights activists feel that the Sino-Africa relations are benefiting China more than African countries given the

215

fact that Africa is a market that China feels it can tap into for its production and trade. Besides, the idea of markets, China has made it a point that countries that relate with it must renounce relations with Taiwan. Denouncing Taiwan is good for China as it rallies support from developing countries, especially Africa, which happens to have the majority support at the United Nations.[2]

China's hands-off approach in Africa has implications for the type of governments, political parties, civil society actors, and development partners that the continent is likely to have. In the area of governance and human rights, some of the gains may be reversed as dictators find a haven in China's approach. China is known for its restrictions on citizens' freedom and intolerance of dissent. The European Union (EU) has long frowned at China's action in Africa for not requiring respect for human rights as a condition for aid and thus promoting a Chinese-inspired authoritarian Africa.[3] For example, China has stood with Zimbabwe since the ruling party came to power in 1980, and through the period since 2002 after it was slammed with sanctions for seizing white-owned farms in a controversial land reform program.

THE BASIS AND RATIONALE FOR CHINA'S HANDS-OFF APPROACH TO AFRICAN POLITICS

China's relation with Africa started with an ideological link and it dates back to the Bandung conference of 1955. The cooperation between China and most African countries drew inspiration from shared experiences of fighting Western imperialism and hegemony.[4] Over the years, the relations between China and Africa have evolved to include commercial, diplomatic, social, and military reasons. China's closeness to most African countries is a remnant of the time that China bankrolled most revolutionary movements against colonialism. The support given by China included training of liberation fighters under Mao Zedong. French (2007) argues that China's renewed interest and cooperation with Africa at the beginning of the twenty-first century expressed through the establishment of FOCAC was less political as it had to do more with its economic growth aimed at getting copper from Zambia and the Democratic Republic of Congo, Oil from Angola, Sudan and South Sudan, and iron ore from Gabon.[5] China has refuted claims that it is in Africa to exploit its resources. According to the Chinese Ministry of Foreign Affairs, China's aid to Africa is based on the following principles: sincerity, friendship, and equality, mutual benefit, reciprocity, common prosperity, mutual support, close coordination, learning from each other, and seeking common development.[6] China has argued that it is after "mutual benefit" as evidenced by "no strings attached" to its aid to Africa. China has also refuted allegations that they are taking over jobs meant for locals in African countries arguing that they only bring in their labor to quicken the delivery of expected results.[7]

Over the years, with a growing and diversifying global influence, it has been increasingly difficult for Beijing to stick to its noninterference foreign policy especially when a lot is at stake after some major political or economic instability in an African country. Africa has become a testing ground for the sustainability of the hands-off foreign policy approach by China. In countries such as Sudan and South Sudan, where there it has oil interests, China has found itself having to do shuttle diplomacy between government, opposition groups, and civil society representatives.[8] In 2011, China as a permanent member of the UN Security Council surprisingly backed the UN Resolution 1973 on Libya as it took into consideration the positions of Arab countries, the African Union, and the Organization of Islamic conference that condemned the serious human rights violations by Colonel Gaddafi's regime. Thus, China supported the underlying principle of the responsibility to protect (R2P) but was reluctant about the use of force to implement it. China refrained from using its veto power in the UN Security Council Resolution to authorize military action, against the Libyan government. Both in the case of Sudan and Libya, it can be argued that China deviated from its traditional stance of noninterference and resorted to a new direction in its diplomacy.[9] Another sign of pragmatism in response to a fast-changing world was witnessed in 2014 when China opened its first military base in Djibouti and began UN peacekeeping missions in 2015.

In the period after 2000, China's policy shift toward Africa was a result of realizing several economic and political advantages in working with the continent. First, Africa has the numbers when it comes to supporting multilateral forums when it comes to "bloc voting."[10] This is evidenced in African countries backing China's application for a seat in the Security Council. Second, China noted the diminishing interest and influence of the West in Africa. Third and in terms of China's economic growth, Africa is a growing source of energy and natural resources for China.[11] Fourth, for international diplomacy and foreign policy, which is aimed at isolating Taiwan in Africa.

It is worth noting that with its expanding global reach China is caught between supporting problematic regimes and pressure from the international community to act against them. In the case of Libya, where the regime had undoubtedly committed atrocities and failed to protect civilians causing unnecessary bloodshed, China did not want to put its reputation at risk by blocking the United Nations Security Council Resolution. Vetoing the resolution and supporting Libya would have meant China would be criticized for sabotaging international community efforts to protect civilians.[12] In most of its voting at the United Nations Security Council, China seeks to differentiate itself from the interests of hegemonic superpowers: the United States of

America, the United Kingdom, and France. In complicated cases, China has sought to use "soft power," which includes private communication and quiet persuasion. In line with this, Beijing has offered education scholarships and opportunities for students from developing countries. It is estimated that more than 100,000 African students are studying in Chinese universities and military institutes, and China is sending more than 900 Chinese doctors to African countries as well as establishing more than 100 new Confucius Institutes, which are culture and language centers.[13] Some scholars argue that China [with the use of its "non-interference policy" or "soft power"] is also trying to set itself up as a leader on the world stage, in opposition to the West and the United States.

China's noninterference and go global policies have helped it to become an emerging political and economic giant, as well as one of the largest trading partners for the fifty-four countries within Africa. By investing in infrastructure, agriculture, and energy in African countries such as Rwanda, Angola, and Equatorial Guinea without setting conditionalities, China is getting more international allies which will help its rise to the position of being a superpower ahead of the United States. It can be argued that China through its hands-off approach is helping African countries to regain economic power without relinquishing political power, which happens when they yield to Western demands for reforms in governance and human rights. "Unsurprisingly, a growing number of African leaders look at the Chinese approach to aid and investment with relish. Even those who have established lucrative relationships with the West, like Djibouti, are willing to sign up for Chinese monetary incentives and collaborate with its geostrategic goals."[14]

China's economic cooperation with African countries has differed from one country to the other, depending on the type of governance and economics that the country is pursuing. Ghana and Rwanda give us two different narratives of bilateral engagements, a variance in resources, and the different outcomes achieved thereof. Ghana is considered to be rich with gold and cocoa, democratic, given its commitment to human rights promotion and protection, while Rwanda is not resource-endowed, regarded to be authoritarian, given the heavy-handedness power is exercised by the Kagame regime since the 1994 genocide. Ghana has enjoyed relative stability, ranked high on most governance and economic performance indicators. The two examples should provide a road map of what matters for Beijing and what does not.

SINO-GHANA COOPERATION

Ghana was the first country to get independence in sub-Saharan Africa and as such, it was the first to engage China as well as taking a lead in transforming itself from military rule to multiparty politics. Since the 1960s, China and Ghana enjoy good bilateral relations within the framework of noninterference in each other's internal politics. China like Communist Russia offered military training in Ghana in the use of explosives and guerrilla tactics to many freedom fighters from across Africa in the 1960s and early 1970s. In the twenty-first century, Ghana's economic deals with China have evolved around assistance to finance high-profile infrastructure projects (road, airline, telecommunication, railway, water supply, and dam projects), diversification and transformation of its economy through gas, education, expanded access to new technologies, and proposed oil-driven industrialization. Ghana has reciprocated with the provision of raw materials, voting in favor of the retention of China's seat at the United Nations and the One-China policy. China currently buys 60 percent of Ghanaian metal exports and trade between the two countries, which was boosted by the discovery of oil in Ghana in 2007.[15] Politically, Ghana supports China's foreign interest, while China backs Ghana's economic transformation and regional integration efforts through boosting its oil production, mining, and construction sectors. The deepening of bilateral relations between China and Ghana has to an extent involved the strengthening of interpersonal and cultural exchanges.

Unlike the Chinese, Ghanaians have unfailingly disallowed dictatorial rule and state abuse of office. Their relations with China remain historical and in international issues only. Despite its friendship with China, Ghana remains a fledgling democracy, which has held periodic elections and made strides toward enhancing the rule of law and good governance as the basis of democracy. Ghana is considered as one of the success stories of democratization in Africa—a "functioning, multi-ethnic democracy" with considerable progress in human development.[16] Ghana has worked with other development partners like the U.S. Agency for International Development (USAID) to strengthen inclusion, accountability, and participatory mechanisms at both local and central government levels.

Ghanaians unlike Chinese and other African peers have managed to make their democracy go beyond electoral participation to holding duty bearers to account when they assume office after elections. Political voice, which is citizens freely taking part in politics, has been key to consolidating democracy. There is the increased use of the media, think-tanks, political parties, civil society organizations, community-based organizations, and individuals influencing policy-making, and hold those holding public offices accountable for their actions.[17] For example, Ghanaian civil society campaigned about illegal gold mining by the Chinese, and resultantly government took action and that was stopped.[18] Increased popular participation and the peaceful handover of power from one regime to the other has made Ghana different from most countries that the Chinese have been engaging in the continent. Ghana's system of governance has created citizens' faith in the political system and the country experiences higher voter turnout in every election. Unlike in China and most African countries, citizens in Ghana still influence economic policies by the party that forms government after elections. However, several challenges to Ghana's democracy remain in the areas of traditional practices such as witchcraft accusations, harmful widowhood rites, and female genital mutilation.[19]

CHINA-RWANDA RELATIONS

Rwanda is another example of a government that China has helped improve its national development without interfering in its internal affairs, though at the expense of the right to protect citizens from state excesses, promoting good governance and human rights. The Rwanda-China engagement has been described as a win-win situation though Rwanda is less endowed with natural resources.[20] China has assisted Rwanda under the South-South cooperation umbrella in the areas of infrastructure, telecommunications, and power generation-areas that Western aid donors have been reluctant to fund. In the area of infrastructure, China has helped to put up the much-needed buildings, roads, and bridges in Rwanda, while Zhongxing Telecommunication Equipment Corporation (globally known as ZTE) assisted local telecom operators MTN and TIGO, and Huawei providing the information technology equipment. Besides these projects, China opened a Confucius Institute in Kigali to teach Chinese language and culture to the Rwandan community. An Agro-veterinary secondary school was also built in Rwanda's Western province. In 2015, a Chinese garment firm, C&H Garments with previous operations in Kenya, opened a factory in Kigali, introducing new experiments in technology transfer and training. Zhang (1996) maintains that most of the development assistance offered to Rwanda by China is in the form of grants, state-sponsored investments, noninterest loans, concessional loans, and debt cancellations.[21] Generally, China's bilateral aid is in the form of loans, grants, and debt relief, while the loans are both noninterest and concessional. In return for such support, Rwanda together with other African countries support China in its "One China policy" and its retaining of a permanent seat at the United Nations Security Council. Chinese aid has been described by the Rwandese government as flexible when compared to the West and above all China is commended for been consistent with the principles of "equality and mutual benefits/win-win" and "non-interference in internal affairs." President Paul Kagame, who is a renowned critic of aid to Africa, described China's aid and investment strategy as "deeply transformational" and respectful of Africa's global position.[22]

China's rule just like most African leaders, including Rwanda is strongly associated with the shrinking of civil society space by government, heavy control of the internet, and the incarceration of dissenting voices, especially human rights activists and lawyers.[23] Despite the progress made in assisting Rwanda with developmental work, the Chinese hands-off approach in Rwanda has not helped to improve its system of governance and human rights. In Kagame's twenty-four years as the de facto leader of Rwanda, most of his critics have been incarcerated, tortured, assassinated, or fled into exile. Human Rights Watch and Amnesty International notes that most critics of the Kagame regime especially investigators, journalists, and opposition politicians have been found dead in mysterious circumstances.[24] President Kagame has administered foreign aid with a strict autocratic hand and Beijing has turned a blind eye to this. Most Rwandese have remained silent beneficiaries of the development efforts by their President fearing to speak out lest they lose their lives. Opposition leaders contesting for presidency in Rwanda are not free to openly criticize President Kagame. President Kagame is known for having shut down both local and foreign media houses and human rights institutions—including programs run by Transparency International, Lawyers without Borders, and the Rwandan League for the Promotion and Defense of Human Rights that reported on government policy failures, extravagances and viciousness.[25] Although donors, including the International Monetary Fund, and governments of the United States and Britain have showered praises on President Kagame as leading a rising star in African development, they have ignored the authoritarian methods used to achieve it. There is no doubt that economic cooperation between Rwanda and China has grown considerably, promoted mutual benefit, and has the potential to transform Rwanda's economy, though having serious deficits in human rights and governance.

CHINA'S INFLUENCE AT THE UNITED NATIONS

As a member of the United Nations Security Council, China has maintained consistency in pursuing its foreign policy principles of noninterference and respect for national sovereignty. At the multilateral and bilateral levels, China presented its diplomacy as safeguarding the interests of sovereignty, security, and development, which promotes a multipolar world, and the prudential management of major power relations.[26] To China, global power is shifting from West to East and from established to emerging economies and states. At the United Nations, China has as part of advancing the right to protect committed itself to uphold international peace and good order. Within the UN

Security Council, China has used its veto power to shed light on their particular political interests.[27] Most vetoes and abstentions have aligned China with Russia on issues of particular interest to them as emerging powers or in support of the developing world, especially Africa.

Recent vetoes pertain to the ongoing conflict in Syria, where China did not support an investigation into the use of chemical weapons and also sided with Russia in condemning Western strikes in Syria. In 2008, China vetoed a proposal that threatened sanctions against the government of Zimbabwe over electoral violence and intimidation. Due to its economic interests, in 2018, it abstained from voting on two resolutions that sought to impose an arms embargo and extend sanctions on South Sudan.[28] For Zimbabwe and Sudan, China cognizant of historical relations, the geostrategic positions of the countries and the economic consequences of the sanctions, opted to save them from such punishment by the international community. It should also be noted that China has been choosy when it comes to deploying its peacekeepers. In Africa, when deploying peacekeepers, China has shown great interest in the Democratic Republic of Congo, Liberia, and Sudan given the endowment of these countries with some natural resources.

It can be argued that China's voting pattern within the UN Security Council, especially the abstentions are a sign that it is not ready to be a global leader. The vetoing seems to demonstrate that China with its hands-off approach does want to keep a low profile when it comes to tackling global challenges. UN records indicate between 1995 and 2005, of the five permanent members of the UN Security Council, it has the highest abstentions, totaling fifty-one. Its use of veto power seems to suggest a reluctance to become involved in time and resource-consuming efforts to manage international crises, leaving the world to yield to the dominant voices and values of the Western countries.[29] This could be its obsession with prudence and its principles of equality and sovereignty. However, several challenges to Ghana's democracy remain in the areas of traditional practices such as witchcraft accusations, harmful widowhood rites, and female genital mutilation. At the United Nations, China is known to be pursuing three policy goals: defending its national interest, engaging the major global powers (i.e., the United States in particular), and addressing international threats to peace and stability. China together with Russia has ensured that the United Nations and global institutions are balanced in structure and operation—not held hostage by Western ideas and excesses. For example, China ensured that in the 2011 Libya military intervention, NATO's wings were curbed and was not given the mandate to do as the West wished. Thus, China is pushing for more global consensus-building and respect of the values: justice, equality, respect for human rights, and inclusiveness.

CHINA'S COOPERATION WITH OTHER
INTERNATIONAL BODIES

China's voting behavior at the UN Security Council has been greatly influenced by the regional bodies of developing countries. For instance, China in 2011 sided with the African Union's position on the establishment of a no-fly-zone in Libya. China in line with its policies of seeking peace and stability in the globe has supported UN initiatives meant to strengthen regional bodies like the African Union.[30] As part of its preventive diplomacy, China has gone on to insist that issues of conflict in Africa must first be dealt with by the African Union and the United Nations must be guided by the positions being taken by the African Union. To this end, the annual joint meetings between the UN Security Council and the Peace and Security Council of the African Union have served to strengthen cooperation with regional organizations in Africa. For China, the global security governance system is better and well-developed if it is coordinated through various regional security arrangements. The establishment of a UN Multidimensional Integrated Stabilization Mission in Mali (MINUSMA) reflected such a cautious and pragmatic approach on China's part.[31] In 2013, China supported the African Union deferral of the International Criminal Court (ICC) cases against the Kenyan president and the vice president and the motion that no sitting head of state or government should be prosecuted by the ICC. China, though it had its reservations on the African Union suggestions, supported calls for the reform of the UN Security Council including an enhanced role of African countries within the Council as laid out in the 2005 Ezulwini Consensus.[32] According to the Ezulwini Consensus, African countries are requesting to have at least two permanent members with veto rights and five nonpermanent members at the United Nations.

With its "hands-off approach," China has used different platforms to establish links with developing countries, especially those in Africa. The Group of 77 (G77) developing nations and the South-South Cooperation are some of the platforms where China has established areas of cooperation with African countries in the name of solidarity. China is not a member of G77 but offers political and financial support to the group and its members. In most cases, China has presented itself as the leader of the developing world. For example, at the Doha round of trade negotiations, China took a lead in siding with developing countries to demand the end of rich-country agricultural subsidies. Notions such as "We believe that China and Africa are a community with a shared future. China is the largest developing country. Africa is the continent with the most developing countries"[33] have been echoed and cherished among Africa leaders.

One of the high-level dialogue mechanisms to attain international peace being advanced by China at the international level, for the benefit of African countries, is the Strategic and Economic Dialogue (S&ED).[34] The US-China Strategic and Economic Dialogue established by President Obama and Chinese President Hu in April 2009 has helped promote the positive, constructive, and comprehensive relationship between the two countries, which in turn would benefit Africa and other developing countries. Some of the key global issues discussed between China and the United States are climate change-reduction of carbon footprint. Consensus and bargains between the two nations have been key to get certain global processes to work for the entire world. Both the United States and China are not interested in Africa's stability just for access to markets for their products but also in their pursuit of global leadership. On the other hand, a trade war between China and the US brings both opportunities and harm to African countries. It may mean Africa's less dependence on these two economic giants, opportunities to fill the export gap to the United States, and even to fill some commodities export gaps left by the United States in China itself.[35]

A CRITIQUE OF THE CHINESE APPROACH

Some scholars have accused China of neocolonialism, depicting China's investment in the continent as a second scramble for Africa. Langan (2017) argues that China is an imperial power seeking to advance its interest in Africa through the use of aid and trade. Similarly, Michael Sata, the fifth Zambian president, accused China of neocolonial tendencies seeking to bribe Africa leaders, exploit the continent's resources and advance its interests.[36] China is also accused of back-rolling up rogue and corrupt states in Africa. Most dictatorial regimes that the West has denied development aid based on their political, economic, and human rights records have turned to China for assistance. China due to its hands-free approach is regarded as an "All-weather friend." For example, President Mugabe who ruled Zimbabwe between 1980 and 2017, and was under Western sanctions openly said, "We have turned east, where the sun rises and given our back to the west, where the sun sets."[37] To shore up its domestic legitimacy and legacy as a freedom fighter and liberator, as well as assert its role as an important international actor, Zimbabwe's ruling party, the Zimbabwe African National Union Patriotic Front [ZANU (PF)] under Mugabe's leadership adopted a Look East Policy (LEP).[38] China ignored Mugabe's appalling human rights and international calls for him to stand trial at the International Criminal Court in the Hague. Instead, at the height of such calls in 2014, China invested $4bn in Zimbabwe and awarded him with the Confucius Prize-equivalent to a Nobel Peace Prize in Europe.

Critics of the Chinese policies have also cited Sudan as another example of a rogue state enjoying Chinese protection through its hand off approach. Sudan, which has been on U.S. sanctions since 1995 for harboring terrorists like Osama bin Laden is a good ally of China. China has investment deals in Sudan in the areas of oil, trade, mining, and construction. It is argued that China's first African investment was in Sudan.[39] By claiming to be not interfering in the internal affairs of these countries, China absolves itself of any guilt. China has been accused of siding with the Sudanese government in its atrocities allegedly committed in Darfur. China went to the extent of defending the alleged genocidal criminal activity by blocking the UN Security Council sanctions against President Bashir and even his arrest by the International Criminal Court.[40] The ruling party, the National Congress Party (NCP), where President Bashir hails from, has been in power since 1989 and is determined the retain power at all costs, although accused of stifling democracy and blocking human rights work in the country. Hammond (2017) notes that the NCP is very close to Beijing and because it follows and emulates the Chinese model of development it has been sending most of its students to universities in China and ensuring that some representatives of the Chinese Communist Party attend its party special congresses and events.[41]

China's involvement in the continent has not been without controversy. Issues of unfair labor practice, unscrupulous arms deal, and environmental degradation have been cited in many countries. Pertaining to labor issues, China has been on record for not complying. In countries such as Ethiopia, Algeria, and Zambia, the Chinese have been victims of xenophobic attacks for taking over jobs meant for locals. The Chinese nationals have taken over local jobs and do accept low pay than locals. In Sudan, although the law stipulates that 80 percent of labor in foreign companies should be nationals, the Chinese have floated this threshold. The government insists that despite the failure by Chinese companies to comply with this, the Sudanese benefit more from Chinese companies than locals in other African countries.[42] In the area of peace and stability, the Chinese are accused of fuelling the conflict by supplying arms to corrupt African leaders in exchange for exploitation rights or other forms of access to raw materials. According to arms dealers' records, a total of twenty-two sub-Saharan African countries procured major arms from China in 2013–2017, and China accounted for 27 percent of sub-Saharan African arms imports in that period (compared with 16 percent in 2008–2012).[43]

China's environmental practices on the continent, especially in mining, energy, and fishing have been widely criticized. Chinese investors do little to promote environmental sustainability, which would promote stable, long-term growth in the continent. In countries without good, strong, and democratic political institutions, China and other investors get to continue with their actions, with no ramifications. Laurence (2017) argues that this is mostly possible due to bribery and corruption practices between government and Chinese officials. The Chinese officials "go straight to the top officials and bribe them lavishly, and then nobody can stop them."

RECOMMENDATIONS

In line with the above discussion on China's hands-off policy, the following recommendation has been made to better the engagement between China and Africa:

- There is a need for African governments to fully understand China's policy context and maximize the benefits as well as avoid the pitfalls thereof.
- The African Union and its member states need to identify their individual and collective needs before engaging China. They also need to develop strategies to ensure that cooperation with China is mutually beneficial.
- It is important for African leaders to continuously measure and analyze the trends around Chinese aid. This will assist them to know if they are progressing in the utilization of the aid they are receiving and not getting unnecessarily indebted in the process.
- African countries need to be guided by their constitutions in their engagements with China, especially that which speaks to labor law and environmental protection. A deviation to please China is detrimental and sending the wrong message. A country must be able to engage China based on its valued principles and not lose its national values and norms to secure Chinese cooperation. A wholesome embracement of the Chinese model is suicidal and detrimental, a country needs to go for its strategic needs and leave out the unnecessary stuff.
- Greater engagement between African think tanks and civil society with their Chinese counterparts should be promoted to enable professional assessment of the partnership and developmental progress.

CONCLUSION

Both China and Africa appear to be complex continents run by sophisticated men and women. Things that have worked for China in some parts of Africa have attracted criticism and disrepute in others. Rwanda among other African countries seems to be praised for having taken a development path, though with less human rights promotion, while countries like Zimbabwe have neither experienced development without democracy nor fully embraced Westernized development, which is coupled with human rights. Sino-African relations have differed from one country to the other, even with the actors involved. The emergence of China and its entry into the aid systems and global development discourse in Africa is fundamental but yet to be fully explored. The hands-off approach has been characterized by incrementalism and gradualism, with a marked preference for stability and gradual change in the status quo.

NOTES

1. Jianbo and Hongming (2014). Jianbo, L. and Hongming, Z. (2014). *China-Africa Relations: Review and Analysis, Volume 1*. Paths International Limited.
2. Taylor (2006) Taylor, I. (2006). *China and Africa. Engagement and Compromise*. New York/ London: Routledge.
3. Fabian Wagner (2018) EU is as comfortable as China with the African thugs and dictators. See https://www.euractiv.com/section/development-policy/opinion/wed-eu-is-so-comfortable-with-african-thugs-and-dictators/ (Accessed 8 December 2018).
4. Anshan (2007: p. 70).
5. French, H. (2007). China and Africa. African Affairs, 106(422), pp. 127–132.
6. Chinese MOFA, China's African Policy, January 2006. http://www.fmprc.gov.cn/eng/zxxx/t230615.htm (Accessed 17 December 2018).
7. Muekalia, D. (2007). Africa and China's strategic partnership. *African Security Review*. 13(1), pp. 1–8.
8. Financial Times, Zimbabwe Crisis Turns Spotlight on China's Role in Africa, November 21, 2017. Harare.
9. The Economist, Bamboo Capitalism: The Rise of Entrepreneurial China, 10 March 2011.
10. Ministry of Foreign Affairs of the People's Republic of china, "China's Africa Policy," 2006 http://www.fmprc.gov.cn/eng/zxxx/t230615.htm (Accessed 13 October 2018).
11. Rotberg (2008, p. 1) Rotberg, R. (2008). *China into Africa. Trade, Aid and Influence*. Washington DC: Brookings Institution Press.
12. PacNet (2011) China's Acquiescence on UNSCR 1973: No Big Deal March 31, 2011 see https://www.pacforum.org/sites/default/files/tmp/pac1120.pdf (Accessed 3 October 2018).
13. Council for Foreign Affairs. (2006). China's Soft Power Initiative, at https://www.cfr.org/backgrounder/ chinas-soft-power-initiative (Accessed 23 December 2018).
14. Uju Okoye. In Africa, China's Human Rights Concerns Don't Apply, Diplomatic Courier, April 29, 2017. See https://www.diplomaticourier.com/africa-chinas-human-rights-concerns-dont-apply/ (Accessed 23 January 2019).
15. African Center for Economic Transformation. (2009). "*Looking East: China-Africa Engagements: Ghana Country Case Study*. See http//acetforafrica.org/wp

-content/uploads/2010/08/looking-East-Ghana-China-Study-2010.pdf. (Accessed 23 January 2019).

16. Overseas Development Institute. (2015). "Ghana, the Rising Star: Progress in Political Voice, Health And Education." London: ODI papers.

17. Lindberg. S. (2010) "What accountability pressures do MPs in Africa face and how do they respond? Evidence from Ghana," *Journal of Modern African Studies* 117: 48.

18. Fick, M (2017). Ghana crackdown on illegal gold mining inflames tensions with Beijing. https://www.ft.com/content/cb032036-2a63-11e7-bc4b-5528796fe35c. (Accessed 15 February 2019).

19. USAID, Democracy, Human Rights, and Governance, see https://www.usaid .gov/ghana/democracy-human-rights-and-governance.

20. Foster, W., Butterfield, W., Chen, C., Pushak, N. (2009). Building Bridges: China's growing role as infrastructure financier for Sub-Saharan Africa. World Bank: trends and policy options. No 5: July.

21. Zhang, C. (1996). The Foreign aid work develops in the course of the reform. Almanac of China's Foreign Economic Relations and Trade, 1996–97. Beijing: China Economics Publishing House and Economic Information & Agency.

22. The East African, Rwanda's Kagame endorses Chinese investment in Africa, Tuesday, September 2018. See https://www.theeastafrican.co.ke/news/ea/Rwanda-Pa ul-Kagame-endorses-Chinese-investment-Africa/4552908-4742800-5brualz/index. html (Accessed 4 October 2018).

23. The Sudanese Tribune, China's Political and Economic Exploitation of Sudan in http://www.sudantribune.com/spip.php?article66193 (Accessed 17 November 2018).

24. Timothy Longman, "Limitations to Political Reform: The Undemocratic Nature of Transition in Rwanda," in Remaking Rwanda: State Building and Human Rights after Mass Violence, Scott Straus and Lars Waldorf (ed.s), pp. 40–41; Rachel Hayman, 'Funding Fraud? Donors and Democracy in Rwanda', in Remaking Rwanda, p. 118.

25. Anjan Sundaram, Rwanda: The Darling Tyrant in *Politico Magazine*, March/ April 2014.

26. Wang, Jisi (2011) China's Search for a Grand Strategy: A Rising Great Power Finds Its Way, Foreign Affairs, Vol. 90, No. 2, pp.68–79.

27. China power. Is China contributing to the United Nations' mission? See https ://chinapower.csis.org/china-un-mission/ (Accessed 29 January 2018).

28. Independent, Russia and China reject new sanctions against South Sudan, April 25 2017. See https://www.independent.ie/world-news/north-america/russia -and-china-reject-new-sanctions-against-south-sudan-35654336.html (Accessed 15 February 2019).

29. Dai, Ying and Xing, Yue (2007) China Has Not Attempted to Softly Balance the US in the UN, *Quarterly Journal of International Politics*, Vol. 3, pp. 19–51.

30. Xue Lei (2014) China as a Permanent Member of the United Nations Security Council, FES Occasional Paper, Berlin.

31. UN Security Council, S /RES/2100 (2013), adopted at 6,952nd meeting, 25.3.2013.

32. https://au.int/sites/default/files/decisions/31274-assembly_au_dec_605-620_xxvii_e.pdf (Accessed 11 February 2019).

33. Beijing Declaration-Toward an Even Stronger China-Africa Community with a Shared Future. See https://www.focac.org/eng/zywx_1/zywj/t1594324.htm (Accessed 23 January 2019).

34. Wang Yizhou (2012) Creative involvement: a new direction in Chinese diplomacy, in European Council on Foreign Relations, edited by Mark Leonard, pp. 106–111.

35. Bonnie Girard, What Will the US-China Trade War Mean for Africa? in The Diplomat, October 25, 2018.

36. Langan, M. (2017). *Neo-colonialism and the poverty of 'development' in Africa*. Cham, Switzerland: Palgrave Macmillan, p. 40.

37. The Guardian, Mugabe Looks to the East, in, see https://www.theguardian.com/world/2005 /apr/18/zimbabwe (Accessed 26 November 2018).

38. Jeremy Youde (2007) Why Look East? Zimbabwean Foreign Policy and China. *Africa Today* Vol. 53, No. 3 (Spring, 2007), pp. 3–19, Indiana University Press.

39. Joseph Hammond (2017) Sudan: China's Original Foothold in Africa, in The Diplomat, June 14, 2017. See also https://thediplomat.com/2017/06/sudan-chinas-original-foothold-in-africa/ (Accessed 12 December 2018).

40. The Sudanese Tribune, China's Political and Economic Exploitation of Sudan in http://www.sudantribune.com/spip.php?article66193 (Accessed 17 November 2018).

41. Joseph Hammond (2017) Sudan: China's Original Foothold in Africa, in The Diplomat, June 14, 2017. See also https://thediplomat.com/2017/06/sudan-chinas-original-foothold-in-africa/ (Accessed 12 December 2018).

42. Ibid.

43. ZIPRI (2018) Trends in International Arms Transfers, SIPRI Fact Sheet. 2017. Page 7. See https://www.sipri.org/sites/default/files/2018-03/fssipri_at2017_0.pdf (Accessed 24 November 2018).

BIBLIOGRAPHY

African Economic Outlook (2017*)* *Political and Economic Governance in Africa*. Washington DC: The World Bank Group

Amanor, K. S (2013) "Chinese and Brazilian Cooperation with African Agriculture: The Case of Ghana." Future Agricultures Consortium Working Paper 52. Brighton, Sussex: IDS.

Ampratwum, E, Armah-Attoh, D & Ashon, MA (2012) "Public expenditure tracking survey in education: Tracking possible leakages in the distribution of textbooks in public primary schools in Ghana," CDD-Ghana Research Paper No. 20. Accra: Ghana Centre for Democratic Development.

Anshan, L (2007). "China and Africa: Policy and Challenges." In *Afro-Chinese Relations: Past, Present and Future,* Kwesi Kwaa Prah (Ed.). South Africa: Centre for Advanced Studies of African Society (CASA)

Anshan, L (2008) "China's New Policy towards Africa. In China into Africa, Trade, Aid and Influence." Edited by Rotberg I Robert. Washington DC: Brookings Institution Press.

Dai, Y. and Xing, Y. (2007). "China Has Not Attempted to Softly Balance the US in the UN," *Quarterly Journal of International Politics*, Vol. 3, pp. 19–51.

Frimpong, S. K (2012). *"Research on Relationship between China and Ghana"*: Trade and Foreign Direct Investment (FDI). *Journal of Economics and Sustainable Development,* Vol 3.

Firoze, M and Stephen, M (2007) *African Perspectives on China in Africa.* Cape Town, Nairobi and Oxford: Fahamu-Networks for Social Justice.

Langan, M. (2017). *Neo-colonialism and the Poverty of "Development" in Africa.* Cham, Switzerland: Palgrave Macmillan.

Lindberg. S. (2010) "What Accountability Pressures do MPs in Africa Face and How Do They Respond? Evidence from Ghana." *Journal of Modern African Studies* Vol. 117, p. 48.

Mbondenyi, MK (2010) *International Human Rights and Their Enforcement in Africa.* Nairobi: Law Africa Publishing.

Shambaugh, D (2013): *China Goes Global: The Partial Power.* Oxford: Oxford University Press.

Taylor, I. 2007. *Governance in Africa and Sino-African Relations: Contradictions or Confluence? Politics—Ian Taylor.* Vol. 27 No. 3, pp. 139–146 [online] Journals .sagepub.com. Available at: http://journals.sagepub.com/doi/full/10.1111/j.146 7-9256.2007.00293.x#aHR0cDovL 2pvdXJuYWxzLnNhZ2VwdWIuY29tL2R vaS9wZGYvMTAuMTExMS9qLjE0NjctOTI1Ni4yMDA3LjAwMjkzLnhAQE Aw [Accessed 19 Nov. 2019].

Wang, J (2011). "China's Search for a Grand Strategy: A Rising Great Power Finds Its Way," *Foreign Affairs*, Vol. 90, No. 2, pp. 68–79.

Wang, Y (2012) *Creative Involvement: A New Direction in Chinese Diplomacy, in European Council on Foreign Relations,* edited by Mark Leonard. Berlin: European Council on Foreign Relations.

Xue, L (2014), "China as a Permanent Member of the United Nations Security Council." Berlin: FES Occasional Papers.

Youde. J (2007) "Why Look East? Zimbabwean Foreign Policy and China." *Africa Today* Vol. 53, No. 3 (Spring, 2007), pp. 3–19, Indiana: Indiana University Press.

Part III

CHINA'S REGIONAL FOOTPRINTS

Chapter 11

Reporting the Dragon

A Thematic Study of Anti-Chinese Sentiments in "China in Africa" News Coverage

Surajudeen Oladosu Mudasiru and
Abdul-Gafar Tobi Oshodi

BACKGROUND

China's presence in Africa is no longer news. Chinese financial support, infrastructure, and the periodic Forum on China-Africa Cooperation (FOCAC) have all become a common feature of contemporary Sino-African encounter. The value of Sino-Africa "exports and imports surged from US$ 676.5 and 227.4 million in 1980 to 43.3 and 52.9 billion in 2008"[1] Sino-Africa trade galloped to US$220 billion in 2014,[2] and by 2015, China was on course to become Africa's largest trading partner with over $200 billion trade, a figure some forecasted to reach $400 billion in 2020.[3] Expectedly, China's presence in Africa, or what was earlier conceptualized as "Chinese Africana,"[4] has therefore continued to attract commentaries in Africa, China, and elsewhere. But while China's presence in Africa is no longer news, what remain newsworthy are its manifold implications for Africa, China, and other actors. As such, commentaries on Sino-Africa encounters vary. While many are optimistic about China's presence in Africa, others like the former *New York Times* journalist and Columbia University scholar, Howard French, argue that Sino-Africa relations are "entering a new and much more skeptical phase."[5] This skepticism play-outs in numerous theatres. One of these theatres has been in the news space. Our chapter interrogates this online news arena.

Bearing in mind the varying commentaries on Sino-Africa encounter,[6] this chapter highlights the themes in anti-Chinese sentiments in online news.

In doing this, however, the chapter will not do two things. First, it will not narrate (and therefore repeat) the history of China's entry into Africa. The task of constructing this history have been carried out by, for instance, Anshan[7] who periodized Sino-African relations into ideological beginnings (1949–1978), diversification (1979–1982) and the spirit of codevelopment of the current era; Adisu, Sharkey and Okoroafor[8] who periodized the relations into colonial phase (1850–1950), political phase (1960–1980), and economic phase (1990–till date); and Konings[9] who divides these phases into Maoist era of ideological and strategic considerations, Deng Xiaoping era of economic modernization and era of neoliberal globalization. Second, the chapter will not debate—especially within pessimistic, optimistic, and cautious perspectives—the developmental benefit (or otherwise) of Sino-Africa relations.[10] Instead, the chapter set out to achieve two goals in this chapter. First, the chapter highlights six themes in Sino-pessimistic coverage of China's activities in Africa. These include labor practices, deindustrialization and debt, corruption, racism and colonialism, environmental issues, and the inactions of African governments. Second, using a Kenyan case, we will interrogate the extent to which some of these reports qualify as developmental journalism.

To achieve the aforementioned two goals, the rest of this chapter is structurally divided into four sections. The second section deals with conceptual and contextual issues. The third section highlights six themes in Sino-pessimism as discernible in online news media. This is followed by a section that engages one of the themes within the context of developmental journalism. Here, we use a case of reports on a Chinese restaurant in Kenya. The fourth section is a conclusion which essentially calls for the deepening of knowledge on the role of online news media in particular and news media in general on Sino-African relations.

THE NEWS MEDIA AND CHINA IN AFRICA: A BRIEF COMMENTARY

The discourse on the construction and manufacturing of news is not new.[11] By this, what is generally accepted to be "the news" is largely a social construction. While this may be viewed as exaggerated, there is no gainsaying that the slants and reportage of news media are influenced by several factors. News media are influenced by gatekeepers such as the owners of the outfits, the journalists and editors, the nature and system of government, the (enlightened) public, the advertisers, and the views of opinion leaders. These gatekeepers are themselves influenced by other factors.[12] The interplay between these actors determines the ideological slant of news media outfits.

For one, while these actors do not always possess an equal level of influence, governments are usually interested in the activities of the news media. Even when some governments find it difficult to directly control the news media within their territories owing to legal provisions and/or the nature of the state, other governments have directly interfered in the activities of both private and public news media. An example of the latter scenario is observable in China.[13]

But beyond the fact that the state and Chinese Communist Party control the Chinese media environment, the importance of the news media in particular and other media in general in promoting and/or shaping Sino-Africa relations cannot be overemphasized. Suffice to mention three important reasons the media occupies a crucial position in this regard. The first reason is practical, while the second is more traditional. The practical utility of the news media is hinged on the barriers to accessing the information on Africa-China relations. The so-called "noninterference policy" of the Chinese government and the difference in a language all the more makes accessing information difficult for many African analysts. Hence, the media is left—at least in many instances—to shape our understanding of the state of Africa-China relations. The utility of the Media-Based Data Collection (MBDC) methodology, which creates "a comprehensive database of Chinese development finance flows to Africa from 2000–2011"[14] provides support for the foregoing argument.

A second reason the news media represents a critical element in Africa-China relations is hinged on their traditional capacity to frame image. Traditionally, the news media inform and educate their audience. Even if they are considered to be instruments used to perpetuate certain agenda, they can only do so because they wield a certain power to influence, popularize, criticize, and/or mute news or government's policies and actions. The media is a powerful tool to perpetuate or even showcase people in a certain light. From *The Economist*'s front page that described Africa as "The hopeless continent" in 2000 to its "African rising" portrayal of the same continent in 2013, the media are a powerful force in shaping the perceptions of Africa. Bunce, Franks, and Paterson's[15] and Gallagher[16] provide useful insight into the power of the media in the creation and negotiation of the image of Africa. But the media power is not only one of framing the image of Africa to the world, but it also shapes the image of foreign powers on the continent. China is not unaware of the latter role of the media.[17] Third, what is considered as stories in the media, sometimes, are often sources from experts in the field. It is not uncommon for experts in Sino-Africa relation to be interviewed by the media or for their opinions to be published in the features section of the media. Linkages between the academia and the media are also enhanced by the emerging need for science popularization, often promoted by many research funders, in news and social media.

Conscious of the important role of news media within China and in its soft power projection, Beijing's internationalization policy takes cognizance of this element of Africa-China relations.[18] As one expert on China in Africa media studies puts it: "the entry of Chinese media into Africa is an integral part of Chinese media spreading tentacles globally."[19] In addition to the traditional state-owned news media such as the China Central Television (CCTV), *China Daily* and *Xinhua* that are now available online to an international audience, Beijing launched Nairobi-based CCTV Africa in 2012. While CCTV Africa is available on satellite television providers like DSTV, Chinese owned StarTimes and Zuku, the English-language news channel run by the Chinese state broadcaster, CCTV, also have an online presence (on cctv-africa.com, on tweeter, and with numerous clips available on Youtube).

Though CCTV Africa was chiefly set up to present a more positive face of Sino-Africa relations,[20] China and Chinese companies have not escaped strong criticisms in other news media. These criticisms range from those of private Chinese citizens and companies to those against the Chinese government. Regardless of their direction, they present negative representations of China in Africa. Needless to say that just as the broader contestations between Sino-pessimism and Sino-optimism often boils down to the question of the extent to which China can support Africa's development,[21] Sino-pessimism in online news media could also qualify as developmental journalism. We will return to this point shortly. But suffice to note that it is not new for a news media to be described as an agent for development: developmental journalism. What then is developmental journalism?

From a simplistic perspective, developmental journalism is a practice where news media—through the activities of journalists and other gatekeepers of media practice—carry out their responsibility in such a manner that supports development in a country. Two traditions of developmental journalism are discernible. First is the statist argument that views the media as a *servant of government* in the development process. In this sense, the media does not challenge the government's actions, but rather it operates as an instrument to mobilize the people for development.[22] Developmental journalism is thus viewed within a purview of national media theory where the state is the chief architect of development, and therefore, it is the responsibility of the state to push for development journalism. This is understandable given that governments—at least in their public pronouncements—tend to declare support for national development by initiating programs and strategies to ensure development. From this statist perspective, certain regulations are put in place to ensure that the news media goes along with the developmental agenda of the state. This is the case in China. This perspective of developmental journalism has thus attracted criticisms "as one of the most insidious threats to press freedom."[23]

The second tradition of developmental journalism has a populist interpretation. As Gunaratne[24] notes, developmental journalism is that "analytical interpretation, subtle investigation, constructive criticism and sincere association with the grass-roots (rather than with the elite)." In this sense, because the state is not the only interested party in the development process, news media, as well as other nonstate actors, act as an independent mechanism to promote development. Here, the media—rather than being an instrument of the state—holds the government accountable for its development promises to the people and thus criticizes the government when it is not living up to its expectations. Thus, Sino-pessimism is developmental journalism only to the extent that the news media hold the government and/or China accountable to the African people. In this sense, "Grass-roots activism and vibrant independent media are, everywhere, the ultimate check on corrupt legislators and on foreigners who get lucrative but unsound deals by handing over bags of cash."[25] Yet, just as the news media is influenced by a multiplicity of gatekeepers, it follows that even where China is criticized, such criticisms could be nothing but enlightened self-interest of parties within or outside Africa. When this is the case, determining that Sino-pessimism or anti-Chinese sentiments are development journalism becomes a tricky task business.

Meanwhile, journalism, like all human activities, is not static. It changes with time and technology. Developmental journalism thus cannot also be static. For one, the internationalization of local news media—for example, as manifested in online versions and live streaming services—confirms this dynamism. Similarly, international media can set the agenda for national action given its online presence and availability of audiences in many countries. International media run programs that are relayed on national news media platforms that further blur the divide between the two. For instance, the British broadcaster, BBC, has agreed with many local African stations for the relay of their programs to local audiences in Africa. The BBC is reported to currently have access to about 122 million people in Africa.[26] Our concern here is the online news media broadly defined within the context of new media.

It is necessary to emphasize that new media is not disconnected from traditional media. As Wekesa[27] notes, traditional print media are reinventing themselves through online media. Many television and radio stations are launching online streams, making their programs available to an international audience. Given this convergence of new and old media, any discussion of online news and their possible developmental usefulness will be holistic only to the extent that our definition of new media is crafted in its loosest and borderless sense. Thus, even when an online magazine, for instance, had reported the discriminatory practice of a Chinese restaurant in Kenya that barred African customers from entering it after 5:00 p.m., the British

Broadcasting Cooperation's (BBC) program, *Have Your Say*, relayed the same story both on its World Service radio and on its Facebook page, generating comments from across the world. This convergence that has been described as "flow of content across multiple media platforms"[28] blurs the accentuating divide between old and new media. Yet, new media is generally defined as follows:

> those methods and social practices of communication, representation, and expression that have developed using the digital, multimedia, networked computer and the ways that this machine is held to have transformed work in other media: from books to movies, from telephones to television.[29]

But for our purpose, while the aforementioned new media broadly accommodates "digital, multimedia, networked computer and the ways that this machine is held to have transformed work in other media," our focus interrogation of the themes of Sino-pessimism only focuses on online news. By online news, we refer to new and traditional news media with a presence on the Internet. The central advantage of online news platforms being that news items can be accessed from anywhere with a potentially higher cross border following. Having said this, what are the themes of Sino-pessimism in online news?

THEMES IN SINO-CRITICISM IN THE MEDIA

News media is just one of the numerous theatres for the contestation between Sino-pessimism and Sino-criticism—other theatres including academic and press conferences, summits, government boardrooms, the publishing world, and students' classrooms. It must be stressed, again, that even where criticisms and pessimism are presented as drawbacks or dangers in Africa-China encounters, there is certainly no universal agreement as to the *real* role of China in Africa and neither is there a single representation of China in Africa.[30] In no sense, therefore, are China's activities on the continent the same or equally perceived across the board. Thus, while some Chinese state-owned companies, for instance, observe best practices on the continent, others run foul. Similarly, the interest of China varies across the continent from oil and infrastructure to tourism and agriculture. Just as the financial implications of these varied interests differ so does the behavior of actors (Chinese and Africans) differ across contexts. For sure, many themes are discernible in the literature on China in Africa. They range from those that focus on the ideological backdrop of China's relations with Africa, social networks and communities; language, ethnicity, and racialized identities; the agency of African governments and other actors; the role of third parties in Africa-China engagement; contemporary arts; and labor relations.[31]

Despite the crucial role of news media in the shaping of contemporary Africa-China encounter, there is still relatively little academic interest in the framing of China in Africa in the news. There are a few efforts in this regard. For instance, Bob Wekesa studied the framing of China in East-Africa, "with a view to determining positive, negative, and weak perceptions by applying a content analysis approach."[32] Using the economic consequences and conflict frames, he found that there were more positive than negative frames in the four newspapers sampled. However, Wekesa's goal was not to critically unpack the frames or themes broadly categorized as "positive" and "negative." This section contributes to filling this gap, albeit within the negative frames here interchangeably referred to as Sino-pessimism or anti-Chinese sentiments in the media. The six themes highlighted include labor practices, deindustrialization and debt, corruption, racism and colonialism, environmental issues, and the actions of African governments. The six themes are selected not only because they represent a recurring element in most negative or anti-Chinese online news but because a few of them have also necessitated a strong response from Beijing and its embassies in Africa.

Labor Practices in Africa

While several Chinese companies maintain a high standard of labor relations, others have generated bad press for Sino-Africa relations. From the news story of a Chinese boss, Mike Jackson and his cousin, Tony Jackson, breaking the head of Adeleke Owolabi, an African worker,[33] to a report of another African worker, Maaji Meriga, allegedly being "kicked . . . on his testicles and punched . . . on the ear to prove who is boss" by his Chinese boss at China Civil Engineering and Construction Company (CCECC), Marcho Chin,[34] to inhumane shifts and poor working conditions for workers,[35] Chinese bosses and companies are depicted in a negative light in these reports.[36] Examples of headlines in this regards include, for example, the following: "Chinese Expats Treat Nigerian Employees as Punching Bags,"[37] "Labour Movements Pickets, Install Workers Union in Foreign Companies That Denies Workers' Welfare,"[38] "Chinese Labour Practices Haunt Zim Factory Workers"[39]; "Man Accuses Chinese Boss of Brutality"[40]; "Police detain Chinese for assaulting an employee in Ogun,"[41] "China in Zambia: Trouble Down in the Mines,"[42] and "We're treated like slaves but we're afraid of losing our jobs—Nigerians in Chinese, Indian companies."[43] While these news stories tend to present Chinese bosses as brutal and inconsiderate, news reports often do not state the version of the Chinese bosses. The absence of this creates an impression of these bosses as being above the local laws.

Development Issues

At least three subissues are often raised, and they include unemployment, importation of Chinese labor, and growing debt. On unemployment, Chinese companies, owing to their ability to out-compete their African counterparts, are presented as a danger to Africa's nascent industries. By outcompeting their African counterpart, this reality increases rather than reduce the rate of unemployment. A news report noted that "China's emergence as a major source of cheap textiles has been particularly devastating for small developing countries with less diversified economies, especially Africa."[44] Another news report, on the impact of Chinese importation on South Africa, concludes thus: "Since 2003, there has been a 480% increase in clothing imports from China. In the same period, there have been 62 000 job losses in the textile industry."[45] This line of argument—that is, Chinese imports destroys Africa's industries—is common. Other reports link China's interest in Africa's raw materials as a cause. A Reuters report, quoting the African Development Bank, noted that "most minerals mined in Africa are exported raw, meaning the jobs and wealth from processing them is created elsewhere."[46] Aside from reports of how Chinese companies create unemployment in Africa, other reports stress that Chinese companies import labor from China. By this, "China provided infrastructure but brought own workforce."[47] Regarding debt, news media reports highlight the growing debt African countries owe China. Though denied by Beijing,[48] headlines such as "China loans create 'new wave of Africa debt,'"[49] "Debt by African countries to China growing,"[50] and "Debt colonialism: Is China trying to buyout Africa's resources?"[51] continuously draw attention to the growing debts African countries owe China.

Corruption

What is referred to as Beijing consensus is essentially marked by a view of development wherein state sovereignty and social harmony are the most important guiding philosophy? As a consequence, Beijing's foreign policy and its provision of financial support to African governments comes with a bias for state sovereignty and "constitutionally uneasy about dealing with independent actors like advocacy groups, labor unions, and independent journalists"[52]; an approach that is often believed exposes Chinese companies to allegations of corruption. Indeed, several journalists have reported cases and allegations of corruption involving Chinese companies and individuals. Headlines include "Hu Jintao's son linked to corruption probe,"[53] "China's aid to Africa funds corruption, says report,"[54] and "Corruption concerns taints burgeoning China-Africa trade."[55] But far from accepting this depiction as a supporter of corrupt African governments, China often rejected the allegation. Apart from arguing that the governments they deal with in Africa are the representatives of the people, the Chinese-constructed "bridge and the hospital are not built for the president or officials but are for the common people."[56]

Racism and Colonialism

While the aforementioned news reports about the treatment of Africans in Chinese companies in some sense suggests a subtle inferior-superior relationship that allows Chinese bosses to harass their African workers, other news coverages allege racism and colonialism in Sino-Africa relations. Even if commentaries on Chinese prejudice and racism against Africans in China have been reported,[57] the reference to Chinese racism in Africa—for instance, as alleged in reports on a Kenya-based Chinese restaurant which barred Africans from visiting after 5:00 p.m. unless they were "accompanied by Chinese, Europeans or Indian patrons"[58]—is rare. But headlines on possible Chinese colonialism are relatively more common. Though the assumptions of Chinese colonization thesis (CCT) remain highly debatable,[59] the growing Chinese influence and the presence of over one million Chinese citizens in Africa which have led to the so-called "China's second continent" description[60] have been reflected in China's economic colonization of Africa narrative. News reports of "Chinese colonialism" vary and often differ, ranging from titles like "Teaching Mandarin at African schools 'will colonize SA anew'—Sadtu,"[61] "Africa will not put up with a colonialist China"[62] to "Why China is trying to colonize Africa."[63] These reports often suggest that China is either trying to or has, colonized the African continent. Though many of the reports are by Africans, many others are a reflection of the views of other powers; powers sometimes contesting with China. More directly, negative news could become an instrument not just from *outside* but *within* Africa. John Bolton aptly captures this point when he announced America's new African policy in 2018:

> China uses bribes, opaque agreements, and the strategic use of debt to hold states in Africa captive to Beijing's wishes and demands. Its investment ventures are riddled with corruption, and do not meet the same environmental or ethical standards as US development projects.[64]

Environmental and Conservation Issues

Headlines along this line include: "China's presence in Africa blamed for new threat to rhino,"[65] "Report: Africa ivory smuggled on China visit,"[66] "Chad suspends China's local oil unit for the environment,"[67] "China illegally fishing off West Africa—Greenpeace,"[68] "Environmental group accuses Chinese diplomats on state visits of smuggling Tanzanian ivory,"[69] and "China's colonialist behavior in Africa could be a 'disaster' for the environment, Jane Goodall warns, as she says Beijing is pillaging continent for raw materials."[70] China, ordinary Chinese and Chinese companies have been accused of involvement in illegal poaching and/or the destruction of the environment. Thus, while *Al Jazeera*'s report described China as "the world's largest importer of smuggled tusks,"[71] the *BBC* referred to Chinese bottom trawlers as "one of the most destructive fishing vessels in the industry."[72] In its editorial of June 1, 2014, entitled "China's pollution of Africa finally merits a penalty," *The Boston Globe*, stressed that "China's role in Africa is based far more on self-interest than consideration of Africa's concerns, or anyone else's." The editorial was essentially based on a decision by the government in Chad, in May 2014, to suspend work by China National Petroleum owing to its environmental damage. While the editorial noted that African governments are beginning to discover that Chinese aid comes with its complications, it noted that "Chad's willingness to put some teeth into its environmental protections should reverberate through Africa and beyond." Allegations of the involvement of Chinese state officials, criminal gangs, corrupt African officials, and the reductions in existing biological species have come to typify China's criticism in this regard.

African Governments' Inactions

Even where the foregoing themes essentially criticize China in its relations with Africa, negative news stories also report the role of African governments. The failure of the African state to act in some cases where Chinese interest negatively clashes with those of the local people is what has been described as "points of exit" of African governments.[73] The news media is one of the nonstate actors that have taken up the challenge of holding China accountable via "points of engagement."[74] Thus, some news reports have drawn attention to the allegations of corruption involving African governments and Chinese companies. For instance, "corrupt Tanzanian officials" were noted to be a part of the trade involving the illegal smuggling of ivory.[75] Other news reports mention the inaction or the delayed actions of the African government's failure in coming to the rescue of local workers at Chinese companies. For instance, in the case of the physical attack on Mr. Owolabi by his Chinese boss (referred to above), *The Punch* noted the failure of the Nigerian police to act swiftly. Similarly, in Zambia, Chinese mines operated twelve-hour shifts per week despite the existence of a law that workers can only work for forty-eight hours per week.[76] Yet, as demonstrated in Kenya, Chinese firms too "cite corruption as major hurdle" t their business in Africa.[77]

At this juncture, suffice to stress that rather than compartmentalized themes, the aforementioned six themes highlighted above sometimes interact with one another. For instance, as reported by the Associated Press in 2014, "Chinese-led criminal gangs conspired with corrupt Tanzanian officials to traffic huge amounts of ivory, some of which were allegedly loaded in diplomatic bags on Xi's plane during a presidential visit in March 2013." In this case, themes such as corruption, environmental issues, and host government's inaction are discernible. While some of these news reports are not news in other theatres of contestation on the "real" role of China in Africa, news reports are what they are: news stories that are reflections of the opinion of individuals, groups, organizations, or even countries at a particular time. But even where they are mere reports, the role of the news media in shaping opinion and influencing discussions cannot be overemphasized. In this case, owing to the real-time nature of online transmission of news, the role of the news media in shaping the opinion of ordinary Africans about China and Chinese people cannot be underestimated. But does Chinese criticism in the media mean developmental journalism? In other words, does criticizing Chinese activities in Africa equates developmental journalism? This is the focus of the next section.

PROBLEMATICS OF SINO-CRITICISM AS DEVELOPMENTAL JOURNALISM

Normally, governments often prefer supportive news media than an antagonistic one. As such, many governments not only employ media advisers and official spokespersons, but they also establish and/or maintain state-owned media to air its side of the story. Chinese and African governments are not immune to this preference. Given this understanding, it is expected that Sino-Africa relations, at least from the perspectives of both the Chinese government and their African counterpart, will prefer supportive news stories that present both parties as benefiting from a "win-win" partnership. Therefore, it is not unexpected that China—like any reasonable government—will remain sensitive to accusations of colonialism, torture, smuggling, and racisms in Africa. Even where the African government continues to look forward to China for development assistance, China is conscious of the impacts of negative perceptions and depiction of its activities on the continent and the emerging responses from ordinary Africans. Yet Sino-criticism in the media does not in itself imply developmental journalism. But as will be discussed below, critical news reports about China or Chinese businesses have the potential to generate reactions not only within individual African countries but from across the globe leading to unexpected actions. This is more possible where news stories are published to an online audience. Such stories could spur the government to act. This possibility seems to be buttressed in the case of a Chinese restaurant based in Nairobi, Kenya. In this case, the Chinese restaurant owned by Ms. Zhao Yang introduced a racist order that unaccompanied Kenyans—and by extension, black Africans—are not allowed into the restaurant's premises after 5:00 p.m.

The intro for one of the first news reports on the restaurant's policy reads thus: "'*Masaa ya Waafrika yameisha*,' (The time for Africans is over) a guard at a Chinese restaurant in Nairobi's Kilimani neighborhood tells *Nation* reporters when they get there at 7:00 pm."[78] According to the *Daily Nation*'s report, the restaurant's management introduced the policy "because Africans pose a security threat to its Chinese patrons."[79] The restaurant's relations manager, Ms. Esther Zhao, was reported to have said: "We don't admit Africans that we don't know because you never know who is Al-Shabaab and who isn't."[80] The newspaper report added that "Only taxi drivers or Africans accompanied by Chinese, European or Indian patrons are allowed into the compound."[81]

The restaurant's discriminatory policy had been introduced in 2014 when six armed (African) men broke into the restaurant, robbing the restaurant of Sh600,000 (about US$6,170), robbing its patrons, and injuring a chef. The restaurant's relations manager added that the Chinese embassy had issued a warning to Chinese businesses to be vigilant owing to the threat of Al-Shabab terrorists. She continued: "The Chinese people who stay here or come to dine want to feel safe . . . They also have families back in China and they don't want to be in harm's way during their stay in Kenya . . . As management, it is our duty to ensure their safety."[82] Ms. Zhao, however, noted that "In the future, we are considering rolling out a membership scheme and give cards to some of our loyal African customers so that they can be admitted after 5:00 pm."[83] In the same report, the reporter had interviewed Kenyan Ombudsman, Mr. Otiende Amollo, who stated that the restaurant's policy is "illegal and unconstitutional." He maintained that the actions of the restaurant's management amounted to racial and ethnic profiling as it "has in it the inherent assumption that Africans are inevitably pre-disposed to be robbers." He added that victims of the policy could sue for discrimination or approach the Kenyan National Commission on Human Rights. He hinted that his Commission could put pressure on the county government "to revoke the licences of a private company that has been accused of discrimination."[84]

Given this narration, to what extent does the reports of *Daily Nation*,[85] one of the first newspapers to break the news of the aforementioned Chinese restaurant and others qualify as developmental journalism? As noted earlier, public responses to Sino-criticism could be unexpected but since the break of the story by such online newspapers like the *Daily Nation*, numerous online news platforms from the less known to popular ones like CNN and BBC have reported the story of the restaurant, further popularizing the story and leading to numerous follow-ups.

From a populist perspective of developmental journalism, three positive effects were achieved with the restaurant's news story. First, the media report highlighted the racial policy of a Chinese restaurant—though not representative of other Chinese restaurants—that discriminate against Kenyans and blacks in Kenya. If development embodies dignity in human lives,[86] to the extent that the story highlighted the indignity of barring black Africans from a restaurant located in an African country, the media shed light on the inappropriateness of the restaurant's policy. The internationalization of the story via the online presence of *Nation* newspaper particularly increased access to the news story.

Thus, while Nigeria-based *Vanguard* newspaper, on March 25, 2015, captioned the story "'No blacks' Chinese restaurant shut down in Kenya," a blog run by *The Washington Post* in the United States simply captioned it thus: "This Chinese restaurant in Kenya is open for dinner, as long as you're not African."[87] The BBC captioned the story as "Chinese restaurant in Africa has a 'no black Africans' policy,"[88] CNN captioned it thus: "Chinese restaurant owner in Kenya arrested after 'No Africans' uproar,"[89] *The Telegraph* captioned it as "Restaurant owner in Nairobi who bars Africans from entering establishment is arrested,"[90] and *Yahoo News*, relaying an AFP report, captures it as "'No blacks' Chinese restaurant shut down in Kenya."[91] In all these cases, the report by the *Nation* is cited and sometimes linked as a source, thus underscoring the potential of a local newspaper—with an online version—to highlight a negative episode of Sino-Africa encounter and for such news stories to be reported across the globe within less than forty-eight hours. These online platforms provided netizens an opportunity to engage with the story from varying perspectives, ranging from comments below stories to full opinion pieces.

Second, as an aftermath of the story, it led to a response from the Chinese authority and an official decry of the restaurant's policy by representatives of the Chinese government.[92] For instance, by March 26, 2015, the Chinese Embassy in Kenya had apologized to Kenyans for the restaurant's policy. Mao Yizong, the spokesperson for the Embassy had stated thus:

> On behalf of the Embassy, I declare that the conduct reported was wrong and unbecoming. It has caused unnecessary, yet avoidable, misunderstandings and threatened to jeopardize the mutual trust and friendship between the Chinese and Kenyan people . . . The Embassy has thus far raised its concerns to and reprimanded the owner of the restaurant.[93]

The statement, which was also fully reported in *China Daily* newspaper, further noted that the management and owners of the restaurant have learned lessons and urged other Chinese restaurants to take note. It adds that: "We do not expect such reckless conduct from Chinese businesspeople in Kenya forthwith. We shall deal with any repeat of such misconduct with the severity, firmness, and the alacrity that it deserves."[94]

Third, the restaurant's story, since allegations of racial profiling of Africans in Chinese restaurants began to surface from March 17, 2015,[95] led to some level of Kenyan government action. For one, the Kenyan Tourism Regulatory Authority and Tourist police stormed the Chinese restaurant for allegedly not paying the annual Sh45,000 since 2011.[96] It soon became reported that the restaurant lacked several licenses. As one report puts it: "The restaurant in Kilimani did not have a liquor license, a health license, and a change-of-use license—having been converted from a residential house to a restaurant."[97] Evans Kidero, Governor of Nairobi County, while admitting that the city inspectorate officers failed to ensure compliance, was reported to have noted that thorough inspection would be conducted to ensure that hotels and restaurants operating within the city abide by its laws.[98]

In attracting the public, Chinese and Kenyan governments to the story, the news coverage of the restaurant yielded some positive development: developmental journalism *a la* populist view. Yet, the news report also led to some negative and unintended consequences. For instance, following the restaurant's news story, on March 26, 2015, a mob attacked the Chinese restaurant in question, destroying its property and looting items like electronics, utensils, and drinks.[99] Violence rather than rule of law and mob action rather than peaceful protest cannot be said to be a positive political development in a country that practices democracy. Given that Kenya (and other African states) could use more Chinese investment, promoting mob justice—rather than rule of law—could be counterproductive for encouraging Chinese investors and businesses. As a commentator noted: the "excitement and subsequent damage to property that was generated by biased reports must make them (Chinese investors) and others think twice."[100]

It is also interesting that news reports on the restaurant did not make further effort to interrogate the fears of the Chinese restaurant especially in terms of whether or not its owners requested the Kenyan government for some sort of security guarantee following the 2014 robbery attack. Giving that they had treated their African customers equally for years, a statement by the restaurant's management had noted thus: "Because of the concern of the business environment at night and the bad memory of . . . 2013, we adopted certain measures. Unfortunately, some of the measures were inappropriate, we sincerely apologize for this."[101] Was the restaurant's policy response to the failure of the government to respond to security fears? Virtually none of the news reports investigated this dimension of the story.

Ultimately, the Kenyan restaurant's episode suggests that online news can spread and move African governments, their citizens, netizens, and even China into some sort of action. Yet it must be stressed that it is not always clear whether it was the online news story or comments by netizens, for instance, on such platforms like Facebook and tweeter, that generated the aforementioned responses. Nevertheless, the fact that many international media often cited local news reports in the Kenyan case suggests that the news media remains an important factor in the shaping of Sino-Africa relations.

CONCLUSION

In this chapter, we have highlighted six themes in anti-Chinese reports in the news media. We specifically highlighted labor practices, development issues, corruption, racism and colonialism, environmental and conservation issues, and the (in)actions of African governments. While these themes individually represent some of the most reported negative stories on China/Chinese activities in Africa, each theme sometimes exists alongside the others. However, two caveats suffice. First, the cliché *China in Africa* does not necessarily mean that China is equally present in Africa. The themes we have highlighted here are thus in themselves mainly examples of negative stories that have reoccurred in several instances. They are not necessarily the norm. Second, this article is largely anecdotal to the extent that it draws attention to the themes and role of news media in Africa-China encounters. In providing this anecdotal commentary on Sino-criticism, we have attempted to contribute to broadening an emerging research interest into the media dimension of the reality of China in Africa. Though negative stories may ordinarily be viewed as a drawback, it could also motivate state and nonstate actors to act as the Kenya case discussed demonstrates. Thus, while negative media reports can create and subvert the image of China in Africa, we must be careful not to generalize that negative news are in themselves only detrimental to the continent.

From the foregoing, we conclude that news media is an important factor in the deepening of Africa-China encounters in terms of government-to-government and people-to-people relations. By highlighting the negative actions of China and Chinese companies in Africa, the online news media plays a developmental role as with the case of the Chinese restaurant in Kenya. Whether it is the issue of environmentally destructive gold mining in Ghana or the harassment of local workers in Nigeria, online news media remains an important factor in shaping and highlighting the perceptions of China and Chinese citizens in Africa. As was the case with the Chinese restaurant in Kenya, news reports provide an opportunity for ordinary Africans to air their views about China and Chinese businesses in Africa via the comment section. In most cases, where there is a negative news report on China's presence in Africa (or in an African country), there is often a tendency for comments below such reports to view China as an imperialist, environmental polluter, inhumane, and corrupt player in Africa. Yet while our focus has mainly been anecdotal, further research is needed to deepen existing understanding of the undercurrents in media organizations with respect to reporting China in Africa and how possible extraneous factors can shape what is being reported as news stories.

NOTES

1. De Grauwe, P., Houssa, R. & Piccillo, G. (2012). "African trade dynamics: is China a different trading partner," *Journal of Chinese Economic and Business Studies*, 10:1, 15–45.

2. Eom, J., Brautigam, D., & Benabdallah, L. (2018). BRIEFING The Path Ahead: The 7th Forum on China-Africa Cooperation. Retrieved from https://static1.squarespace.com/static/5652847de4b033f56d2bdc29/t/5b84311caa4a998051e685e3/1535389980283/Briefing+paper+1+-+August+2018+-+Final.pdf.

3. Shanggang, Liang & Qidi, Feng (2015). Africa Focus: China, Africa to deepen cooperation: Chinese envoy. *Xinhua.* http://www.focac.org/eng/zfgx/jmhz/t1247696.htm. See also Young, J. (2014). "Corruption concerns taints burgeoning China-Africa trade." *Voice for America.* September 1. http://www.voanews.com/content/corruption-concerns-tain-buregeoning-china-africa-trade/2432469.html.

4. Oshodi, A. T. (2012a). "Does China's activities in Africa mean colonization?" *The Constitution*, 12: 3, 1–54. See also Oshodi, A. T. (2013). "Chinese Africana versus Chinese international: Africanising the Chinese Option." In A. Odukoya (Ed.), *Alternative Development Strategies for Africa.* Lagos: CBAAC and Concepts Publications, pp. 217–242. See also Oshodi, A. T. (2015a). "Sino-pessimism versus Sino-optimism: Which way for Chinese Africana?" In Charles Quist-Adade & Vincent Dodoo (eds). *Africa's many divides and Africa's future: Pursuing Nkrumah's vision of Pan-Africanism in an era of globalisation,* Newcastle: Cambridge Scholars Publishing, pp. 190–216. See also Oshodi, A. T. (2015b). "Between the dragon's gift and its claws: China in Africa and the (un)civil fostering of ILO's decent work agenda." In A. Marx, J. Wouters, G. Rayp, & L. Beke (eds). *Global governance of labour rights.* Edward Elgar, pp. 190–208.

5. French, H. W. (2014a). "Into Africa: China's Wild Rush," *The New York Times,* May 16. http://www.nytimes.com/2014/05/17/opinion/into-africa-chinas-wild-rush.html?_r=0.

6. Broadly, three views have surfaced with contemporary China in Africa. These include optimism, pessimism, and caution (see Oshodi, 2013). While Sino-optimism sees the positives of Sino-Africa relations, Sino-pessimism highlights the dangers. The cautious view is situational in the sense that Africa, it is believed, could

benefit from China when certain conditions—such as good governance, investment in critical sector(s), and support of existing powers—are ensured.

7. Anshan, L. (2007). "China and Africa: Policy and Challenges." *China Security*, 3:3, 69–93.

8. Adisu, K., Sharkey, T. & Okoroafo, S. (2010). "The Impact of Chinese Investment in Africa." *International Journal of Business and Management*, 5:9, 3–9.

9. Konings, P. (2007). "China and Africa in the Era of Neo-liberal Globalisation." *CODESRIA Bulletin*, 1:2, 17–22.

10. See Oshodi, A. T. (2012a). "Does China's activities in Africa mean colonization?" *The Constitution*, 12: 3, 1–54. See also Oshodi, A. T. (2015a). "Sino-pessimism versus Sino-optimism: Which way for Chinese Africana?" In Charles Quist-Adade & Vincent Dodoo (eds). *Africa's many divides and Africa's future: Pursuing Nkrumah's vision of Pan-Africanism in an era of globalisation*. Newcastle: Cambridge Scholars Publishing, pp. 190–216.

11. See Schudson, M. (1989). "The sociology of news production." *Media, Culture and Society*. 11, 263–282.

12. Chang, T. & Lee, J. (1992). "Factors affecting gatekeepers' selection of foreign news: A national survey of newspaper editors." *Journalism & Mass Communication Quarterly*, 69: 3, 554–561.

13. Stockmann, D. & Gallagher, M. E. (2011). "Remote control: How the media sustain authoritarian rule in China." *Comparative Political Studies*. 20:10, 1–32.

14. Strange, Austin, Park, Bradley, Tierney, Michael J., Fuchs, Andreas, Dreher, Axel & Ramachandran, Vijaya (2013). "China's Development Finance to Africa: A Media-Based Approach to Data Collection. Center for Global Development Working Paper No. 323. https://ssrn.com/abstract=2259924.

15. Bunce, Mel, Franks, Suzanne & Paterson, Chris (2017). *Africa's Media Image in the 21st Century: From the "Heart of darkness" to "Africa rising."* London: Routledge.

16. Gallagher, Julia (2015). Images of Africa: Creation, negotiation and subversion. Manchester: Manchester University Press.

17. Leslie, Michael (2016). "The dragon shapes its image: A study of Chinese media influence strategies in Africa." *African Studies Quarterly*, 16:3/4, 161–174.

18. Ibid.

19. Wekesa, Bob (2017). "New directions in the study of Africa–China media and communications engagements," *Journal of African Cultural Studies*, 29:1, 11–24.

20. As at 2015, the station's website notes that "CCTV News wishes to promote communication and cooperation between China and African countries on politics, economy, trade and culture" (see http://english.cntv.cn/program/africalive/20120111/117620.shtml).

21. Oshodi, A. T. (2015a). "Sino-pessimism versus Sino-optimism: Which way for Chinese Africana?" In Charles Quist-Adade & Vincent Dodoo (eds). *Africa's many divides and Africa's future: Pursuing Nkrumah's vision of Pan-Africanism in an era of globalisation*. Newcastle: Cambridge Scholars Publishing, pp. 190–216.

22. Doh, M. V. (2010). "The Mass Media and Social transformation: Development journalism in the People's Republic of China—An example to the World."

In *Global Communication, Local Perspectives*. Hong Kong: China Association of Communication, Chinese Communication Association Department of Media and Communication, City University of Hong Kong & National Center for Radio and Television Studies, Communication University of China, pp. 70–81.

23. Fitzgerald, Mark (1988). "The Problem with 'Developmental Journalism," *Editor & Publisher*, 121:24, p. 74.

24. Gunaratne, Shelton A. (1998). "Old Wine in a New Bottle: Public Journalism, Developmental Journalism, and Social Responsibility," *Annals of the International Communication Association*, 21:1, 277–322.

25. French, H. W. (2014a). "Into Africa: China's Wild Rush," *The New York Times*, May 16. http://www.nytimes.com/2014/05/17/opinion/into-africa-chinas-wild -rush.html?_r=0.

26. Malekezo, Feston (2018). "BBC signs agreement with Malawi's Times Group." The Times Group, August 24. http://www.times.mw/bbc-signs-agreement-with-malawis-times-group/.

27. Wekesa, Bob (2013). "The media framing of China's image in East Africa: An exploratory study," *Africa East-Asia Affairs*, 1, 15–41.

28. Jenkins, H. (2006). *Convergence culture: where old and new media collide*. New York and London: New York University Press.

29. Lister, M., Dovey, J., Giddings, S., Grant, I. & Kelly, K. (2009). *New Media: a critical introduction* (2nd Edition). London and New York: Routledge.

30. Oshodi, A. T. (2015b). "Between the dragon's gift and its claws: China in Africa and the (un)civil fostering of ILO's decent work agenda." In A. Marx, J. Wouters, G. Rayp, & L. Beke (eds). *Global governance of labour rights*. Edward Elgar, pp. 190–208.

31. Large, Daniel (2008). "Beyond 'dragon in the bush': The study of China–Africa relations," *African Affairs*, 107:426, 45–61. See also Monson, Jamie & Rupp, Stephanie (2013). "Introduction: Africa and China: New Engagements, New Research," *African Studies Review*, 56:1, 21–44. See also Oshodi, A. T. (2015b). "Between the dragon's gift and its claws: China in Africa and the (un)civil fostering of ILO's decent work agenda." In A. Marx, J. Wouters, G. Rayp, & L. Beke (eds). *Global governance of labour rights*. Edward Elgar, pp. 190–208.

32. Wekesa, Bob (2013). "The media framing of China's image in East Africa: An exploratory study," *Africa East-Asia Affairs*, 1, 15–41.

33. Akintuotu, E., (2014a). "Man accuses Chinese boss of brutality." *The Punch*. 20th January. http://www.punchng.com/metro-plus/man-accuses-chinese-boss-of-bru tality/.

34. *Sahara Reporters*. (2011). Chinese expats threat Nigerian employees as punching bags. 18 October. http://saharareporters.com/report/chinese-expats-treat-nigerian-employees-punching-bags.

35. *Mail & Guardian*, (2012). "Chinese labour practices haunt Zim factory workers." January 6. http://mg.co.za/article/2012-01-06-chinese-labour-practices-haunt-zim-factory-workers/. See also Smith, D. (2011). "Chinese Mining Firms in Zambia Under Fire for Mistreating Workers," *The Guardian*, November 3, http:// www.theguardian.com/global-development/2011/nov/03/chinese-mining-zambia-m istreating-workers. See also Smith, D. (2012). "Workers Claim Abuse as China Adds

Zimbabwe to its Scramble for Africa," *The Guardian*, January 2, http://www.theg uardian.com/world/2012/jan/02/china-zimbabwe-workers-abuse.

36. Oshodi, A. T. (2015b). "Between the dragon's gift and its claws: China in Africa and the (un)civil fostering of ILO's decent work agenda." In A. Marx, J. Wouters, G. Rayp, & L. Beke (eds). *Global governance of labour rights*. Edward Elgar, pp. 190–208.

37. *Sahara Reporters*. (2011). Chinese expats threat Nigerian employees as punching bags. 18 October. http://saharareporters.com/report/chinese-expats-treat-nigerian-employees-punching-bags.

38. *Sahara Reporters*. (2013). Labour movements pickets, install workers union in foreign companies that denies workers' welfare. 8th October. http://saharareporte rs.com/gallery/photonews-labor-movements-picket-install-workers-union-foreign-co mpanies-deny-workers-welfar.

39. *Mail & Guardian*, (2012). "Chinese labour practices haunt Zim factory work-ers." January 6. http://mg.co.za/article/2012-01-06-chinese-labour-practices-haunt -zim-factory-workers/.

40. Akintuotu, E., (2014a). "Man accuses Chinese boss of brutality." *The Punch*. 20th January. http://www.punchng.com/metro-plus/man-accuses-chinese-boss-of-bru tality/.

41. Akinkuotu, E., (2014b). "Police detain Chinese for assaulting employee in Ogun." *The Punch*. 31 January. http://www.punchng.com/metro-plus/police-detain -chinese-for-assaulting-employee-in-ogun/.

42. Wells, M., (2011). China in Zambia: trouble down in the mines. *Huffington Post*, 21st November. http://www.hrw.org/news/2011/11/21/china-zambia-trouble -down-mines.

43. Falayi, K., (2014). "We're treated like slaves but we're afraid of losing our jobs –Nigerians in Chinese, Indian companies." *The Punch*. 8 February. http://www .punchng.com/news/nigerians-who-work-in-chinese-indian-lebanese-companies-w ere-treated-like-slaves-but-were-afraid-of-losing-our-jobs/.

44. IRIN (2005). "South Africa: Fallout as China sews up textile market." IRIN. June 29. http://www.irinnews.org/report/55156/south-africa-fallout-as-china-sews-up-textile-market.

45. SABC (2006). "COSATU Warns of Job Losses on SA-China Trade Deal." *SABC News*, April 13. http://www.bilaterals.org/spip.php?page=print&id_ar ticle=4413. See also Jannah, Chijioke (2018). "AfDB reveals what China is doing to African companies." *Daily Post*, November 4. http://dailypost.ng/2018/11/04/afdb -reveals-china-african-companies/.

46. Flynn, D. (2013). "China brings goods and roads, now Africa wants jobs." *Reuters*, July 21. http://www.reuters.com/article/africa-china-idUSL6N0FI3TE201 30721.

47. Ibid.

48. Blanchard, Ben (2018). "Corrupt government? You voted for them—China pushes back at Africa summit." *Reuters*, September 5. https://www.reuters.com/articl e/us-china-africa-summit-analysis/corrupt-government-you-voted-for-them-china-pu shes-back-at-africa-summit-idUSKCN1LL0EV.

49. Beattie, A. & Callan, E. (2006). "China loans create 'new wave of Africa debt.'" *Financial Times*. December 7. http://www.ft.com/intl/cms/s/0/640a5986-863a-11db-86d5-0000779e2340.html#axzz3cqM4UvsG.

50. AsiaNews (2006). "Debt by African countries to China growing." *AsiaNews*. December 12. http://www.asianews.it/news-en/Debt-by-African-countries-to-China-growing-8029.html.

51. Daniel, Luke (2018). "Debt colonialism: Is China trying to buyout Africa's resources?" *The South African*, September 3. https://www.thesouthafrican.com/debt-colonialism-china-africa-resources/.

52. French, H. W. (2014a). "Into Africa: China's Wild Rush," *The New York Times*, May 16. http://www.nytimes.com/2014/05/17/opinion/into-africa-chinas-wild-rush.html?_r=0.

53. Berger, S. & Moore, M. (2009). "Hu Jintao's son linked to corruption probe," *The Telegraph*, July 17. http://www.telegraph.co.uk/news/worldnews/asia/china/5851056/Hu-Jintaos-son-linked-to-African-corruption-probe.html.

54. Migiro, K. (2015). "China's aid to Africa funds corruption, says report." *BusinessDay Live*, January 25. http://www.bdlive.co.za/africa/africannews/2014/11/20/chinas-aid-to-africa-funds-corruption-says-report.

55. Young, J. (2014). "Corruption concerns taints burgeoning China-Africa trade." *Voice for America*. September 1. http://www.voanews.com/content/corruption-concerns-tain-buregeoning-china-africa-trade/2432469.html.

56. Blanchard, Ben (2018). "Corrupt government? You voted for them—China pushes back at Africa summit." *Reuters*, September 5. https://www.reuters.com/article/us-china-africa-summit-analysis/corrupt-government-you-voted-for-them-china-pushes-back-at-africa-summit-idUSKCN1LL0EV.

57. A report noted that Chinese racism against Africans dates to the 1960s when African students began to travel to China to study at Chinese universities with the 1988 violent mob attack on African dormitory at Nanjing University being one of the most nasty (Jaffe, 2012). Dick Wilson, in an opinion piece in the *New York Times* of April 15, 1992, opens with the following paragraph: "The human race, according to a Chinese legend, was created by a divine potter who left his clay figure of a man too long in the kiln. When it came out burned and black, he threw it away as far as he could—and it landed in Africa. The second one he pulled out too soon: It was too white. So, he threw that one away, more gently, and it landed in Europe. Now he knew the correct timing. The third man was a gorgeous yellow, and from him the East Asian races descended."

58. Shankar, S. (2015). "Chinese restaurant in Kenya shut down after refusing service to Africans," *International Business Times*, March 25. http://mg.co.za/article/2015-04-08-teaching-mandarin-at-school-will-colonise-sa-anew-sadtu.

59. See Oshodi, A. T. (2012a). "Does China's activities in Africa mean colonization?" *The Constitution*, 12: 3, 1–54.

60. French, H. W. (2014b). *China's second continent: How a million migrants are building a new empire in Africa*. New York: Knopf.

61. Nkosi, B. (2015). "Teaching Mandarin at African schools 'will colonise SA anew'—Sadtu," *Mail & Guardian*, April 8. http://mg.co.za/article/2015-04-08-teaching-mandarin-at-school-will-colonise-sa-anew-sadtu.

62. Mbaye, S. (2011). "Africa will not put up with a colonialist China." *The Guardian*, February 7. http://www.theguardian.com/commentisfree/2011/feb/07/china-exploitation-africa-industry.

63. Blair, D. (2007). "Why China is trying to colonise Africa," *The Telegraph*, August 31. http://www.telegraph.co.uk/comment/personal-view/3642345/Why-China-is-trying-to-colonise-Africa.html.

64. Borger, Julian (2018). "US unveils new Africa policy to counter 'predatory' Russia and China." *The Guardian*, December 13. https://www.theguardian.com/us-news/2018/dec/13/us-john-bolton-africa-policy-russia-china.

65. Taylor, J. (2011). "China's presence in Africa blamed for new threat to rhino," *The Independent*, January 14. http://www.independent.co.uk/environment/nature/chinas-presence-in-africa-blamed-for-new-threat-to-rhino-2184340.html.

66. Al Jazeera (2014). "Report: Africa ivory smuggled on China visit," November 6. http://www.aljazeera.com/news/asia-pacific/2014/11/report-africa-ivory-smuggled-china-visit-2014116163317314744.html.

67. Mjamba, K. O. (2014). "Chad suspends China's local oil unit for environment," *This is Africa*, May 23. http://thisisafrica.me/chad-suspends-chinas-local-oil-unit-environment/.

68. BBC (2015). "China illegally fishing off W Africa—Greenpeace," *BBC News*, May 20. http://www.bbc.com/news/world-africa-32817193.

69. Associated Press (2014). "Environmental group accuses Chinese diplomats on state visits of smuggling Tanzanian ivory." *Fox news*, November 6. http://www.foxnews.com/world/2014/11/06/environmental-group-accuses-chinese-diplomats-on-state-visits-smuggling/.

70. Allen, E. (2014). "China's colonialist behaviour in Africa could be a 'disaster' for environment, Jane Goodall warns, as she says Beijing is pillaging continent for raw materials," *Mail Online*, February 18. http://www.dailymail.co.uk/news/article-2562001/China-pillaging-Africa-raw-materials-like-old-colonialists-says-chimp-expert-Jane-Goodall.html.

71. Al Jazeera (2014). "Report: Africa ivory smuggled on China visit," November 6. http://www.aljazeera.com/news/asia-pacific/2014/11/report-africa-ivory-smuggled-china-visit-2014116163317314744.html.

72. BBC (2015). "China illegally fishing off W Africa—Greenpeace," *BBC News*, May 20. http://www.bbc.com/news/world-africa-32817193.

73. Oshodi, A. T. (2015b). "Between the dragon's gift and its claws: China in Africa and the (un)civil fostering of ILO's decent work agenda." In A. Marx, J. Wouters, G. Rayp, & L. Beke (eds). *Global governance of labour rights*. Edward Elgar, pp. 190–208.

74. Ibid., pp. 200–202.

75. Associated Press (2014). "Environmental group accuses Chinese diplomats on state visits of smuggling Tanzanian ivory." *Fox news*, November 6. http://www.foxnews.com/world/2014/11/06/environmental-group-accuses-chinese-diplomats-on-state-visits-smuggling/.

76. Smith, D. (2011). "Chinese Mining Firms in Zambia Under Fire for Mistreating Workers," *The Guardian*, November 3, http://www.theguardian.com/global-development/2011/nov/03/chinese-mining-zambia-mistreating-workers.

77. Wangalwa, E. (2015). "Kenya-based Chinese firms cite corruption as major hurdle," *CNBC*, February 12. http://www.cnbcafrica.com/news/east-africa/2015/01 /21/chinese-firms-kenya/.

78. Chege, N. (2015). "Only 'loyal' African patrons are allowed in Chinese restaurant after sunset." *Daily Nation*, March 23. http://www.nation.co.ke/counties/na irobi/Chinese-restaurant-no-African-after-5pm/-/1954174/2662642/-/svixtnz/-/index .html.

79. Ibid.

80. Ibid.

81. Ibid.

82. Ibid.

83. Ibid.

84. Ibid.

85. The *Daily Nation* newspaper published numerous follow-ups on the story. On March 23, 2015 alone it had captions such as "Only 'loyal' African patrons are allowed in Chinese restaurant after sunset" (Chege, 2015) and "Restaurant has no licence: Agency" (Chege and Wachira, 2015). Subsequently, for the rest of the month, the newspaper, which has an online presence, followed with such titles as "Nairobi county govt closes 'racist' Chinese restaurant" (Karanja, 2015), "Chinese envoy condemns looting of Chinese restaurant" (Cherono, 2015), and "Manager of city Chinese restaurant at centre of racism row released on bond" (Agoya, 2015).

86. Sen, Amartya (2000). Why human security? *International Symposium on Human Security* in Tokyo, 28 July. http://sicurezzaambientale.gruppi.ilcannocchiale .it/mediamanager/sys.group/447/filemanager/Sen2000.pdf.

87. Tharoor, I. (2015). "This Chinese restaurant in Kenya is open for dinner, as long as you're not African," *The Washington Post*, March 24. http://www.washingto npost.com/blogs/worldviews/wp/2015/03/24/this-chinese-restaurant-in-kenya-is-ope n-for-dinner-as-long-as-youre-not-african/.

88. Nsubuga, J. (2015). "Chinese restaurant in Africa has a 'no black Africans' policy," *BBC Newsday*, March 24. http://bbcnewsday.com/world-news/chinese-rest aurant-in-africa-has-a-no-black-africans-policy/#axzz3ctYvK7L3.

89. McKindy, E. (2015). "Chinese restaurant owner in Kenya arrested after 'No Africans' uproar." *CNN*, March 25. http://edition.cnn.com/2015/03/25/africa/kenyan -chinese-restaurant-discrimination-arrest/.

90. Findlay, S. (2015). "Restaurant owner in Nairobi who bars Africans from entering establishment is arrested." *The Telegraph*, March 25. http://www.telegraph .co.uk/news/worldnews/africaandindianocean/kenya/11494613/Restaurant-owner-in -Nairobi-who-bars-Africans-from-entering-establishment-is-arrested.html.

91. AFP (2015). "'No blacks' Chinese restaurant shut down in Kenya." *Yahoo News*, March 25. http://news.yahoo.com/no-blacks-chinese-restaurant-shut-down -kenya-082940084.html.

92. Kennedy Kangethe (2015). "Kenya: Chinese embassy slams restaurant over racism." *Capital FM*, March 26. http://allafrica.com/stories/201503271093.html.

93. Correspondent (2015). "'Racist' restaurant policy was wrong, says Chinese Embassy." *Daily Nation*, March 26. http://www.nation.co.ke/news/China-Embassy -Restaurant-Kilimani-Nairobi/-/1056/2666586/-/q6535pz/-/index.html.

94. Yizong, M. (2015). "Equal treatment for customers in Kenya, China's embassy says." *China Daily*. March 26. http://www.chinadaily.com.cn/china/2015-03 /26/content_19921212.htm.

95. See Jambo (2015). "The Chinese restaurant in Nairobi that does not take Africans after 7pm." *Jambonewspot.com*. March 17. http://www.jambonewspot.com /the-chinese-restaurant-in-nairobi-that-does-not-take-africans-after-7pm/.

96. Chege, N. & Wachira, M. (2015). "Restaurant has no licence: Agency." *Daily Nation*, March 23. http://www.nation.co.ke/news/Restaurant-has-no-licence-Agenc y/-/1056/2663520/-/cg20di/-/index.html.

97. Karanja, S. (2015). "Nairobi county govt closes 'racist' Chinese restaurant." *Daily Nation*, March 24. http://www.nation.co.ke/counties/nairobi/Chinese-Restau rant-Kilimani-Racism/-/1954174/2664382/-/rbns4a/-/index.html.

98. Ibid.

99. Cherono, S. (2015). "Chinese envoy condemns looting of Chinese restaurant." *Daily Nation*, March 27. http://www.nation.co.ke/news/Youths-raid -racist-Chinese-restaurant-in-Nairobi/-/1056/2667760/-/format/xhtml/-/mywqeu/-/i ndex.html.

100. Owino, K. (2015). "Chinese restaurant saga revealed Kenyans' ability to accommodate contradictions." *Daily Nation*, April 2. http://www.nation.co.ke/oped/b logs/dot9/kwame/-/2274474/2673510/-/k0gl6nz/-/index.html.

101. Karanja, S. (2015). "Nairobi county govt closes 'racist' Chinese restaurant." *Daily Nation*, March 24. http://www.nation.co.ke/counties/nairobi/Chinese-Restau rant-Kilimani-Racism/-/1954174/2664382/-/rbns4a/-/index.html.

BIBLIOGRAPHY

Adisu, K., Sharkey, T. & Okoroafo, S. (2010). "The Impact of Chinese Investment in Africa." *International Journal of Business and Management*, 5:9, 3–9.

AFP (2015). "'No blacks' Chinese restaurant shut down in Kenya." *Yahoo News*, March 25. http://news.yahoo.com/no-blacks-chinese-restaurant-shut-down-kenya -082940084.html.

Agoya, V. (2015). "Manager of city Chinese restaurant at centre of racism row released on bond." *Daily Nation*, March 31. http://www.nation.co.ke/news/Chines e-Ms-Zhao-Yang-out-on-bail/-/1056/2671612/-/x1nlqvz/-/index.html.

Akinkuotu, E., (2014b). "Police detain Chinese for assaulting employee in Ogun." *The Punch*. 31st January. http://www.punchng.com/metro-plus/police-detain-ch inese-for-assaulting-employee-in-ogun/.

Akintuotu, E., (2014a). "Man accuses Chinese boss of brutality." *The Punch*. 20 January. http://www.punchng.com/metro-plus/man-accuses-chinese-boss-of-bru tality/.

Al Jazeera (2014). "Report: Africa ivory smuggled on China visit," November 6. http://www.aljazeera.com/news/asia-pacific/2014/11/report-africa-ivory-smug gled-china-visit-2014116163317314744.html.

Allen, E. (2014). "China's colonialist behaviour in Africa could be a 'disaster' for environment, Jane Goodall warns, as she says Beijing is pillaging continent for raw materials," *Mail Online*, February 18. http://www.dailymail.co.uk/news/art icle-2562001/China-pillaging-Africa-raw-materials-like-old-colonialists-says-chi mp-expert-Jane-Goodall.html.

Anshan, L. (2007). "China and Africa: Policy and Challenges." *China Security*, 3:3, 69–93.

AsiaNews (2006). "Debt by African countries to China growing." *AsiaNews*. December 12. http://www.asianews.it/news-en/Debt-by-African-countries-to-China-growing-8029.html.

Associated Press (2014). "Environmental group accuses Chinese diplomats on state visits of smuggling Tanzanian ivory." *Fox news*, November 6. http://www.foxn ews.com/world/2014/11/06/environmental-group-accuses-chinese-diplomats-on-s tate-visits-smuggling/.

BBC (2015). "China illegally fishing off W Africa—Greenpeace," *BBC News*, May 20. http://www.bbc.com/news/world-africa-32817193.

Beattie, A. & Callan, E. (2006). "China loans create 'new wave of Africa debt.'" *Financial Times*. December 7. http://www.ft.com/intl/cms/s/0/640a5986-863a-11db-86d5-0000779e2340.html#axzz3cqM4UvsG.

Berger, S. & Moore, M. (2009). "Hu Jintao's son linked to corruption probe," *The Telegraph*, July 17. http://www.telegraph.co.uk/news/worldnews/asia/china/58 51056/Hu-Jintaos-son-linked-to-African-corruption-probe.html.

Blair, D. (2007). "Why China is trying to colonise Africa," *The Telegraph*, August 31. http://www.telegraph.co.uk/comment/personal-view/3642345/Why-China-is-tryin g-to-colonise-Africa.html.

Blanchard, Ben (2018). "Corrupt government? You voted for them—China pushes back at Africa summit." *Reuters*, September 5. https://www.reuters.com/articl e/us-china-africa-summit-analysis/corrupt-government-you-voted-for-them-china -pushes-back-at-africa-summit-idUSKCN1LL0EV.

Borger, Julian (2018). "US unveils new Africa policy to counter 'predatory' Russia and China." *The Guardian*, December 13. https://www.theguardian.com/us-news /2018/dec/13/us-john-bolton-africa-policy-russia-china.

Bunce, Mel, Franks, Suzanne & Paterson, Chris (2017). *Africa's Media Image in the 21st Century: From the "Heart of darkness" to "Africa rising."* London: Routledge.

Chang, T. & Lee, J. (1992). "Factors affecting gatekeepers' selection of foreign news: A national survey of newspaper editors." *Journalism & Mass Communication Quarterly*, 69: 3, 554–561.

Chege, N. & Wachira, M. (2015). "Restaurant has no licence: Agency." *Daily Nation*, March 23. http://www.nation.co.ke/news/Restaurant-has-no-licence-Agency/-/1 056/2663520/-/cg20di/-/index.html.

Chege, N. (2015). "Only 'loyal' African patrons are allowed in Chinese restaurant after sunset." *Daily Nation*, March 23. http://www.nation.co.ke/counties/nairobi /Chinese-restaurant-no-African-after-5pm/-/1954174/2662642/-/svixtnz/-/index .html.

Cherono, S. (2015). "Chinese envoy condemns looting of Chinese restaurant." *Daily Nation*, March 27. http://www.nation.co.ke/news/Youths-raid-racist-Chinese-rest aurant-in-Nairobi/-/1056/2667760/-/format/xhtml/-/mywqeu/-/index.html.

Correspondent (2015). "'Racist' restaurant policy was wrong, says Chinese Embassy." *Daily Nation*, March 26. http://www.nation.co.ke/news/China-Embassy-Restaur ant-Kilimani-Nairobi/-/1056/2666586/-/q6535pz/-/index.html.

Daniel, Luke (2018). "Debt colonialism: Is China trying to buyout Africa's resources?" *The South African*, September 3. https://www.thesouthafrican.com/deb t-colonialism-china-africa-resources/.

Eom, Janet, Brautigam, Deborah & Benabdallah, Lina (2018). "The path ahead: The 7th Forum on China-Africa Cooperation." *China-Africa Research Initiative Briefing Paper*, No. 1, Johns Hopkins School of Advanced International Studies (SAIS), pp. 1–10. https://static1.squarespace.com/static/5652847de4b033f56d2bd c29/t/5c467754898583fc9a99131f/1548121941093/Briefing+Paper+1+-+August +2018+-+Final.pdf.

De Grauwe, P., Houssa, R. & Piccillo, G. (2012). "African trade dynamics: is China a different trading partner." *Journal of Chinese Economic and Business Studies*, 10:1, 15–45.

Doh, M. V. (2010). "The Mass Media and Social transformation: Development journalism in the People's Republic of China—An example to the World." In *Global Communication, Local Perspectives*. Hong Kong: China Association of Communication, Chinese Communication Association Department of Media and Communication, City University of Hong Kong & National Center for Radio and Television Studies, Communication University of China, pp. 70–81.

Donohew, L. (1967). "Newspaper gatekeepers and forces in the news Channel." *The Public Opinion Quarterly*, 31:1, 61–68.

Falayi, K., (2014). "We're treated like slaves but we're afraid of losing our jobs— Nigerians in Chinese, Indian companies." *The Punch*. 8th February. http://www .punchng.com/news/nigerians-who-work-in-chinese-indian-lebanese-companies-w ere-treated-like-slaves-but-were-afraid-of-losing-our-jobs/.

Findlay, S. (2015). "Restaurant owner in Nairobi who bars Africans from entering establishment is arrested." *The Telegraph*, March 25. http://www.telegraph.co.uk /news/worldnews/africaandindianocean/kenya/11494613/Restaurant-owner-in-Na irobi-who-bars-Africans-from-entering-establishment-is-arrested.html.

Fitzgerald, Mark (1988). "The Problem with 'Developmental Journalism." *Editor & Publisher*, 121:24, p. 74.

Flynn, D. (2013). "China brings goods and roads, now Africa wants jobs." *Reuters*, July 21. http://www.reuters.com/article/africa-china-idUSL6N0FI3 TE20130721.

French, H. W. (2014a). "Into Africa: China's Wild Rush," *The New York Times*, May 16. http://www.nytimes.com/2014/05/17/opinion/into-africa-chinas-wild-rush .html?_r=0.

French, H. W. (2014b). *China's second continent: How a million migrants are building a new empire in Africa*. New York: Knopf.

Gallagher, Julia (2015). Images of Africa: Creation, negotiation and subversion. Manchester: Manchester University Press.

Gunaratne, Shelton A. (1998). "Old Wine in a New Bottle: Public Journalism, Developmental Journalism, and Social Responsibility." *Annals of the International Communication Association*, 21:1, 277–322.

IRIN (2005). "South Africa: Fallout as China sews up textile market." IRIN. June 29. http://www.irinnews.org/report/55156/south-africa-fallout-as-china-sews-up-texti le-market.

Jaffe, G. (2012). "Tinted prejudice in China." *CNN*, July 24. http://edition.cnn.com /2012/07/24/world/asia/china-tinted-prejudice/.

Jambo (2015). "The Chinese restaurant in Nairobi that does not take Africans after 7pm." *Jambonewspot.com*. March 17. http://www.jambonewspot.com/the-chinese-restaurant-in-nairobi-that-does-not-take-africans-after-7pm/.

Jannah, Chijioke (2018). "AfDB reveals what China is doing to African companies." *Daily Post*, November 4. http://dailypost.ng/2018/11/04/afdb-reveals-china-africa n-companies/.

Jenkins, H. (2006). *Convergence culture: where old and new media collide*. New York and London: New York University Press.

Karanja, S. (2015). "Nairobi county govt closes 'racist' Chinese restaurant." *Daily Nation*, March 24. http://www.nation.co.ke/counties/nairobi/Chinese-Restaurant-Kilimani-Racism/-/1954174/2664382/-/rbns4a/-/index.html.

Kennedy Kangethe (2015). "Kenya: Chinese embassy slams restaurant over racism." *Capital FM*, March 26. http://allafrica.com/stories/201503271093.html.

Konings, P. (2007). "China and Africa in the Era of Neo-liberal Globalisation." *CODESRIA Bulletin*, 1:2, 17–22.

Large, Daniel (2008). "Beyond 'dragon in the bush': The study of China–Africa relations." *African Affairs*, 107:426, 45–61.

Leslie, Michael (2016). "The dragon shapes its image: A study of Chinese media influence strategies in Africa." *African Studies Quarterly*, 16:3/4, 161–174.

Lister, M., Dovey, J., Giddings, S., Grant, I. & Kelly, K. (2009). *New Media: a critical introduction* (2nd Edition). London and New York: Routledge.

Mail & Guardian, (2012). "Chinese labour practices haunt Zim factory workers." January 6. http://mg.co.za/article/2012-01-06-chinese-labour-practices-haunt-zim-factory-workers/.

Malekezo, Feston (2018). "BBC signs agreement with Malawi's Times Group." The Times Group, August 24. http://www.times.mw/bbc-signs-agreement-with-malaw is-times-group/.

Mbaye, S. (2011). "Africa will not put up with a colonialist China." *The Guardian*, February 7. http://www.theguardian.com/commentisfree/2011/feb/07/china-exploi tation-africa-industry.

McKindy, E. (2015). "Chinese restaurant owner in Kenya arrested after 'No Africans' uproar." *CNN*, March 25. http://edition.cnn.com/2015/03/25/africa/kenyan-chinese -restaurant-discrimination-arrest/.

Migiro, K. (2015). "China's aid to Africa funds corruption, says report." *BusinessDay Live*, January 25. http://www.bdlive.co.za/africa/africannews/2014/11/20/chinas -aid-to-africa-funds-corruption-says-report.

Mjamba, K. O. (2014). "Chad suspends China's local oil unit for environment," *This is Africa*, May 23. http://thisisafrica.me/chad-suspends-chinas-local-oil-unit-enviro nment/.

Monson, Jamie & Rupp, Stephanie (2013). "Introduction: Africa and China: New Engagements, New Research." *African Studies Review*, 56:1, 21–44.

Nkosi, B. (2015). "Teaching Mandarin at African schools 'will colonise SA anew'—Sadtu," *Mail & Guardian*, April 8. http://mg.co.za/article/2015-04-08-teaching-m andarin-at-school-will-colonise-sa-anew-sadtu.

Nsubuga, J. (2015). "Chinese restaurant in Africa has a 'no black Africans' policy," *BBC Newsday*, March 24. http://bbcnewsday.com/world-news/chinese-restaurant -in-africa-has-a-no-black-africans-policy/#axzz3ctYvK7L3.

Oshodi, A. T. (2012a). "Does China's activities in Africa mean colonization?" *The Constitution*, 12: 3, 1–54.

Oshodi, A. T. (2012b). "ECOWAS and the Chinese Option." In Simeon Koffi, Lambert did galadjo Bamba, Gervasio Semedo (eds.) *Sortir Du Sous-Développement: Quelles Nouvelles Pistes Pour L'afrique De L'ouest ? (Tome 2)*, Paris: L'Harmattan, pp. 71–96.

Oshodi, A. T. (2013). "Chinese Africana versus Chinese internationa: Africanising the Chinese Option." In A. Odukoya (Ed.), *Alternative Development Strategies for Africa*. Lagos: CBAAC and Concepts Publications, pp. 217–242.

Oshodi, A. T. (2015a). "Sino-pessimism versus Sino-optimism: Which way for Chinese Africana?" In Charles Quist-Adade & Vincent Dodoo (eds.) *Africa's many divides and Africa's future: Pursuing Nkrumah's vision of Pan-Africanism in an era of globalisation*. Newcastle: Cambridge Scholars Publishing, pp. 190–216.

Oshodi, A. T. (2015b). "Between the dragon's gift and its claws: China in Africa and the (un)civil fostering of ILO's decent work agenda." In A. Marx, J. Wouters, G. Rayp, & L. Beke (eds) *Global governance of labour rights*. Edward Elgar, pp. 190–208.

Owino, K. (2015). "Chinese restaurant saga revealed Kenyans' ability to accommo-date contradictions." *Daily Nation*, April 2. http://www.nation.co.ke/oped/blogs/ dot9/kwame/-/2274474/2673510/-/k0gl6nz/-/index.html.

SABC (2006). "COSATU Warns of Job Losses on SA-China Trade Deal." *SABC News*, April 13. http://www.bilaterals.org/spip.php?page=print&id_article=4413.

Sahara Reporters. (2011). Chinese expats threat Nigerian employees as punching bags. 18th October. http://saharareporters.com/report/chinese-expats-treat-nigerian -employees-punching-bags.

Sahara Reporters. (2013). Labour movements pickets, install workers union in for-eign companies that denies workers' welfare. 8th October. http://saharareporte rs.com/gallery/photonews-labor-movements-picket-install-workers-union-foreign -companies-deny-workers-welfar.

Schudson, M. (1989). "The sociology of news production." *Media, Culture and Society* 11, 263–282.

Sen, Amartya (2000). Why human security? *International Symposium on Human Security* in Tokyo, 28 July. http://sicurezzaambientale.gruppi.ilcannocchiale.it/med iamanager/sys.group/447/filemanager/Sen2000.pdf.

Shanggang, Liang & Qidi, Feng (2015). Africa Focus: China, Africa to deepen cooper-ation: Chinese envoy. *Xinhua*. http://www.focac.org/eng/zfgx/jmhz/t1247696.htm.

Shankar, S. (2015). "Chinese restaurant in Kenya shut down after refusing service to Africans," *International Business Times*, March 25. http://mg.co.za/article/2015-0 4-08-teaching-mandarin-at-school-will-colonise-sa-anew-sadtu.

Smith, D. (2011). "Chinese Mining Firms in Zambia Under Fire for Mistreating Workers," *The Guardian*, November 3, http://www.theguardian.com/global-develo pment/2011/nov/03/chinese-mining-zambia-mistreating-workers.

Smith, D. (2012). "Workers Claim Abuse as China Adds Zimbabwe to its Scramble for Africa," *The Guardian*, January 2, http://www.theguardian.com/world/2012/ja n/02/china-zimbabwe-workers-abuse.

Stockmann, D. & Gallagher, M. E. (2011). "Remote control: How the media sustain authoritarian rule in China." *Comparative Political Studies* 20:10, 1–32.

Strange, Austin, Park, Bradley, Tierney, Michael J., Fuchs, Andreas, Dreher, Axel & Ramachandran, Vijaya (2013). "China's Development Finance to Africa: A Media-Based Approach to Data Collection. Center for Global Development Working Paper No. 323. https://ssrn.com/abstract=2259924.

Taylor, J. (2011). "China's presence in Africa blamed for new threat to rhino," *The Independent*, January 14. http://www.independent.co.uk/environment/nature/ch inas-presence-in-africa-blamed-for-new-threat-to-rhino-2184340.html.

Tharoor, I. (2015). "This Chinese restaurant in Kenya is open for dinner, as long as you're not African," *The Washington Post*, March 24. http://www.washingtonpost .com/blogs/worldviews/wp/2015/03/24/this-chinese-restaurant-in-kenya-is-open -for-dinner-as-long-as-youre-not-african/.

The Boston Globe (2014). "China's pollution of Africa finally merits a penalty." Editorial, June 1, 2014. http://www.bostonglobe.com/opinion/editorials/2014/05 /31/china-pollution-africa-finally-merits-penalty/4rsDElo9fU7nPsN5AyyqoN/stor y.html.

Vanguard (2015). "'No blacks' Chinese restaurant shut down in Kenya," [online], March 25. http://www.vanguardngr.com/2015/03/no-blacks-chinese-restaurant-s hut-down-in-kenya/.

Vines, S. (2009). "China's black pop idol exposes her nation's racism." *The Guardian*, November 1. http://www.theguardian.com/world/2009/nov/01/lou-jing-chinese-tal ent-show.

Wangalwa, E. (2015). "Kenya-based Chinese firms cite corruption as major hurdle," *CNBC*, February 12. http://www.cnbcafrica.com/news/east-africa/2015/01/21/c hinese-firms-kenya/.

Wekesa, Bob (2013). "The media framing of China's image in East Africa: An exploratory study." *Africa East-Asia Affairs*, 1, 15–41.

Wekesa, Bob (2017). "New directions in the study of Africa–China media and com-munications engagements." *Journal of African Cultural Studies*, 29:1, 11–24.

Wells, M., (2011). China in Zambia: trouble down in the mines. *Huffington Post*, 21st November. http://www.hrw.org/news/2011/11/21/china-zambia-trouble-down -mines.

Wilson, D. (1992). "Asian racism: cold truths are beginning to surface." *The New York Times*, April 15. http://www.nytimes.com/1992/04/15/opinion/15iht-eddi.html.

Xin, Z. (2014). "Why Africans resent the Chinese." *Worldcrunch*. November 3. http://www.worldcrunch.com/opinion-analysis/why-africans-resent-the-chinese/trade-partner-tzr-africa-zheng-he-sustainability-employment/c7s17217/#.VYU2DPmqqkp.

Yizong, M. (2015). "Equal treatment for customers in Kenya, China's embassy says." *China Daily*. March 26. http://www.chinadaily.com.cn/china/2015-03/26/content_19921212.htm.

Young, J. (2014). "Corruption concerns taints burgeoning China-Africa trade." *Voice for America*. September 1. http://www.voanews.com/content/corruption-concerns-tain-buregeoning-china-africa-trade/2432469.html.

Chapter 12

Chinese Economic Development Projects in Zimbabwe

Charity Manyeruke

INTRODUCTION

Economic development has been depicted to be the crux through which a country's status quo is defined, thus explaining why there is a lot of pandemonium when it comes to attempts by African countries to develop their nations. The boisterous winds of "underdevelopment" have sadly enveloped Africa, and thus China has been turned to by many African countries such as Zimbabwe to free her from theses dire straits and come up with a new developmental trajectory. As a result, in 2003, Zimbabwe officially opened its doors to Chinese enterprises in an initiative dubbed the "Look East Policy," (LEP) which has seen Zimbabwe not look back in engaging China in terms of its economic development projects. The "Look East Policy" came about as a result of the inadequacies that were prevailing in the Zimbabwean economy and its lack of capacity to come up with the resources it on its own. Youde is of the view that these circumstances, coupled with Zimbabwe being denied technical assistance by western donors prompted the government to look for assistance elsewhere.[1] This resulted in the pronunciation of the "Look East Policy" (LEP) by the government, which has arguably brought about some level of economic development in some sectors of Zimbabwe's economy.

China's goal in Zimbabwe and other developing countries in the world is premised on the belief that it views itself as a "big brother" in terms of fighting colonialism and aiding toward self-determination, cooperation, and economic development. Cape notes that China is founded on the belief that the economy is the pivotal drive of development in any specific country.[2] This explains why China has been taken up the initiative to assist Zimbabwe in its developmental efforts.[3] The most substantial aspect of the Chinese economic projects in Zimbabwe is that they do not only benefit Zimbabwe on an economic level, but they also cascade into on all other aspects of life that are of paramount importance such as the social, technological, economic, and political spheres. Interestingly, what even made it easier for the nations to develop deep ties is the fact that China from the onset presented itself with a series of features and characteristics that made it attractive to the Government of Zimbabwe (GOZ). Of note is China's role as the largest importer of Zimbabwe's tobacco, which made China a strategic and important economic partner for the country. Also, China's economic success allowed her to be an important provider of foreign direct investment (FDI) which Zimbabwe so much needed. Most importantly, Schumpeter notes that, unlike the Western governments, China does not involve itself in the governance issues of the nation it is assisting.[4] Also, the historical ties between China and Zimbabwe, particularly during the liberation struggle of Zimbabwe, solidified China's future position as Zimbabwe's "all-weather friend" so to speak.

However, the strong ties that now exist between China and Zimbabwe have attracted a lot of controversies within the international system. Several Western nations are not particularly thrilled with how China has assisted Zimbabwe to develop, rendering the sanctions that were illegally imposed on Zimbabwe null and void as they failed to make the government learn from their "supposed" mistakes. More so, Chingono, as cited in the China Monitor, is of the view that The LEP has manifested both intangible and tangible benefits, but not without impediments and condemnation.[5] There has been a general belief by the ordinary Zimbabweans that the challenges they are experiencing are attributed to the failure of the diplomatic paradigm shift from the Western bloc to the Eastern bloc. Furthermore, the LEP has not received much public support as it should as Zimbabwe is currently experiencing excessive poverty that is characterized by a high unemployment rate, continuous deindustrialization, cash crisis, and dilapidating infrastructure among other things. This chapter, shall, therefore, look at some of the Chinese Economic Development projects implemented in Zimbabwe in the aspects of mining, infrastructure, foreign direct investment (FDI), employment, ICT developments, agriculture, energy and transport, textile, and well as in the aspect of tourism. The impact of these projects shall also be analyzed on both the positive and the negative fronts.

HISTORICAL DEVELOPMENT OF
CHINA-ZIMBABWE RELATIONS

As previously highlighted, China has always had the aim of aiding African nations and freeing them from the shackles of their colonizers and setting them on a path of self-sustenance and self-determination. According to Manyeruke and Mhandara, contrary to general belief, China-Zimbabwe relations were not established during the Chimurenga warfare, rather the relations were established as far back as 600 years ago.[6] During this time, the Chinese established trade relations with the Munhumutapa State. This means that this relationship is certainly not a new phenomenon.

China's contemporary interactions with Zimbabwe began with its support of Zimbabwe's liberation struggle against colonialism and racial oppression, when China helped the Zimbabwe African National Union (ZANU), one of the movements that fought for the liberation of Zimbabwe in the early 1960s.[7] The Chinese rendered their support to liberation movements in Zimbabwe through the provision of arms to ZANU PF against the European colonizers. This was a critical time for Zimbabwe where they had to fight white settlers for their identity. As a result, a mutual relationship developed, and this also laid very strong foundations for the future relationship between China and Zimbabwe. When the liberation war was over and finally won by ZANU, the Sino-Zimbabwe relations did not come to an end, but they further blossomed into a new era albeit at a much slower pace as in the early years of independence the ties remained lukewarm. This was because of Mugabe's desire to maintain good relations with the West from where most of his aid came.

All the same, Chun points out that, the China-Zimbabwe relationship grew through loans, projects, and further visits.[8] Through this, Beijing was reaping the political capital it had sown in the 1960s and was invited to construct hospitals and the National Sports Stadium in the 1980s. The former president of Zimbabwe, Mugabe again traveled to China in 1985 and received $55m in loans. After a while, the relations began to sour for a while. However, Zimbabwe's reaction to the Chinese Tiananmen Square Massacre of 1989 had a major bearing on the development of the Zimbabwe-China relations in the twenty-first century. When the Chinese government received immense condemnation from the West for the massacres, China actively sought African support for its position on human rights issues on the international platform. Mugabe immediately obliged by defending China's actions.

In return, China stretched out a desperately needed hand of friendship to Zimbabwe as from 2000 when Mugabe was bashed by the West for his land reform policy and gross Human Rights abuses. The land reform program coupled with the growing concern by Western countries of gross human rights abuse in Zimbabwe further increased the rift between Zimbabwe and the Western allies. This led Zimbabwe to shift its attention to more receptive partners. The noninterference policy by China was very much welcomed by Zimbabwe and they seized the opportunity to grow economically despite the sanctions imposed by Western countries. Thus, the Chinese act helped in strengthening the bonds of friendship between the two countries at the turn of the century. To show his appreciation for this gesture of friendship (comradeship) Mugabe came up with the LEP. The policy, which on paper aimed to expand bilateral and trade relations and offer priority to investors from Malaysia, Singapore, Vietnam, Japan, South Korea, India, and Russia, focused increasingly on China, to the exclusion of other countries.

As a result of the Fast Track Land Reform Programme (FTLRP) of 2000, the USA imposed sanctions upon Zimbabwe through the Zimbabwe Democracy and Economic Recovery Act (ZIDERA) which was implemented in 2001.[9] ZIDERA led to bitter relations between Zimbabwe and the USA as it prohibited the USA from supporting International Financial Institution (IFI), loans, or grants to the government of Zimbabwe. There were also placed upon aid programs to Zimbabwe through this act. As a result of ZIDERA and the sanctions that came with it, Zimbabwe was left in-between a rock and a hard place as the economy was already rapidly descending, and the country's economic development was being stifled. Confronted with numerous challenges resulting from the ZIDERA sanctions, the Government of Zimbabwe (GOZ) decided to "look east" where the sun rises and not west, where it sets as Mugabe put it, to try and revive the country's economy.

FORUM ON CHINA AFRICA COOPERATION (FOCAC) AND ZIMBABWE

With the growing need to formalize relations between China and Africa, the African leaders agreed on trade and economic development under what was termed FOCAC. Jansson points out that, "the Forum for China-Africa Cooperation (FOCAC) is a multilateral platform for collective, pragmatic consultation and dialogue."[10] FOCAC was jointly established by Chinese and African leaders in 2000 to further strengthen the friendly cooperation between China and Africa under the new circumstances, to jointly meet the challenge of economic globalization and to promote common development. Youde notes that China adopted its Africa Policy in 2006 and held the FOCAC summit that same year as the first step in seeking external support for its developmental initiative, as well as seeking to strengthen Sino-African cooperation.[11] Under the banner of South-South cooperation in the epoch concerned with economic globalization, China has thus reflected a great interest in the African continent as established over the years. According to Chipaike and Mhandara, FOCAC was therefore established to substantiate key economic sectors such as trade, investment, tourism, energy, and agriculture and also solidify diplomatic marriage between China and Africa.[12]

These relations, according to the Chinese are purportedly based on fairness, corporation, and consultation emphasized by the standard of noninterference in the internal affairs of other partners. FOCAC came out of the realization by both the African and Chinese leaders that they could no longer afford to ignore the issue of development in the international arena. The common history shared between Africa and China made this initiative even more popular amongst the two parties. Enuka states that that the result of this was a mutually beneficial relationship where China would obtain natural resources and energy to feed her growing industrialization and economic growth from Africa and Africa would attain a partner to help grow her industries and economies in the form China which by now has mastered the art of economic development.[13]

It would be incomplete to discuss the relationship between Zimbabwe and China in the context of the LEP alone without discussing FOCAC and what it means for Zimbabwe. Interestingly enough, the establishment of FOCAC transpired at the same time the relationship between Zimbabwe and Western nations turned sour following Zimbabwe's implementation of the Fast Track Land Reform Program (FTLRP) at the dawn of the millennium. Zimbabwe then took this opportunity to launch its policy to focus on the Far East Asian countries as potential economic development partners especially China. Since the launch of the LEP in 2003, Zimbabwe has had significant gains from the loans, grants, and projects implemented by the Chinese in Africa through the FOCAC initiative which was launched in 2006.[14] The FOCAC initiative continues to gain momentum as was witnessed in the recent FOCAC meeting held in 2018,[15] which President Mnangagwa attended and where China availed more funds for investment in Africa's economic development initiatives.

THEORETICAL AND CONCEPTUAL CONSIDERATIONS

Complex Interdependence Theory

The world in the twenty-first century is going through an economic revolution with a shift in the economic paradigm between nations. The complex economic interdependence theory posits that states pursue their economic foreign policies to ensure that a relationship enables importation as well as exportation of goods. Complex economic interdependency means that the purpose of economic foreign policy must be pursued to ensure resource flows from end to end. The trade among nations has significantly increased within the past fifty years. It has been noted that the motivation of complex economic interdependence is both a simple and powerful tool, designed to improve wealth through an economic transition. Awad argues that "in a world infested by politics, economic interdependence is a symbiotic economic dependence between states."[16] Awad further highlights that "within this system, there is an increased economic dependence by both consumers and producers."[17]

According to Ndimande and Moyo, "it has been argued that the makers of Zimbabwe's foreign economic policy explicitly designed their foreign policy towards China for economic gains and development above all else."[18] Zimbabwe has natural resources in abundance and China is increasingly becoming a global economic and manufacturing powerhouse. This relationship is meant to interdepend on each other through the exchange of natural resources, goods, and services. Complex economic interdependence is thus characterized by mutual dependency. It can, therefore, be noted that Zimbabwe's LEP and China's FOCAC initiative can both be best described using the economic interdependency theory which assumes that states engage to benefit their economies. However, it must be noted that achieving economic interdependency is very difficult if not impossible. Most times due to the uneven power dynamics, developing countries often get a lesser share in most arrangements with developed nations getting the larger share and benefiting the most. There should, therefore, be in existence of a system where nations on the same level must interdepend on each other more to avoid the pitfalls of dependency.

Concept of Economic Development

The term "economic development" is more often used in social and political circles. Bartrik holds the view that "the term 'Economic Development' has its roots in the period preceding the 2nd World War in 1949."[19] During this period, there was exacerbated economic destruction, which left the world with no option but to rebuild the nations that had suffered immense destruction after the war. Economic development has been deemed a key dominant feature to ensure that the standard of living of the people of a specific polity id of high quality inclusive of an improvement of the Gross Domestic Product (GDP), employment rates, fiscal capital. Economic development ensures a secure economy in terms of being. Das notes that "economic development is measured by economic indicators that are inclusive; gross domestic product (GDP), rising real per capita income, the levels of employment, distribution of wealth in a state, goods and services as well as the levels of production."[20]

Schumpeter views economic development differently and is of the view that "it comprises of transferring capital from established means of production to new, innovative, productivity-enhancing methods."[21] In Schumpeter's view, economic development involves an essential transformation of an economy. This includes the alteration of the industrial arrangement and the educational, occupational characteristics of the citizens of a nation and the social and institutional fabrication. Despite this, of the various choices, there are for measuring economic development, the state-level GDP per capita is the most commonly accepted and commonly available indicator there is. In most cases, economic development is often associated with robust industries, an attractive infrastructure, a literate populace, and so many other aspects. According to Hodzi, "the interests and national development goals are important to economic development and these should be achieved following the aim of adding value to the way people live."[22]

CHINESE ECONOMIC DEVELOPMENT PROJECTS IN ZIMBABWE

Infrastructure

The infrastructural advancements that have been initiated by the Chinese in Zimbabwe lie at the center of the economic development projects that they have initiated within Zimbabwe. It has been argued that a country's infrastructure largely determines the trajectory of its economic development. China has been assisting Zimbabwe to resuscitate its aging infrastructure. Some of the infrastructure projects include the Harare City's water infrastructure rehabilitation program undertaken with funding from China's Exim Bank. This project cost about US $144m and it aimed to rehabilitate Harare's Morton Jaffrey Water Treatment Plant, and increased its capacity to over 520 million liters per day, up from 400 million liters a day.[23]

There are further plans by China Railway Corporation Company to establish a railway project stretching from Harare to Bulawayo, which will be one of the most advanced railways in Africa when upon its completion. One other notable infrastructure project that was undertaken with assistance from China is the construction of Long Cheng Plaza, a highly esteemed mall in Zimbabwe, which was constructed by Anhui Foreign Economic Construction Corporation (AFECC), a Chinese company at an estimated cost of over $200m.[24] This project, however, has caused a lot of controversies as it has been alleged that the construction site was a presumed wetland upon which no construction should take place. The AFECC further provided US$98m for the construction of the National Defence College in Harare, which was a three-year project.[25] The funds for this project were secured through a loan from the China Export and Import Bank and they will be repaid after twenty years at a 2 percent interest. The improvement made to the Robert Mugabe International Airport Road was made with assistance from another Chinese company, Augur Investments Company. Also, the Chinese Dalian Technical Group initiated the Matabeleland Zambezi Water Pipeline Programme. This program gave access to water for over two million people. China's EXIM bank also provided US $864m toward this project.[26]

China also initiated the Daniel Academy Hatcliffe School project. This school was previously known as the Zimbabwe-China Friendship High School and worth about $US2m was handed over by the Chinese government to Zimbabwe and later renamed to Daniel Academy Hatcliffe School.[27] The school has been said to have the capacity to enroll up to 960 students at a time and employs 50 teachers. Speaking during the handover ceremony, Primary and Secondary Education Minister Professor Paul Mavima thanked the Chinese government for the kind gesture by saying:

> "I feel a sense of gratitude to be here on behalf of the Government of the Republic of Zimbabwe, receiving this state-of-the-art school, the Hatcliffe China-Zimbabwe Friendship Government High School," he said. "This noble project is a gift to us from the People's Republic of China. It is testimony to the immense friendship that exists between our two governments and indeed the peoples of the two great nations."[28]

The government has further managed to secure about US $680m from the Chinese government toward the construction of the much anticipated Kunzvi-Musami Dam which will be incorporated into Harare's water supply system, in a bid to solve the capital city's water challenges.[29] It is apparent that the list of infrastructural developments is expansive, but these are just some of the projects worth noting.

Mining

The mining sector in Zimbabwe has been identified as one of the most dominant sectors of the economy that has been identified by Chinese companies. Chinese companies have contributed immensely to the mining sector in terms of machinery and expertise to the Zimbabwean mining companies. Zimbabwe prides itself to be rich in natural resources particularly rich and expansive mineral deposits. Diamonds and gold are some of the minerals that are constantly given a lot of attention to in Zimbabwe's mining sector. Zimbabwe's mineral deposits have drawn several investors showing interest, especially from China. Many Chinese firms have come in to play a part and claim a stake in the supposed development of Zimbabwe's mining sector. Mvutungayi highlights that, in 2008, the Mineral Marketing Corporation of Zimbabwe (MMCZ) signed a memorandum of understanding with the Chinese Nickel Company, Jinchuan Nickel Mining Company of China.[30]

Jinchuan is the biggest producer of nickel and cobalt in China with an annual production capacity of 130,000 tons of nickel, 200,000 of copper, and 6,000 tons of cobalt and it is reported that the deal required Zimbabwe to sell these minerals to China.[31] Chun notes that the Chinese diamond mining firm Anjin is in a partnership with Zimbabwe Mining Development Corporation, which is operating in the Marange diamond fields, and China International Mining Group is interested in investing US$21.2m in Bindura Nickel Corporation, a company that had ceased operations due to operational difficulties in Zimbabwe and a sharp decline in the price of nickel.[32] China CAMC Engineering Company has made available the requisite machinery to Zimbabwe to allow for the mining of nickel, gold, and diamonds. This firm has further provided expertise to some Zimbabweans in the form of technology transfer of technical information on the use of this machinery.

Selling minerals to China means that Zimbabwe once more has a ready market for their minerals and improves its prospects of bringing in the much-needed revenue to the ailing economy. However, these Chinese companies have been criticized for only in taking the resources and initiating any meaningful developmental projects to improve the country's infrastructure and lives of the locals. Scholars have argued that most Chinese deals have been concentrated on minerals and this has been viewed and questioned by some as a way of looting natural resources from the country. There has further been a lot of controversy in the Marange area, especially on the deteriorating environment due to the extraction of diamonds and damage to the road infrastructure because of the over usage of roads. The sentiments around communities are that the Chinese are doing more damage than any actual development. There have been concerns raised in Bindura over how the Chinese have been treating locals working in the mines which some have labeled it an unfair labor practice. Guma highlights that "Anjin Investment dismissed a total of 1 500 workers in a day after the workers engaged in a legal strike for higher pay and better working conditions in its diamond mine."[33] The dismissal shocked the workers and other interested groups and made many headlines.[34] It can be noted that many Zimbabweans employed by some of these Chinese mining firms have leveled allegations of unfair labor practices against them.

Foreign Direct Investment (FDI)

Foreign Direct Investment (FDI) refers particularly to the money and funds, a specific entity inject into a country to allow for the economic development of a state. FDI is usually injected into an economy by foreign firms or a foreign country. Zimbabwe as part of President Mnangagwa's "*Zimbabwe is open for business*" mantra has been on a renewed drive to attract more FDI into the country. The FDI from China is in the spheres of mining, construction, agriculture, trade, tourism, and other spheres of the economy. The Chinese FDI into Zimbabwe is driven by the Bilateral Investment Promotion and Protection Agreement (BIPPA) which was signed by several companies that include Tianze, China Tobacco Import and Export Corporation, and Anhui Agricultural Cooperation amongst others.[35] It has been noted that the increased flow of FDI coming into Zimbabwe from China has been as a result of the historic and strategic partnership that exists between the two nations. These investments have been had positive connotations in the form of foreign currency injection into the local economy. There has been a steady increase in the amount of FDI coming into the country over the past decade.[36] In 2008, the country received FDI in the region of US $35m from China, in 2010 the amount had increased to US $45m and by 2011 the amount had increased sharply to US $460m, which depicts the increased growth of the economic ties between China and Zimbabwe.[37] The FDI that has come into Zimbabwe has had several advantages for the country such as increasing its access to foreign currency, employment creation, access to foreign skills and expertise, technological transfer, acquisition of new machinery as well as a general boost and improvement of the economy.

Employment Creation

Employment creation has been viewed as an equally important indicator of the attainment of economic development in any country. It is of importance to establish how much the Chinese have contributed toward employment creation in Zimbabwe. It should be noted that there is a symbiotic relationship between employment creation and FDI in a country. Hellström notes that "FDI accelerates an astounding growth in business opportunities and improves business operations which in turn usually has the effect of increasing employment opportunities."[38] Therefore, since there has been a considerable amount of Chinese FDI coming into Zimbabwe, some employment has been created. According to an employee from the RNH Company, several Chinese companies and businesses are willing to employ as many local Zimbabweans as they can and there is a low proportion of Chinese employees especially in those companies that needed technicians and specialists who are not found in Zimbabwe.[39] Chinese firms have created more than 20,000 jobs for local Zimbabweans in their business ventures.[40] Since the coming in of Chinese firms into Zimbabwe, local employees have made vital contributions to the development of Chinese businesses, and in most of those businesses, the locals have become the backbone of the companies. Ndimande and Moyo highlight that employment creation has been a positive implication of the Chinese economic development initiatives in Zimbabwe especially considering the high unemployment rate that is prevalent and which was over 90 percent according to both official and unofficial statistical reports.[41]

Agriculture

China's contributions in Zimbabwe's agricultural sector is of critical importance since agriculture in Zimbabwe contributes over 50 percent of the
GDP.[42] The Chinese government supported Zimbabwe's Fast Track Land
Reform Programme (FTLRP) at a time the initiative was condemned by a
host of Western nations. The land reform program is arguably one of the most
important reasons why relations soured between Zimbabwe and its Western
allies. Without the backbone from the West coupled with climate change,
poor policies, and the failing economy, Zimbabwe was faced yet with another
crisis in this very important sector. The move to look east was driven by the
desire to revitalize this sector.

In a bid to stimulate Zimbabwe's agricultural output especially after the
FTLRP, in 2001 China provided low-cost agricultural equipment for newly
resettled farmers worth more than US$2,41,000.[43] They provided for US$24m,
424 tractors and 50 trucks toward the reparations of the FTLRP.[44] In recent
years, China has availed support to Zimbabwe in the form of expertise and
technical assistance. Mvutungayi further notes that, in 2007, the Chinese
government extended a credit facility of US$200m in support of Zimbabwe's
agriculture.[45] The facility was mainly used to acquire farming equipment from
China which included 1,000 tractors, and an assortment of combine harvesters,
irrigation pumps, disc harrows, and planters, among others.[46] This also saw
the extension of land given for tobacco products in the country. According to
Eisenman in 2011 the Chinese state-owned company China International Water
and Electricity had been contracted to farm about 2,50,000 acres in southern
Zimbabwe to produce a yield of 2.1 million tons of maize each year[47]. This
agreement would also result in the construction of a massive irrigation system.[48] It has been claimed that this project will be paid for by Zimbabwe using
tobacco, which China already purchases in large quantities from Zimbabwe.
Between January and October 2007, 13,000 tons of tobacco was sold to China.

Furthermore, Tianze, a Chinese company has been at the forefront of
developing a farming business in Zimbabwe to stimulate economic growth
and has been playing a pivotal role in this regard. To date, Tianze is believed
that has invested over US$100m to stabilize the agricultural sector in
Zimbabwe.[49] Anhui Agricultural Reclamation Company has been another
player involved in agricultural projects in Zimbabwe particularly wheat
production.[50] The company has so far had a notable positive impact as it has
succeeded in increasing the country's wheat production per hectare as noted
by the fact that in 2017, the company increased the production of wheat to 5
tons per hectare compared to 2 tons per hectare in the previous year, 2016.[51]

Since tobacco is one of the main agricultural products that bring in large
sums of foreign currency to the country, China has been actively involved in

the country's tobacco sector through the China Tobacco Import and Export Corporation. This company has also allowed for the importation of machinery and loans to the small-to-medium scale tobacco farmers in Zimbabwe. Through this company, China has become the largest importer of Zimbabwe's tobacco. To support Zimbabwe's tobacco production, in 2007, China promised a loan of US$58m to the Zimbabwean government intended to purchase farming inputs and tools on condition that Zimbabwe will deliver 110,000 tons of tobacco to China in two years.[52] Hubei Agricultural Reclamation Company in correlation with the Shondong Jinfang Cotton Industry Company have also initiated projects in the cotton production sector through the provision of loans and fertilizers toward Zimbabwe's cotton industry. Cotton is considered a very important commodity in the agricultural sector. Despite all the efforts, the agriculture sector is still challenged by corruption and poor weather conditions. There is still overreliance on manual methods of farming in comparison to adopting new methods.

Energy

The energy in Zimbabwe is one sector that has been faced with a lot of challenges ranging from power cuts, underutilization of the available resources to the advantage of the country, and also relying on outdated infrastructure that is failing to contain the ever-growing population. To that end, China has been strongly involved in the development of Zimbabwe's energy sector. Companies such as China's National Aero-Technology Import and Export Corporation (CATIC) and China North Industry Cooperation (NORINCO) have signed and expressed their willingness to finance a multibillion dollar expansion project by the Zimbabwe Electricity Supply Authority (ZESA) and Hwange Colliery Company.[53] Zhang notes that between 2000 and 2004, ZESA signed a deal with Chinese energy companies which provided them with affordable solar energy equipment.[54] This signaled a new beginning of the two countries' partnership in energy development. Under that same deal, contracts were concluded between Zimbabwe and China for the construction and development of power plants and the installation of generators worth US$368m.[55] The same agreement further provided for the expansion of the Hwange Power plant with two new production units of 300 MW each.[56] In June 2006, Zimbabwe entered into an agreement estimated at US$1.3bn with China Machine Building International Corporation to mine coal and build two new thermal power units at the Hwange thermal plant.[57] This was seen as a solution to cut the dependence on electricity from neighboring Mozambique and South Africa. The Kariba South Hydro-Power Station Extension is also one of the major energy projects that are being undertaken with the assistance of China to enable Zimbabwe to increase its electricity output and be self-sufficient in terms of energy. China has shown a lot of interest in assisting in the energy sector.

Tourism and Transport

Zimbabwe's tourism sector plays a somewhat significant role in bringing in foreign currency into the country. To facilitate the country's tourism sector, China has been assisting Zimbabwe to revamp its transport sector especially its international airports to enable the smooth flow of tourists coming in and out of the country. The Chinese initiated the modernization of the Victoria Falls Airport. This was done with funding from China's Export and Import Bank (EXIM) which in April 2013 provided a US \$150m loan to construct the airport's new runway, taxiway, and a terminal to advance the airport's internal capacity from 500,000 passengers to 1.7 million annually.[58] The airport has an operating system of twelve hours per day, with immigration and customs services being made available within operating hours. It has to offer airport services, such as aircraft parking, cargo, and passenger handling, refueling, weather information, restaurants, and duty-free shops and banking facilities. China further facilitated the creation of flights between Harare and Beijing and also Harare and Guangzhou to create a direct link between the two nations and allow the Chinese to travel easily from China to Zimbabwe and also allow tourism to lower the costs of bringing Chinese tourists into the country. Chigora and Chisi note that as a result, "the tourism sector has seen a huge influx of visitors from China into Zimbabwe and the number of Zimbabwean visitors to China has also increased."[59]

COMPREHENSIVE STRATEGIC PARTNERSHIP OF COOPERATION (CSPC) UNDER THE NEW DISPENSATION

This is a well-esteemed paradigm shift that was established under the New Dispensation. Zimbabwe's foreign policy under President Emmerson Mnangagwa has shifted from focusing on the political toward the economic. Ndimande and Moyo note that "the country's foreign policy has been designed in such a manner which promotes Zimbabwe's economic recovery, facilitates economic growth, creates employment, and encourages a climate conducive to attracting FDI into the country."[60] The CSPC was an agreement made between China and Zimbabwe in Beijing at the Great Hall of People in China, where, President Mnangagwa visited China in person to initiate a fresher and stronger relationship between the two countries. Under the CSPC agreement, the two countries pledged to strengthen bilateral ties in terms of top-level planning and cooperation, development strategies, people to people, and cultural exchange. Among the cooperation was an exchange of views on state governance, expansion of cooperation, trade, technology, telecommunication, infrastructure, and people-to-people exchanges. The friendship of Zimbabwe and China has stood the test of time, and because of the new dispensation, the initiation of the CSPC was to strengthen this bond with Zimbabwe moving forward as the second Republic. This, therefore, further strengthens the future relationship between Zimbabwe and China.

CHINESE ENGAGEMENT WITH ZIMBABWE: ANALYSIS

Positive Impact of Chinese Economic Development Projects to Zimbabwe

The Chinese Economic Developmental projects in Zimbabwe have brought in many positive aspects. Projects initiated by Chinese firms such as the Anhui Agricultural Reclamation Company, Sinotex, Anjin Diamond Mine Company, and China Railway International have resulted in significant employment opportunities for the locals with over 20,000 Zimbabweans having gained employment from these firms. Infrastructural Development lies at the center of economic development and the Chinese have managed to make a notable contribution to this sector in Zimbabwe with projects such as Long Cheng Plaza, Zimbabwe Defence College, Zimbabwe-China Hatcliffe School, and the National Sports Stadium among others. The assistance China has rendered to Zimbabwe's Agricultural sector has had a massive impact on the country attaining food security. Production of goods and services is also on the rise due to the Chinese economic development projects in Zimbabwe.

Demerits of Chinese Economic Development Projects in Zimbabwe

In as much as the Chinese economic projects in Zimbabwe have brought much positivity to the country, they have not been without their share of negative implications. Looking into the projects being done by China in Zimbabwe, there is often a misconception between agreements and actual commitment. African governments are coming from a background where they have low bargaining power because of the lagging economic development. Zimbabwe is not spared on this. It is worth noting that Chinese companies usually import their expertise from China and shun local expertise. Environmental degradation has raised a lot of concern especially from the local communities in which Chinese mining and construction firms especially are engaged in. Concerns have been raised particularly in the activities of mining firms in Marange and on the construction of the Long Chen plaza on top of a wetland. Dependency syndrome comes about as a result of interdependency. Over interdependency often results in dependency. More so, some of the economic development projects lead toward substandard goods flooding the Zimbabwean economy. This being asserted, Zimbabwe then becomes a dumping ground for cheap goods, these cheap goods are like a wolf in sheep's clothing. There is a further risk of looting and plundering of the nation's natural resources by some of these large Chinese mining firms.

The alleged looting of minerals by the Chinese is a clear sign that when the negotiations were done there was no proper monitoring and evaluation of minerals beneficiation and calculating the value of the minerals before signing the deal. There have also been concerns raised over the welfare of employees in the employment of some of these Chinese firms. There have been allegations that the Chinese employers constantly mistreat their local employees and disregard fair labor practices completely with long working hours, dangerous working conditions, arbitrary dismissals, and very little compensation. However, it is worth noting that, not all Chinese companies have been deemed to be treating their employees in this manner. More so, the business culture of the Chinese has been called into question. The Chinese have been criticized for failing to comply with some of the country's laws. They have been accused of avoiding taxes and externalizing money among a host of other allegations

CONCLUSIONS AND RECOMMENDATIONS

Zimbabwe is one of the recipients of Chinese aid but not the biggest, however. There has been a lot of agreements signed between China and Zimbabwe, some of which have brought about some benefits to the Zimbabwean population. Much talk has been on whether the relationship is bringing about mutual benefits or is one in which one is benefiting more than the other. In this case, scholars have argued that China, since is getting raw natural resources, is getting more out of the relationship. The resources are then processed and sold back to Zimbabwe as finished products at very high prices. The question that a lot raise is, is the relationship worth pursuing considering that there have been so many allegations surrounding the diamond deals in the Marange area. It is of interest that a lot of people have questioned how the investments from China sometimes have faced criticisms especially on workmanship and durability of the infrastructure. In light of that, some scholars have argued that when Zimbabwe negotiates with China they do so with a "begging bowl," forgetting that they are not the only ones that stand to benefit from the relations but also the fact that China is also looking for mineral resources as well as a market for their finished products.

The first major step perhaps in trying to improve the relations and perceptions is to work around the policies, and how negotiations are done. It is important to also realize that when those huge deals are made engagement should be done by the Zimbabwean government with the private sector to carry out independent monitoring and evaluation of the resources. Constant audits need to be done to ensure that what was agreed to initially is religiously adhered to by both parties. Corruption is one of the major challenges that Zimbabwe faces, and if it is not dealt with properly, then some of the deals that are signed will not properly reap the intended fruits. The mega-deals that are being signed are not necessarily going to deliver Zimbabwe from the economic challenges, but the way Zimbabwe deals with corruption will change a lot. The corrupt tendencies had become systematic to a level that it was regarded as normal. The government should also realize that the Chinese alone cannot foster economic development in the country and the government should thus engage other nations as well to partner with. The government of Zimbabwe must come up with strategies that allow for the sustainable economic development of the country to occur over a long period.

NOTES

1. Jeremy Youde, "Why Look East? Zimbabwean Foreign Policy and China." *Africa Today* 53, No. 53 (2007): 4.

2. Cape, A. *China will Step in Place of the G8. Africa*, 2006.

3. Shinn, David H. *A Long-term Stable China-Africa Relationship All-round Cooperation*, China Ministry of Foreign Affairs, Published: Nov 17 (2000).

4. Schumpter, J.A. *The Theory of Economic Development: An Inquiry into Profits, Capital, Credit, Interest and the Business Cycle*, California: Stanford University Press, 1961.

5. Chingono, H. *Zimbabwe's "Look East Policy."* The China Monitor. The Centre for Chinese Studies 3, No. 57 (2010): 4–8.

6. Manyeruke, C and Mhandara, L. Zimbabwe's Views on Current Transformation of the International System. *Global Review* 1 (2011): 85–91.

7. Chun, Z. "China: Zimbabwe Relations: A model of China-Africa Relations." *South Africa Institute of International Affairs* (2014): 6.

8. Ibid, 7.

9. Chigodora, P. *Zimbabwe's Look East policy in the New Millenium*, 2015 http://www.osrea.net/publictions/newsletter/oct6/article9/2015.

10. Janssa, J. *The forum on China-Africa Coperation (FOCAC)*. Centre for Chinese studies. University of Stellenbosch, 2009.

11. Youde, *Why Look East? Zimbabwean Foreign Policy and China*, 4.

12. Mhandara, L and Chipaike, R. "Chinese Investment in Africa: Opportunities and Challenges for Peace and Security." *Institute of Peace and Security* 1 (2010):211–224.

13. Enuka, C. *The forum on China-Africa Cooperation (FOCAC): A framework for China's re engagement with Africa in the 21st century*. China: Jilin University, 2010, 2.

14. Obert Hodzi A, Leon Hartwell B and Nicola de Jager. "'Unconditional aid': Assessing the impact of China's development assistance to Zimbabwe," *South African Journal of International Affairs*, 19:1 (2012): 79–103.

15. Youde, *Why Look East? Zimbabwean Foreign Policy and China*, 4.

16. Awad, E. *Economic Interdependency, Trade and War: A Theoretical and Empirical Analysis*. Rotterdam: University of Rotterdam, 2013, 10.

17. Ibid.

18. Ndimande, J. and Moyo, K.G. "Zimbabwe is Open for Business': Zimbabwe's Foreign Policy Trajectory under Emmerson Mnangagwa," *Afro Asian Journal of Social Sciences* IX, No II (2018): 1.

19. Timothy, J. Bartrik. *Management Policies in Local Finance*. Washington DC: International City/ County Management Association, 2004.

20. Das, A. Socio-Economic Development in India: A Regional Analysis. *Reserve Bank of India* 28, No. 2 (2009): 313–345.

21. Schumpeter, *The Theory of Economic Development: An Inquiry into Profits, Capital, Credit, Interest and the Business Cycle*.

22. Hodzi, *Unconditional aid: Assessing the impact of China's development assistance to Zimbabwe*, 80.

23. Interview by Research Assistant.

24. Ibid.

25. Ibid.

26. Ibid.

27. Interview by Research Assistant.

28. *Professor Paul Mavima Speech*.

29. Interview by Research Assistant.

30. Mvutungayi, T. *China in Zimbabwe: exploring the political and economic impacts of Chinese engagement in the Zimbabwean crisis*. South Africa: Witwatersrand University, 2010, 26.

31. Ibid.

32. Chun, *China: Zimbabwe Relations: A Model of China-Africa Relation*, 33.

33. Guma, L. Zimbabwe: Anjin Fires 1500 Workers, Tells Them to Re-Apply. *SW Radio Africa*, 6 August, allafrica.com/stories/201208070405.html.

34. Ibid.

35. Mudavanhu, S.B. A "Critical Analysis of Whether Zimbabwe can Achieve Economic Development Through it 'Look East Policy,'" *African Journal of Political Science and International Relations* 8, No. 8 (2014): 280–287.

36. Ndimande and Moyo, *Zimbabwe is Open for Business: Zimbabwe's Foreign Policy Trajectory under Emmerson Mnangagwa*, 14.

37. Interview by Research Assistant.

38. Jerker Hellström. China's emerging role in Africa: A strategic overview. *FOI Studies in African Security* (2009).

39. RNH employee interviewed by Research Assistant.

40. Interview by Research Assistant.

41. Ndimande and Moyo, *Zimbabwe is Open for Business': Zimbabwe's Foreign Policy Trajectory under Emmerson Mnangagwa*, 14.

42. Interview by Research Assistant.

43. Ibid.

44. Mvutungayi, *China in Zimbabwe: exploring the political and economic impacts of Chinese engagement in the Zimbabwean crisis*, 29.

45. Ibid.

46. Ibid.

47. Joshua Eisenman, "Zimbabwe: China's African Ally." *China Brief* 5 (2011): 9–11.

48. Ibid, 2.

49. Interview by Research Assistant.

50. Ibid.

51. Ibid.

52. Mvutungayi, *China in Zimbabwe: exploring the political and economic impacts of Chinese engagement in the Zimbabwean crisis,* 29.

53. Eisenman, *Zimbabwe: China's African Ally,* 3.

54. Zhang Chun, "China-Zimbabwe Relations: A Model of China-Africa Relations?" *Global Powers and Africa Programme, Occasional Paper* 205 (2014): 4.

55. Ibid.

56. Ibid.

57. Ibid.

58. Interview by Research Assistant.

59. Chigora, P.A. and Chisi, T.H. "The eight years of interaction: lessons from Zimbabwe's look east policy and the future of African countries and Asia-Pacific Region." *Dev Affairs* 10, No. 4 (2009): 147–161.

60. Ndimande and Moyo, *Zimbabwe is Open for Business: Zimbabwe's Foreign Policy Trajectory under Emmerson Mnangagwa*, 14.

BIBLIOGRAPHY

Awad, E. *Economic Interdependency, Trade and War: A Theoretical and Empirical Analysis*. Rotterdam: University of Rotterdam, 2013, 10.

Cape, A. *China will Step in Place of the G8*. Africa, 2006.

Chigodora, P. "*Zimbabwe's Look East policy in the New Millennium*," 2015 http://www.osrea.net/publictions/newsletter/oct6/article9/2015.

Chigora, P.A. and Chisi, T.H. "The eight years of interaction: lessons from Zimbabwe's look east policy and the future of African countries and Asia-Pacific Region." *Dev Affairs*, 10 (4), (2009): 147–161.

Chingono, H. *"Zimbabwe's 'Look East Policy.'"* The China Monitor. The Centre for Chinese Studies 3, No. 57 (2010): 4–8.

Chun, Z. "China: Zimbabwe Relations: A model of China-Africa Relations." *South Africa Institute of International Affairs* (2014): 6.

Chun, *China: Zimbabwe Relations: A model of China- Africa Relation*, 33.

Das, A. Socio-Economic Development in India: A Regional Analysis. *Reserve Bank of India*. 28, No. 2 (2009): 313–345.

Eisenman, J. *Zimbabwe: China's African ally. Jamestown Foundation: China Brief*,5 (15), (2005).

Enuka, C. 2010. *The forum on China-Africa Cooperation (FOCAC): A framework for China's reengagement with Africa in the 21st century.* China: Jilin University, 2010, 2.

Guma, L. Zimbabwe: Anjin Fires 1500 Workers, Tells Them to Re-Apply. *SW Radio Africa*, 6 August, allafrica.com/stories/201208070405.html.

Hodzi, O., Hartwell, L., and de Jager, N. 'Unconditional aid': Assessing the impact of China's development assistance to Zimbabwe, *South African Journal of International Affairs*, 19 (1), (2012): 79–103.

Janssa, J. *The forum on China-Africa Cooperation (FOCAC).* Centre for Chinese studies. University of Stellenbosch, 2009.

Jeremy Youde, "Why Look East? Zimbabwean Foreign Policy and China." *Africa Today*, 53, No. 53 (2007): 4.

Jerker Hellström. China's emerging role in Africa: A strategic overview. *FOI Studies in African Security* (2009).

Joshua Eisenman, "Zimbabwe: China's African Ally." *China Brief*, 5, (2011): 9–11.

Manyeruke, C and Mhandara, L. Zimbabwe's Views on Current Transformation of the International System. *Global Review*1 (2011): 85–91.

Mhandara, L and Chipaike, R. "Chinese Investment in Africa: Opportunities and Challenges for Peace and Security." *Institute of Peace and Security* 1 (2010): 211–224.

Mudavanhu, S.B. A "Critical Analysis of Whether Zimbabwe can Achieve Economic Development Through it 'Look East Policy,'" *African Journal of Political Science and International Relations*, 8 (8), (2014): 280–287.

Mvutungayi, T. *China in Zimbabwe: exploring the political and economic impacts of Chinese engagement in the Zimbabwean crisis.* South Africa: Witwatersrand University, 2010, 26.

Mvutungayi, *China in Zimbabwe: exploring the political and economic impacts of Chinese engagement in the Zimbabwean crisis*, 29.

Ndimande, J. and Moyo, K.G. "Zimbabwe is Open for Business': Zimbabwe's Foreign Policy Trajectory under Emmerson Mnangagwa," *Afro Asian Journal of Social Sciences* IX, No. II (2018): 1.

Ndimande and Moyo, *Zimbabwe Is Open for Business: Zimbabwe's Foreign Policy Trajectory under Emmerson Mnangagwa*, 14.

Obert Hodzi A, Leon Hartwell B and Nicola de Jager. "'Unconditional aid': Assessing the impact of China's development assistance to Zimbabwe," *South African Journal of International Affairs* 19, No. 1 (2012): 79–103.

Schumpter, J.A. *The Theory of Economic Development: An Inquiry into Profits, Capital, Credit, Interest and the Business Cycle.* California: Stanford University Press, 1961.

Shinn, David H. A *Long-term Stable China-Africa Relationship All-round Cooperation,* China Ministry of Foreign Affairs, Published: Nov 17 (2000).

Timothy, J. Bartrik. *Management Policies in Local Finance.* Washington DC: International City/County Management Association, 2004.

Youde, J. Why Look East? Zimbabwean foreign policy and China. *Africa Today,* 53 (3), Spring 2007): 3–19.

Zhang Chun, "China-Zimbabwe Relations: A Model of China-Africa Relations?" *Global Powers and Africa Programme, Occasional Paper* 205 (2014): 4

Chapter 13

The March of the Red Dragon

The Geographic Footprints of Chinese Presence in Africa

Elisha J. Dung and Augustine Avwunudiogba

INTRODUCTION

The world has witnessed tremendous economic output and development since the beginning of the industrial revolution. This has led to general growth in productivity, income, and quality of life. Most of the gains of the economic miracles of the past century have been largely manifested in advanced countries of Western Europe, North America, and a few Asian countries including Japan, South Korea, Singapore, and Indonesia. While this has enabled these countries and some Latin American countries to move into the high- and middle-income status by World Bank classification, African countries, to a large extent, have remained rooted at the low-income level. Recently, a few low-income countries, including China, India, Brazil, and Malaysia, have benefited from the recent economic liberalization and globalization movements because of the integration of their economies to the global economy. As a result, they have enjoyed beneficial investment and favorable trade agreements from industrialized countries of Western Europe and North America. In contrast, African economies are weakly integrated into the global economic system.

Consequently, African countries have not benefited from these global trends. On the contrary, except for a few countries such as Nigeria, South Africa, Egypt, Algeria, Morocco, Angola, Kenya, Ethiopia, Tanzania, and Ghana, most African countries have witnessed minimal improvement in gross domestic product (GDP) even in the face of the widely acclaimed impact of trade liberalization and globalization.[1] Nevertheless, African countries continue to witness an upswing in population growth. Indeed, most of the increase in the world population in the coming decades is expected to come from the African continent. The rapid population growth of Africa in the face of dwindling or stagnant economic fortunes means that African countries require foreign investments. In its quest to bolster economic development and create jobs for an increasingly jobless and restless youth population, most African countries are opening their economies to the outside world. In the last few decades, Chinese presence in Africa has grown exponentially. This is evident in the fact that state-owned and private Chinese companies have become major investors in all the regions of the continent.

There are about 3,171 Chinese companies in Africa with a direct investment of about $66.4 billion (bn) for 705 projects in 2015 alone.[2] There are more than 10,000 Chinese firms in Africa, about 90 percent of which are privately owned. This is about nine times more than is reported by the Chinese Ministry of Commerce.[3] Chinese footprints can be observed from the southern region of the continent to the Horn of Africa and the West African subregion. This forward and persistent match of China over the continent has raised concerns among academics, policy, and decision-makers in Africa in particular, as well as countries in Europe and North America.

Why is China interested in Africa? What are the implications of Chinese incursions and expansion in Africa for the continent and its people? The answer to these fundamental questions has become imperative and urgent, given the recent colonial history of Africa. This chapter examines the spatial pattern and trends of Chinese presence in Africa from a variety of perspectives, including economic, demographic, social, cultural, political, military, trade, telecommunication, and diplomatic ramifications. The chapter focuses on the lingering issues of what this means to the continent. Is this a new scramble for the resources and strategic importance of Africa or is it a new dawn of mutually beneficial relationship between Africa and China? Furthermore, will Africa become a new battleground for the fight between China and the West in their quest for world economic and political dominance? Drawing theoretical inspiration from colonial/neocolonial theory and the core-periphery model, this chapter attempts to address these questions with special emphasis on the implications for the economic development of African countries.

THEORETICAL FRAMEWORK

Different theories and models have been put forward by economists, political economists, developmental theorists, and economic geographers to explain the disparity in the global and regional patterns of world economic development. These theories or models include the colonial dependency/ neocolonial dependency, and the core-periphery models.

Scholars of South-South development have put forth different theories to explain the spatial disparity between the level of development of countries in the global North or Western Europe and North America and the developing countries of Africa, Latin America, and Asia. One of the explanations from the delay in the economic, technological, political, and social development of these countries has been attributed to the long period of colonial rule.[4] It is argued that this colonial dependency created an economic, political, technological, and social structure that was designed to serve the interest of the respective colonial powers to the detriment of the development of the colonized countries.[5] Thus, for several centuries, the natural and human resources of these countries were exploited and appropriated for the development of the Western colonial capital and economy. Colonial policies discouraged the emergence of indigenous technological know-how and home-grown political institutions that would have catalyzed the process of social and political development in the developing world. Similarly, punitive economic policies were put in place to prevent or slow down the industrial transformation of the economies of these countries. As a result, countries of the Global South largely became exporters/providers of natural industrial raw materials at a very low economic cost to their respective colonial masters.

The meager investments of colonial powers on infrastructures such as railways, seaports, airports, and roads were designed to swiftly transport raw material from the hinterland to the coast for an onward journey to Europe. Consequently, the economies of these countries during the colonial period were nothing more than mere appendages to those of their colonial masters. Whereas there was a massive flow of raw materials to European colonial powers, in return, the colonies became markets for the sale of manufactured goods produced overseas. Thus, the colonial powers set both the price of the raw natural resources as well as the finished products. One of the major ramifications of this prolonged economic and social arrangement was the creation of long-lasting structures and institutions that continued to promote European economic and political interests.

Thus, even after political independence, countries of the Global South still largely depend on their former colonial powers in what has been actively described in the developmental literature as a neocolonial dependency syndrome.[6] According to this viewpoint, politically dependent countries of the Global South except for a few, are yet to cut the "umbilical cord" that tie them to their former colonial masters. Postcolonial economic policies of the ruling elites in these countries have been designed to perpetuate the interest of their former colonial masters. This, coupled with internal mismanagement, has meant that many countries continue to depend on their former colonial masters for economic survival. Some of the ramifications of these include the dependence on their former colonial power for foreign direct capital investment, technological know-how and political patronage to provide basic infrastructural facilities such as road networks, hospitals, electricity, water supply, and waste management for their people.

The former colonial powers continue to use this unequal relationship as leverage through the organs of the international financial, monetary systems such as the World Bank, International Monetary Fund (IMF), and World Trade Organization (WTO) to extract favorable political and economic policies that continue to serve their interest. It has been argued, therefore, that developing countries of Africa, Latin America, and Asia will continue as a matter of practicality to depend on the rich countries of the Global North.[7] It is within this context that the emergence of China as an alternative source of developmental aid to African countries is being viewed largely negatively in Western and North American capitals. Critics of China's involvement in Africa see this as nothing more than another episode of colonial and neocolonial programatization of African countries in the twenty-first century.

Closely related to the colonial and neocolonial theories is the core-periphery model for the explanation of the spatial disparity between Western Europe and developing countries of Africa, Latin America, and Asia.[8] Proponents of the core-periphery model of development argue that Western European powers and North American countries have amassed significant advantage from the prolonged period of the industrial revolution which took early hold in Europe and enabled them to develop economically and obtain superior technological know-how. This development coupled with the gains of European colonization of many regions of Africa and Latin America have subsequently created a global spatial system in which European and North American countries became the "Core" while developing countries became the "Periphery." Like the relationship between the large metropolis and their hinterland where the flow of agricultural resources and human capital moves from the hinterland to the metropolis, African countries serve as the hinterland of the core European and North American countries. This spatial arrangement, it is argued, ensures that the periphery countries will always exist to serve the economic interest of the core countries. In other words, the current arrangement will always constraint their development, and hence, they must as a matter of necessity continue to look up to the core countries. Critics argue that the core countries will never relinquish this economic advantage; rather, they will continue to perpetuate it through series of international policies that ensure that the periphery countries remain at the periphery and therefore maintain the constant outflow of human and natural capital from these countries to service the core countries.[9]

One of the recent economic policies that emanated largely from the Core countries of Western Europe and North America is that of trade liberalization and globalization. In a nutshell, it was argued that economic liberalization and the integration of South-South countries into the global economic system will usher in shared economic development and progress to the economies of the world, including those of the developed countries.[10] One of the pillars of this model is 'open markets' in which barriers to trade such as tariffs, was largely reduced or eliminated to ensure the unimpeded movement of goods and services throughout the global economy. While European and North American countries have benefited from this policy to a large extent, its positive impact on the economies of some developing countries has not been realized.

Consequently, scholars of international economic development have argued that trade liberalization and globalization have produced winners and losers, with developed countries as the winners and developing countries as the losers.[11] Part of the reason for this outcome has been blamed on the unequal economic exchange, the result of trade agreements that were designed within the context of the WTO to be favorable to these countries to the detriment of the developing world, including African countries. In the section that follows, we examine the pattern of Chinese investment in Africa bearing in mind its ramifications for the economic development of the continent.

THE STATE AND PATTERN OF CHINESE INVESTMENT IN AFRICA

Although available data on Chinese investment in Africa is comparatively recent, our analysis of available data reveals some interesting results. The trend in the pattern of Chinese foreign direct investment (FDI) to Africa between 2003 and 2017 shows consistent upward growth. Between 2003 and 2010, growth in FDI was relatively modest, ranging from US$0.5bn to an impressive US$13bn. Starting from 2011, the FDI shows a dramatic increase of US$16.2bn peaking at US$43.3bn in 2017 (see figure 13.1).

The last decade, therefore, has witnessed an increase in the intensity of Chinese involvement in the countries of the African economy when FDI is used as the metric. Given the current commentary by political economists in Western Europe and North America about the growing influence of China in the economic affairs of the African economy, it will be interesting to compare the FDI of China and that of Western Europe/ North America in Africa. For instance, in 2015, China's FDI to Africa was US$32bn, and that of the United States was US$79bn, while that of Europe was US$141bn. Between 2010 and 2014, though, China's FDI to Africa experienced a 25 percent growth compared to 10 percent and 17 percent for the United States and

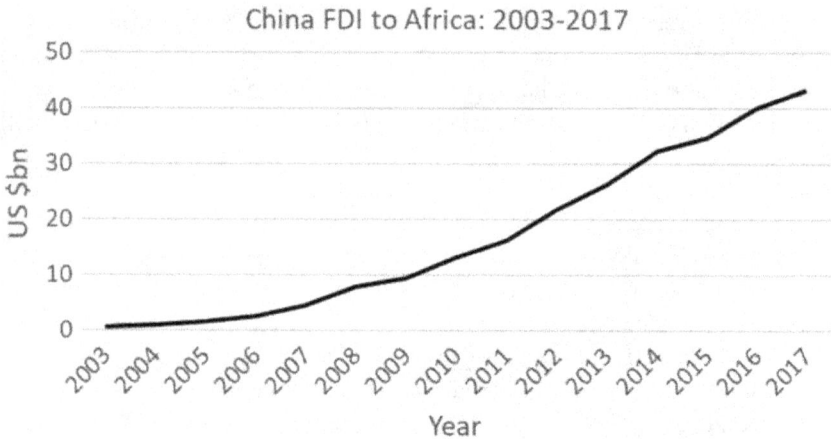

Figure 13.1 China Foreign Direct Investment (FDI) To Africa: 2003-2017.

Europe respectively.[12] Furthermore, the relative importance of China and the traditional Western democratic countries in the recent economy of African countries can be gleaned from comparing US Import/Export to and from Africa relative to that of China.

Figure 13.2 shows the trend in the US and China imports from Africa between 2013 and 2017. The data suggests a slightly higher import by China compared to the United States for all the years under consideration. In 2013, for example, US imports from Africa were approximately US$90bn compared to about US$110bn of Chinese imports from Africa. The figures for

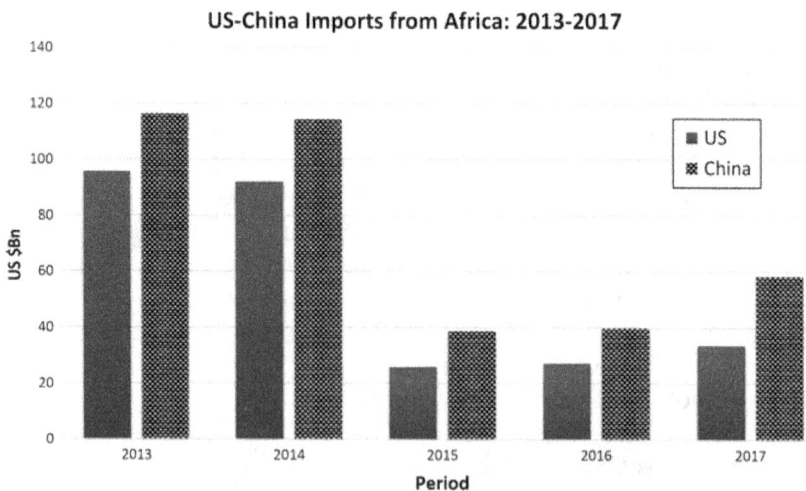

Figure 13.2   US-China Imports from Africa: 2013-2017.

US-China Exports to Africa: 2013-2017

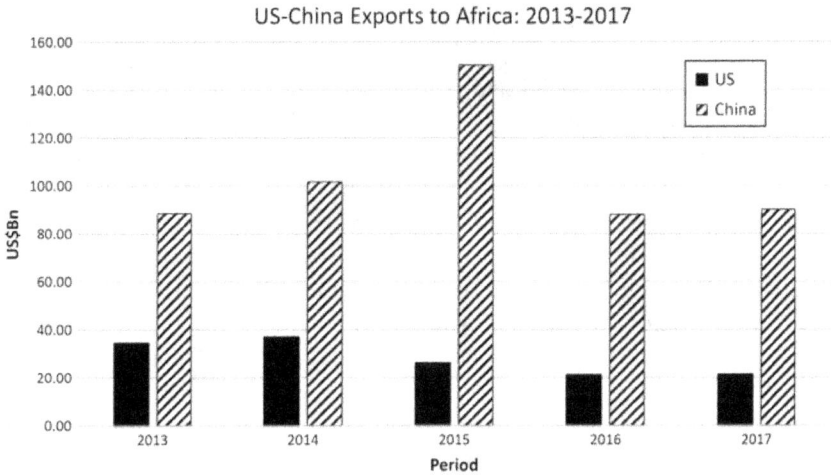

Figure 13.3   US-China Exports to Africa: 2013-2017.

2014 are comparable. Nevertheless, a worrying trend in the data is the fact that a dramatic drop in the value of imports from Africa by both China and the United States can be observed in 2015, 2016, and 2017. In 2017, for instance, US imports from Africa were a meager US$30bn, while that of China was about US$58bn. This represents a 52 percent and 33 percent drop in imports from Africa for the United States and China respectively using 2013 as a base year. This declining trend translates to a decrease in the incoming foreign exchange flow to Africa's economies. This problem may be further exacerbated by the fact that the corresponding US and China exports to Africa have shown an upward increasing trend (see figure 13.3).

Figure 13.3 shows the US and China exports to Africa between 2013 and 2017. In contrast to the import data, the US and China exports have been steady over the period under consideration. However, a detailed analysis indicates that China has a clear dominance over the United States in terms of exports to Africa throughout the years under review. For example, in 2013, US exports to Africa were about US$35bn in contrast to about US$85bn from China. In 2015, US exports of about US$23bn were completely dwarfed by that of China which stood at about US$145bn. Furthermore, the Chinese exports to Africa show an overall upward trend compared to that of the United States which shows a steady declining trend. Although the period under review is relatively short, the tentative conclusion from the pattern revealed from the data suggests that China is playing a more significant role in the economy of African countries when export data is used as a metric. Due to the unavailability of import/Export data of Western European countries to Africa at the time of this analysis, the conclusion here should be regarded as preliminary. This is because, historically, African countries have a long history of economic trade between Europe compared to the United States because of previous colonial and present neocolonial ties. Therefore, a permanent conclusion about the dominance of China in the African economy can only be made with a full complement of data from the European economic bloc.

Nevertheless, there is no doubt of the increasingly influential role of China when it comes to foreign exports to African countries.[13] From a global perspective, if the current surplus of trade between the United States and China, and Western Europe and China, which is largely in favor of China, is taken into consideration, it might be plausible to suggest that China will continue to play a dominating role in terms of exports to African countries for the foreseeable future. The implication of this trend is that of increasing foreign exchange outflow from African countries to China. This is particularly troubling given the fact that the value of Chinese imports from Africa is comparatively lower than the value of Chinese exports (see figures 13.2 and 13.3). This suggests that most African countries will experience a trade deficit to China, a condition that may create foreign exchange flight. If this is the case, the overall economic benefit of China/African relations may not be perfectly mutual. Put simply, it might be argued within the scope of the limited data, that China stands to gain more from the current fledging economic bromance. This situation is not so much dissimilar from the current economic relationships between Africa and the European and North American trading blocs. Therefore, it can be argued that Africa is seen as an economic opportunity to be exploited by both the West and China. This state of affair is at least, economically disadvantageous and at worst, has serious political implications for African countries. Will this lead to a second scramble for Africa? This question is outside the scope of this chapter, but nevertheless pertinent for exploration by scholars interested in African affairs.

The potential impact of Chinese presence in Africa can be further appreciated by examining the sectoral allocation of their FDI investment efforts in the economy of African countries. This consideration is important from a strategic point of view. A detailed analysis unravels the impact and focus of Chinese FDI to Africa between 2003 and 2017. As shown in figure 13.4, the overall Chinese FDI to selected major sectors of the African economy shows an increasing trend.

Construction and mining received the greatest share of Chinese FDI, followed by manufacturing, financial investments, and information technology. The greater share of the FDI in the construction sector shows that African countries are still grappling with the issue of providing fundamental infrastructure such as transportation, communication, and water supply, which requires massive capital outlay given the underdeveloped state of African

CHINESE FDI TO AFRICA BY SECTOR: 2013-2017

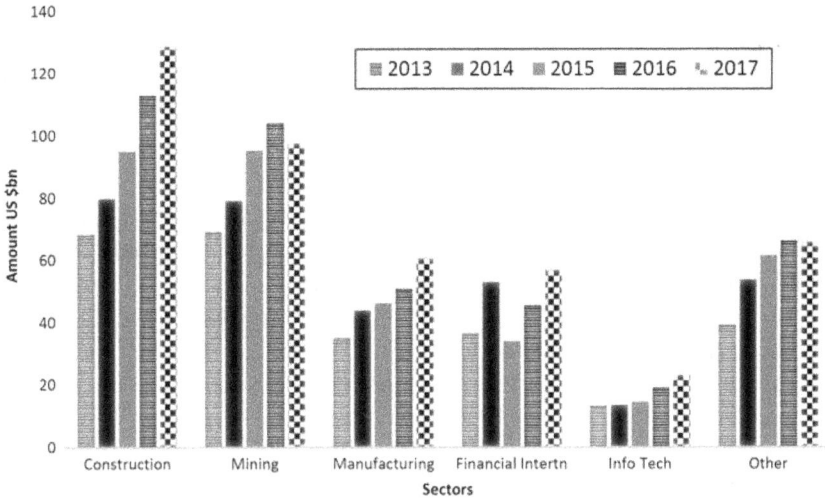

Figure 13.4   Chinese FDI to Africa by Sector: 2013-2017.

infrastructural facilities. The position of mining in terms of Chinese FDI is not surprising given the recent appetite of China for natural resources such as Iron Ore, petroleum and other raw material that is required to fuel the growing Chinese industry and economy.[14] An additional analysis of the sectoral pattern of Chinese loans to Africa suggests that China seem to adopt a strategic choice in their investment pattern. Figure 13.5 shows Chinese loans to

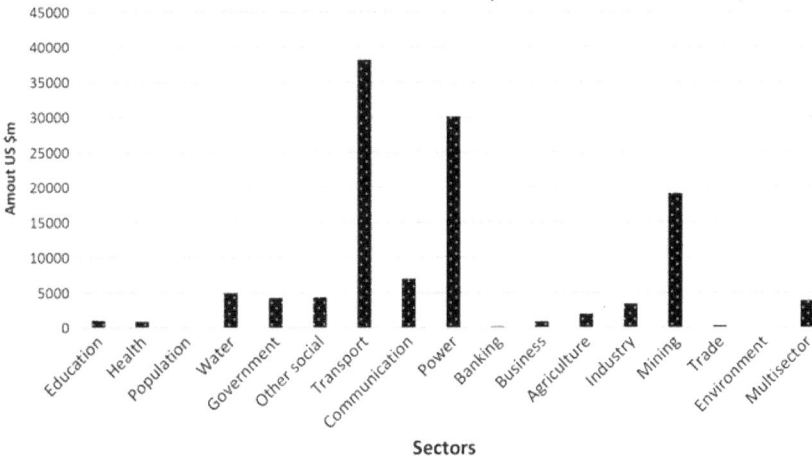

Figure 13.5   Chinese Loans to Africa by Sector: 2000-2016.

Africa by sector. Three prominent sectors rank highest, including transport, power, and mining. Other notable sectors with modest loans include water, government, communication, industry, and agriculture.

The preeminence of transportation and power is not surprising since most African countries are still in the process of developing basic transportation and power infrastructure. It is expected, therefore, that they seek more loans in this regard to enable them to provide these services to their people. This might have implications on the ability of these countries to repay the loans as these sectors are not necessarily profit-oriented. This is because they are social services provided by the government. The trend in loans to agriculture and mining suggests Chinese interest in the natural resource base of African countries. A detailed analysis of the structure of the loans in terms of the lending agencies to these sectors is imperative to understand the extent to which the benefits are accruable to African countries or otherwise.

Figure 13.6 shows an increasing trend in Chinese loans to Africa through different avenues; and these include the China Export-Import Bank (EXIMBANK) and the China Development Bank (CDB). Others are direct Chinese government investments, Chinese commercial banks, and Chinese contractors. Between 2000 and 2006, Chinese loans to Africa were relatively modest. Starting from 2007 significant increase, especially from EXIMBANK is apparent. EXIMBANK emerges as the largest lender followed by the CDB and other Chinese lenders. This trend probably reflects Chinese emphasis on the export of finished products from China and the import of raw material from

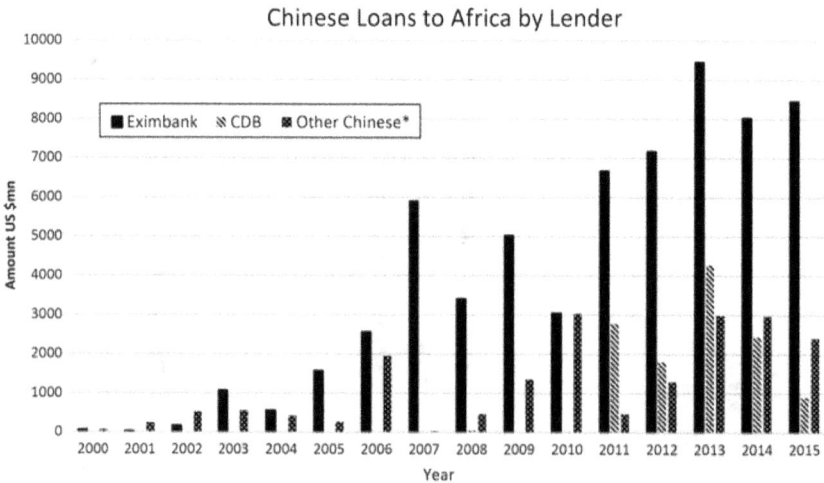

Figure 13.6   Chinese Loans to Africa by Lender.

Africa. Nevertheless, significant increases in loans from the CDB, starting from 2011 (figure 13.6) suggests an increased focus on the financing of long-term development projects such as roads, transportation infrastructure, utilities, and bridges. Although lending from other Chinese sources is relatively modest, the increasing trend suggests an increasing interest and participation from the Chinese private sector in the economy of Africa. This is a significant development because until recently, private investments in Africa have largely come from multinational/transnational corporations in Europe and North America.

THE SPATIAL PATTERN OF CHINESE INVESTMENT IN AFRICA

To further appreciate the extent of Chinese foothold on the African continent, an analysis of the spatial pattern of Chinese investments is imperative. Figure 13.7 shows the Chinese footprints on the African continent. Except for Libya, Somalia, and Western Sahara, China has a presence in the entire continent. The "Red Dragon" is marching across the continent with deliberate and persistent intention.

The greatest impact is in the Southern African region, with an average FDI of US$2-6bn. Part of the countries straddling East and Central Africa to the horn of the African region received an average FDI of up to US$2bn. The swat of countries in West Africa and the Sahelian Zones received an FDI of US$2-5bn (figure 13.7). This observed pattern may be partially explained by the spatial variability of the natural resource endowment of the countries in these regions, level of economic development, level of political acceptance, and domestic reception of Chinese participation in the economy of the country. Nevertheless, the fact that only three countries/territories, lack Chinese presence, confirms the increasing role that China is playing and is likely to play in the foreseeable future in the economies of African countries. This is remarkable because, although, China and African countries have long had close political ties, the intensity in economic ties is a relatively recent phenomenon compared to the long-existing trade relationships with Western Europe and North America. This pattern is not unrelated to the recent emergence of China as a global economic superpower. Given some available projections which suggest that the Chinese economy will exceed the US and European Union economies in terms of GDP by the year 2030,[15] it is reasonable to conclude that we will witness an increase in the intensity of this pattern in decades to come.

This projection is plausible when viewed against the trend of returns on Chinese investments in Africa. Figure 13.8 shows an increasing trend in

China FDI to Africa: 2003-2017

LEGEND

FDI in $bn

Negative Investment

Zero Investment

Up to 2 $bn

2 to 5 $bn

6 + $bn

Figure 13.7   China FDI to Africa: 2003-2017.

Chinese revenue from projects in Africa. Between 1998 and 2006, Chinese revenue was relatively modest with an average of less than US$10bn per annum.

In 2007, revenue exceeded the US$10bn mark for the first time and has continued an upward trajectory. From 2014 to 2017, revenue has exceeded US$50bn. This data clearly shows that Chinese involvement in Africa is not solely based on developmental aid, but also to generate revenue. It should be interesting to see how much of the Chinese revenue impacts the local economy of African countries. If this revenue is repatriated back to China

Chinese Revenues from Projects in Africa

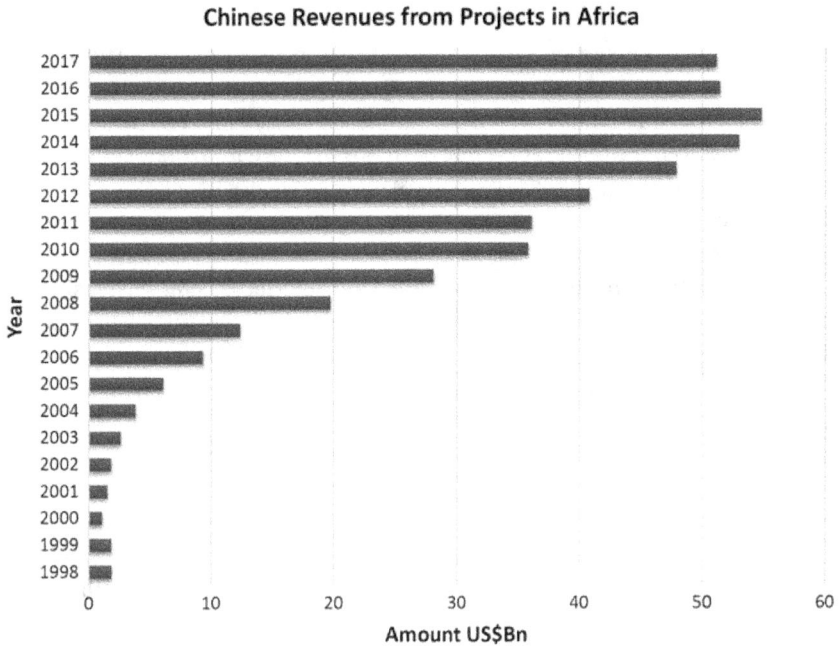

Figure 13.8   Chinese Revenues from Projects in Africa.

as is expected, then the economic multiplier effect will not be realized in the African country's economy. In general, compared to Chinese monetary value investments in Africa, the data presented in figure 13.8 suggests that China gets more returns from the investments.

WHY IS CHINA INTERESTED IN AFRICA?

The data in sections 3 (Chinese investments) and 4 (Chinese revenue) clearly shows that China has an interest in the African continent. China has not attempted to disguise or underplay her interest in Africa. In the past ten years, China has organized and hosted African economic forums in Beijing. This is in addition to the increase in the number of bilateral economic meetings with different African countries.[16] The fundamental question, therefore, is why is China interested in Africa? Is this interest a signpost for a new scramble for the resources of Africa? Or is its new dawn of a mutually beneficial South-South relationship? The answers to these questions require a brief historical exploration of the relationship between Africa, the "Lion" continent, and China, the country of the "Red Dragon." Historically, from a political perspective, China has always maintained a cordial relationship with African countries. The vote and cooperation of African countries were instrumental in China, securing the position of a veto power in the United Nations (UN).

Except for Swaziland, no African country has recognized Taiwan as an independent country, a situation that is in alignment with China's one nation policy concerning the political status of Taiwan. Built from this historical perspective, the African continent can be regarded as a friend of China, but is China a friend of Africa? The critical examination of this relationship has only come to the forefront recently because of the increasing physical presence of the footprints of the 'Dragon' in the African continent. There are two schools of thought that have tried to explain the nature of this relationship. On the one hand, some have argued that China's renewed active interest in Africa, is nothing short of a new colonial trend in which China is seeking the natural resources of the African continent to satisfy its developmental needs especially within the context of its ever-rising middle class.[17] The argument goes that as China has witnessed the tremendous transformation of its standard of living of its people in the past three decades, there has been a corresponding rapid increase in the middle class. This large population of individuals has led to an increase in its consumption pattern, and China is constantly looking toward Africa as a source of cheap natural resources to satisfy the needs of this expanding middle class. In other words, this relationship is merely a form of twenty-first-century colonialism. Interestingly, this is a viewpoint that is widely held by scholars and political commentators in Western European and North American countries,[18] which is an irony.

On the other hand, some argue that the Chinese approach to Africa differs significantly from those of European colonial experience.[19] The argument goes that in the first place, African countries are politically independent and are therefore in a stronger position to negotiate the nature of the relationship between their countries and China. It is significant to note that, unlike postcolonial European and North American developmental efforts in Africa that comes largely with conditionalities that force African countries to adopt certain policies, e.g. multiparty democracies, human rights reforms and other socioeconomic reforms that are beneficial to them; Chinese economic aid and development has come with largely no 'strings attached'. Indeed China, believes that countries should be allowed to develop their political system according to their unique circumstances. Consequently, it appears that China does not discriminate on its investments based on any political ideology and is not interested in meddling in the political affairs of any African country. Thus, Chinese investment in Africa can be seen in countries such as Zimbabwe, which Western countries have traditionally labeled as having very poor human rights records, and democratic governance and institutions. Hence, this relationship is purely an economic one that is mutually beneficial to the continent of Africa and China.

IMPLICATIONS OF CHINESE INVESTMENT IN AFRICA

Giving the narratives, this section examines some of the broad economic, demographic, social, cultural, and political implications of Chinese presence in Africa.

The current Chinese presence in Africa has profound economic consequences. Whether the economic consequences are going to be positive or negative in the long run is yet to be seen. Based on the results of the analysis of the available data in this paper, African countries have received FDI capital investments into the African economy. This has the potential to catalyze economic growth and development if judiciously and strategically spent. The multiplier impact of Chinese FDI will also depend partly on the terms of the loans and financial transactions. Nevertheless, the fact that African countries are receiving the highly needed foreign infusion of capital from China is a positive development. This is significant given the recent decline in the foreign exchange flow into the African economy from its traditional European and North American trading blocs. It might be argued that Chinese FDI to Africa at least, in the meantime, does not come with political conditionalities such as demand for multiparty democracy, political and human rights reforms. This is evident from the spatial pattern of Chinese presence in African countries. If African countries learn from the lessons of the debt crises imposed by their interactions with traditional international monetary institutions of the West (Bretton wood, IMF, World Bank, etc.), they might be able to obtain favorable loan agreements from China. In an era when Western countries and the United States are beginning to look inward, Chinese FDI to Africa should not be dismissed outright as another form of colonialism. This relationship has the potential to transform the African economy.

This relationship may also have some demographic implications. Recently, Chinese citizens have started to settle in most parts of Africa. Although the rate of Chinese immigration to Africa may be considered as negligible in terms of numbers, the phenomenon is nevertheless, remarkable. China compared to other countries is a relatively closed country with a largely homogenous population lacking cultural diversity compared to developed countries such as the United States and Europe. The settlement of Chinese citizens, especially in the rural parts of Africa, may pose challenges at the local community level. Although not widespread, there are reported cases of intermarriages between Chinese nationals and their African counterparts.[20] Whether this is going to be an emerging trend is yet to be seen, but it is certainly incredible.

Whatever the case, this emerging trend may help to strengthen the social and cultural ties between China and Africa. Already, there seems to be an increase in cultural and educational exchange activities between the Chinese Government and African countries.[21] In the last couple of years, the Chinese government has hosted the annual China-Africa forum in Beijing. This is in addition to several bilateral meetings with individual African countries. It is also noteworthy that the number of African residents in China has been on the rise. Although the residential status may not be clearly defined, there is no doubt that a significant number of Africans are participating in the sports (especially professional football) and trading sectors of the Chinese economy. Whether China and Chinese citizens are willing to embrace multiculturalism is a matter of debate.

There is currently a fierce debate over the political consequences of increasing tight relationships between China and Africa. Some argue that this relationship may develop into another form of colonialism in which the African countries are nothing more than a means for China to exert political influence on the global stage.[22] In particular, United States and Western European Countries have become nervous about the growing influence of China in the economic affairs of African countries. Although China has indicated her noninterest in the internal politics and affairs of African countries, there is the suspicion from the West that African countries might be tempted to adopt the Chinese political-economic model as an alternative model for economic development and prosperity. Such reasoning is not farfetched given the rapid economic progress made by China in the recent decade that has enabled her to move many of its citizens into the middle income. There is the danger, therefore, that Africa may become once more the battleground for ideological supremacy in which China and the Western democracies carry out proxy wars to the detriment of the already fragile political stability and security of African countries.

At another level, it has been argued, especially by Western commentators that the lack of discrimination by China in its association with African Governments, may help to suppress progress in democratic and human rights reforms in Africa since Chinese investments and aids do not normally come with conditionalities in contrast to that of the United States and Western Europe that have been used as a leverage to extract certain democratic and political reforms from African countries. Nevertheless, political analysts from the Global South have argued that such conditionalities have only been used as a tool to advance the economic and political interest of the Western countries.[23] Therefore, the Chinese policy of nonpolitical conditionality in their investment and aids to Africa should be welcomed with open arms.

In addition to its economic progress, China is also becoming a military superpower. Given the lukewarm attitude of Western democratic countries when it comes to giving military aids to African countries, especially countries with so-called poor human rights records, African countries may increasingly seek military cooperation with China. Such cooperation may include areas of training, purchase of advanced military weapons, joint military exercises, and military pacts (fashioned along the lines of NATO-like agreements to defend member countries). In the long run, such an agreement may result in the establishment of military bases in Africa by China. Currently, China's only military presence in Africa is a very small military base in Djibouti.

This relationship has the potential to expand trade in a positive way between China and Africa. However, the fact that the major export items of African countries are primary raw material and agricultural products is rather worrisome. Realistically, the maximum economic benefit is greater from the export of processed and manufactured products, whose monetary value increases due to the added value. The process of exporting manufactured products helps to develop the industrial base of a country, provide employment opportunities, and improve the overall quality of life. The data from this chapter suggests that African countries are currently experiencing a trade deficit concerning China. African countries must deemphasize the export of raw material and insist on technological assistance from China to enable them to develop a robust manufacturing base. The time to seek such an arrangement is now when China is still trying to develop a stronghold on Africa. Failure to do this may result in African countries becoming the new periphery of China, an arrangement whereby African countries only exist to service the growing appetite of China for raw economic resources.

The closed ties between Africa and China may help Africa to develop its telecommunications infrastructure. As a relatively developing country, China is uniquely placed to address some of the telecommunication challenges of African countries by providing affordable telecommunication equipment and logistics. For example, Chinese telecommunications companies have established factories in Ethiopia, where they manufacture equipment such as affordable Cell phones.[24] This will help to increase accessibility to communication services, especially in rural Africa. Finally, the current trade relationships between China and African countries may help to solidify and consolidate the already existing strong diplomatic relationships between African countries and China and help China to uphold its status as one of the veto powers in the UN.

SUMMARY AND CONCLUSION

In summary, this current bromance between China and Africa is a complex relationship that requires careful navigation by African countries to ensure a mutually beneficial outcome that will advance African countries' economic, political and sociocultural interests within the global economy. African countries must, of necessity, draw heavily from their recent colonial and neocolonial experience to navigate this emerging relationship with China who is destined to become a superpower. African countries must avoid the mistakes and miscalculations of the developmental policy that is heavily built on the providence of "benevolent" foreign power. In this regard, they must ensure that cooperative agreements are not entered, which will be to the detriment of the economic wellbeing of their people. Economic projects and financial arrangements with unfavorable terms should be avoided at all costs. African countries must resist political interference in their affairs from China. Military cooperation must be skeptically examined for any political ramifications. African countries should develop their political ideology that is uniquely based on their political, historical, and cultural experience. The African continent cannot afford a second incident where the ideological-political turf war is fought. If properly managed, this new relationship could be mutually beneficial to Africa and China.

NOTES

1. International Monetary Fund (IMF) World Economic Outlook. *Challenges to Steady Growth* (New York: IMF, October 2018).
2. Sarah Nassiri, "China's Investments in Africa," *Infomineo.* May 7, 2017. Infomineo is a business research company, focusing on Africa and the Middle East. The company provides its clients, including the majority of the leading global management consulting firms and several Fortune Global 500 companies, with ad hoc data on countries, markets, companies and people gathered through primary and secondary research. Accessed May 3, 2019. https://www.howwemadeitinafrica.com/chinas-investment-africa/.
3. Jayaram Kartik, Omid Kassiri and Irene Yuan Sun, "The Closest Look Yet at Chinese Economic Engagement in Africa," Mckinsey Field Survey of Chinese Firms in 8 African Countries, November 2016–March 2017. Field interviews with more than 1,000 Chinese companies provide new insights into Africa-China business relationships. Accessed May 3, 2019. https://www.mckinsey.com/featured-insights/middle-east-and-africa/the-closest-look-yet-at-chinese-economic-engagement-in-africa.
4. Nicola Phillips, "Power and Inequality in the Global Political Economy," *International Affairs* 93, no. 2, (2017): 429–444.
5. Young Namkoong, "Dependency Theory: Concepts, Classifications, and Criticisms," *International Area Review* 2, no. 1 (1999): 121–150.
6. Andrew Shepherd, Dhana Wadugodapitiya, and Alice Evans, "Social Assistance and the 'Dependency Syndrome,'" *Chronic Poverty Research Centre Policy Brief* No. 22 (2011). Accessed April 23, 2019. http://dx.doi.org/10.2139/ssrn.1765933.
7. Eric Kehinde Ogunleye, "African Trade and Integration: Longer-term Prospects," In *The Future of South-South Economic Relations*, ed. Adil Najam and Rachel Thrasher (New York and London: Zed Books, 2012).
8. Stephen P. Borgatti and Martin G. Everett, "Models of Core/periphery Structures," *Social Networks* 21, no. 4 (2000): 375–395; see also; Derek Gregory,

Ron Johnston, Geraldine Pratt, Michael Watts and Sarah Whatmore, eds. *The Dictionary of Human Geography* (John Wiley & Sons, 2011).

9. Robert Potter, Tony Binns, Jennifer A. Elliott, and David W. Smith, *Geographies of Development: An Introduction to Development Studies* (New York: Routledge, 2017).

10. Ndumbe J. Anyu. and J.P.A. Ifedi, "China's Ventures in Africa: Patterns, Prospects, and Implications for Africa's Development," *Mediterranean Quarterly* 19, no. 4 (2008): 91–110.

11. Bradley Jones, "Support for Free Trade Agreements Rebounds Modestly, But Wide Partisan Differences Remain," *Pew Research Center.* April 25, 2017. Accessed March 4, 2019. http://www.pewresearch.org/fact-tank/2017/04/25/su pport-for-free-trade-agreements-rebounds-modestly-but-wide-partisan-differences-remain/.

12. United Nations, Department of Economic and Social Affairs, Population Division, *World Population Prospects: The 2015 Revision* (New York: United Nations, 2015).

13. Miria Pigato and Julien Gourdon, "The Impact of Rising Chinese Trade and Development Assistance in West Africa," *Africa Trade Practice Working Paper Series*, no. 4 (2014).

14. Deborah Brautigam and Haisen Zhang, "Green Dreams: Myth and Reality in China's Agricultural Investment in Africa," *Third World Quarterly* 34, no. 9 (2013): 1676–1696.

15. Emilio Casetti, "Power Shifts and Economic Development: When Will China Overtake the USA?" *Journal of Peace Research* 40, no. 6 (2003): 661–675; see also; Malcolm Scott, and Cedric Sam, "Here's How Fast China's Economy Is Catching Up to the U.S.," *Bloomberg.* May 21, 2019. Accessed May 26, 2019. https://www.blo omberg.com/graphics/2016-us-vs-china-economy/.

16. Yoon Jung Park, Ben Lampert and Winslow Robertson, "China's Impacts on Africa's Development," *African Review of Economics and Finance* 8, no. 1 (2016): 3–11.

17. Domingos J. Muekalia, "Africa and China's Strategic Partnership," *African Security Studies* 13, no. 1 (2004): 5–11.

18. David N. Abdulai, *Chinese Investment in Africa: How African Countries Can Position Themselves to Benefit from China's Foray into Africa* (London, UK: Routledge, 2016).

19. Peter Kragelund, "Knocking on a Wide-open Door: Chinese Investments in Africa." *Review of African Political Economy* 36, no. 122 (2009): 479–497.

20. Howard W. French, *China's Second Continent: How a Million Migrants Are Building a New Empire in Africa* (New York: Knopf Borzoi Books, 2014).

21. Deborah Brautigam, *The Dragon's Gift: The Real Story of China in Africa* (Oxford University Press, 2009).

22. Barry Sautman and Yan Hairong, "Friends and Interests: China's Distinctive Links with Africa," *African Studies Review* 50, no. 3 (2007): 75–114.

23. Michael Meidan, "China's Africa Policy: Business Now, Politics Later," *Asian Perspective* (2006): 69–93.

24. Yomi Kazeem, "The Biggest Mobile Phone Maker in Africa Is Going Public in China," *Quartz Africa*. March 29, 2019. Accessed on May 28, 2019. https://qz.com/africa/1583473/chinas-transsion-of-african-tecno-phones-to-ipo-in-shanghai/.

REFERENCES

Abdulai, David N. *Chinese Investment in Africa: How African Countries Can Position Themselves to Benefit from China's Foray into Africa*. Routledge. London, UK, 2016.

Anyu, J. Ndumbe. and J.P.A, Ifedi. "China's Ventures in Africa: Patterns, Prospects, and Implications for Africa's Development." *Mediterranean Quarterly* 19, no. 4 (2008): 91–110.

Brautigam, Deborah. *The Dragon's Gift: The Real Story of China in Africa*. Oxford University Press, 2009.

Brautigam, Deborah, and Hansen Zhang. "Green Dreams: Myth and Reality in China's Agricultural Investment in Africa." *Third World Quarterly* 34, no. 9 (2013): 1676–1696.

Borgatti, Stephen P., and Martin G. Everett. "Models of Core/periphery Structures." *Social Networks* 21, no. 4 (2000): 375–395.

Casetti, Emilio. "Power Shifts and Economic Development: When will China Overtake the USA?" *Journal of Peace Research* 40, no. 6 (2003): 661–675.

French, Howard W. *China's Second Continent: How a Million Migrants Are Building a New Empire in Africa*. New York: Knopf Borzoi Books, 2014.

Gregory, Derek, Ron Johnston, Geraldine Pratt, Michael Watts and Sarah Whatmore, eds. *The Dictionary of Human Geography*. John Wiley & Sons, 2011.

International Monetary Fund (IMF) World Economic Outlook. *Challenges to Steady Growth*. New York: IMF, October 2018.

Jones, Bradley. "Support for Free Trade Agreements Rebounds Modestly, But Wide Partisan Differences Remain." *Pew Research Center*. April 25, 2017. Accessed March 4, 2019. http://www.pewresearch.org/fact-tank/2017/04/25/support-for-free-trade-agreements- rebounds-modestly-but-wide-partisan-differences-remain/.

Kartik, Jayaram; Omid Kassiri and Irene Yuan Sun. "The Closest Look Yet at Chinese Economic Engagement in Africa." *Mckinsey Field Survey*. Accessed May 3, 2019. https://www.mckinsey.com/featured-insights/middle-east-and-africa/the-closest-look-yet-at-chinese-economic-engagement-in-africa.

Kazeem, Yomi. 2019. "The Biggest Mobile Phone Maker in Africa Is Going Public in China." *Quartz Africa*. March 29, 2019. Accessed on May 28, 2019. https://qz.com/africa/1583473/chinas-transsion-of-african-tecno-phones-to-ipo-in-shanghai/.

Kragelund, Peter. "Knocking on a Wide-open Door: Chinese Investments in Africa." *Review of African Political Economy* 36, no. 122 (2009): 479–497.

Meidan, Michael. "China's Africa Policy: Business Now, Politics Later." *Asian Perspective* (2006): 69–93.

Muekalia, Domingos J. "Africa and China's Strategic Partnership." *African Security Studies* 13, no. 1 (2004): 5–11.

Namkoong, Young. "Dependency Theory: Concepts, Classifications, and Criticisms." *International Area Review* 2, no. 1 (1999): 121–150.

Nassiri, Sarah. "China's Investments in Africa." *Infomineo*. May 7, 2017. Accessed May 3, 2019. https://www.howwemadeitinafrica.com/chinas-investment-africa/.

Ogunleye, Eric Kehinde. "African Trade and Integration: Longer-term Prospects." In *The Future of South-South Economic Relations*, edited by Adil Najam and Rachel Thrasher. New York and London: Zed Books, 2012.

Park, Yoon Jung, Ben Lampert, and Winslow Robertson. "China's Impacts on Africa's Development." *African Review of Economics and Finance* 8, no. 1 (2016): 3–11.

Phillips, Nicola. "Power and Inequality in the Global Political Economy." *International Affairs* 93, no. 2 (2017): 429–444.

Pigato, Miria, and Julien Gourdon. "The Impact of Rising Chinese Trade and Development Assistance in West Africa." *Africa Trade Practice Working Paper Series*, no. 4 (2014).

Potter, Robert., Tony Binns; Jennifer A. Elliott; and David W. Smith. *Geographies of Development: An Introduction to Development Studies*. New York: Routledge, 2017.

Sautman, Barry. and Yan Hairong. "Friends and Interests: China's Distinctive Links with Africa." *African Studies Review* 50, no. 3 (2007): 75–114.

Scott, Malcolm, and Cedric Sam. "Here's How Fast China's Economy Is Catching Up to the U.S." *Bloomberg*. May 21, 2019. Accessed May 26, 2019. https://www.bloomberg.com/graphics/2016-us-vs-china-economy/.

Shepherd, Andrew, Dhana Wadugodapitiya, and Alice Evans. "Social Assistance and the 'Dependency Syndrome.'" *Chronic Poverty Research Centre Policy Brief* no. 22 (2011). Accessed April 23, 2019. http://dx.doi.org/10.2139/ssrn.1765933.

United Nations, Department of Economic and Social Affairs, Population Division. *World Population Prospects: The 2015 Revision*. New York: United Nations. 2015.

Chapter 14

China: Africa's New Wise Men from The East?

An Analysis of Africa's Non-State and State Actors' Perceptions of China and the Chinese

Emmanuel Matambo

INTRODUCTION

Currently, apart from the customary counter-slandering between the ruling political party and its detractors, the most prominent political subject in Zambia is that country's relationship with China. The ruling Patriotic Front (PF) made headways during its opposition days by accusing the former ruling party—the Movement for Multiparty Democracy (MMD)—of giving China carte blanche in Zambia and yielding the country's sovereignty in the process. Michael Sata, the founder of the PF and Zambia's president from 2011 to 2014, was the most charismatic critic of Zambia-China relations. At the time, the MMD government situated Zambia-China relations in the broader Africa-China scope wherein African countries, left disappointed by Western tutelage, had turned to the East as an alternative.[1]

While contact between Africa and China dates back many centuries, the first formal relations between China and an African country were with Egypt in 1956 following the Bandung Conference of 1955 in Indonesia. The Bandung Conference was held a decade after the end of the Second World War and the beginning of the Cold War when ideological fissures deepened between the capitalist West and the socialist East. The main belligerents were the United States and the Union of Soviet Socialist Republics (USSR). Economically smaller players had negligible political influence and did not feature prominently in this jostling for global dominance. Thus, Bandung "came to represent the mythical moment when the combined dynamism of the newly decolonized, independent states of Asia and Africa monopolized the center stage in international relations."[2] It also testified "to the 'agency' of the newly independent states in shaping the post-war international order."[3] It is noteworthy that in 1955, most of the African countries were under colonial or settler rule.

One of China's main stated interests in Africa was to help the continent to defeat colonial and minority rule. Members of African liberation movements were feted by China from the 1950s onwards.[4] At the time, China was a poor country, having been ravaged by more than two decades of war culminating in the establishment of the People's Republic of China in 1949. That a poor country managed, through propaganda and modest material support, to shore up Africa's anticolonial crusade endeared the country to Africa and cultivated an appealing identity that still lingers. One of the African countries with which China has had a longstanding but controversial and chequered relationship is Zambia. This relationship was instituted in October 1964, less than a week after Northern Rhodesia gained independence from Britain and was christened the Republic of Zambia. The ensuing chapter focuses on the evolution and changing dynamics and contours of Sino-Zambian relations. One of the major changes in Sino-Zambian relations—often overlooked—is the deepening interaction between non-state actors from the two countries.

This chapter bases its arguments and analyses on the premise that the quality of relations among nations is heavily influenced by convergent or divergent ideas, norms, identities, and interests that states ascribe to or are associated with. The chapter seeks to deconstruct the identities that people attribute to China from a Zambian perspective. Furthermore, the study looks at identities that China evokes from Zambian citizens, depending on their socioeconomic and political station. The chapter seeks to ascertain whether or not the Sino-optimism that African governments express percolates to the African citizenry. A similar study was undertaken by Jura et al. in *Events over Endeavours*.[5]

The rhetoric that has become attendant to Africa-China relations at state-to-state interaction presents China as the proverbial wise partner from the East bearing gifts such as infrastructure and foreign direct investment (FDI) that Africa needs. However, Zambia-China relations have been sullied by sundry disputes which have occasionally engendered killings of both Chinese and Zambian nationals. More recently, the word "xenophobia" has been used to describe the sentiment that ordinary Zambians express toward the Chinese.[6] These illustrations demonstrate that, while African governments gush over China's involvement in Africa, this optimism is not invariably shared by Africans who do not interact with China at the state level but rather interact with Chinese nationals who are not state agents and hence come to Africa of their own volition, pursuing individual interests and thus embodying different identities from China's institutional identities.[7]

The chapter is divided into four main parts. The first part is a brief presentation of the methodology used and constructivism —a theoretical approach that underpins the arguments and conclusions drawn in this study. The second section gives a background of Zambia-China relations through successive Zambian governments. The third part looks at the impressions of non-state actors on Zambia-China relations. Throughout the different epochs and dimensions of Zambia-China relations, readers are invited to note the changes and continuities in terms of China's identity in Zambia and the increasing opinion of non-state actors to exert their voice on national affairs. The fourth part demonstrates that this is not the first time when the effect and opinions of non-state actors on Africa-China relations have received attention; in 2014, Howard French did so in *China's Second Continent.*[8] In 2009, Patrick Chabal, in *Africa: The Politics of Smiling and Suffering,*[9] advocated analyzing African politics from the level of non-state actors, preferably ordinary Africans, rather than from the level of the Big Men. The two books influenced the ensuing arguments: one looks at the impact of ordinary Chinese citizens on Africa and the other sponsors a perspective of African politics that is influenced by the daily experiences of Africans, respectively.

METHODOLOGY AND CONSTRUCTIVISM

The chapter used the interpretivist, otherwise known as the constructivist, research paradigm. This paradigm was named thus because it argues that social phenomena are interpreted or constructed through social practice and behavior.[10] Actors, whether as individuals, groups, or nations, are agents of constructing social reality and in doing so are influenced by a confluence of historical, cultural, and sociopolitical circumstances.[11] This is important for the current chapter because one of its essential arguments is that depending on where they stand politically, socially, or economically, Zambians presumably have a variety of concordant and contradictory identities that they attribute to China.

Apart from its obvious appropriateness for studying social phenomena, the interpretivist approach was chosen because the current chapter does not dwell on statistical analysis or positivist inquiries of Zambia-China relations. Thus, the research approach elected for the current chapter was the qualitative approach, and the methods of gathering primary data were interviews. Three focus group discussions were conducted. The size of the sample chosen for the research is by no means representative of entire Zambia. However, typical of qualitative research, the chapter involved "collecting a large amount of data on a rather small, purposive sample."[12] In the fourth part of the chapter, primary data will be tested against secondary literature and the author's interpretation of China's identity in Zambia to answer the question: Is China the proverbial bearer of gifts for an impoverished partner or just another exploiter of a developing country? The theoretical approach used to analyze the different views is constructivism.

Constructivism gained its prominence as an approach for studying international relations after the end of the Cold War. It has several features that set it apart from more entrenched theories of international relations. While conceding the presence of anarchy, political structures, and national interest in relations among nations, constructivism is distinct by its argument of how these features come into being. Classical realism, for example, argues that relations among nations are driven by immanent and unchanging egoism, while neorealism refers to the anarchic nature of the international system as the determinant of politics and conflict among nations. Constructivism underlines the role of social dynamics and norms as influential elements of international relations. In other words, if the world is dominated by self-serving egoists (à la classical realism) or by players who act in response to anarchy (à la neorealism), it is because these actors have created that atmosphere through social practice. Thus, self-serving inclinations and anarchy are not exogenously imposed on nations. Alexander Wendt sums this up aptly when he says, "anarchy is what states make of it."[13]

The chapter used constructivism as a theoretical approach for understanding Zambia-China relations, the shifting identities of China, and the diversity of views from Zambians. This approach will nevertheless eschew one crucial tendency of mainstream theories of international relations, including constructivism: the proclivity to consign analyses of international politics to the perceptions of state actors. The chapter notes the growing opinion of non-state actors on international relations. It cannot be gainsaid that traditional political principals are the ultimate deciders of relations among nations. However, in countries where democracy has been established and reinforced, governments are more likely to hearken to the concerns of electorates.

The disenchantment of Zambians regarding the growing presence and influence of China and its citizens could translate into a change in voting preferences. Disillusionment among non-state actors stems from the fact that their constructions of China's identity are not dependent on the pronouncements of state actors. Non-state actors generally interact with non-state actors from China who exude identities and pursue interests that are not necessarily in tandem with the image and interests that the Chinese government claims to uphold. Thus, the current research retains the prominent role of social interaction and identity creation in international relations as proposed by constructivism. A variation of this chapter is that it considers the impressions of non-state actors and how their constructions of identity and interest could have bearing on international relations.

The quality of relations among nations, according to constructivism, is mostly based on how nations regard each other. States that regard each other as allies are more likely to forge a relationship that enhances mutual growth and development. Zambia-China relations have been shaped by intersecting identities and interests which are mainly constructed by state actors. Identities are often shaped through interaction, though at times they emerge from observed conduct. Interests in relations proceed from identities that countries share. Constructivism thus differs from the rationalist approach which seems to suggest that nations relate according to a portfolio of *a priori* identities and interests. The importance of the current chapter resides in the fact that China has become Zambia's main trade partner. The relationship between the two countries is likely to influence Zambia's political and economic landscape to a greater extent than the other way around.

THE HISTORY OF ZAMBIA-CHINA RELATIONS

The Chinese Communist Party (CCP) seized power in 1949 at the expense of the nationalist government that fled to the island of Taiwan to establish the Republic of China (ROC). The CCP proclaimed mainland China as the People's Republic of China (PRC). The country was conceived under challenging circumstances. Being socialist pitted it against the Western capitalist bloc. Its weak economy at the time forced it to play second fiddle to the Soviet Union in the socialist camp. China's acceptance of a less influential place in the socialist bloc is encapsulated in Mao's admission that the Soviet Union was a teacher of socialism and that the CCP modeled its praxis on the Communist Party of the Soviet Union.[14] The pent-up reservations that China harbored against Soviet socialism only came to the open after the death of Joseph Stalin. Another inauspicious factor prevalent immediately after the institution of the PRC was international recognition. After the formation of the United Nations, China, under the nationalists, became one of the five permanent members of the United Nations Security Council (UNSC).

When the nationalists fled to Taiwan, they retained China's seat at the Security Council. For this reason, one of the PRC's consuming aspirations was to assume the Security Council seat, thereby usurping Taiwan's international recognition.[15] Before 1949, Taiwan was a part of mainland China. It is this that underscores China's insistence that the island remains an inalienable, albeit renegade, part of mainland China. The One-China Policy is one of the sacrosanct conditions for establishing diplomatic relations between any country and the PRC. China has used a multiplicity of overtures to win its diplomatic competition with Taiwan.[16] During the Cold War, a period that largely coexisted with anticolonial agitation, China used its history of being an economically weak and peripheral actor, to support African countries. Africa had the requisite number of countries that could significantly influence decisions at the United Nations. Ergo, courting the continent was a huge political insurance for China, and the best way of securing African support was through anticolonial solidarity. It is this that reinforced relations between Zambia and China.

When the Republic of Zambia was founded, a number of its neighbors in Southern Africa were still many years away from gaining independence. It was flanked by Portuguese colonies in Angola and Mozambique. South Africa was under the Afrikaner-led apartheid government and Zimbabwe (at the time known as Rhodesia) was under settler rule. Being a landlocked country, Zambia depended on its coastal neighbors for sending exports and receiving imports. This was a fraught situation for a country that was decidedly anticolonialist and anti-settler rule. Zambia's interest in ending colonial and minority rule resonated with China's. Intersecting identities (such as self-identification as developing countries) and ideas were at play in relations between the two countries. The political situation in Zimbabwe and South Africa demanded that Zambia lessens or stops its dependency on the two countries for conveying exports and imports (Leslie 2016, 90–91).[17]

Together with Tanzania, Zambia had mooted the idea of constructing an alternative route for channeling exports and imports, a route that would go north and hence provide a solution to the route that passed through settler-ruled Rhodesia and apartheid South Africa. Julius Nyerere of Tanzania and Kenneth Kaunda of Zambia had reportedly approached Western actors for assistance to build a railway line for this purpose. Their supplications were unsuccessful, and the reasons given ranged from infeasibility to inordinate expenses. Nyerere and Kaunda then made independent appeals to China for assistance, and China readily agreed to lead the project, offering both finances and human labor even though China was itself 'very poor' at the time.[18] Meine Pieter van Dijk reports that the Tanzania-Zambia Railway (TAZARA) "was built by the Chinese because no other donor was willing to provide the necessary support to the socialist government of Tanzania."[19]

China's decision to fund the TAZARA project is attributable to a number of reasons, considering the circumstances of the time. To Zambia and Tanzania, it was China's munificent demonstration of solidarity with the struggle for liberation and self-reliance in the developing world. Committing to the TAZARA was an exception because China's contribution to liberation struggles was "largely rhetorical."[20] Zambia's gratitude for this project features prominently to this day whenever state actors from the two countries seek to buttress the argument that Zambia-China relations are characterized by win-win cooperation and mutual benefits. This argument appeals to Beijing and it continues to strengthen the general Africa-China relationship.[21]

Another possible reason for undertaking the TAZARA project was China's attempt to undercut Soviet influence in Africa.[22] The TAZARA came at the time when China and the Soviet Union were locked in the throes of bitter ideological conflict. China accused post-Stalinist Soviet socialism of being an apostate of socialism. "Revisionist" was the sobriquet widely used to describe the Soviet Union and actors in the developing world that were recipients of Soviet largesse.[23]

Zambia was to form part of the Frontline States, a group of African countries that was formed to wage a concerted struggle against apartheid. In retrospect, this enhanced the importance of the TAZARA line as a countervailing initiative to using South Africa as a conduit for Zambia's exports and imports. In sum, the first epoch of Zambia-China relations was largely steeped in the ideological fervor of the Cold War. The two countries self-identified as part of the developing world, and their intersecting interests ranged from fighting colonial dependency, imperialism, and settler-cum-minority rule. The Mao era in China was heavily influenced by ideology and the consolidation of the CCP's rule.

China's ideological forays into Africa and its tangible contributions through projects like the TAZARA were accepted with alacrity by liberation movements and newly independent African countries. In 1971, independent African countries demonstrated their support for China by overwhelmingly voting in its favor to take over the permanent seat at the UNSC as the *de jure* representative of Chinese people, thereby effectively ending Taiwan's diplomatic status at the UN.[24] After the death of Mao in 1976 and the readmission of Deng Xiaoping in the high echelons of the CCP, China embarked on a series of economic reforms whose reach and implications are extant. The following section deals with what could be termed the second epoch of Zambia-China relations, an era that was characterized by economic reforms in China and economic and political reforms in Zambia.

CHINA AND THE MOVEMENT FOR MULTIPARTY DEMOCRACY

After twenty-seven years in power, Kenneth Kaunda and his party, the United National Independence Party (UNIP), were resoundingly voted out of office in 1991. The election was a result of the reintroduction of multiparty contestation which the UNIP government had ended in 1973. Zambia was the first country in Southern Africa where a liberation movement was voted out of power after the wave of multiparty democracy swept through the region (Renwick 2018, 158). It is politic to consider the context that forced Kaunda to reintroduce multiparty politics. His futile experiment with structural adjustment programs in the 1980s provoked an avalanche of protests by citizens who had their subsidies reduced. Besides, the trade union movement was becoming bolder, and eventually, Frederick Chiluba, the head of the Zambia Congress of Trade Unions (ZCTU), became an active politician and president of the MMD, the party that defeated Kaunda and ruled Zambia from 1991 to 2011.

Another possible reason for Kaunda's capitulation is more ideological. Though as early as 1966 he had expressed contempt for opposition political parties, dismissing them as "a ragbag of disgruntled individuals and tribalists" (Kaunda 1966, 107),[25] he also cited his commitment to the liberation struggle as one of the reasons for proscribing opposition political parties. His pretext was that for Zambia to wage the struggle for Southern African independence with single-minded determination, it did not need an opposition that can inflame the notion that, rather than catering for a newly liberated and impecunious populace, the government was more interested in catering for citizens of its neighboring countries.

This last reason was increasingly losing its basis starting from 1980 when Zimbabwe gained independence. In the twilight years of the 1980s, apartheid South Africa relinquished its control over Southwest Africa, and the Republic of Namibia was established in 1990. In the same year, F. W. de Klerk, the last Nationalist president of South Africa, rescinded the ban on liberation movements and started releasing political prisoners. These developments had a telling impact on Kaunda's One-party's raison d'être. Once in power, the MMD assumed the task of repairing a ravaged economy and entrenching the tenets of multiparty democracy. Zambia's return to multiparty democracy was an internal matter with which China undertook not to interfere (Taylor 2006).[26] The 1990s also came at the time when China had been implementing economic reforms for more than a decade. Zambia embarked on its reforms of privatizing enterprises that had been state-owned.

Zambia-China relations during the MMD government coincided with the emergence of the United States as the unrivaled superpower of the international system after the dissolution of the Soviet Union. This unipolar world order created a conducive climate for the emergence of middle powers that could play the role of de facto leaders in their regions.[27] Chief among these have been Brazil, China, India, Russia, and South Africa, a group of countries that would later form BRICS.[28] The post-Cold War order has also enhanced the salience of nomenclature such as "Global South" to refer to the developing world and South-South cooperation as an ideally mutually beneficial relationship among the developing world as a counterbalance to the much-abhorred North-South relationship. Like many African countries, Zambia is quick to take umbrage at alleged Western interference and hawkish demeanor in the affairs of weaker and smaller economies.[29]

At the 2007 Africa-EU summit in Portugal, President Levy Mwanawasa of Zambia intimated that Africa had turned to the East because the West had turned its back on the continent.[30] Western attitudes toward the developing world are usually governed by conditions of economic practice and political behavior that are inserted as requirements for trade, aid, and investment. These conditions have been interpreted as unjust and intrusive by the developing world. Consequently, China's policy of noninterference appeals to countries that have endured Western punishment, sanctions, and criticism. China's industrialization occasioned a massive need for more energy and mineral resources. Thus, the emerging Sino-Zambian relationship was more driven by practical necessities rather than the ideological affinity of the Cold War era. Secondly, Zambia's privatization, especially of the mining industry, created room for foreign multinational corporations and state-owned enterprises to buy operations in Zambia's economic mainstay. Chiluba was one of the few African heads of state that participated in the inaugural Forum on China-Africa Cooperation (FOCAC) Conference in 2000 in Beijing. The participants signed the Beijing Declaration, a statement of intent for Africa-China relations, which was also an indictment on "serious destabilizing factors in the world and a huge gap between the rich North and the poor South and that peace and development are far from being fully realized" (FOCAC 2000).[31]

This era also coincided with the increasing number of Chinese nationals who are coming to Zambia for private reasons and to possibly settle permanently. This was in stark contrast to the Chinese who came as state agents and contract workers during the Kaunda years and had to go back to China at the end of their state-led missions. Hannah Postel of the Migration Policy Institute estimated that between 2009 and 2015, there was a 60 percent increase of Chinese nationals coming to Zambia for a variety of reasons. Furthermore, Postel noted that "Zambia does not have a separate permit for family reunion—family members enter on the same permit as the initial holder. This complicates the collection of accurate statistics, as only the individual granted a permit is written into the immigration records."[32] Thus, the number of Chinese residing in Zambia is presumably higher than official records indicate.

CHINA AND THE PATRIOTIC FRONT GOVERNMENT

After ten years as an opposition party, the Patriotic Front finally came to power in 2011. As an opposition party, it was well known for its propaganda against alleged kowtowing of the MMD government to China. During the tenure of Levy Mwanawasa as the president of both the MMD and Zambia from

2001 to 2008, the MMD reinvented itself as an organization that was determined to stymie corruption. Mwanawasa's success in convincing Zambians that the new MMD was a stark contrast to the Chiluba-era one forced the opposition to find another Achilles heel in the MMD. For the Patriotic Front, China's growing presence in Zambia provided a formidable object of attack. Sata went as far as describing Taiwan as an independent country. This was an indirect threat that once elected as president, he would seek to establish relations with Taiwan.[33] This meant severing ties between Zambia and China because of the nonnegotiable One-China policy by the PRC which dictates that no country can have simultaneous formal relations with China and Taiwan. Guy Scott, Sata's acolyte, added to anti-Chinese sentiment by asserting that China was out to exploit Africa and to win Africa's support at international platforms. Li Baodong, the Chinese ambassador to Zambia from 2005 to 2007, warned that China would withdraw from Zambia if Sata won the 2006 election. According to Kopiński and Polus, "This was the very first time China openly violated its 'non-interference rule.'"[34] There were "extensive anti-Chinese riots in the capital city Lusaka and in the Copperbelt region in 2006, following an election that Michael Sata lost."[35]

After the death of Mwanawasa in 2008, the PF lost the ensuing presidential by-election to the MMD's Rupiah Banda. Contrary to his predecessor's administration, Banda's presidency was dogged by allegations of corruption. For this reason, the PF reduced is criticism of Zambia-China relations and revived accusations of elite corruption against the MMD government.[36] The success of the PF's campaign was borne out by the fact that Rupiah Banda and the MMD lost to the PF in the 2011 general election and Sata became president of Zambia. Even though, as already mentioned, Sata had reduced his anti-Chinese rhetoric in the three years before assuming the presidency, his victory was still seen in some quarters as confirmation that Zambians were increasingly critical of and uncomfortable with China's presence and possible impact in Zambia.

Since coming to power, the PF government has increased its economic relations with China. It was during the tenure of the PF, in 2012, that Zambia and China agreed to embark on an ambitious road network project known as Link Zambia 8000. The project was estimated to take between five and eight years and cost K31.42 billion. The Link Zambia 8000 could be described as a contemporary version of the TAZARA, albeit being a road project. It aims to build and enhance 8000 kilometers of roads in Zambia so that the country can be transformed from being landlocked to a "land-linked" country.[37] Contrary to what many would have expected, Sata had changed tack on China; the first dignitary he invited to State House was the Chinese ambassador.[38] He expressed the oft-repeated refrain that China should confine itself to sending only Chinese with skills that are scarce or absent in Zambia. In 2012, the

Zambian government decided to double mineral royalties and to charge tax based on production rather than sales.[39] This move was arguably an assertion of Zambian agency in the Zambia-China relationship considering that China has started making inroads in Zambia's mining sector though the sector is still largely dominated by non-Chinese investors from India, Canada, and Switzerland.

Ironically, non-state actors, civil society organizations, and opposition political parties have taken over the anti-Chinese sentiment that the current ruling party had successfully promoted in its days as an opposition party. This sentiment has become more common under the presidency of Edgar Lungu, starting from 2016. Rumors are rife of China taking over strategic government parastatals such as airports, broadcasting enterprises, and the forest industry. These have been fueled by rumors that the Zambia government is failing to service the huge debts owed to China. Shortly after the conclusion of the 2018 FOCAC Summit in China, speculation seemed to have reached a fever pitch, especially on social media, and in opposition circles that it was only a matter of time before China would completely take over Zambia. Mr. Emmanuel Mwamba, Zambia's ambassador to Ethiopia and permanent representative to the African Union, has come out to rebut speculations that China threatens Zambia's sovereignty.[40]

Mwamba argued that colonizing other regions has never been in China's DNA because, even centuries ago when China was in a position to colonize Africa and establish slavery, it did not do so.[41] Mwamba referred to the expeditions of Chinese Admiral Zheng He who made several expeditions to Africa without colonizing the continent or taking slaves. Reportedly, there was an exchange of an African giraffe and indigenous medicines between the Chinese voyagers and their African hosts. "Due to the fact that Zheng's expeditions were not motivated by a colonial or aggressive rationale, China has been able to draw on these ancient accounts in contemporary relations."[42] Isaac Mwanza, a former student leader, also supported Zambia-China relations claiming that in the SADC region Zambia is China's "strongest and best partner."[43] Similar to what will be presented in the section dealing with trade union participants, Mwanza asserts that nongovernmental commentators who besmirch Zambia-China relations are unwittingly doing the bidding of Western media and former colonizers who have exhausted their influence of dictating to Africa.[44]

In November 2018, Hakainde Hichilema, Zambia's main opposition leader, gave a radio interview during which it was alleged that he said China had taken over Zambia Forestry and Forest Industries Corporation (ZAFFICO), a state-owned enterprise. This allegation provoked spates of attacks on Chinese-owned businesses on the Copperbelt province. Some Chinese nationals fled from Zambia. The Chinese ambassador delivered a formal

missive of complaint to Zambia's State House complaining about xenophobic attacks on Chinese nationals.[45] Lungu enjoined Zambians "to ignore the
misleading headlines that seek to malign Zambia's relationship with China by
mischaracterizing the economic cooperation to mean colonialism."[46]

Lungu's assurances contest with the conviction of his detractors and are
at variance with some of the government's actions. For example, in early
September 2018, the Zambian government denied Patrick Lumumba, a
Kenyan academic, entry into Zambia for "security reasons." This was interpreted as capitulating to China's subtle pressure as Lumumba was to make a
speech at a local university, whose content was centered around Africa-China
relations.[47] One who reads political developments in a linear or deterministic
manner could find the PF's behavior as confounding or hypocritical at worst
because it is the party that played a pioneering role in brewing hostility
toward China. However, as Ebrahim Harvey noted, "the world of politics and
power is fraught with shifting sands as events shape and change perceptions
of leaders. Sometimes there is tension between what is said at one moment
and what is said at another."[48]

NON-STATE ACTORS AND THE CHINESE QUESTION

Emmanuel John Hevi, a Ghanaian national who studied in China during
Mao's chairmanship, is possibly one of the earliest non-state actors of African
origin to construct an identity of China that was decidedly antithetical to the
identity that African state actors constructed.[49] Hevi described the Chinese as
inveterate liars, who were desirous of colonizing Africa after the demise of
European colonialism and imperialism. He also decried the Chinese determination to indoctrinate their citizens to fortify the CCP's rule against detraction
and criticism. He expressed concern that Kwame Nkrumah's growing frustration with social expressions such as religion and his antipathy for political
opposition could be traced to the influence that China exercised on him. One
of the pithy cautions of Hevi's work was that colonialism is not inherently
linked with people of certain races and economic ideologies. This caveat was
aimed at warning African leaders against an unthinking embrace of Eastern
political and economic proclivities simply because their purveyors had never
colonized Africa.

The shift of many postcolonial leaderships toward socialism was sponsored by African communitarian economics and also by the solidarity that the
Soviet Union and China had shown toward Africa during the struggle against
capitalist colonialism. This chapter concurs with Hevi that there is no intrinsic
kinship between economic ideology and colonialism (see also Matambo and
Mtshali 2016).[50] Even further, while China may never colonize Africa in the

same way that Europe did, it can nevertheless exercise influence on Africans that is equally damaging.[51] Thus, while ordinary Zambians who are leery of the presence of Chinese citizens usually cite colonialism as a possible outcome, there could be many ways in which control over Zambia could be expressed. Also, while the ruling elite presents identities and interests that are befitting for state-level interaction, national identity, and rhetoric recede when individual interests are paramount. Non-state actors do not act in conformity to constraints that circumscribe the behavior of state actors. The following subsections present the data gathered from non-state actors in Zambia. The non-state actors interviewed included representatives of a congress of trade unions, a focus group of Zambian employees in a Chinese enterprise, and another focus group of ordinary Zambians, predominantly from the Copperbelt province, a mineral-rich region where most foreign investment in mining is concentrated.

VIEWS FROM TRADE UNION REPRESENTATIVES

Labor practices and unfair competition between Chinese traders and their Zambian counterparts have been the main facet of a growing concern for the presence of Chinese in Zambia. Trade union representatives situated China's growing unpopularity in Zambia in the international competition, between the West and the East, for Africa's resources. The respondents put the media and Western analysts and observers of China's presence in Zambia under the shed of what is called Sino-pessimism. One respondent argued that the media has played a part in influencing "the mind-set of most Zambians to think that [the Chinese] are bad."[52] Furthermore, one of the respondents described China as a developing country whose economy has only recently begun to grow. In effect, the respondent was endorsing the similarity in identities that Zambia-China state actors promote. The description of China as a developing power has been repudiated by Western actors, for example, Marco Rubio, who claims that China, as the second-biggest economy in the world, scarcely fits the identity of a developing country.[53]

On the question of Chinese labor practices that have become a thorny issue, the respondents once again looked at them from a broader perspective of many other actors. Like Sautman and Yan,[54] trade union representatives opined that investors of different nationalities have also flouted labor legislation in Zambia. The sources of concern, they said, were the levels of enforcement and compliance. This came on the back of the argument that Zambia has sufficient labor laws that could protect workers, irrespective of who they work for.

Reference to the alleged unlawful labor practices of non-Chinese firms was indirectly aimed at suggesting bias in the manner in which the media and the West report on Chinese or labor practices in general. There was also an approving observation that after the release of Anthony Yaw Baah and Herbert Jauch's book, Chinese Investments in Africa: A Labour (2009),[55] staff members of China's embassy volunteered a meeting with the ZCTU to address the concerns that usually bedevil China's labor practices in Zambia.[56] This willingness was hailed by respondents who also added that while some labor practices are unsavory in Zambia and occasionally lead to fatalities, the conditions for Chinese laborers in China are probably more trying than those of Zambians and that Chinese labor workers probably encounter more work-related deaths.

ZAMBIAN WORKERS ON THEIR CHINESE EMPLOYERS

Much of the popular and publicized condemnation that has marred China's presence in Zambia has related to mining issues. The Beijing General Research Institute of Mining and Metallurgy (BGRIMM) explosion that happened at a Chinese-run explosive plant, killing more than fifty Zambian workers in 2005, has been cited as the illustration of China's safety and work-place insouciance. The current chapter takes a departure from mining-related research to include a relatively under-researched facet of Chinese investment in Zambia, ascertaining the impressions of Zambian workers in Chinese clothing and fabric firms. The participants were drawn from Kamwala Market in Lusaka.

The respondents had a realistic understanding of China's interests in Zambia through experiences with their employers. They invariably stated that the primary interest of the Chinese coming to Zambia is economic profit. A permanent settlement was also cited as another reason for the increasing number of Chinese nationals, though the respondents argued that immigration of Chinese nationals should be painstakingly monitored and reduced (Ruth Nyirenda). This sentiment had also been expressed by Chishimba Kambwili during his time as Zambia's Minister of Foreign Affairs.[57]

One of the participants feared that a huge number of Chinese nationals in Zambia could lead to a "dictatorship."[58] Upon further interrogation, it was established that what she meant by dictatorship was colonialism. Despite these concerns, the workers were grateful for having employment—courtesy of Chinese entrepreneurs. In terms of work conditions, the participants, like the representatives of trade unions, argued that Chinese are being singled out when even some Zambian employers are scornful of labor laws.[59] By and large, China is being touted as a redeemer for Zambians who would otherwise be unemployed.[60]

CHINA'S IDENTITY IN ZAMBIA:
VIEWS FROM ORDINARY CITIZENS

Through social media and raids on Chinese businesses, ordinary Zambians have arguably been the loudest critics of the presence of China and Chinese citizens in Africa. During his ten years as an opposition leader, Sata had managed to galvanize urban-based Zambians against China's presence.[61] However, the widespread odium that China has increasingly incurred is the consequence of the current PF government's failure to mitigate Chinese permeation of many sectors of Zambia, from the media to small-scale entrepreneurship. The chorus of non-state condemnation of China has been reinforced by civil society organizations and opposition political parties, the latter motivated by a mixture of real concerns and political opportunism. The focus group comprising ordinary citizens yielded a concoction of both optimistic and pessimistic observations of China and the Chinese in Zambia.

Trying to situate Zambia-China amity in history, one of the interviewees referred to the ideological convergence of Mao-era socialism to Kaunda's ideology of humanism which mixed elements of African tradition, Christianity and socialism.[62] The same participant went on to state how China and Zambia have made marked departures from erstwhile ideological moorings and have embraced market economics. The Mao era was characterized by 'brainwashing the entire population of' China.[63] Ideology was an overriding factor during the Mao era and that is why even the construction of the TAZARA, which the participants commended, was justified using ideological arguments. China's commitment to Zambia bred trust and what Howard French describes as "lingering gratitude in Zambia."[64] Despite the enduring appreciation, certain sections of Zambian citizens are growing increasingly alarmed at the possible effect of China's and Chinese presence in Zambia.

Predictably, one of the participants, who hails from Chambishi, where the BGRIMM explosion referred to earlier took place, expressed concerns about the possible adverse effects that China and its citizens might have on Zambians.[65] The explosion attracted international attention and gave Sino-pessimists ammunition to attack China and the MMD government. The participant who referred to that event concluded that in their current form, Sino-Zambian relations are exploitative in China's favor. This percolates even to the level of non-state interaction where Chinese employers are abusive toward their employees both in terms of emoluments and general conduct.[66]

Ultimately, the respondents argued that because the Zambian government is more attuned to the Zambian economic and political situation, the "onus" to leverage Zambia-China relations in a more balanced and mutually beneficial nexus resides with the Zambian government.[67] This assertion forms part of a growing call for Africa's agency in its relations with China. Some writers have argued that there are cases where African governments, and Zambia in particular, have demonstrated agency in their dealings with China, rather than being passive partners as Western observers, media, and governments are wont to characterize them. For example, Sata's fulminations as an opposition leader and his request, as president, to Chinese dignitaries that only Chinese with critical skills are preferred in Zambia defied "Afropessimism—a predominantly Western view that Africans lack the ability to push for their development."[68]

On a few occasions, the Zambian government has called for the arrest of errant Chinese employers, and in one instance, the government conducted a sting operation which eventuated in the arrest of four Chinese nationals who were offering bribes to obtain the consent of farmers who had vetoed Tiang Mining Zambia Limited's intent to start a quarry mine in Shimabala.[69] From the foregoing, it is evident that the Zambian government has tried to promote and enforce adherence to Zambian legislation from Chinese investors. However, in comparison to views from the trade union federation (ZCTU) and from workers in a Chinese firm, the participants of the group comprising ordinary citizens were more circumspect in commending China, accusing it of flooding Zambia, inundating the country with substandard Chinese products and taking advantage of desperation and lack of employment to hire Zambians that are resigned to accepting pittances.[70] The following section will put into perspective the views generated from primary and secondary data and give possible explanations for China provoking a variety of appraisals from different political players in Zambia.

A CONSTRUCTIVIST ANALYSIS OF ZAMBIA-CHINA RELATIONS

The current research used constructivism as a tool for analyzing Zambia-China relations. It did so first by dividing these relations into three epochs. The first epoch was from 1964 to the end of the Cold War and the reintroduction of multiparty democracy in Zambia. The first epoch was characterized by ideological positions such as nonalignment that were encouraged by the Bandung Conference, the Non-Aligned Movement, and the Organisation of African Union.[71]

Constructivism characterizes relations among nations as being synonymous with any form of social relations, mostly interpersonal relations. Thus, what constructivism adds to rationalist analyses of relations among nations is that it considers the social dimension of relations.[72] It is through social interaction and stereotypes that identities that shape relations emerge. Social forces that forge identities are mostly steeped in historical vicissitudes. It is thus not surprising that international players that have historical, social, and political experiences that are at variance with China's look askance at China and its growing influence on global affairs. The West has not been sanguine about China's growth and its consequent growing footprint in Africa, a continent that the West regards as an impressionable region that is susceptible to the whims and political tastes of more powerful players.

However, social perceptions, even within Africa, have at certain times been consonant with perceptions that generally typify Western notions of Africa-China relations. What could be deduced from the material used in this chapter is that among the different sources, respondents from the trade union sector and the government are more inclined toward painting a generous picture of Chinese presence in Zambia. They also converged on the idea that China's negative identity has been a construct of Western propaganda and the media. The identities attributed to China by non-state actors, in the form of civil society organizations, opposition political parties, and ordinary Zambians, have provoked a curious scenario that has forced the Zambian government to be a spirited apologist of China against its own (Zambia's) citizens. The Zambian government has effectively been accused of pursuing a complaisant attitude toward the Chinese government. In a wider scheme of analysis, the Zambia government and its Chinese counterpart have pitted themselves against Zambians who are neither state actors nor adherents of Zambia's ruling party. The identity of China that non-state actors have is that of non-state actors of Chinese stock who are venturing into spheres of enterprise that bring competition to Zambians. China, thus, is a usurper of opportunity, but it has to be borne in mind that, since the targeted immigrants are not agents of their government, Zambians are uncomfortable with the Chinese rather than China.

During its days in opposition, the PF constructed an unsavory identity of China. It should be mentioned that during the reign of the MMD, relations between China and Zambia experienced a spike in economic terms, which has grown even more after the assumption of the PF to power. Judging from the PF's robust defense of Sino-Zambian relations, one can question whether the PF's initial anti-Chinese vitriol was an authentic protest against a marauding would-be colonizer or whether it was a cleverly crafted ruse, calculated to attract the support of a frustrated citizenry. To use Steven C. Dubin's description of how Rwanda media stoked genocide, it is arguable that Sata was adroitly "generating a negative climate of opinion" about the Chinese.[73]

"Africa is a lucrative partner and a rich source of raw materials for China's expanding economy."[74] Latterly, Zambia-China relations have been driven more by China's demand for resources that Zambia has and to Zambia, China's investment and expertise have been a long-overdue antidote to Zambia's poor and inadequate infrastructure. While it is understandable, for diplomatic stability, for the Zambian government to pacify China as a response to anti-Chinese sentiment, it should also address what spawns such sentiments in the first place. Stereotypes about China's threat to Zambia are not incorrect; they are generalizations of observed phenomena. They are founded in real experiences of Zambians alongside their Chinese counterparts. The possibility that China is a surrogate target for Zambians whose government has failed to boost and diversify the economy and provide employment for its citizens cannot be dismissed. Indeed, the more favorable identity that workers in a Chinese firm attributed to China was a construct that was influenced by resignation and fatalism by the youth who would otherwise have been jobless without their Chinese employers.

In *Africa: The Politics of Smiling and Suffering*, Patrick Chabal advocated an approach to African politics that emanates from the daily lives and experiences of ordinary Africans instead of perspectives peddled by Africa's "Big Men."[75] The current chapter advocated such an approach to understanding Zambia-China relations. In a democracy such as Zambia, the government serves at the pleasure of the voters, and hence decisions made at the level of political elites should ideally reflect the views and sensitivities of the electorate. When an agency is talked about, it is mostly a state agency that is under discussion. State actors are prone to burnishing Zambia-China relations, presenting China as the proverbial wise guest from the East without the colonial badge. This identity is not invariably supported by non-state actors.

While Chabal proposed a reading of African politics that is grounded in the experiences of ordinary Africans,[76] Howard French's *China's Second Continent* argues that China's presence in African should be looked at from the perspective of the swelling number of non-state actors from China who are making their way to Africa.[77] The subtitle of his book, *How A Million Chinese are Building a New Empire in Africa*, is an instructive indication of French's position on the argument of whether or not China is a herald of a new colonial or imperial edifice in Africa. His main departure from the common view is that it is ordinary Chinese who are likely to institute an empire in Africa rather "than any carefully planned action by the Beijing government to build state power and reinforce national prestige."[78]

Chabal's and French's arguments fit together with the main argument of this chapter: the importance of the constructions of China's identity and interests by non-state actors. For reasons of expediency, economics, and diplomacy, successive governments in Zambia have constructed identities of China that appeal to politically correct behavior. As shown, however, China evokes multiple identities to Zambians. The more accommodating position of workers in a Chinese firm was partly influenced by resignation in the face of the Zambian government's failure to provide sufficient employment. It was not purely based on the understanding that China is the latter-day wise actor from the East bearing gifts for Africa. The perceptions of non-state actors should be given more importance because the consequences of Africa-China relations are felt more acutely by them. Secondly, Chinese citizens, who hold no brief for their government, are more likely to be honest in their intentions, whether stated or demonstrated, rather than pander to the diplomacy of their government's proclamations. That ordinary Zambians interact mostly with ordinary Chinese enhances the importance of their views even more.

CONCLUSION

The article used the analogy of the biblical Magi, more famously known as the Wise Men from the East who came to pay homage to Jesus shortly after his nativity. China, itself coming from the East, has been accepted with alacrity in Africa because of its habit of tying its identity, history, and interests with Africa and by highlighting its unqualified partnerships with other nations. By offering the much-needed infrastructure to Zambia, China is understandably treated as a bearer of gifts and a bailout option for countries that endure the debilitating consequences of experimenting with economic and political prescriptions that are of Western origin. Zambia-China relations are braided together by an intersecting suspicion of Western politics and intentions. However, significant changes have happened since 1964.

The stupendous economic growth that China has undergone has seen it being compared to Western powers and erstwhile colonialists, whether it is being presented as different from them or as heralding a new colonial empire in Africa. At the level of state interaction, relations between China and Zambia are determinedly driven by the same ideals that Kaunda and Mao espoused. The repeated references to China's role in the TAZARA railway line are a wistful attempt to sanitize a relationship that has frayed at the level of non-state-actor interaction. David Monyae offers a valid recommendation that in relating to China, "policy formation should be based on long-term African goals and prospects as opposed to only historical links."[79]

The sui generis nature of the Zambia-China relationship is demonstrated through its longevity that has enhanced the two countries' liberation credentials. However, the relationship has also experienced violence unprecedented anywhere on the African continent. This is because China's identity has been evolving and has acquired more dimensions that non-state actors from Zambia find ominous. The Zambian government is dependent on China for its debt and infrastructure and hence does not wish to run afoul of such an important partner. Non-state actors do not have to be equally guarded in their appraisal of China. As demonstrated in previous sections, the current state of anti-Chinese sentiment is palpable among Zambian non-state actors, and hence for this section of Zambia, China is hardly a wise partner from the East.

NOTES

1. Asia News. 2009, "China's economic colonisation of Africa." http://www.asia news.it/news-en/China%E2%80%99s-economic-colonisation-of-Africa-15856.html

2. Shimazu, Naoko. 2014. "Diplomacy as Theatre: Staging the Bandung Conference of 1955." *Modern Asian Studies*, 48(1): 225–252. doi:10.1017/ S0026749X13000371.

3. Acharya, Amitav. 2016. "Studying the Bandung conference from a Global IR perspective." *Australian Journal of International Affairs*, 70(4): 342–357.

4. Ellis, Steven. 2012. External Mission: The ANC in Exile, 1960-1990. Johannesburg: Jonathan Ball.

5. Jura, Jaroslow, Kaja Kaluzynska and Paulo de Carvalho. 2015. *Events over Endeavours: Image of the Chinese in Zambia and Angola.* Krakow: Jagiellonian University Press.

6. Zambia Daily Mail. 2018. Stop primitive attacks on Chinese. http://www.dail y-mail.co.zm/stop-primitive-attacks-on-chinese/.

7. Ibid, Jura et al. 2015.

8. French, Howard William. 2014. *China's Second Continent: How a Million Migrants Are Building a New Empire in Africa.* New York: Alfred A. Knopf.

9. Chabal, Patrick. 2009. *Africa: The Politics of Suffering and Smiling.* London: Zed Books.

10. Dasgupta, Meeta. 2015. "Exploring the Relevance of Case Study Research." *Vision*, 19(2): 147–160.

11. Howells, Karen and David Fletcher. 2015. "Sink or Swim: Adversity- and Growth-related Experiences in Olympic Swimming Champions." *Psychology of Sport and Exercise*, 16(3): 37–48.

12. Hox, Joop J. and Hennie R Boeije. 2005. "Data Collection, Primary vs. Secondary." *Encyclopedia of Social Measurement*, 1(1): 593–599.

13. Wendt, Alexandra. 1992. "Anarchy Is What States Make of It: The Construction of Power Politics." *International Organisation*, 41(3): 391–425.

14. Schrecker, John E. 2004. *The Chinese Revolution in Historical Perspective.* Westport: Praeger.

15. Chaponnière, Jean-Raphaël. 2009. "Chinese Aid to Africa, Origins, Forms and Issues." In. *The New Presence of China in Africa*, edited by Meine Pieter van Dijk, 55–82. Hilversum: University of Amsterdam Press.

16. Mthembu, Philani. 2018. *China and India's Development Cooperation in Africa: The Rise of Southern Powers.* Cham: Palgrave Macmillan.

17. Leslie, Agnes Ngoma. 2016. "Zambia and China: Workers' Protest, Civil Society and the Role of Opposition Politics in Elevating State Engagement." *African Studies Quarterly*, 16(3–4): 89–106.

18. Chen, Xiangming. and Garth Myers. 2013. *China and Africa: The Crucial Urban Connection.* Trinity College, https://digitalrepository.trincoll.edu/cgi/viewcon tent.cgi?article=1100&context=facpub.

19. van Dijk, Meine Pieter. 2009. "Introduction: Objectives of and Instruments for China's New Presence in Africa." In *The New Presence of China in Africa*, edited by Meine Pieter van Dijk, 9–30. Hilversum: University of Amsterdam.

20. Renwick, Robin. 2018. *How to Steal a Country: State Capture and the Hopes for the Future in South Africa.* Johannesburg: Jacana.

21. Vhumbunu, Clayton Hazvinei. 2016. "Enabling African Regional Infrastructure Renaissance through the China-Africa Partnership: A Trans-Continental Appraisal." *International Journal of China Studies*, 7(3): 271–300.

22. Ibid, Chaponnière 2009, 58.

23. Anshan, Li. 2007. "China and Africa: Policy and Challenges." *China Security*, 3(3): 69–93.

24. Ibid, Leslie 2016.

25. Kaunda, Kenneth. 1966. *A Humanist in Africa: Letters to Colin Morris.* London: Longmans Green.

26. Taylor, Ian. 2006. *China and Africa: Engagement and Compromise.* Abingdon: Routledge.

27. Nkoana-Mashabane, Maite. 2009. Speech at the Heads of Missions Conference, 13 August 2009. http://www.dfa.gov.za/docs/speeches/2009/mash 0813.html.

28. Ibid, Mthembu 2018, 16.

29. Reuters. 2010. Zambian president says donors must not interfere. 26 June. http://www.reuters.com/article/idININdia-49672220100626.

30. Ibid, Asia News 2009.

31. Forum on China-Africa Cooperation, 2000. Beijing Declaration of the Forum on China-Africa Cooperation. https://www.focac.org/eng/zywx_1/zywj/t606796.htm.

32. Postel, Hannah. 2015. Following the Money: Chinese Labor Migration to Zambia. https://www.migrationpolicy.org/article/following-money-chinese-labor-m igration-zambia.

33. Mukwita, Anthony. 2017. "Lessons from Zambia-China 'bitter-sweet' rela-tions." Zambia Daily Mail, June 10. http://www.daily-mail.co.zm/lessons-from-zamb ia-china-bitter-sweet-relations/.

34. Kopiński, Dominik, and Andrzej Polus. 2011. "Sino-Zambian Relations: 'An All-weather Friendship' Weathering the Storm." *Journal of Contemporary African Studies* 29(2): 181–192.

35. Carmody, Pádraig, and Peter Kragelund. "Who Is in Charge-State Power and Agency in Sino-African Relations." *Cornell Int'l LJ* 49 (2016): 1–23.

36. Bowman, Andrew. 2011. "Can Zambia Stand Up To China?" New Internationalist, December 1. http://newint.org/sections/agenda/2011/12/01/chinese -investment-in-zambia/.

37. Road Development Agency. 2016. Annual Report. http://www.rda.org.zm/ind ex.php/reports/annual-reports.

38. Ibid, Bowman 2011.

39. England, Andrew. 2011. Zambia to double mine royalties. Financial Royalties, 12 November. https://www.ft.com/content/5a64a96c-0c8c-11e1-88c6-00144feabdc0.

40. Mwamba, Emmanuel. 2018. China-Zambia: An Intricate Relationship. The Zambian Observer, 16 September. https://www.zambianobserver.com/emmanuel -mwamba-zambia-china-an-intricate-relationship/.

41. Kissinger, Henry. 2012. On China. London: Penguin Books.

42. Ibid, Mthembu 2018, 30.

43. Mwanza, Isaac. 2018. China – Is She a Friend or Enemy of Africa? Lusaka Times, 19 November. https://www.lusakatimes.com/2018/11/19/china-is-she-a-f riend-or-enemy-of-africa/.

44. Ibid, Mwamba, Emmanuel. 2018.

45. Lusaka Times. 2018. State House says it has received an official complaint from China over victimization of Chinese People. 19 November. https://www.lusakati mes.com/2018/11/19/state-house-says-it-has-received-an-official-complaint-from-c hina-over-victimization-of-chinese-people/.

46. Lusaka Times. 2018. It is Regrettable for President Lungu to Defend China at Expense of Citizens - Shimunza. 20 September. https://www.lusakatimes.com/20 18/09/20/it-is-regrettable-for-president-lungu-to-defend-china-at-expense-of-citizens -shimunza/.

47. Lumumba, Patrick L. O. 2018. Prof PLO Lumumba explains why he was denied entry into Zambia. https://www.youtube.com/watch?v=sXR9GGkkP1k.

48. Harvey, Ebrahim. 2012. *Kgalema Motlanthe: A Political Biography.* Johannesburg: Jacana.

49. Hevi, Emmanuel. 1963. *An African Student in China.* London: Pall Mall Press.

50. Matambo, Emmanuel, and Khondlo Mtshali. 2016. "The Relevance of Emmanuel Hevi: China in Contemporary Sino-African Relations." *Africology: The Journal of Pan African Studies*, 9(4): 219–237.

51. Lumumba, Patrick L. O. 2018. Prof PLO Lumumba explains why he was denied entry into Zambia. https://www.youtube.com/watch?v=sXR9GGkkP1k.

52. Kamanisha, Muleka. 2017. Interview with research assistant. 6 February. Lusaka.

53. Rubio, Marco. 2018. China's threat to U.S. national security is not a game. https://www.youtube.com/watch?v=UiRAW66wdV0.

54. Sautman, Barry, and Yan Hairong. 2011. "Gilded Outside, Shoddy within: The Human Rights Watch Report on Chinese Copper mMining in Zambia." *The Asia-Pacific Journal*, 9(52): 1–15.

55. Baah, Anthony Yaw and Herbert Jauch. 2009. *Chinese Investments in Africa: A Labour Perspective.* Accra: Africa Labour Research Network.

56. Ibid, Muleka Kamanisha, 2017.

57. Sautman, Barry. 2013. "Chinese Defilement Case: Racial Profiling in an African Model of Democracy." *Rutgers Race & L. Rev* 1: 87.

58. Nkumbwa, Mulenga. 2017. Interview with author. 7 July. Lusaka.

59. Mwamulima, Shigala. 2017. Interview with author. 7 July. Lusaka.

60. Nyirenda, Ruth. 2017. Interview with author. 7 July. Lusaka.

61. Ibid, Leslie, Agnes Ngoma, 2016.

62. Kafwilo, Mutale. 2017. Interview with author. 20 May. Pietermaritzburg.

63. Ibid, Kafwilo, Mutale. 2017.

64. Ibid, French, Howard William. 2014.

65. Zulu, Elvis. 2017. Interview with author. 20 May. Pietermaritzburg.

66. Muwema, John Lwandamo. 2017. Interview with author. 20 May. Pietermaritzburg.

67. Mwale, Brian. 2017. Interview with research assistant. 13 February. Lusaka; See also Chongwe, Lukonde. 2017. Interview with author. 20 May. Pietermaritzburg.

68. Sautman, Barry. 2015. "Racialization as Agency in Zambia-China Relations." In *Africa and China: How Africans and their Governments Are Shaping Relations with China*, edited by Aleksandara W. Gadzala, 127–148. London: Rowman & Littlefield.

69. Times of Zambia. Four Chinese Arrested. 10 January 2015. Available: http://www.times.co.zm/?p=48129.

70. Ibid, Kafwilo, Mutale. 2017.

71. Schaufelbuehl, Janick Marina, Sandra Bott, Jussi Hanhimäki & Marco Wyss. 2015. "Non-Alignment, the Third Force, or Fence-Sitting: Independent Pathways in the Cold War." *The International History Review*, 37(5): 901–911.

72. Checkel, Jeffrey T. 1998. "The Constructivist Turn in International Relations Theory." *World Politics*, 50(2): 324–348.

73. Dubin, Steven. C. 2012. *Spearheading Debate: Culture Wars and Uneasy Truces*. Johannesburg: Jacana.

74. Ibid, Dubin 2012, 48.

75. Ibid, Patrick Chabal 2009.

76. Ibid, Patrick Chabal 2009.

77. Ibid, Howard French 2014.

78. Ibid, Howard French 2014, 6.

79. Monyae, David. 2017. The US, Russia, China and Africa in the evolving global order. Policy Brief, 3. Johannesburg: The University of Johannesburg Confucius Institute.

REFERENCES

Acharya, Amitav. "Studying the Bandung Conference from a Global IR Perspective." *Australian Journal of International Affairs* 70, no. 4 (2016): 342–357.

Anshan, Li. "China and Africa: Policy and Challenges." *China Security* 3, no. 3 (2007): 69–93.

AsiaNews. "China's Economic Colonisation of Africa." China-Africa. Asia News, July 22, 2009. http://www.asianews.it/news-en/China's-economic-colonisation-of-Africa-15856.html.

Baah, Anthony Yaw, and Herbert Jauch. "Chinese Investments in Africa: A Labour Perspective." Globalization Monitor, June 12, 2009. https://www.globalmon.org.hk/content/chinese-investments-africa-labour-perspective.

Bowman, Andrew. "Can Zambia Stand up to China?" New Internationalist, December 1, 2011. https://newint.org/sections/agenda/2011/12/01/chinese-invest ment-in-zambia/.

Carmody, Pádraig, and Peter Kragelund. "Who Is in Charge? State Power and Agency in Sino-African Relations." *Cornell International Law Journal* 49 (n.d.): 1–23.

van Dijk, Meine Pieter, and Jean-Raphaël Chaponnière. "Chinese Aid to Africa, Origins, Forms and Issues." In *The New Presence of China in Africa*. Hilversum: University of Amsterdam Press, 2009.

Checkel, Jeffrey T. "The Constructive Turn in International Relations Theory." *World Politics* 50, no. 2 (1998): 324–348.

Chen, Xiangming, and Garth Myers. "China and Africa: The Crucial Urban Connection." The European Finacial Review, December 28, 2013. https://digital repository.trincoll.edu/cgi/viewcontent.cgi?article=1100&context=facpub.

"China and Africa: The Crucial Urban Connection." Trinity College Trinity College Digital Repository, September 25, 2009. https://digitalrepository.trincoll.edu/cgi/vi ewcontent.cgi?article=1100&context=facpub.

French, Howard. *Chinas Second Continent: How a Million Migrants Are Building a New Empire in Africa*. New York: Alfred Knopf, 2015.

Dasgupta, Meeta. "Exploring the Relevance of Case Study Research." *Vision: The Journal of Business Perspective* 19, no. 2 (2015): 147–160.

Dubin, Steven. *Spearheading Debate: Culture Wars and Uneasy Truces*. Chicago: Ipg-Academic, 2013.

Editor, Web. "Stop Primitive Attacks on Chinese." Zambia Daily Mail, November 21, 2018. http://www.daily-mail.co.zm/stop-primitive-attacks-on-chinese/.

Ellis, Stephen. *External Mission - the ANC in Exile, 1960-1990*. London: C Hurst & Co Publishers Ltd, 2015.

England, Andrew. "Zambia to Double Mine Royalties." Financial Times, November 12, 2011. https://www.ft.com/content/5a64a96c-0c8c-11e1-88c6-00144feabdc0.

Harvey, Ebrahim. *Kgalema Motlanthe: A Political Biography*. Chicago: Jacana Media, 2013.

Hevi, Emmanuel John. *An African Student in China*. London, Dunmow: Pall Mall Press, 1964.

Howells, Karen, and David Fletcher. "Sink or Swim: Adversity- and Growth-Related Experiences in Olympic Swimming Champions." *Psychology of Sport and Exercise* 16 (2015): 37–48.

Hox, Joop J., and Hennie R. Boeije. "Data Collection, Primary vs. Secondary." *Encyclopedia of Social Measurement*, 2005, 593–599.

"It Is Regrettable for President Lungu to Defend China at Expense of Citizens-Shimunza." Lusaka Times, September 20, 2018. https://www.lusakatimes.com/20 18/09/20/it-is-regrettable-for-president-lungu-to-defend-china-at-expense-of-cit izens-shimunza/.

Jura, Jaroslaw, Kaja Kaluzynska, and Paulo de Carvalho. *Events over Endeavours: Image of the Chinese in Zambia and Angola*. Kraków: Jagiellonian University Press, 2015.

Kaunda, Kenneth David. *A Humanist in Africa: Letters to Colin M. Morris from Kenneth D. Kaunda, President of Zambia.* London: Longmans, Green, 1969.

Kissinger, Henry. *On China.* Toronto: Penguin Canada, 2012.

Kopiński, Dominik, and Andrzej Polus. "Sino-Zambian Relations: 'An All-Weather Friendship' Weathering the Storm." *Journal of Contemporary African Studies* 29, no. 2 (2011): 181–192.

Leslie, Agnes Ngoma. "Zambia and China: Workers' Protest, Civil Society and the Role of Opposition Politics in Elevating State Engagement." *African Studies Quarterly* 16, no. 3–4| (December 2016): 89–106.

Matambo, Emmanuel, and Khondlo Mtshali. "The Relevance of Emmanuel Hevi: China in Contemporary Sino-African Relations." *Africology: The Journal of Pan African Studies* 9, no. 4 (July 2016): 219–237.

Monyae, David. "US, Russia, China and Africa in the Evolving Global Order." *Changing Societies & Personalities* 2, no. 4 (2018): 351–365.

Mthembu, Philani. *China and India's Development Cooperation in Africa: The Rise of Southern Powers.* Cham: Palgrave Macmillan, 2018.

Mukwita, Anthony. "Lessons from Zambia-China 'Bitter-Sweet' Relations." Zambia Daily Mail, June 10, 2017. http://www.daily-mail.co.zm/lessons-from-zambia-china-bitter-sweet-relations/.

Mwale, Sylvester. "Four Chinese Arrested." Times of Zambia, January 10, 2015. http://www.times.co.zm/?p=48129.

Mwamba, Emmanuel. "China-Zambia: An Intricate Relationship." The Zambia Observer, September 16, 2018. https://www.zambianobserver.com/emmanuel-mwamba-zambia-china-an-intricate-relationship/.

Mwanza, Isaac. "China—Is She a Friend or Enemy of Africa." Lusaka Times, November 19, 2018. https://www.lusakatimes.com/2018/11/19/china-is-she-a-friend-or-enemy-of-africa/.

Nkoana-Mashabane, Maite. "Speech at the Heads of Missions Conference." Department of International Relations and Cooperation - South Africa. Government of Zambia, August 13, 2009. http://www.dfa.gov.za/docs/speeches/2009/mash0813.html.

Postel, Hannah. "Following the Money: Chinese Labor Migration to Zambia." migrationpolicy.org, August 16, 2018. https://www.migrationpolicy.org/article/following-money-chinese-labor-migration-zambia.

Renwick, Robin. *How to Steal a Country: State Capture and Hopes for the Future in South Africa.* London: Biteback Publishing, 2018.

"Road Development Agency 2016 Annual Report." Government of Zambia, 2016. http://www.rda.org.zm/jdownloads/Annual Reports/RDA Annual Report 2016 Email.pdf.

Rubio, Marco. "China's Threat to U.S. National Security Is Not a Game." Youtube, May 23, 2018. https://www.youtube.com/watch?v=UiRAW66wdV0

Rwizi, Lenon. "Prof PLO Lumumba Explains Why He Was Denied Entry into Zambia. Failure of Pan Africanism." Youtube, October 6, 2018. https://www.youtube.com/watch?v=sXR9GGkkP1k.

Sautman, Barry, and Yan Hairong. "Gilded Outside, Shoddy Within: The Human Rights Watch Report on Chinese Copper Mining in Zambia." *The Asia-Pacific Journal* 9, no. 52 (2011): 1–15.

Sautman, Barry. "Chinese Defilement Case: Racial Profiling in an African Model of Democracy." *Rutgers Race & Law Rev* 14, no. 87 (2013).

Sautman, Barry. "Racialization as Agency in Zambia-China Relations." In *Africa and China: How Africans and Their Governments Are Shaping Relations with China*, edited by Aleksandara W Gadzala, 127–48. London: Rowman & Littlefield, 2015.

Schaufelbuehl, Janick Marina, Sandra Bott, Jussi Hanhimäki, and Marco Wyss. "Non-Alignment, the Third Force, or Fence-Sitting: Independent Pathways in the Cold War." *The International History Review* 37, no. 5 (2015): 901–911.

Schrecker, John E. *The Chinese Revolution in Historical Perspective*. Westport, CT: Praeger, 2004.

Shimazu, Naoko. "Diplomacy As Theatre: Staging the Bandung Conference of 1955." *Modern Asian Studies* 48, no. 1 (2013): 225–252.

"State House Says It Has Received an Official Complaint from China over Victimization of Chinese People." Lusaka Times, November 19, 2018. https://www.lusakatimes.com/2018/11/19/state-house-says-it-has-received-an-official-complaint-from-china-over-victimization-of-chinese-people/.

van Dijk, Meine Pieter. "Introduction: Objectives of and Instruments for China 's New Presence in Africa." In *The New Presence of China in Africa,* edited by Meine Pieter van Dijk, 9–30. Hilversum: University of Amsterdam, 2009.

Vhumbunu, Clayton Hazvinei. "Enabling African Regional Infrastructure Renaissance through the China-Africa Partnership: A Trans-Continental Appraisal." *International Journal of China Studies* 7, no. 3 (2016): 271–300.

Wendt, Alexander. "Anarchy Is What States Make of It: The Social Construction of Power Politics." *International Organization* 46, no. 2 (1992): 391–425.

"Zambian President Says Donors Must Not Interfere." Reuters. Thomson Reuters, June 26, 2010. http://www.reuters.com/article/idINIndia-49672220100626.

Chapter 15

Chinese Investments in Africa

"Chopsticks Mercantilism"

George B. N. Ayittey

In the early parts of the twenty-first century, China became an important source of finance for African development. The continent's infrastructure was in disrepair; it had crumpled after decades of abject neglect and destruction from senseless civil wars. A substantial investment was—and still—needed to rebuild this infrastructure. According to a World Bank Report (2009), "the poor state of infrastructure in Sub-Saharan Africa—its electricity, water, roads and information and communications technology (ICT)—cuts national economic growth by two percentage points every year and reduces productivity by as much as 40 percent." To close the infrastructure gap, an annual spending of $93 billion would be required. As we noted above, Africa must spend US$360 billion on infrastructure by 2040, according to the African Development Bank (AfDB).

Africa, however, did not have the funds but had natural resources, which China needed to feed its economic machine galloping at a dizzying 9 percent clip in 2006. So, China went looking for resources in Africa and elsewhere, wooing African leaders with diplomatic platitudes about "equal terms" and lofty promises of foreign aid without conditions. It declared 2006 the "Year for Africa" and convened an Africa Conference in Beijing in November. That was music to the ears of African leaders, miffed at the West's insistence on conditionalities for its aid. Operating on the fallacious notion that "the enemy of my enemy is my friend," forty-eight African heads of state—mostly from Sub-Saharan Africa—tripped over themselves to the conference, threw caution to the wind, and began signing a blizzard of "infrastructure-for-resources" deals or exchanges. These deals were touted as win-win for both. As Benjamin (2017) noted,

Within a decade some 1 million Chinese had moved to Africa, while Chinese-African trade rose by a factor of 10, to $115 billion. Chinese direct investment skyrocketed to more than $9 billion from less than $0.5 billion in 2003 (although the United States remains the continent's biggest investor overall). China is now the largest trading partner for the continent (including North Africa). Chinese trade with Africa hit $222 billion in 2014, making China the region's biggest trading partner for a sixth consecutive year.[1]

Among the Chinese projects are the Husab uranium mine in Namibia, a Chinese military base in Djibouti, an $8 billion high-speed railway through Nigeria and a $4 billion, 466-mile transnational railway from Djibouti to Addis Ababa in Ethiopia are just a few of the Chinese projects already built or underway across the continent.[2] Chinese mining investments have increased 25-fold in just 10 years, from stakes in a few mines to more than 120 in 2015.[3]

However, in 2015 China's economy hit the skits, reducing demand for Africa's raw materials. To help ameliorate the discomfort, Chinese president Xi Jinping pledged $60 billion to the continent over three years in loans, export credits, and grants in December 2015.[4] Well-intentioned perhaps, but China is unlikely to remain an important source of finance for SDGs. Even then, new evidence has unfortunately emerged that questions the credibility of the Chinese source of finance.

Chinese investments in Africa did not produce the glorious "win-win" results most analysts had expected. In many countries, the "infrastructure-for-resources" deals were of dubious nature. Under many of those deals, some shady Chinese middlemen or syndicates undertook feasibility studies, estimated the cost of the infrastructure project, and then sought financing from China's EX-IM bank. For repayment, they demanded a quantum of the African country's resources to be shipped to China—essentially a barter deal.

Under this scheme, there was every incentive to inflate the cost and make the deal as "gargantuan" as possible. The higher the cost estimate, the larger the loan, and the larger the loan, the greater the quantum of resources that must be shipped to China for repayment. A high cost estimate obviously benefited the Chinese company that would undertake the construction as that translated into huge profits. And the more gargantuan the loan, the more swollen-headed the African head of state, who stood to extract much political mileage from it. For example, China offered ex-president, Capt. Moussa Dadis Camara of Guinea, a $7 billion "infrastructure-for-resources" deal in 2009. Guinea's GNP was only $4.5 billion. Throughout its history, no entity has given Guinea such a huge loan—and even one that exceeded its GNP; not even the World Bank came close.

What the recipient African country got in return was infrastructure at a grossly inflated cost that might or might not be delivered and some political

PR mileage. And if the African government wavered, the Chinese were willing to build a presidential palace or a sports stadium as "gifts from China."

Ordinarily, such a deal would be flagged by auditors and civil society, but in many cases, it was essentially a "closed shop" deal, shrouded in secrecy, and signed with mostly autocratic regimes. The deals were often opaque with no open and competitive bidding—all stacked in China's favor. If approved, it was a Chinese company that undertook the infrastructure projects with its own materials and workers, generating scant employment opportunities for the locals. And there was no protection against cost over-runs. A year or more later, the Chinese company could jack up the cost estimate, saying it erred in its initial estimation. Such was the case with the Bui Dam Project in Ghana. The total cost of the dam's construction was initially estimated at $622 million in 2009, but a cost review conducted in 2012 raised that amount by $168 million.[5]

We discuss three case studies.

A $23 BILLION DEAL FOR NIGERIA

A typical case was the $23 billion deal China signed with Nigeria—an oil-producing country that does not produce enough refined petroleum products for its people and must import 85 percent of them. China was to build three refineries with a combined capacity of 750,000 barrels a day that would exceed the domestic demand of some 450,000 b/d. In exchange, China wanted to grab one-sixth of Nigeria's 36 billion barrels of oil reserves.[6] The price tag of $8 billion for a refinery with the capacity of 250,000 b/d was outrageous as compared to these prices:

- In October 2002, President Obasanjo laid the foundation stone of the $1.5 billion Tonwei Refinery in Bayelsa State. The Tonwei Refinery will have an initial capacity of 100,000 bbl/d and it can be expanded to 200,000 bbl/d.[7]
- In Egypt, China will build a $2 billion refinery that would be the largest such plant in the Arab nation and Africa. The capacity of the refinery will annually amount to 15 million tons or 105 million barrels of oil or 287,671 bbl/d.[8]

Clearly, the price that China charges for building oil refineries varies wildly among African countries. Even more outrageous was what China was demanding in exchange—a sixth of Nigeria's 36 billion oil reserves. A simple multiplication by the price of oil at $107 a barrel in 2010 yielded $642 billion, which was what China was demanding for a $23 billion infrastructure project. In July 2012, Nigeria signed a memorandum of understanding with

Vulcan Petroleum Resources for a $4.5 billion project to build six refineries with a combined 180,000 barrel a day capacity. Vulcan, an affiliate of New York-based private equity firm Vulcan Capital Corp, aimed to have two of the refineries finished in under a year.[9]

A $3 BILLION DEAL FOR GHANA

In 2012, China offered Ghana a $3 billion loan on barter terms. The loan was to be used to rehabilitate portions of Ghana's dilapidated railway system, build infrastructure to capture gas that would otherwise be flared from oil production and the reconstruction of roads. In exchange for the loan, China demanded a daily supply of Ghana crude of 13,000 barrels—the entire portion of the Government of Ghana's share in Jubilee Oilfields—for the next fifteen and half years! The ruling NDC government, which had a majority in Parliament, agreed to sign the deal.[10] A few strokes on a cheap calculator would reveal that over the fifteen and half year period, 74 million barrels of oil would be shipped to China. The value at the price of crude oil of $107 in 2010 per barrel, works out to be $8.1 billion. Nice repayment for a loan of $3 billion.

THE $4 BILLION "LUNATIC EXPRESS" IN KENYA

On June 6, 2017, President Uhuru Kenyatta's opened a $4 billion on a 300-mile railway connecting the capital, Nairobi, to the Indian Ocean port of Mombasa—the most expensive infrastructure project since Kenya's independence 54 years ago and one-fifth of its national budget. China's Eximbank provided about 90 percent of the funding for the Nairobi-Mombasa project. The loan has already pushed the Kenyan debt above 50 percent of GDP, and imports of Chinese supplies and materials required to build the railway are making people anxious about Kenya's worsening trade imbalance with China.[11] Pamphlets heralding the arrival of the Express were in Chinese. Some staff members wore uniforms of red and gold — the colors of China's flag. Even the music on the train was not Kenyan. And to add insult to injury, a sculpture of Mao Zedong at the Mombasa station was actually that of Zheng He, a fifteenth-century Chinese explorer who sailed to East Africa.[12] In a related railway project, the launch of the Madaraka Express inter-county train was postponed because the managing director Atanas Maina said, "China Road and Bridge Corporation employees, who were key to the operations, had just arrived in the country and needed time to "go through the handover process."[13]

"SWEET AND SOUR" DEALS

In those "sweet and sour" deals (sweet for China but sour for Africa), there were additional costs. Since the deals were signed with mostly autocratic African governments, they were not transparent or subject to scrutiny. In many cases, they were secured through secrecy, outright bribery, kickbacks—for example, building a presidential palace for Sudan's despot, donating the blue tiles that adorn Robert Mugabe's new £7 million palace in Harare, a large Namibian presidential palace in Windhoek, and sports stadiums in Congo DR and Guinea.[14]

In July 2008, there was an outcry over the China-Niger oil deal. Civil rights groups called for a parliamentary inquiry into the $5 billion (£2.5 billion) contract and for scrutiny of how funds would be spent. China's state oil company was given oil exploration rights in Niger in June. "A mining union in Niger said the deal with China took place in the greatest of secrecy and with contempt for regulation."[15] In November 2011, Niger vowed to commission an audit of the Soraz oil refinery being built by Chinese oil company, CNCP, with a capacity of 20,000 barrels per day, after the price tag rose to $980 million from $600 million.[16] It may be noted that the same refinery with the same capacity built by China in Chad cost only $60 million.[17]

In July 2009, Namibian prosecutors began investigating allegations of bribery kickbacks on government contracts with China. One involved a contract to supply Namibia with scanners at security checkpoints. The Beijing-based Nuctech Companies Limited that makes the scanners, was headed until 2008 by the son of Hu Jintao, China's president. Nuctech was accused of living and paid $4.2 million in kickbacks to a Namibian front company.[18] Another investigation involved a Chinese contract to build a key railroad link as prosecutors burrowed through a web of corruption on deals with China.

On July 4, 2010, Luanda's general hospital evacuated 150 patients over worries that the four-year-old, $8 million Chinese-built structure could collapse, Angola's state radio reported.[19] In Guinea, the Chinese syndicate, Queensway, set up a joint venture, African Development Corporation (ADC), with 85 percent share and the government with the remaining 15 percent. Guinea has the world's largest reserves of bauxite and its largest untapped reserves of high-grade iron ore. ADC won exclusive rights to new mineral concessions in Guinea, including the right to negotiate oil-production contracts in the Gulf of Guinea. In return, the syndicate promised to invest up to $7 billion in housing, transport, and public utilities. Guinea's GDP is about $4.5 billion. Queensway syndicate was so pleased that it gave Guinea's military ruler, Captain Moussa Dadis Camara, a helicopter as a gift.

In Zimbabwe, the syndicate created a new company, called Sino-Zimbabwe Development Limited, which received rights to extract oil and gas and to mine gold, platinum, and chromium. In return, the company publicly promised to build railways, airports, and public housing. These pledges were valued at $8 billion by Mr. Mugabe's government.

But as *The Economist* (Aug 13, 2011) noted,

> Queensway syndicate failed to meet many of the obligations. Zimbabwe is still awaiting even a fraction of its promised infrastructure. Chinese goods sent to Africa are notorious for their poor quality. None of a shipment of 50 buses to Zimbabwe worked and an order for 250 more was suspended. Of three MA60 passenger jets the Chinese sent to Mugabe, one never managed to fly, one had to make an emergency landing at Victoria Falls, injuring many passengers, and the third caught fire on take-off in Harare in Nov 2008. All were grounded. And Guinea never received the 100 public buses that were meant to arrive within 45 days of the 2009 deal.[20]

The achievement of some SDGs would be difficult with the influx of Chinese goods and workers. Clothing manufacturers in Lesotho, Nigeria, and Zambia complain bitterly of cheap Chinese goods destroying their markets and jobs. In Nigeria, the flood of Chinese products has devastated Kano's manufacturing sector. In 1982, 500 factories churned out textile products in Kano, but fewer than 100 remain operational today, most at far less than full capacity. Kano's Kwari textile market, the biggest in West Africa, now trade Chinese fabrics and clothing. A decade ago, 80 percent of the fabric sold at Kwari was made in Nigeria, compared with 5 percent in 2012.[21] There are more beggars and other visible signs of poverty in Kano than ever before. It is not far-fetched to link the collapse of the textile industry in northern Nigeria with the rise of the terrorist group, *Boko Haram.*

Textile factories no longer offer Africa's youth employment opportunities and youth unemployment has now become a ticking time bomb in Africa. Disenchanted youth disillusioned over lack of jobs started the Arab Spring in 2011.[22] Other youth left their countries and embarked on dangerous crossings across the Sahara Desert to seek greener pastures in Europe, with thousands drowning in the Mediterranean Sea. Still, other unemployed youth fell prey to radical ideas and were recruited by terrorist groups.

Unable to compete with Chinese imports, textile factories in Lesotho closed in 2003 and 2004, throwing over 5,000 workers out of their jobs. In South Africa, the textile union said some 100,000 jobs have been lost as Chinese synthetic fabrics replaced cotton prints in street markets across Africa. In 2007, the unions threatened to boycott anyone selling Chinese products.[23] In Ghana,

> there were more than 20 textile firms that employed more than 20,000 people in 1995. In 2012, the industry had only 4 textile factories, employing less than

3,000 Ghanaians. The country's once-thriving textile market is now flooded with Chinese substandard textile products, therefore surging the unemployment rate. The situation has further deteriorated with the textile companies currently in operation now employing some 2,961 people.[24]

Africans derived little benefit from the "infrastructure-for-resources" deals with China since they offered scant employment opportunities. Not only did they destroy textile jobs, but China brought its workers into Africa. The Chinese also invaded sectors traditionally reserved for locals. In July 2011, shop owners in Uganda's capital, Kampala, shut their businesses to protest against a weakened currency and the influx of Chinese traders."[25] In August 2011, Ghana began arresting foreign nationals, mostly Chinese, illegally engaged in artisanal gold mining.

Twenty-seven Chinese nationals engaged in illegal gold mining activities, popularly called "galamsey" operating in the Ankobra River at Kutukrom, near Prestea, Sikane-Asem and Tumantu in the Western Region, have been arrested by a joint military-police-immigration team. The police also seized from them three pump action rifles, 41 pieces of BB live cartridges, two walkie-talkies, 19 Chinese passports, four mobile phones, a metal safe with keys and their machines.[26]

Further, the Chinese deals enriched the corrupt ruling elites. Angola, Nigeria, Sudan, and Zimbabwe are examples where the trade and oil deals with China have not benefited the poor. Recall the plunder of the Marange diamond fields in Zimbabwe, adjudged to be one of the largest in the world. Chinese investments and aid, disingenuously described as with no strings attached, is doing grave harm to Africa. First, it has been propping up hideously repressive regimes in Guinea, Sudan, and Zimbabwe.[27] Second, China's increased engagement with Africa impedes the continent's halting steps toward democratic accountability and better governance. The West made its aid conditional on progress toward reform in several areas, including democratic pluralism, the rule of law, human rights, reduction of graft, and improved access to education. China never required these challenging commitments. Any rogue regime that spits venom at World Bank conditionalities was welcomed by China.

Indeed in 2002, an International Monetary Fund (IMF) team went to Angola to help the country put its financial affairs in order. It was flabbergasted by Angola's robber economy and even more by the nonchalance of its leading officials. Though the regime contracted $3 billion worth of loans in 2001 alone, one senior official told the IMF team that Angola had taken out no commercial loans in recent years.[28] In March 2002, the IMF reported that despite years of assistance, the government's finances remained hopelessly opaque, that officials had fended off all demands for reform and thus that "it would be very difficult for Angola to formulate a meaningful poverty-reduction strategy." A "donors' conference" was scheduled for that July. But after the IMF report, the United States and Britain pulled out, and Angola, still deeply in debt despite billions in oil revenue, was left to bitterly contemplate its options. Luckily for Angola, a new benefactor had just materialized. China came to the rescue with a $2 billion oil deal.

Several other African countries told Western donors and multilateral financial institutions to jump into the Atlantic Ocean. Most disturbing, the West caved. Alarmed by the inroads China was making in Africa, the European Union hurriedly convened an EU-Africa Summit in April 2014. It brought together more than 60 EU and African leaders, and a total of 90 delegations, to discuss the future of EU-Africa relations and reinforce links between the two continents. Not to be outdone, the United States organized its own US Africa Summit in August 2014, with heads of state and senior government officials from 50 African countries. Nowhere on the two summit agendas was reform even mentioned—a clear license to dictators to do what they wanted. But there has been some backlash. The continent that suffered so much from Western exploitation and oppression is not likely to take another form of exploitation from any foreign quarter.

RISING ANTI-CHINESE SENTIMENTS

China is not to blame for deals that went sour. It knows what it wants in Africa and cares less about what it takes to get it. It will bribe if it must. It built a $200 million glitzy new headquarters for the African Union in Addis Ababa.[29] China sees no evil nor hears no evil in Africa—precisely the kind of posture African dictators, tired of Western lectures, relish.

China drives a hard bargain and should not be faulted.[30] The problem has been African leaders who adamantly refuse to learn from their history, which teaches that every foreign entity that goes to Africa does so to pursue its interest. Americans go to Africa to pursue American interests, the French to pursue French interests, Arabs, Arab interests, and so on. Certainly, the Chinese are not in Africa because they love Africans so much. This is a perspective that African leaders needed to understand.

Africa leaders seldom pursued African interests, except their own, which is stirring up discontent in many countries. The initial enthusiasm that greeted China in Africa has now cooled. "There is mounting objection to China's deepening forays into Africa," said *News Africa* (March 2007). Former president Thabo Mbeki of South Africa warned against allowing

China's push for raw materials to become a "new form of neo-colonialist adventure" with African raw materials exchanged for shoddily manufactured imports and little attention to developing an impoverished continent.[31] Rene N'Guetta Kouassi, the head of the African Union's economic affairs department echoed this warning: "Africa must not jump blindly from one type of neocolonialism into Chinese-style neo-colonialism."[32] Some African commentators are less charitable, denouncing what they see as "chopsticks mercantilism," alluding to the chopsticks dexterity with which China picks off at its leisure platinum from Zimbabwe, copper from Zambia, and oil from Angola, Nigeria, and Sudan.

The backlash against Chinese investments has been particularly strong in Zambia due to workplace accidents, poor working conditions and below-minimum wage pay at Chinese-run copper mines. More than 50 Zambian workers died in a 2005 mine explosion and dozens of others were sacked by Chinese security guards in 2006. In the run-up to Zambia's general election in September 2006, the opposition leader Michael Sata made China's investment in the country a campaign issue. According to Sata, Chinese businesses employ relatively few Zambians. "Our Chinese don't bring in any equipment or create any sensible employment. In fact, to every Zambian in a Chinese company, there are about 15 Chinese. Sata called the Chinese profiteers, not investors, in a country where unemployment is about 50 percent, and more than 73 percent of people live in poverty. Chinese investment has not added any value to the people of Zambia," he charged.[33] In a blatant show of arrogance, Chinese Ambassador Li Baodong warned Zambians that China might sever diplomatic ties with Zambia if Sata became president and recognized Taiwan. The ambassador also raised the specter of a halt in Chinese investment. But Zambians were unfazed; they elected Michael Sata in Sept 2011, but he died in October 2014. It is probably too late for Zambia. When it defaulted on its loans, China seized control of ZESCO, the country's power utility company, and the Kaunda International Airport (*The Lusaka Times*, September 4, 2018). China was also poised to seize control of Kenya's port of Mombasa after loan default in a strategy widely criticized as deep debt-trap diplomacy.

Militants in Nigeria's volatile oil-producing region detonated a car bomb in May 2006 and issued a warning that investors and officials from China would be "treated as thieves" and targeted in future attacks. A spokesman for the Movement for the Emancipation of the Niger Delta (MEND) said in an e-mail sent to news organizations that the car-bomb attack was "the final warning" before the militants turned their attention to oil workers, storage facilities, bridges, offices, and other "soft oil industry targets."[34] In Ethiopia, the Ogaden National Liberation Front (ONLF) has warned Chinese energy exploration companies against operating in the Ogaden Region. In April

2007, nine Chinese workers were killed in an attack by armed men on an oil field in eastern Ethiopia.[35]

We have discussed this Africa-China relationship at length because this turn of events is alarming and must be condemned in no uncertain terms. Trade with China or any other foreign nation should bring benefits to both parties. Attacks on the Chinese in Africa will not rectify the imbalance. Perversely, Chinese forays into Africa have had a beneficial effect. It has drawn others—the EU, Russia, India, Turkey, and some Middle Eastern countries—to Africa in what *The Economist* magazine (March 7, 2019) called "the new scramble for Africa."

> Chinese expansion has worried other Asian powers. Japan is enlarging its base in Djibouti. India is developing a network of radar and listening posts around the Indian Ocean, though plans for a base in Seychelles were blocked by the archipelago last year. In March the Indian army will host its first military exercises with a number of African countries, including Tanzania, Kenya and South Africa. (*The Economist*, March 7, 2019)

NOTES

1. Benjamin, Matthew. "Sub-Saharan Africa: Will It Regain Its Economic Footing?" *Sage Business Researcher*, June 7, 2017.

2. See *The New York Times*, May 13, 2017, http://tinyurl.com/la2a8nl.

3. See *The New York Times Magazine*, May 2, 2017, http://tinyurl.com/msm8eyx.

4. See *The Wall Street Journal*, December 4, 2015, http://tinyurl.com/my4g8ko.

5. See "China is building a third of Africa's new power capacity" Climate Home, April 7, 2016 www.hydroworld.com/articles/2008/09/china-signs-financing-for-gha nas-400-mw-bui.html.

6. See *Financial Times,* May 15, 2010: http://on.ft.com/wkh4vn.

7. See *Vanguard*, October 21, 2002. http://allafrica.com/stories/200210230287 .html.

8. See *Reuters*, May 2, 2010. http://af.reuters.com/article/newsOne/idAFJOE 64105S20100502.

9. See Tim Cocks and Camillus Eboh, "Nigeria signs $4.5 bln refineries deal with Vulcan Petroleum," Reuters, July 3, 2012 http://www.reuters.com/article/ozatp-nig eria-refineries-idAFJOE86200820120703.

10. See *Daily Guide*, February 29, 2012: http://bit.ly/xfmQdP.

11. See Kimiko de Freytas-Tamura, "Kenyans Fear Chinese-Backed Railway Is Another 'Lunatic Express,'" *The New York Times*, June 8, 2017. https://mo bile.nytimes.com/2017/06/08/world/africa/kenyans-fear-chinese-backed-railway -is-another-lunatic-express.html?mwrsm=facebook&referer=http%3a%2f%2fm.fac ebook.com.

12. Ibid.

13. See "Launch of Madaraka Express Inter-county Train Postponed" *Daily Nation*, June 30, 2017 http://www.nation.co.ke/news/Madaraka-Express-inter-county -train-launch-postponed/1056-3994696-ruedmqz/index.html.

14. See RW Johnson, "China Empire-Builder Sweep Up Africa's Riches," *The Sunday Times*, July 16, 2006 https://www.thetimes.co.uk/article/chinas-empire-b uilders-sweep-up-african-riches-lgr0ngvlmms.

15. See, "Outcry Over China-Niger Oil Deal," *BBC*, July 30, 2008 http://news.bbc .co.uk/2/hi/africa/7534315.stm.

16. See *Reuters*, November 24, 2011.

17. See *Reuters*, November 24, 2011.

18. See Sharon LaFraniere and John Grobler, "China Spreads Aid in Africa, With a Catch," *The New York Times*, September 21, 2009; p.A1 and A12. http://www.nyti mes.com/2009/09/22/world/africa/22namibia.html?_r=1&ref=africa.

19. "Chinese-built Hospital Risks Collapse," *AFP*, June 6, 2010 http://www.terr adaily.com/reports/Chinese-built_hospital_risks_collapse_in_Angola_state_radio_9 99.html.

20. "The Queensway Syndicate and the Africa Trade." *The Economist*, August 13, 2011. https://www.economist.com/briefing/2011/08/13/the-queensway-syndicate- and-the-africa-trade.

21. See Center for Research and Development, September 20, 2012. "The Collapse of the Textile Industry in Kano affects Africa's largest textile market" http: //www.crdng.org/the-state-of-kano-textile-industries-and-its-effect-on-the-nigerian-e conomy-a-study-of-the-kantin-kwari-market-in-kano-state/.

22. It was triggered by this self-immolation of an unemployed graduate called Mohammed Boazizi, a Tunisian. Unable to find work, he set up a fruit cart by a roadside to sell some vegetables. A policewoman demanded to see his permit; he did not have any. Thereupon, the policewoman seized his cart. When he protested, the policewoman's allegedly spat in his face—a contumacious indignity in the Arab world. When he went to the Ministry of interior to complain, the door was slammed in his face. Thereupon, he doused himself in gasoline and lit a match on December 10, 2010. Street protests erupted across Tunisia. Within one month, longtime dictator, Ben Ali, had fled to Saudi Arabia. The revolution spread to Egypt, Libya, and the rest of the Arab world.

23. See *Progressive Economy*, July 30, 2010 http://tasceconomists.blogspot.com/ 2010/07/china-iii-beijings-scramble-for-africa.html.

24. *See Daily Graphic*, April 30, 2012, p.40.

25. See "Uganda Traders Close Shops in Protest," *BBC*, July 6, 2011 http://www .bbc.com/news/world-africa-14053516.

26. See *Daily Graphic*, March 12, 2012.

27. Three strings are attached. First, the recipient or borrower shall have no dip- lomatic relationship with Taiwan. Second, construction of infrastructure must be undertaken by Chinese firms. Third, all the materials and labor must be Chinese. In other words, China's loans are 100 percent tied.

28. See James Traub, "China's Africa Adventure," *New York Times Magazine*, Nov 19, 2006 http://www.nytimes.com/2006/11/19/magazine/19china.html.

29. It was widely speculated that every room is bugged. Indeed, "The African Union's shiny new headquarters was built and paid for by the Chinese government, as a gift to its "African friends." But when the building was officially opened in 2012, China left a backdoor into the African Union's computer network, allowing it to access the institution's secrets at will. "According to several sources within the institution, all sensitive content could be spied on by China," wrote Le Monde. "It's a spectacular leak of data, spread from January 2012 to January 2017." Once the problem was discovered, African Union officials acted quickly to fix it. The organization acquired its own servers, and began encrypting its communications" *(Mail&Guardian*, January 29, 2018 https://mg.co.za/article/2018-01-29-how-china -spied-on-the-african-unions-computers).

30. Remember the aphorism, "no one can exploit you without your consent."
31. See *AFP*, September 30, 2009.
32. See *AFP*, September 30, 2009.
33. See *The Washington Post*, September 25, 2006; p.A16.
34. See *Washington Post*, May 1, 2006; P.A15.
35. See *China Daily*, April 24, 2007 http://www.chinadaily.com.cn/china/2007-04 /24/content_858956.htm.

REFERENCES

"9 Chinese Workers Killed in Ethiopia." *China Daily*, April 24, 2007. http://www .chinadaily.com.cn/china/2007-04/24/content_858956.htm.

Allison, Simon. "How China Spied on the African Union's Computers." *The Mail & Guardian*, January 29, 2018. https://mg.co.za/article/2018-01-29-how-china-spied -on-the-african-unions-computers.

Benjamin, Matthew. "Sub-Saharan Africa: Will It Regain Its Economic Footing?" *Sage Business Researcher*, June 7, 2017.

"China Signs Financing for Ghana's 400-MW Bui." *Hydro Review*, September 2, 2019. http://www.hydroworld.com/articles/2008/09/china-signs-financing-for-g hanas-400-mw-bui.html.

"Chinese-Built Hospital Risks Collapse in Angola." *State Radio*, July 6, 2010. http: //www.terradaily.com/reports/Chinese-built_hospital_risks_collapse_in_Angola_ state_radio_999.html.

Cocks, Tim. "Nigeria Signs $4.5 Bln Refineries Deal with Vulcan Petroleum." *Reuters*. Thomson Reuters, July 3, 2012. http://www.reuters.com/article/ozatp-nig eria-refineries-idAFJOE86200820120703.

Darby, Megan. "IEA: China Is Building a Third of Africa's New Power Capacity." *Climate Home News*. Climate Home, February 5, 2016. https://www.climatec hangenews.com/2016/07/05/iea-china-has-built-a-third-of-africas-power-capac ity/.

"Egypt to Build Its Largest Oil Refinery: Agency." *Reuters*. Thomson Reuters, May 2, 2010. http://af.reuters.com/article/newsOne/idAFJOE64105S20100502.

Freytas-Tamura, Kimiko de. "Kenyans Fear Chinese-Backed Railway Is Another 'Lunatic Express.'" *The New York Times*. Accessed March 9, 2020. https://mo bile.nytimes.com/2017/06/08/world/africa/kenyans-fear-chinese-backed-railway -is-another-lunatic-express.html?mwrsm=facebook&referer=http://m.facebook. com.

Johnson, R W. "China's Empire Builders Sweep up African Riches." *The Sunday Times*, March 16, 2010. https://www.thetimes.co.uk/article/chinas-empire-builders -sweep-up-african-riches-lgr0ngvlmms.

LaFraniere, Sharon, and John Grobler. "China Spreads Aid in Africa, With a Catch." *The New York Times*, September 21, 2009. http://www.nytimes.com/2009/09/22/w orld/africa/22namibia.html?_r=1&ref=africa.

Larmer, Brook. "Is China the World's New Colonial Power?" *The New York Times*, May 2, 2017. http://tinyurl.com/msm8eyx.

"Madaraka Express Inter-County Train Launch Postponed." *Daily Nation*, June 30, 2017. http://www.nation.co.ke/news/Madaraka-Express-inter-county-train-launch -postponed/1056-3994696-ruedmqz/index.html.

McGroarty, Patrick. "China's Xi Pledges $60 Billion for Africa Development Over Three Years." *WSJ. The Wall Street Journal*, December 4, 2015. http://tinyurl.com /my4g8ko.

Oyadongha, Samuel. "Nigeria: Obasanjo Lays Foundation Stone of First Private Refinery." *Vanguard Newspaper*, Nigeria. AllAfrica, October 21, 2002. https://al lafrica.com/stories/200210230287.html.

Perlez, Jane, and Yufan Huang. "Behind China's $1 Trillion Plan to Shake Up the Economic Order." *The New York Times*, May 13, 2017. http://tinyurl.com/la2a8nl.

Ross, Will. "Outcry over China-Niger Oil Deal." *BBC News*. BBC, July 30, 2008. http://news.bbc.co.uk/2/hi/africa/7534315.stm.

Sweeney, Paul. "China (III) - Beijing's Scramble for Africa." progressive-economy@ tasc, July 30, 2010. http://tasceconomists.blogspot.com/2010/07/china-iii-beijings -scramble-for-africa.html.

Traub, James. "China's African Adventure." *The New York Times*, November 19, 2006. http://www.nytimes.com/2006/11/19/magazine/19china.html.

"The Queensway Syndicate and the Africa Trade." *The Economist*, August 13, 2011. https://www.economist.com/briefing/2011/08/13/the-queensway-syndicate-and-t he-africa-trade.

"Uganda Traders Close Shops in Protest." *BBC News*. BBC, July 6, 2011. http://www .bbc.com/news/world-africa-14053516.

Conclusion

The Chinese and a Continent
Made Fragile by Its Leaders

Sabella O. Abidde and Tokunbo A. Ayoola

INTRODUCTION

Africa cannot and must not close its doors to international engagements—be it political, social, cultural, or economic. And especially in this instance, she must not close its door to, but instead, engage China and its state-owned enterprises, governmental and nongovernmental organizations and private individuals that wants to invest in and or partner with their African counterparts. The fact is that Africa cannot afford to be and should not be a closed society. However, in her engagement with the Chinese and other nations, nationals, and economic and political entities, she must be smart and proactive. States and societies on the continent must pay attention—but more than paying attention, they must pursue their national interest and the interest of future generations. Furthermore, Africans must not for a second or a day think that China, the United States, the Europeans, or any non-Africans will come to rescue them in terms of growth and development. Only Africans can and must rescue Africa and Africans.

For several decades, Africans have relied on colonial-Europe. That reliance has not stopped. The economic dependency is such that the Europeans—alone or in concert with the United States—could bring the entire continent on its knees. That the African economy is wholly dependent on the West is incontrovertible. This is also the case with Africa's political system. Most African leaders cannot formulate and/or implement public policy without the say-so of Western capitals. From the colonial era until now, most African leaders have been puppets: obedient servants of Western governments and leaders, and so also are the elites. As with the political leaders, most of the elite class do not have a strong and independent mind. They worry most about their private interest and gain and the gain and interest of their friends and

345

family—to the detriment of the national interest and the interest of most of their fellow citizens.

Even though one might be worried about the motives and motivation of the Chinese, the greatest concern is the motives and motivation of many of the leaders and elites on the continent. During the Trans-Atlantic Slave Trade, many leaders—economic, political, religious, and traditional—did not do right by their fellow African. They were complicit in the slave trade just as they were complicit during the colonial era. In the years since independence, one can only point to a few who have been true patriots who genuinely love their respective country and people and did what was commendable most of the time for the benefit of their respective countries and societies. Their greed, excesses, maladministration, stealing, and stupidity have been unrivaled anywhere in the world. The Chinese need not worry: many leaders and their proxies will make the first move—encourage the Chinese to short-change the government and the people.

THE UNITED STATES AND EUROPE: FEIGNING CONCERN FOR AFRICA

The allegations against Beijing, Chinese companies, and individuals engaged with/in Africa are legion: (1) that Chinese enterprises employ Chinese at the upper/managerial level while employing Africans only at the lower level; (2) that China ferociously grabs lands; (3) that Chinese investments are designed to trap African governments; (4) that the Chinese are indifferent to bad governance and weak institutions, growing theft, and corruption; (5) that China is interested only in Africa's resources; and (6) that in the long run, China is interested in dominating and colonizing Africa.[1] Finally, China, the Europeans and the United States argue, is only interested in economic gains and not the growth and development of the continent. In the opinion of the West, the totality of these allegation points to a bad strategy that will not help African states and societies.

The recent expression of concern for Africa by the United States and the European countries is should be considered hypocritical—especially on the part of the Europeans who had been on the continent for more than a century; yet, they have not had an enviable impact on the continent. Other than the pitiable investments, minuscule FDI, and negligible provision of infrastructures—what did colonial-Europe do for Africa other than carting away its resources and subjugating the people? What had postcolonial Europe done for Africa other than the puppetization of African leaders and the pauperization of the people? On all counts, Western Europe has been bad for Africans and so have the United States who, under the guise of freedom, democracy, and open markets, has joined in impoverishing Africa.

Furthermore, since the end of the Cold War, at least, Western Europe and the United States seem to have given up on Africa.[2] China's rise and the wars in the Middle East also pulled away resources and attention. And now, with Washington raising doubts about global agreements on issues like free trade and climate change, Beijing has more leverage to push its initiatives and show its capacity for global leadership. President Trump's disdain for the Trans-Pacific Partnership has already made Beijing's trade proposals, which exclude the United States, more appealing.[3]

Even long before this time, the continent is seen as a backwater, the Dark Continent, an unknowable place that was only good for their resources, and as a dumping ground for excess and/or inferior goods. The West did not consider Africa in its long-term plan. But instead, they encouraged corruption, encouraged illiberal regimes, and encouraged many of the economic and political excesses African leaders and elites engaged in. With the Chinese— at least on the surface, things seem different: they have publicly expressed respect and appear to consider African sensibilities. The reason for this may be because China, like Africa, was a poor and struggling economy and for a while, fighting against colonialism and injustice.

So, if China is in Africa to serve its own economic and political interest, it is no different from what the Europeans did and continues to do which has lasted more than 100 years. The West, it spears is vexed because China seems to be doing what they could not do, and in the process acquiring power and influence that might soon exceed the collective power and influence of the West. At this point, there is nothing to suggest that China will loosen its grips on the continent, or that the West will accelerate to catch up or surpass the Chinese. In all of this, however, it is up to states and societies in Africa to wise up—not only to China but also to the West. To do this, Africans must look for a new generation of leaders to renegotiate with the global hegemon, redefine their role and place within the international system, and earn the respect of the global community. As things are neither China nor the West would ever voluntarily behave righteously toward a weak and submissive people.

Africans and their leaders, for the most part, put themselves in their current position—a position that is not likely to change for the better anytime soon. According to Sanders Moody, "It is up to African governments to maximize the endowment of natural resources when entering into business relationships with China. A specific recommendation to African governments and leaders is that they should negotiate better deals and concessions with China guaranteeing better employment for locals including higher wages, development, and patronage of local businesses, adherence to labor standards, environmental degradation, and internship for African students and young professionals."[4] Moody went on to say that:

African leaders and government officials must be politically mindful that for the Chinese Communist Party to stay in power the Chinese economy must continue to grow and the Chinese population must be supplied with the consumer goods it needs and increasingly desires. The magnitude of China's demand for African natural resources is enormous. This leverage is in the hands of African leaders. Africa's leaders and government officials must use their enormous leverage to their advantage for the benefit of the people of Africa.[5]

AFRICA: ITS LEADERS AND ITS FUTURE

The typical African head of government is lily-livered, spineless. About the only time they exhibit courage is when they are stealing, or when fanning the amber of ethnic or religious antagonism—or when they are about to plunge their country into senseless wars. Many of these leaders cannot look at their foreign counterparts in the eyes. Many do not dare to say "No!" and walk away if the prevailing condition does not favor their country and its people. And far too many of them do not have the moral credential or authority to condemn internal or external abominations. When you take a critical look at the continent, you cannot but be dismayed and dejected by what you see — not just in terms of poverty and hopelessness—but also by the scale of human suffering and man's inhumanity to man. Africa, Robert Rotberg tells us,

> has long been saddled with poor, even malevolent, leadership: predatory klep-tocrats, military-installed autocrats, economic illiterates, and puffed-up postur-ers. By far the most egregious examples come from Nigeria, the Democratic Republic of the Congo, and Zimbabwe—countries that have been run into the ground despite their abundant natural resources. But these cases are by no means unrepresentative: by some measures, 90 percent of sub-Saharan African nations have experienced despotic rule in the last three decades. Such leaders use power as an end in itself, rather than for the public good; they are indiffer-ent to the progress of their citizens (although anxious to receive their adulation); they are unswayed by reason and employ poisonous social or racial ideologies; and they are hypocrites, always shifting blame for their countries' distress.[6]

And indeed, under these leaders, infrastructure in many African countries has fallen into disrepair, currencies, and the economy have been downgraded, and real prices have inflated dramatically, while job availability, quality health care, and education standards, and life expectancy have declined. Besides, general security has deteriorated, crime and corruption have increased, much-needed public funds have flowed into hidden bank accounts, and officially sanctioned ethnic discrimination has become prevalent.[7] The irony is that

Africans themselves don't think much of themselves, their peoples, and their land, and have, for the most part, contributed to the continuing underdevelopment, chaos, and anarchy that have come to characterize the continent. Long before the Trans-Atlantic and the Indian Ocean slave trade, Africans have been trading and dehumanizing their peoples. Beginning in the 1960s, in one country after another, African presidents and prime ministers have been physically chaining and mentally abusing their people. They collaborate with foreign and domestic agents and saboteurs to loot their resources. Not only are these leaders involved in enslaving their people, but they are also involved in the economic exploitation of the continent. Africans are doing to Africa what despicable Europeans did to Africa from the fourteenth century onward.

The scramble for Africa was necessitated by commercial greed, territorial ambition, proselytism, reckless adventures, and political rivalry. Today, the Chinese and the European need not plan for the partitioning and looting of the continent. African leaders and African elites have been doing the partitioning and economic exploitation on their behalf. The Chinese, the Israelis, the Indians, the Lebanese, and every other big, small, and mid-size powers have been roaming the African woodland, digging into the African soil for minerals, and exploring the oceans and waterways for treasures. For the old and new powerhouses, Africa is their playground, their dumpster, their killing field, their Wall Street, and their spit-bucket. While they are feeding off the fat and riches of the continent, Africans themselves—much like some of their forefathers—are on the sideline as though watching a freak show. There is nothing freakish about what is happening to Africa and Africans. Nothing is amusing about five hundred years of exploitation, servility, and bastardization.

Social historians and chroniclers of events in and around the continent cannot but notice the fact that the average Africans give their leaders permission to exploit and abuse and to steal and mismanage their resources. In their respective countries, African leaders steal and commit all sorts of crimes and iniquities with the full acquiesce of their people. In turn, African leaders green-light foreign powers and foreign entrepreneurs the power to exploit, subjugate, and to steal their continent's resources. From Tunisia to South Africa, from Nigeria to Djibouti, and from Mauritania to Tanzania, the reality of the continent is the same: lacking in economic power, lacking in technological know-how, and lacking in political will.

No one is denying the fact that there have been some improvements. For instance, the incidence of coups has fallen sharply. But they now tamper with the constitution or manipulate members of the congress to enable them to engage in tenure elongation. They are good at jailing, exiling, and killing members of the opposition party or citizens who openly disagree with their vision, policies, and intentions. And when you have leaders who have been in power for more than a decade, you can be sure that such leaders are detrimental to the good and welfare of the state and society. No matter how popular a leader may be—beyond a decade in office—he or she is on the way to becoming a god. Well, you know how gods can be: acquisitive, depraved, temperamental, egotistic, and bloodthirsty. Under these and other inhumane conditions, you cannot speak of an African Renaissance.

CHINESE ACTIVITIES: BLAME AFRICAN LEADERS

That China's engagement with states and societies in Africa is a "win-win" for all is damn lie. That there are no "no strings attached" to China's economic activities on the continent is also a bloody lie. These are two of the greatest lies ever told to and believed by African leaders and the elites. They fell for it. Muhammadu Buhari of Nigeria fell for it. Paul Kagame of Rwanda fell for it. Cyril Ramaphosa fell for it. So did fifty-one other African leaders—and their predecessors. What a gullible lot, a gullible continent, and a gullible people. The relationship with the Chinese, as with the Europeans and the United States, is unequal, a master-servant relationship. No African president can claim to operate or relate to the president of China at the same level. None! The president of Nigeria, as with the president of South Africa, Rwanda, Uganda, Tanzania, Mozambique, Madagascar, Egypt, Sudan, Senegal, or Mauritania all bow before whoever is the general secretary of the Communist Party of China: the supreme leader of China.

They also bow to the premier of the People's Republic of China and other lowly placed members of the Communist Party of China, protocol officers, and diplomatic corps. The Forum on China–Africa Cooperation (FOCAC) is one of the most pitiable forums at which to watch African leaders as they tremble before the Chinese leader, Xi Jinping. The Almighty Leader who beats and dehumanizes their people comes to FOCAC and bows and tremble before the Chinese leader—begging for loans and investment and infrastructures. The tyrants, the absolute leaders, the big men of African politics, the gun-toting buffoons, and the survival strategists—at FOCAC and other forums, they are reduced to boy-boy, errand boys, and bootlickers.

Today, as with the last two or so decades, the Chinese are acquiring millions of acres of land for agricultural and nonagricultural purposes. Acre by acre, they are buying up Africa—without African leaders and the elites raising objections. As in the colonial era when African businessmen, the tribal chief, leaders, and elites looked the other ways when the Europeans where exploiting and looting lands and resources, so are their successors as the Chinese are deviously grabbing lands and resources. This begs the question: how many lands or landed properties do African governments and

Africans own in China? How many acres of lands have they acquired in the last quarter-century? And even if they could afford it, would Beijing allow it? Yet, they are all over Africa grabbing all that is tangible today and that might be tomorrow.

During the colonial era—a time when most Africans could not read or write—a little-read or poorly read European could show up on the continent and lord over the continent's best and brightest. Things have not changed in that regard. Today, a little-read or poorly read Chinese could show up on the continent and instantly becomes the master and lord over some of the best and brightest the continue has to offer. Why? It boils down to poverty, greed, and low self-esteem on the part of the Africans. Beijing would never send its best and brightest to Africa. Well, maybe a sprinkle here and there temporarily. They usually would only send their second, third-rate, or fourth-rate experts. These lower-class members of the Chinese society and government are the same people that would go on to wine and dine with African leaders—same leaders that bark at and bite the best and brightest of their societies.

Even a private Chinese citizen out on his accord could strike it rich and become lord and master within a decade. Why? Because the same African minister, governor, bank manager, or president who refuses to host and listen to the business proposal of a compatriot in the diaspora would gladly welcome the Chinese. Why? Again, it boils down to money and other inducements and poor self-esteem. For most African leaders, foreign is better. Foreign is superior. They see the Chinese; they begin to salivate for money. They see the Europeans and the Americans; they begin to salivate for money and travel visa for themselves and their immediate family members. It is never about the national interest of their country or administration.

The Chinese should be held accountable if their activities are deemed reprehensible. But they and they alone should not shoulder all the blames. But for acquiescing African leaders and elites, they would not dare. Genuine leadership is absent on the continent.[8] They have allowed China and its companies and citizens to overrun the continent. Essentially, therefore, the fault lies with Africans—not the Chinese. Nonetheless, China and its citizens must be careful in terms of how they treat Africans in Africa and Africans who live in China. The blatant and subtle discrimination must stop—the insults, the side-looks, the put-downs, the superciliousness, the violence, the formal and informal shenanigans, and the racial discriminations. All these must stop forthwith. Beijing cannot continue to claim that such behaviors and attitudes by their citizens are isolated and insignificant. No, they are not! Unfortunately for them, and fortunately for Africa, the younger generation of Africans are not as docile as their parents and grandparents were. The cruelty toward Africans living in China, and the ill-treatment of Africans in Africa, is likely to result in equivalent retaliation that would be exorbitant for China to bear.

The older Africans may have tolerated the inhumanity visited on them by the West; the younger generations are not likely to tolerate the rudeness and cruelty of the Chinese. If the government and people of China think they can continue to maltreat Africans, they are helping to hasten the day of reckoning.

CHINA: AFTER AFRICA WHAT'S NEXT, WHERE'S NEXT?

There is a huge presence of China and Chinese state-owned enterprises in many parts of the world. This is especially true in the Global South. And in places like Africa, their hegemonic presence, in the second decade of the twenty-first century, is almost unrivaled. And China—unless there are genuine revolutionary events in Africa—is not like to leave or loosen their grip on the continent. And so the facts remain that the more they invest in Africa, the deeper it will dig into Africa's soil and ocean; the more loans they provide, the greater the return on their investment; the more infrastructure they provide, the more commanding-influence it will have. And should they encounter an unfavorable political or social condition in one country or region, they will hold back until conditions improve while at the same time intensifying their efforts in other countries and regions. China, as with the West, has come to stay. Permanently! Africa is no longer for Africans; Africa now belongs to anyone, any institution, any oligarchy, any crime syndicate, any corporation, and any country bold and clever and cunning and courageous and thuggish enough to venture into its political, economic, and social space.[9] This is not even a second Scramble for Africa,[10] it is the bold-face stealing of the continent's resources and the subjugation of its people which has resulted in the penury of a very substantial portion of humanity.

China, a once backward economy and backward society (in the eyes of the West) have today becoming a global hegemon. Still, some are predicting its collapse as a nation-state or that its economy will collapse and in the process negatively impact the global economic and political system.[11] It is also believed that the continuing growth and the stated and unstated intention of China will, along the way, cause it to collide with the United States thereby precipitating a new era of Cold War or an outright war.[12] On the other continuum are those who are predicting that, eventually, China will replace the United States as the preeminent global power in the twenty-first century.[13] There is no evidence to suggest that China wants to create the world in its image. It is even doubtful—or at least there is no evidence of this—that the People's Republic of China is bent on being the global police or law enforcement officer as the United States is alleged to be. Nations rise and fall, empires rise, and eventually, because of internal and external dynamics, they fall peacefully or violently. The British Empire disintegrated, so did the once-mighty Union of Soviet Socialist Republics (USSR). That is the nature of hegemony: they rise and then collapse. Perpetuity is not possible. So, eventually, the United States will become like every great empire that preceded it. What does China want? What does the post-1949 China want? They wanted Hong Kong and Macau back. They achieved that. And Taiwan? That is different! With the passage of every year and every decade, this aspiration becomes difficult to achieve. Internal conditions in Taiwan make this an impossibility unless of course, Beijing has the stomach for a war it will never truly win. The coalescing and unification of territories aside, China, in the simplest of words, wants to be able to roam the seas and the sky with as little restrictions as possible. China wants to secure and industrialize its economy and society and be able to move several millions of its people out of poverty. And finally, Beijing wants to stand on the same podium with the rest of the West. In other words, China does not want Western nations—especially the United States—wagging its fingers at her. China has come to stay. At the very leaders, in Africa and elsewhere in the Global South, China has come to stay. What happens next is up to Africans—especially their leaders.

NOTES

1. Phinea Bbaala. "Emerging Questions on the Shifting Sino-Africa Relations: 'Win-Win' or 'Win-Lose'?" *Africa Development / Afrique Et Développement* 40, no. 3 (2015): 97–119.

2. Campbell Horace. "China in Africa: Challenging US Global Hegemony." *Third World Quarterly* 29, no. 1 (2008): 89–105.

3. Brook Larmer. "Is China the World's New Colonial Power?" *The New York Times*, May 2, 2017. https://www.nytimes.com/2017/05/02/magazine/is-china-the-worlds-new-colonial-power.html.

4. Sanders Moody. "China in Sub-Saharan Africa: Demand Extracting Supply." *International Affairs Review* 20, no. 1 (Summer 2011).

5. Ibid.

6. Robert I. Rotberg. "Strengthening African Leadership: There Is Another Way." *Foreign Affairs* 83, no. 4 (2004): 14.

7. Ibid.

8. Ibid.

9. Tom Burgis. *The Looting Machine: Warlords, Oligarchs, Corporations, Smugglers, and the Theft of Africa's Wealth.* New York, NY: PublicAffairs, 2016.

10. Padraig Carmody. *New Scramble for Africa 2e.* Cambridge, UK: Polity Press, 2016.

11. Gordon G. Chang. *The Coming Collapse of China.* London: Arrow, 2003; Dinny McMahon. *Chinas Great Wall of Debt: Shadow Banks, Ghost Cities, Massive Loans and the End of the Chinese Miracle.* London, England: Abacus, 2019; See also

James R. Gorrie. *The China Crisis: How Chinas Economic Collapse Will Lead to a Global Depression.* Hoboken: John Wiley & Sons, 2013.

12. Graham T. Allison. *Destined for War: Can America and China Escape Thucydides's Trap?* Boston: Mariner Books/Houghton Mifflin Harcourt, 2018; Miaojie Yu. *China-Us Trade War and Trade Talk.* New York: Springer, 2020.See also Michael Fabey. *Crashback: The Power Clash between the U.S. and China in the Pacific.* New York, NY: Scribner, 2018.

13. Michael Pillsbury. *The Hundred-Year Marathon: Chinas Secret Strategy to Replace America as the Global Superpower.* New York: St. Martins Griffin, 2016.

REFERENCES

Allison, Graham T. *Destined for War: Can America and China Escape Thucydides's Trap?* Boston: Mariner Books/Houghton Mifflin Harcourt, 2018.

Bbaala, Phineas. "Emerging Questions on the Shifting Sino-Africa Relations: 'Win-Win' or 'Win-Lose'?" *Africa Development / Afrique Et Développement* 40, no. 3 (2015): 97–119.

Burgis, Tom. *The Looting Machine: Warlords, Oligarchs, Corporations, Smugglers, and the Theft of Africa's Wealth.* New York, NY: Public Affairs, 2016.

Campbell, Horace. "China in Africa: Challenging US Global Hegemony." *Third World Quarterly* 29, no. 1 (2008): 89–105. https://doi.org/10.1080/01436590701726517.

Carmody, Padraig. *New Scramble for Africa 2e.* Cambridge, UK: Polity Press, 2016.

Chang, Gordon G. *The Coming Collapse of China.* London: Arrow, 2003.

Fabey, Michael. *Crashback: The Power Clash between the U.S. and China in the Pacific.* New York, NY: Scribner, 2018.

Gorrie, James R. *The China Crisis: How Chinas Economic Collapse Will Lead to a Global Depression.* Hoboken: John Wiley & Sons, 2013.

Larmer, Brook. "Is China the World's New Colonial Power?" *The New York Times*, May 2, 2017. https://www.nytimes.com/2017/05/02/magazine/is-china-the-worlds-new-colonial-power.html.

Liang, Guoyong, and Haoyuan Ding. *The China-US Trade War.* Abingdon, Oxon: Routledge, 2021.

McMahon, Dinny. *Chinas Great Wall of Debt: Shadow Banks, Ghost Cities, Massive Loans and the End of the Chinese Miracle.* London: Abacus, 2019.

Moody, Sanders. "China in Sub-Saharan Africa: Demand Extracting Supply." *International Affairs Review* 20, no. 1 (2011): 1–22.

Pillsbury, Michael. *The Hundred-Year Marathon: Chinas Secret Strategy to Replace America as the Global Superpower.* New York: St. Martins Griffin, 2016.

Rotberg, Robert I. "Strengthening African Leadership: There Is Another Way." *Foreign Affairs* 83, no. 4 (2004): 14. https://doi.org/10.2307/20034043.

Yu, Miaojie. *China-Us Trade War and Trade Talk.* New York: Springer, 2020.

Index

Abdel Gamal Nasser, 8, 15–19, 21n26, 22nn29–35, 24, 27

The Abuja Rail Mass Transit system, 167

The Abuja- to Kaduna railway line, 167

Africa Development Bank (ADB), 32, 36, 92–97

Africa Development Fund (ADF), 32, 36

African: debt. *See* debt; governments, 12–13, 52, 60, 62, 73, 93, 98, 103, 115–16, 120, 123, 127, 129–31, 134n22, 143, 146, 148, 151, 177, 216–17, 219–23, 225–26, 234–35, 238–44, 246–47, 264, 266, 270, 274, 276, 278, 305–8, 310–16, 319–23, 327n68, 329–30, 333–36, 338, 347–48, 350; leaders, xv, xx–xxi, xxv, 4, 19, 59–60, 73, 93, 96, 97, 115–16, 120–23, 126–28, 130–31, 152, 162, 166, 167, 169–71, 176–77, 215, 218, 221, 223, 225–26, 266–67, 316, 331, 338, 345–51, 353–54; Union. *See* Organization of African Unity (OAU-AU)

African Policy Paper, 25, 33–35, 40n53, 42–43

Afro-Asian Conference, 4, 18. *See also* Asian-African Conference

Afro-pessimism, xxiv, 96, 320. *See also* Sino-pessimism

agriculture, xxiv, 34, 37, 49, 61, 147, 150, 175–76, 218, 229, 238, 264, 266, 271, 273, 292; agricultural sector, 60, 166, 273–74, 276, 360

aid, 13, 69, 78–79, 96, 98, 106n21, 107nn24–28, 109–11, 121, 127, 129–30, 143, 145, 148, 150, 155n38, 157, 166, 168, 172, 180n42, 189, 207, 211, 215–16, 218, 220, 224, 226–27, 230, 240, 242, 252, 258, 265–66, 277, 279nn14–22, 281, 286, 294, 313, 324n15, 328, 337, 341n18, 343, 360; economic, 25–26, 28, 29–31, 36, 53, 71, 296; food, 169; foreign, 12, 33, 38nn21–23, 41n61, 43, 73, 95, 120, 128, 132, 147, 151, 154n36, 156, 175, 179, 181, 183, 188, 221, 228n21, 331, 358, 361; military, 28; packages, 121, 145, 148; technical, 25–26, 29–33, 38n29, 43, 54, 58, 125, 168–69, 263, 273, 276, 299. *See also* assistance

Aid for Trade, 130

The Ajaokuta-Kaduna-Kano pipeline, 167

Algeria, xxi, 5, 13, 15–16, 21n13, 23, 31, 101, 170, 173–74, 225, 283

About the Editors

Sabella O. Abidde is a professor of Political Science and a member of the Graduate Faculty at Alabama State University. He holds a BA (International Relations) from Saint Cloud State University, Minnesota, and an MA in Political Science from Minnesota State University Mankato, Minnesota. He earned his PhD (2009) in African Studies, World Affairs, Public Policy, and Development Studies from Howard University. He is a recipient of the 2020 MOFA-Taiwan Fellowship awarded to scholars interested in conducting archival research in Taiwan. Dr. Abidde is the author/coauthor/editor/co-editor of several publications including *Fidel Castro and Africa's Liberation Struggle* (Lexington Books, 2020); *Africa, Latin America, and the Caribbean: The Case for Bilateral and Multilateral Cooperation (*Lexington Books, 2018); and *Africans and the Exiled Life: Migration, Culture, and Globalization* (Lexington Books, 2018). Dr. Abidde is a member of the Association of Global South Studies (AGSS); the American Political Science Association (APSA); and the African Studies and Research Forum (ASRF).

Tokunbo A. Ayoola is reader (History and Diplomatic Studies), and chair, Department of History and Diplomatic Studies, Anchor University, Lagos, Nigeria. He holds a PhD (2004) in History and Politics from the University of Manchester, Manchester, UK; an MSc in Political Science from the University of Lagos; and a BA in History/Political Science from the University of Ife (now Obafemi Awolowo University), Nigeria. His publications include "Claude Ake and the Political Economy of Human Rights in Africa," in Adebayo Oyebade and Gashawbeza Bekele (eds.), *The Long Struggle. Discourses on Human and Civil Rights in Africa and the African*

Diaspora (2017); "Post-colonial West African Railroads: State Management, Infrastructural Decay, and Privatization," in Toyin Falola and Jamaine Abidogun, *Issues in African Political Economies* (2017); and "Railway Politics, Colonial Civil Service and Imperialism in Nigeria," in Emmanuel M. Mba and Augustine E. Ayuk, *The African Civil Service Fifty Years after Independence* (2017).

About the Contributors

Augustine Avwunudiogba is an associate professor of geography in the Department of Anthropology, Geography/Ethnic Studies, California State University, Stanislaus. He teaches courses in the regional geography of Africa, Mexico, and Central America. His recent publications on Africa and Latin America include two coauthored chapters in Africa, Latin America, and the Caribbean. He holds an MA in geographical studies from Southern Illinois University, Edwardsville, Illinois, and a PhD in geography from the University of Texas at Austin, Texas.

George B. N. Ayittey obtained his PhD from the University of Manitoba, Winnipeg, Canada, in 1981. He taught at Bloomsburg University, Bloomsburg, PA, from 1985 to 1988. He was selected as a National Fellow in 1989 by the Hoover Institution at Stanford University, California. In 1990, he became a Distinguished Economist in Residence at American University, Washington DC, until he retired in 2010. Dr. Ayittey has written several books on Africa, including *Indigenous African Institutions, Africa Betrayed, Africa in Chaos, Africa Unchained, Defeating Dictators, Applied Economics for Africa.* Africa *Betrayed* won the HL Mencken Award for "Best Book in 1993." He was a contributor to the opinion pages of *The Wall Street Journal, the New York Times, the Los Angeles Times, the Washington Post, and The Times of London.* He was selected among "The World's Top 100 Global Thinkers" by *Foreign Policy* magazine in 2010.

Kudakwashe Chirambwi holds an MA in Peace and Governance from the Africa University, Zimbabwe, and a postgraduate diploma in research methods and a PhD from the University of Bradford, UK. Dr. Chirambwi Kudakwashe is the founder and coordinator of the Peace, Leadership, and

Conflict Resolution Program at the National University of Science and Technology, Zimbabwe. He is a reader on peace, security, and international development with a focus on the intersectionalities between the nature of domestic politics and the neoliberal forces.

Elisha J. Dung is an associate professor of geography in the Department. of Criminal Justice/Social Sciences at Alabama State University. Dr. Dung holds a PhD in Geography from Oklahoma State University, Stillwater, Oklahoma, and teaches courses in World Regional Geography, Cultural Geography, Regional Geography of North America, and the Geography of Africa. His most recent publications have been on African Diaspora, bilateral and multilateral cooperation between Africa, Latin America and the Caribbean, and African migration.

Alecia D. Hoffman currently serves in the Department of History and Political Science at Alabama State University as an assistant professor of political science. She is a 2015 graduate of Clark Atlanta University, where she earned her PhD in political science. Alecia's dissertation research focused on the influence of China's foreign aid policies on the political-economic development of Nigeria between the years of 1979–2010. She is the author of "Blacks in Asia: Identity and Belonging" in *Pan-Africanism a Modern Times: Challenges, Concerns, and Constraints*, edited by Olayiwola Abegunrin and Sabella Abidde; "Africa, Latin America, and the Caribbean: A Shared Historical Connection" in *Africa, Latin America, and the Caribbean: The Case for Bilateral and Multilateral Cooperation.* Sabella Abidde ed. (Lexington Books, 2018).

Charity Manyeruke currently serves as the Ambassador of Zimbabwe to Rwanda. She was a professor of Political Science and dean of the Faculty of Social Studies at the University of Zimbabwe. She is the author of "Regional integration in SADC: Evidence for More Convergence or Divergence" in *Africa, Latin America and the Caribbean, The Case for Bilateral and Multilateral Cooperation*, edited by Sabella Ogbobode Abidde (Lexington Books, 2018). She is also the author of "Pan-Africanism and the Struggle for the Liberation of Zimbabwe," In Africanism in Modern Times, Challenges, Concerns and Constraints, edited by Olayiwola Abegunrin and Sabella Abidde (Lexington Books, 2018). Her latest work, coauthored with Abegunrin, is *China's Power in Africa: A New Global Order* (2019).

Emmanuel Matambo (PhD) is a Zambian national with degrees in philosophy and political science from St Joseph's Theological Institute and the University of KwaZulu-Natal. He is the author and coauthor of academic papers that straddle a range of topics from China-Africa relations, terrorism, conflict resolution, policy implementation, and social cohesion. He is currently a postdoctoral research fellow at the University of Kwa-Zulu Natal and is also a member of the South African Association of Political Science (SAAPS). His main area of research is on the topical China-Africa relations.

Lawrence Mhandara holds a PhD in peace studies from the Durban University of Technology (South Africa). He has been an active participant in international thinks tanks on Africa-China Africa relations. He is currently a lecturer in the Department of Political and Administrative Studies at the University of Zimbabwe where he teaches political science, international security, international conflict management, and strategic studies. He has coauthored articles and book chapters on China-Africa relations. Coauthored publications include "Debating China's new role in Africa's political economy," African East-Asian Affairs, 2013; and "Chinese investment in Africa: An investigation of the opportunities and challenges for peace and security in Zimbabwe," In Berhe, M.G., and Hongwu, L (eds), *China-Africa Relations: Governance, Peace and Security.* Institute of Peace and Security Studies: Ethiopia, pp.146–165.

Regina M. Moorer is an assistant professor of political science at Alabama State University. She is a graduate of Auburn University, where she earned her PhD in public administration and public policy. She has contributed articles to the International Encyclopedia of Social & Behavioral Sciences and the Encyclopedia of Alabama. She joined the faculty at Alabama State University in Fall 2017. Before joining the ASU faculty, she taught political science at Auburn University and Auburn-Montgomery. Dr. Moorer is a member of the American Political Science Association (APSA), the National Conference of Black Political Scientists (NCOBPS), and the Southern Association of Political Scientists (SPSA).

Surajudeen Mudashiru, PhD is an associate professor of Political Science at Lagos State University (LASU). Though his research interest covers a wide spectrum of politics and international relations, he is a peace and conflict specialist. Mudasiru has been Head of Department and currently leads his university's research fund body. He has published widely and made presentations at scientific conferences and other academic fora in many continents including Africa, Europe, and North America. He is scheduled to present a joint-paper entitled "The time for Africans is over? A Discourse Analysis of news reports on a Chinese restaurant in Kenya" at the 2018 IPSA conference in Brisbane, Australia.

Charles Mutasa is an Independent Development Policy consultant and a part-time lecturer in Development Studies of the Zimbabwe Open University. He is the coeditor of *Africa and the World: Bilateral and Multilateral International diplomacy* (2018) and editor of *Africa and the Millennium Development Goals: Progress, Problems, and Prospects* (New York: Rowan Littlefield, 2015); "Aid effectiveness and the question of mutual accountability" in Hakima Abbas and Yves Niyiragira (eds), *Aid to Africa-Redeemer or Colonizer?* (2009) and "A Critique of the EU Agricultural Policy" in Adekeye Adebayo and Kaye Whiteman (eds). Dr. Mutasa has over seventeen years of working nonprofit sector and has been engaged in projects, researches, and publications related to Africa's external relations, including Sino-Africa relations.

Simbo Olorunfemi is a PhD candidate at the University of Lagos, Nigeria. He holds an MA in Political Science and International Law & Diplomacy, and a postgraduate diploma in Journalism. He has published several books which received critical acclaim in and outside of the continent. He won the Association of Nigerian Authors/Cadbury Poetry Prize 2004 for the book— "Eko Ree—The Many Faces of Lagos." His writings are widely published by leading newspapers, online platforms, and magazines in Nigeria, including Premium Times, The Guardian, and This Day. Mr. Olorunfemi presently serves as the Managing Editor of Africa Enterprise; and is also the CEO of HoofbeatDotCom a Strategy, Branding, and Communications Consultancy in Nigeria.

Abdul-Gafar Tobi Oshodi is finalizing his doctoral studies at Centre for Research on Peace and Development (CRPD), KU Leuven, Belgium. Oshodi worked as a journalist for several years at the Vanguard newspapers and taught Political Science at LASU before leaving for his PhD. A fellow of the Social Science Research Council's (SSRC) Next Generation of Social Sciences in Africa program, he presented his first international talk on China in Africa at the Economic Community for West African Countries' (ECOWAS) 2010 Symposium on Ending Underdevelopment in Ouagadougou, Burkina Faso. He has published several articles on China in Africa the latest of which is entitled, "Oscillation of two giants: Sino-Nigeria relations and the Global South," *Journal of Chinese Political Science.*

Priye S. Torulagha is an associate professor of political science and public administration in the Department of Social Sciences, Florida Memorial University, Miami Gardens. He holds an MA in Comparative Politics and Public Administration from Oklahoma State University, Stillwater; and MHR in Counseling and Human Resource Management from the University of

Oklahoma, Norman, and a PhD in political science from the same university. Professor Torulagha writes regularly on Nigerian and African affairs, Third World politics, international terrorism, and democratic governance. He regularly engages students in experiential exercises in parliamentary procedures and diplomacy through the Model United Nations and Model African Union.

Wei Ye is a PhD student at the University of Hong Kong. She also works as a program officer for Chinese government-funded training programs, specializing in ICT innovation in higher education, for researchers, professionals, and government officials from the education sectors of developing countries in 2017 and 2018, responsible for program implementation and quality assurance. Previously, she worked on international exchange and cooperation in different universities in China, responsible for program design and policy research. She obtained an MSc in International Relations from Nanyang Technological University, Singapore in 2013 and, a Bachelor of Law in International Politics from Sun Yat-sen University, China in 2012. Her current research focuses on China's foreign aid to Africa with a specialization in the education sector.